THE PATTERN OF
SOUTH AFRICAN
CULTURE
FROM SETTLEMENT TO APARTHEID

THE PATTERN OF SOUTH AFRICAN CULTURE

FROM SETTLEMENT TO APARTHEID

Edited by
A. L. McLeod

STERLING PUBLISHERS PRIVATE LIMITED

STERLING PUBLISHERS PRIVATE LIMITED
A-59, Okhla Industrial Area, Phase-II, New Delhi-110020.
Tel: 26387070, 26386209; Fax: 91-11-26383788
e-mail: mail@sterlingpublishers.com
www.sterlingpublishers.com

The Pattern of South African Culture
© 2009, Sterling Publishers Pvt. Ltd.
ISBN 978 81 207 4633 6

All rights are reserved. No part of this publication may be reproduced, stored in a retrieval system or transmitted, in any form or by any means, mechanical, photocopying, recording, electronically or otherwise, without prior written permission of the original publisher.

PRINTED IN INDIA

Printed and Published by Sterling Publishers Pvt. Ltd., New Delhi-110020.

For
Kenna and Goody

True sons of Africa are we,
Though bastardized with culture,
Indigenous, and wild, and free
As wolf, as pioneer and vulture—

Our minds like dark destructive engines
Prepare those catapults and slings
In whose preliminary vengeance
The thunder of the Future sings.

– **Roy Campbell**
"Poets in Africa"

Contents

			Page
	Preface		ix
	Introduction	A. L. McLeod	1
1.	Literature	John C. Povey	12
2.	Science	G. G. Cillié	43
3.	Religion	Anna L. Conradie	76
4.	Art and Architecture	Heather Martiennsen	111
5.	Law	Ellison Kahn	138
6.	Language	D. R. Beeton	177
7.	Family Life and Popular Culture	J. B. du Toit	207
8.	Philosophy	Anna L. Conradie	247
9.	Public Address	A. L. McLeod	262
10.	Bantu Culture	F. J. Language	311
	Notes on the Contributors		353
	Index		357

Preface

In 1954 Cornell University Press published *The Culture of France in Our Time* and three years later *The Culture of Contemporary Canada*, both volumes edited by Professor Julian Park of the University of Buffalo (now the State University of New York at Buffalo). These were followed by *The Pattern of Australian Culture* (1963), which was supported by grant from the State University of New York Research Foundation and published also in Australia by Oxford University Press. The same presses issued *The Pattern of New Zealand Culture* in 1968; both of these latter volumes were edited by the present writer.

A subsequent, companion volume on the Union of South Africa (which became the Republic after 1960)—the third of the "Sisters of the South" as Conrad Lighton felicitously described Australia, New Zealand, and South Africa—was planned in preparation for publication in 1972, the midpoint of the era of apartheid; however, financial, political, and editorial considerations resulted in abandonment of the project. But to recognize the considerable effort that had been expended, a small number of copies, without illustrations, were duplicated. That edition has been used as copy-text; consequently, the present publication maintains the American spelling and punctuation of the original.

Contributors, in some cases, arranged for publication of truncated essays elsewhere, and on several occasions inquiries were received requesting copies of the whole text, for South Africa is quite unfamiliar, culturally, to many people who are otherwise quite sophisticated in international political and social affairs.

In earlier times public interest in South Africa was largely restricted to its geography, history, flora and fauna, and mineral deposits; that is, interest was focused upon the land and its strategic location. Subsequently, after the Second World War the focus shifted to race relations, political representation, and membership in the Commonwealth, and these subjects soon diverted attention from the nation's achievements in those several other areas that constituted legitimate elements of its fundamental culture, so that there are numbers of people, both inside the country and elsewhere, who are not well informed about South Africa's cultural heritage prior to 1994, when apartheid ended after the defeat of the National Party.

Until 1994 the vast majority of South Africans were excluded from learning about their nation's cultural heritage or from contributing to its development; few were familiar with the contributions to the dominant culture by minorities or with the sub-cultures that were developed independently or surreptitiously and frequently unacknowledged. It is the intent of this volume to provide an account of the growth of a characteristic South African culture and where possible to assess its individuality and achievement.

While publication some years after original composition may seem unusual, there are copious precedents: John Winthrop's *History of New England*, covering the years from 1630 to 1649, was published only in 1825; Herman Melville's *Billy Budd* was written about 1890 but not published until 1924; Alistair Cooke's *The American Home Front, 1941-1942*, written at that time but published only posthumously in 2007, are examples of this phenomenon in the genres of fiction and general prose.

The chapters in the cultural studies named above are not identical and their subject matters are not all covered in this volume: some areas, such as literature and art are included in all, but others, which seem less significant, such as historiography and music, are omitted. Cultures other than the dominant—the subordinant or subaltern—are considered in separate chapters of each book, so that the Quebeçois, Aboriginal, Maori, and Bantu are considered independently by specialists in those areas.

Preface

Because of prevailing social conditions in South Africa, even scholars in the universities—especially during the half-century of apartheid—were generally reluctant to voice or publish liberal viewpoints insofar as they impinged on race; as a result, it might be conceded that the several chapters in this book represent, in the main, the dominant, conservative positions that prevailed at the time of their composition. And even then, after fifty years of fundamentally British cultural dominance, the Afrikaans culture had not been fully integrated, so that there were, in effect, three cultural traditions rather than a homogenized, single one.

It is a pleasure to acknowledge permission from the following individuals and organizations to reproduce illustrations of which they hold the copyright: *Artlook*, J. H. Boss, Revel Fox, Martin Gibbs, Maggie Laubser, Lippy Lipshitz, Cecily Sash, Lucas Sithole, South African Railways Department of Publicity and Travel, Helmut Starcke.

Rider University   **A. L. McLeod**
Lawrenceville, New Jersey

Illustrations

I   La Provence (c. 1750). Fransch Hoek Valley, Cape Province.

II Old Cape furniture, including a built-in display cabinet. Marie Koopmans de Wet House (c. 1750), Cape Town.

III South African Institute for Medical Research (1912). Sir Herbert Baker, architect. Johannesburg.

IV "Minoan Theme in Yellow and Black." (1964), Cecily Sash.

V   Schlesinger Center (1960). Monty Slack, architect. Johannesburg.

VI "Hollow Torso" (1953). Lippy Lipshitz.

VII "Pregnant Woman" (1960). Lucas Sithole.

VIII "Cat and Nasturtiums" (1932). Maggie Laubser.

IX "Mother of the Tribe" (1969). Walter Battiss.

X   "Hieratic Women" (1966). Alexis Preller.

XI House Le Roux (1950). Revel Fox, architect. Llandudno, Cape Peninsula.

XII "Fire Bird" (1968). Helmut Starcke.

Introduction

In his *Sisters of the South* Conrad Lighton used that felicitous phrase to describe Australia, New Zealand, and South Africa, three settler-dominated countries that faced somewhat similar difficulties in transplanting fundamentally British cultural paradigms to unfamiliar and at times hostile environments. The implication, of course, was that these three "outposts of empire" shared much in common in their sets of interests, behavior, and culture—though he was at pains to differentiate these and demonstrate those nations' individuality, their identifiable cultures.

Unfortunately, definitions of culture are legion: Matthew Arnold depended on a small coterie of his own class to determine what was best in society and thus worthy of being perpetuated and promoted among the inferior groups—the philistines and populace—so that "high culture" would be perpetuated. However, this general dissemination proved impossible, and cultural strata became ever more entrenched through scarcely perceptible distinctions and niceties.

T. S. Eliot, in his *Culture,* settled on a capacious definition: "the characteristic activities and interests of a people," thus including what are nowadays often described as both high and low culture: that of the well-educated, often wealthy, professional, and leisured upper class; and that of the mass of poorly educated, harried, underpaid lower class. Each of these can be subdivided by ethnicity or race or religion or geography.

Clearly the old dictionary definition of culture as "the enlightenment and refinement of taste acquired by intellectual and aesthetic training; the intellectual content of civilization" is no longer sufficient; more to the point is the view offered by Northrop Frye in his *Anatomy of Criticism* (1957), where he says:

> The culture of the past is not only the memory of mankind, but our own buried life, and a study of it leads to a recognition scene, a discovery in which we see not our past lives, but the total cultural form of our present life.... It is the consumer, not the producer, who benefits by culture, the consumer who becomes humanized and liberally educated (345-46).

In effect, culture refers to a system of ideas about the nature of the world and how people in a community should think, act, and react in it; it is learned in childhood as cognitive orientations embedded in a system of symbols, such as laws, religious beliefs, art, language, music, theater, sports, literary texts, dance, and public and private behavior, which can be observed. The origins of culture can be at least partially determined, as can its modifications over time, and the social anthropologist can propose relationships and dependencies based on his observations and research.

How can we explain the culture of contemporary South Africa, a polyglot republic of numerous indigenous black tribes and clans; of several ethnic groups (particularly Dutch-origin Afrikaners and British-oriented Europeans); of bi-racial Cape Coloreds; and of Orientals and Arabs? The most helpful approach is to consider the history of the nation and the implacable forces to which it has been subjected during the past four hundred years.

Ever since the discovery in 1488 by Bartholomew Diaz de Novais, the Portuguese explorer patronized by Prince Henry the Navigator, of what is today known as the Cape of Good Hope, at the southernmost extremity of the African continent, the successive European settlements at this distant outpost of "civilization" have been of prime importance in imperialism, trade, cultural dissemination, and international hegemony.

Shortly after Diaz's landing, Vasco da Gama demonstrated that the Cape, almost midpoint between Iberia and India, was a crucial revictualing location for ships engaged in the elimination of the Arab interdiction of the overland spice trade, in the discovery and development of new lands, and in the spread of Roman Christianity. Accordingly, elements of

Introduction

European culture were being sewn before 1500. Subsequently, Portuguese settlements were supported in East Africa, Mauritius, and India, but the Cape was not substantially developed, and a nominal British occupation in 1616 soon perished.

The first definitive European settlement in South Africa was that led in 1652 by Jan van Riebeeck, a doctor who had had years of commercial experience with the Dutch East India Company, although the firm had established a small station at Table Bay some five years earlier, following the shipwreck there of Leendert Janssen. Because an Anglo-Dutch war was imminent, the Company dispatched some ninety men to erect a fort and develop agriculture in support of its enterprises further east. Willem Jansz had explored the south coast of New Guinea in 1605 and Dirk Hartog and Frederick de Houtman had charted the west coast of what was the Great South Land as far south as present-day Cape Leuwin, while in 1642 Anthony van Diemen, the governor-general of the Company sent Abel Tasman, with two vessels, to explore the uncharted sea between Africa and Terra Australis. Dutch seamen had discovered and largely mapped almost three-quarters of what is Australia.

The effects of the van Riebeeck colony were the importation of slaves for hard labor, the separation of Dutch and Hottentots, the settlement on large farms of "burghers" (independent contractors), the support of a Dutch Reformed Church at Cochin, in India, and later the commercial exploitation of the East Indies. Meanwhile, the Cape became a vital entrepot and attracted ancillary enterprises: shipchandlers, providores, and tradesmen flourished; revictualling encouraged agricultural, pastoral, and viticultural development. Meanwhile, Peter Stuyvesant, as governor of New Netherland, was declaring New Amsterdam (New York) a municipality and placing a Dutch garrison at Fort Good Hope (now Hartford, Connecticut).

British culture was introduced to South Africa after the arrival of a small garrison sent to evict a French contingent that had been encamped during the Napoleonic Wars. The Treaty of Vienna transferred the colony at the Cape to Britain in 1815, and thereafter there existed a fragile coexistence of the prevailing culture and the introduced. In religion—rather more important then than now—the Dutch Reformed Church and the Church of England became symbolic of the division between Boers and Britons, each group resisting cultural intrusions and incursions, each attached to historical precedents and traditions and opposed to innovations and even subtle inconsistencies. It soon became apparent that there was a cultural incompatibility that was becoming untenable. The British authorities soon gave valuable land grants to new settlers, introduced quotas for African laborers, and issued identity cards (the initial "passes"), and encouraged proselytizing by the London Missionary Society.

With the Great Trek of 1835-40 by the Afrikaners, the ethnic Dutch farmers, South African European culture became effectively bifurcated; this led inevitably to the South African (Boer) War of 1899-1902, and that, in turn, to the Union of South Africa in 1910, when the four provinces (Cape, Natal, Orange Free State, and Transvaal) assumed Dominion status within the British Empire.

Louis Botha, Paul Kruger, and Jan Christiaan Smuts, the leading politicians of South Africa, were all fiercely nationalistic and strong individual statesmen; however, they were agreed on the policy of "separate development" (apartheid), that the white and black racial groups should develop their own cultures independently. All believed that white rule would continue in South Africa indefinitely, that it was in accord with natural law, and that this was the best policy to assure that Bantu cultures would be maintained and even developed rather than being absorbed by the dominant cultures. The principal questions were to what extent separation should exist, how it should be maintained, whether in contiguous or discrete areas, and by law or by consensus. These questions were being considered elsewhere at the time.

The situation in South Africa was far from unique. In India the British had early established a de facto apartheid policy in a country that had for centuries accepted the propriety of segregated castes, sanctioned by religion, with the

Untouchables (harijans, dalits) deprived of almost all rights and millions living in virtual slavery and lifelong debt. In the United States, until the late 1950s, it was commonplace to find signs restricting drinking fountains, seating in public conveyances, admission to buildings and recreational facilities to either Blacks or Whites; in Florida and other desirable vacation areas the sign "Preferred Clientele" indicated that neither Blacks nor Jews would be accommodated. And the Black Power advocates even proposed that two or three states become black homelands—this at a time when the Bantustans proposed or created in South Africa were being denounced elsewhere in the world.

In Australia the Commonwealth constitution of 1901 did not even include the indigenes as part of the population; rather, the Aborigines were considered under the rubric of Natural Resources: they were considered a nuisance and an impediment to the full adoption of the White Australia policy that aimed to repatriate Kanaka canefield workers, Chinese farmers and fishermen, and Afghan cameleers who developed Central Australia and the Northern Territory. As towns developed, the original inhabitants were forced into ever-more-undesirable locales, usually arid, rocky regions or isolated, mangroved, coastal enclaves. In Tasmania the Aboriginals had been killed for sport, the women seduced by both troops and the convicts; in the first year of settlement there were perhaps 7000 indigenes, but by 1831 there survived just 190, and they were transported to an island reservation, where they were subjected to Christian indoctrination. The last one died in 1876.

On the mainland, the Aboriginals were forced onto reservations (or church-operated mission stations), often breaking up families and forcing a congeries of unrelated tribes together, thus enforcing a policy of strict segregation that made little or no provision for education or training—except as domestics or farm workers.

The Aborigines had no vote, they were unable to buy land, they were taxed if they earned income but received no social welfare benefits, they were unable to travel without the permission of the local Protector of the Aboriginals (frequently the local policeman), and could be sent to a distant reservation for any insubordination—as happened to Albert Namatjira, the celebrated watercolorist of the Arunda tribe, trained at the Hermansburg Lutheran Mission.

Government policy was predicated on the belief that the indigenes would soon die out; however, by mid-century this was seen as a false premise, and in 1951 assimilation became the new policy: "All Aborigines and part-Aborigines will attain the same manner of living as other Australians, enjoying the same rights and privileges... observing the same customs and influenced by the same beliefs, hopes, and loyalties as other Australians." In effect, Aboriginal cultures were to be eliminated through assimilation into the prevailing white one.

One can understand the attitude of many South African Whites, whether Afrikaners or Britons, who believe that their nation has been subjected to unreasonable discrimination because of its policies regarding the Bantus when other countries have escaped censure though following similar—and even more severely hierarchical—policies of apartheid. Some even point to the situation in Israel (founded in 1948 when the National Party implemented its policy of apartheid), where a small "settler" population established itself within a large population of "others" and implemented exclusionary laws and confiscatory practices.

But even Jan Christiaan Smuts, the founder of the philosophy of Holism; the intellectual behind the establishment of both the League of Nations and the United Nations; the firm believer in cooperation, consensus, and the middle ground between conservatism and progressivism, found opposition within South Africa. Smuts's philosophy of government was a benign paternalism leading to gradual and peaceful assimilation of Bantus into white society with simultaneous development of black homelands under white supervision during a transition period. He had his critics.

One of these was Roy Campbell (1901-57), one of the "angry young men" of his day. (In fact, Campbell introduced the phrase in his "Poets in Africa," written in the early 1920s.) He devoted his romantic, bizarre, frenetic life to championing the underdog, criticizing the salon cliques, and parsing public policies. In *The Flaming Terrapin* (1924), his first long poem, Campbell showed himself to be of a Byronic temper and described his poem as "a symbolic vision of the salvation of civilization," while in *The Wayzgoose* (1928) he focused his attention of the idiosyncrasies of South African culture in these memorable lines:

> Attend my fable if your ears be clean:
> In fair Banana Land we lay our scene—
> South Africa, renowned both far and wide
> For politics and little else beside:
> Where, having torn the land with shot and shell
> Our sturdy pioneers as farmers dwell,
> And, twixt the hours of strenuous sleep, relax
> To sheer the fleeces or to fleece the blacks.

Campbell, William Plomer, Charles Madge, David Wright, and a number of other poets found the South African environment insufficiently stimulating, and they migrated overseas; but away from their native land they lost their originality and, in the case of Plomer, became indistinguishable from the quintessential Englishman.

Contemporary Bantu, unable to emigrate, were nonetheless developing their own literature in English; among these authors were R. R. Dhlomo, *An African Tragedy* (1928); Solomon Plaatje, *Mhudi* (1930), whose work was published in London by the firm of Kegan Paul; and Thomas Mofolo, whose *Chaka the Zulu* (1931) was issued by Oxford University Press and is still in print, though his later works are now collector's items. H. I. E. Dhlomo's play *The Girl Who Killed to Save* (1936) and his long poem *Valley of a Thousand Hills* (1941) both achieved some popularity. Naturally, this literature is not extensive, considering the impediments to literacy and publication, and *Some English Writings by South African Bantu*, compiled by N. M. Greshoff of the School of Librarianship at the University of Cape Town in 1943, lists only 87 items, many leaflets, pamphlets, or academic papers. Lack of education was a major cause.

While it is estimated that perhaps only 18 per cent of Africans are literate in their own language, in South Africa the rate is about 40 per cent. But the statistic requires comment: schooling is compulsory for Whites and Afrikaners from seven to sixteen; it is offered in some places, on a limited scale, for Coloreds; until the Bantu Education Act (1953), which transferred responsibility to the national government, education of Blacks was a provincial matter and unsystematized, noncompulsory, underfunded, and elementary, though one university college, at Fort Hare, provided basic tertiary training, in English.

In a speech explaining the philosophy of the 1953 act, Dr. Verwoerd said that whereas previously church-operated schools for Bantu had used English almost exclusively, future instruction would be in Afrikaans, schools would be run only by the government, and Bantu parents would have to foot the costs. He complained that Bantu liked to "show off their knowledge of English culture" and that this gave them expectations of leaving black communities "for a life outside the community and for posts that do not in fact exist." He continued:

> The economic structure of our country, of course, results in large numbers of Natives having to earn their living in the service of Europeans. For that reason it is essential that Bantu pupils should receive instruction in both official languages from the earliest stages, so that even in the lower primary school they should develop an ability to speak and understand them. Instructions have already been issued to introduce the teaching of Afrikaans immediately.

This is commendable, surely, as a succinct, eminently pragmatic, ingenuous explication of the government's basic philosophy of education—though based on questionable premises.

Notwithstanding the policy of training non-Whites for subservient roles, the National Party government created new university colleges for them: the rationale was to train a small cadre to administer the projected Bantu homelands. The

University of the Western Cape for Coloreds, the University College of Zululand in Natal, the University College of the North, in the northern Transvaal, and a University College for Indians in Durban were created. However, the standards of these non-white institutions are remarkably low, though their numbers are growing almost exponentially. In this they have much in common with the traditionally black educational institutions in the United States: of over one hundred (many founded and financed by black religious denominations), perhaps two have, with charity, any recognized academic quality. And where Blacks have access to multiracial universities, large numbers elect racially segregated colleges because they feel more comfortable in an all-black environment. This obtains even in Pennsylvania, where, on the outskirts of Philadelphia, Cheyney is wholly black and West Chester, a few miles up the road, is white, relics of a century of systematic segregation.

The immense changes in South African society after the 1948 election have been effected by a small majority of the white population, the Afrikaner nationalists, essentially a union of dissident groups rather than a homogeneous, carefully structured and administered one. Yet these various groups obviously have sufficient commonality to provide cohesion and political impact. They share the knowledge that their forebears believed and behaved in certain ways and that these beliefs and behaviors provide the paradigm for anyone claiming to be a true Afrikaner: they constitute the fundamental culture, or way of life. It is, essentially, a rural mindset, one of cohesion, based in large measure on family relationships and on a sense of otherness—of exclusion from the dominant English-speaking community. But this was modified in the 1920s and 1930s, decades of droughts, floods, and the Great Depression, when many Afrikaners had to move into the urban areas for menial jobs that provided some sustenance.

In the cities the "dertigers" (people of the thirties) encountered different values and cosmopolitan mores; the Afrikaner manual laborers encountered for the first time the dominant attitudes of the white population: it was not just country-city, labor-capital, but Afrikaner-British, in essence, and soon had political ramifications. The unifying theme became the existence of a common language, Afrikaans, and a common religion, that of the Dutch Reformed Church, which taught Biblical justification for racial segregation and hierarchy, this at a time when in other countries this was becoming anathema and anachronistic.

The transfer from church to political leadership was brought about substantially by the Fellowship of Afrikaner Brethren, the Afrikaner Broederbond, established in 1920, a highly disciplined leadership organization that has infiltrated almost every sphere of Afrikaner life. In many ways the Broederbond shared the aims and structure of such groups as the United Irishmen of the 1790s and the Irish Republican Brotherhood of the 1890s; and J. C. Smuts himself had proposed settlement of the Irish political situation in 1921 on the basis of "separate development." Its indefatigable membership, seldom fractious, was rewarded by political success in the 1948 elections and the consequent implementation of its ideology. This ideology, not fundamentally different from that which prevailed elsewhere not too long in the past, is nonetheless at variance with what is nowadays almost universally endorsed, and hence subject to criticism and anathematization. We are apt to forget that Woodrow Wilson, that famous advocate of self-determination once told an audience, "Segregation is not a humiliation but a benefit, and ought to be so regarded." South African politicians and statesmen have echoed that statement, but it is no longer seen internationally as an acceptable national policy.

In recent years the churches in South Africa have begun to dissent from government apartheid policies and become vocal, so that missionaries have been expelled from both South Africa and from South West Africa (Namibia). In 1968 the South African Council of Churches actually condemned apartheid, and Dr. Carl-Johan Hellberg, secretary of the department of world missions of the Lutheran World Federation commented that this action "forced individual Christians, as well as congregations and churches, to see government policy against the background of their Christian conviction." He added that Christian leaders in South Africa are apprehensive over a split in their congregations as a result of the stand by the Council of Churches. What this purports for the future of churches remains to be seen.

Meanwhile, South African culture has become identifiable and impressive, so that it is in many respects enviable throughout the continent. Industry, punctuality, frugality, and the other Protestant virtues have permeated the individual psyche, so that the nation has made impressive advances in the extractive industries, in agriculture, and in manufacturing, in science and technology, and in the fine arts (excluding music, ballet, and opera). Culture is not about genes or race; it is about values, beliefs, and attitudes that influence a nation's way of life.

The following chapters will illustrate the dynamics that have created the culture of contemporary South Africa and suggest possible developments and impediments. Whether in sports, literature, art, or medicine, South Africa has much to be proud of; and whether the future holds assimilation or separate development in store, it is assuredly going to continue to impress the world with its achievements.

A. L. McLeod

# 1

Literature

John C. Povey

To discern the essence of South African culture through its literature, it is necessary to seek that writing which most clearly reveals the social and political context of the country, to discover the distinction that it may show rather than only the universality of experience that it also embraces. The absorbing of its unique geography and the historical pressures which mold the individual assumptions of the people will be reflected in the most characteristic writing of the country.

The early situation of nineteenth-century colonial South Africa matches in many ways that of any other area conquered by European colonialists. Settlers were forced by the experience of a different daily life to modify their previous routines until a new cultural nationhood was established. It is perhaps necessary to stress this common identity with the other white settler areas, because recent international attitudes, conditioned in response to South Africa's political and racial philosophies, have stressed the isolated nature of the situation there.

It is easy to demonstrate that, by the mid-twentieth century, racial tensions imposed an increasingly rigorous stress upon the literature of the country and to a large extent controlled the themes available to an author. The internecine color conflict conditions South African writing after 1950 in the same measure as it intrudes on every aspect of South African social existence. But South African writing does not begin with that racial theme; that was to come at a comparatively recent time. The African is understandably a regular feature of the early settler writing, just as in early American literature the existence of the indigenous Indian or the imported slave became part of the implicit social background of the writer; nonetheless, there is a clear sense that the South African writer's real concerns rest elsewhere than race in the earlier period. During the first stages of colonial literature writers are preoccupied with the discovery of new social topography, with recording the variety of the adjustments imposed by a fresh geography, and the complex psychological forces deriving from inevitable changes in nationality and allegiance.

Frost was brilliantly correct when he observed of New England, "The land was ours / Before we were the land's," and his words are appropriate to all settler countries. What the writer has to do is to formulate the concept of a new nationality, forging new assumptions from fresh experiences. So it was with South Africa during the century of settlement until its status as an independent dominion was achieved. Later writers reflect the situation of their racially-rent country, but they do so in the casually confident assumption that they are speaking as South Africans. Defense of nationality is unquestioned, because unnecessary. That certainty of nationality was created as much by a century of literature as by the political events of savage war, out of which the present republic was created.

This early writing was comparable in many ways to the literature of other settler dominions. In South Africa, however, there were special historical circumstances, and this English-language literature was to run parallel not only with spirited and continuous literature in the African languages, both oral and subsequently printed, but also in competition with the well-established Dutch language as it modified itself into the lively new idiom to be called Afrikaans.

As might be anticipated in a settler literature, writing was initially largely in the form of diaries and letters. The frontier was not the ideal place for belles lettres, and the realistic biographical narrative was the first stage of South African writing. In fact, there had been some writing during the period of the first British occupation of the Cape, and the best-known writing from this period are the letters of Lady Anne Barnard, who was the wife of Andrew Barnard, colonial secretary of the Cape from 1797 to 1802. They are marked by a shrewdness and wit and a revealing degree of anti-Dutch prejudice which was to be one of the common principles that marked English-speaking South Africans. These letters still have an immense individual charm, but being letters they can perhaps only posthumously be considered as literary contributions: they were not actually published for nearly a century after they were written.

Although Cape Town must have seemed a very isolated settlement at this time, it was a thriving metropolis compared with the regions that were being settled by the homesteading farmers as they began to farm the Eastern Province regions around Grahamstown after 1820. These men also wrote series of diaries and reports that intriguingly recount the difficulties of their conditions in these pioneer settlements, but few of these have yet been published. The assiduous work of Professor Guy Butler indicates that a large number of fascinating documents of this period are ready to be brought to light, and a plan for printing these important accounts is now established. The best-known of these anecdotal diaries in print is the account of the 1846 Kaffir War, *The Cape and the Kaffirs* (1848), by Mrs. Harriet Ward, and Alfred Whaley Cole's *The Cape and the Kaffirs; or Notes on Five Years' Residence in South Africa* (1852). But these works are surely on the fringe of what we would call a prose literature.

The development of poetry during these years produced little more significant than had appeared in prose, although perhaps the first literature from South Africa must be considered as a remarkable poem called, significantly, "Emigration," an indication of the painful sense of exile that was to permeate a good deal of South African writing at later dates. This poem, published in 1821, is remarkable for nothing more than its primary occurrence, although Sir Rufane Donkin enjoined the attention of the London Colonial Office to this pioneering work, calling it "The First Effort of the African Muse....The First Production of our Parnassus." Although published anonymously, it was in fact the undistinguished work of Herbert Pugh, a Cape Town attorney. His mediocre efforts were followed by similar attempts by other minor versifiers worthy of note only in literary histories aiming at comprehensiveness.

The first poet usually deemed worthy of any literary acclaim in South Africa was Thomas Pringle (1789-1834), who arrived with the first British settlers in 1820. Although Pringle did not in fact remain very long in South Africa, his attempts to absorb the South African scene within his somewhat labored Wordsworthian sonnets at least indicated a determination to draw his poetic sustenance from the roots of his present abode. Even though he cannot in any way be considered a distinguished poet, there are some revealing aspects of his work as he attempts to Africanize, as it were, his subjects in very conventional English poetic diction. His "Ode to Evening" is amusing for this reason:

> Now along the meadows damp
> The enamored firefly light his lamp,
> Link-boy he of woodland green
> To light fair Avon's Elfin Queen;
> Here, I ween, more wont to shine
> To light up the thievish porcupine
> Plundering my melon-bed....

The apparatus of this poem is obviously full of those legendary green woodlands of Avon and of elfin queens in the manner of *A Midsummer Night's Dream*. Yet the actual image he discovers is far from England. There is not only the tropic fruit of the melon, but inescapably African fauna: it is a porcupine and not a squirrel or a rabbit that loots his crop.

Pringle's best-known work is an important one for the future, "Afar in the Desert," a poem much admired by Coleridge. Its significance rests less in the common-place assertion of the moral superiority of the country to the town, or the desirability of God's wide-open spaces to the man-made insalubrious cities. This is a conventional enough Romantic theme, but it does take on a further intensity when applied in the South African context. The continuing yearning for the open expanses of Africa grows more extreme until it receives its merciless pillorying at the hands of Roy Campbell, who truly ridicules the rhetoric concerning the vast imponderable enormities of the African veldt, those "nameless somethings." Pringle's lines are more cautious and more orthodox, yet they move towards this significant South African theme and attitude, which is deep in the cultural consciousness of the country, the passion for "open spaces," the sense of freedom implicit in an unexplored and unsettled geography:

> Afar in the desert I love to ride
> With the silent Bush-boy alone by my side:
> Away, away in the wilderness vast
> Where the white man's foot has never passed.

This sense of the virgin territory open to the pioneer becomes a significant cultural attitude in Southern Africa. Another common topic anticipated by Pringle is the constant explicit contrast established between England and this hard new land:

> No tree, nor cloud, nor misty mount,
> Appears to refresh the aching eye:
> But the barren earth, and the burning sky,
> And the blank horizon, round and round.

Rudyard Kipling remarked, "As to South African verse, it's a case of there's Pringle and there's Pringle, and after that, one must hunt the local papers." This generous praise of Pringle is unfair to other poets. If their work lacked distinction, they occasionally achieved effective verses, which drew upon the South African scene and strengthened the significant sense of national and cultural identity, no matter that many of the verses themselves were not highly inspired. A. S. Cripps, F. C. Slater, and W. C. Scully established at least the basis for the ground from which more inspired South African poetry would spring.

And several of their poems remain of at least passing interest: F. C. Slater (1876-1950) in particular, repeatedly catches the daily beauty of South Africa. A verse from his poem "Milking Kraal" is indicative of his sensitive response to the local scene:

> When stars begin softly to spatter
> Milky drops in the bowl overhead;
> And the wings of brown bats shear obliquely
> The fleece of the dusk;
> In the kraal squatting milkers are stitching
> Each cow to a pail
> With silvery thread.

The first work of real distinction from South Africa is by Olive Schreiner (1855-1920). Her *Story of An African Farm* (1883) is inevitably selected as the work that first comes to mind when one thinks of South African writing. Its intriguing story, reflecting life on an isolated veldt farm, is still most readable.

It raises a number of intriguing non-literary speculations about the nature of this young governess, minimally educated, working with such curious intensity on her first book. The plot of the tale concerns a deeply wronged young girl, Lyndall. In her intensity, she is perhaps too much the idealized woman beloved of woman authors, but there are more unusual virtues in this novel: there is the strange, perhaps significantly South African violence; the grotesque Tant' Sannie, the vicious and unprincipled Blenkins, the strangely agonized young farm boy, Waldo, become the cast of a bizarre social tragedy which is matched in its intensity by the equal savagery of the landscape against which they must act out their restricted and harsh destinies. For all the wild characters, the remarkable thing about this book is the way in which it draws upon the bare, sparse challenge of the South African veldt, which makes a constantly threatening backdrop to the characters' daily action. Always there is the physical presence of the land and its threat:

> The last year of the great drought, the year of 1862. From end to end of the year the earth cried for waters. Man and beast turned their eyes to the pitiless sky, like the roof of some brazen arch overhead...week after week, month after month, the sun

looked down from the sky till the karroo-bushes were leafless sticks broken into the earth, and the earth itself was naked and bare; and only the milk-bushes, like old hags, pointed their shrivelled fingers heavenwards, praying for the rain that never came.

The mixture of violent imagination and commonplace scene seems to have asserted a constant fascination on other writers, though no one has been able to reproduce its haunting quality. Even Schreiner herself, after much travel abroad, became increasingly involved with suffragette causes and she was unable to repeat her first achievement. *Dreams* (1891) is a long and barely readable collection; *Trooper Peter Halkett of Mashonaland* (1897), a kind of parable concerning Rhodes's intervention against the Matabele, has been revived—but more because its dramatic appeal to pacifism and charity sits well with current thought than because it has much integral substance to commend it.

One intriguing aspect is that this important novel was written by a woman and this foreshadows the extreme importance of women writers in the South African context. Perhaps one could pursue reasons for this, speculating on the daily activity which prevented men from giving time to literary endeavor. It remains an obvious and intriguing fact unmatched in most societies.

In the histories of South African literature there are impressive numbers of works listed by the diligent bibliographer, yet few works of this period achieve that most significant individual life that they are read for other than historical reasons. Perhaps the most successful writer to follow Schreiner was the prolific Sarah Gertrude Millin (1889-1968) well known in the world of politics and letters. Only her 1924 novel *God's Stepchildren*, concerning the colored children in Cape Province, seems to have lasting qualities. And even now this appears a little dated in its easy patronage: history has been hard on early South African writing.

A neglected writer of some distinction is Herman Charles Bosman (1903-51). His short stories create a humorous but perceptive vision of the South African scene, his incidents are very closely involved with his country, and in his satirical folk humor he invites a comparison perhaps with Mark Twain, although he can barely stand against such a standard. Lewis Nkosi has argued that the international neglect of Bosman is based upon "the fixed regionality of his characters and the defiant parochialism of the world they inhabited, which insured that the author would present an initial difficulty for the outsider." It is debatable whether this is true of Bosman's humorous stories, but it is a reminder that those tales which most effectively represent the South African scene are most clearly within the extreme of South African culture. Perhaps those which seem the most foreign to the outside reader must be considered as most illustrative of that country.

Bosman's world is a real one, yet it is a distant one, for the progress that he satirizes was to destroy the farmland on which his people depended. He writes of a transitional stage of cultural change, as Twain did; but when that change is totally victorious the past this writer records can be approached only with the nostalgia of social history:

> Afterwards, when they brought the telegraph, when they showed the church elder how they could tap out messages from as far away as Cape Town, the elder shook his head and said he did not give the world a full two hundred years any more. And when he heard a talking machine that could sing songs and speak words just through your turning a handle, the elder said that the end of the world was quite near.

Such a world, of course, was near its end, but it was to be destroyed by international politics as much as anything else: the impact of the First World War was to destroy South Africa's geographic isolation. The South African statesman Jan Smuts was to be one of the major figures in the creation of the League of Nations, and Smuts's own transformation from Boer general to world statesman seems a symbol of the change in South Africa's attitude to the rest of the world.

In its most vigorous form, the break with the tranquil past attended the political changes with which South Africa met the 1920's, and this political decisiveness was matched by an equal literary revolution. It stemmed from the work of a virulent and articulate young man from Natal, Roy Campbell (1901-57). In 1924, with the publication of *The Flaming Terrapin* South Africa at last had a writer of real and consistent international caliber. This work burst like a shell upon an English literary scene that saw the quiet, understated poetry of J. C. Squire's Georgian group as an appropriate contemporary tone for verse. Campbell's flaring, burning lines, savagely rhythmic, dazzling in their multicolored imagery, shocked the effete London world. Lines such as these had not been known in English poetry for two centuries:

> Anarchy, jolted in a rattling car,
> Crested turrets of the storm, and plied
> His crackling whip with forked lash to scar
> Red weals across the gloom: with frantic stride.
> His gusty stallions clenched their bits and tore
> His whirling spokes along the pitchy rack:
> Their gaping nostrils drizzled foam and gore,
> And where they passed the gurly sea grew black.

There are, in fact, good antecedents in British writing for this vigorous and forceful verse. But knowing Campbell was South African, the critics of London seized immediately upon his "colonial" status. It was assumed that it was the violent and exotic land of his birth that lent such fervor to his verse. And it was a pose that Campbell was most willing to adopt. In so doing he indicated one possible method of handling the embarrassing fact of his dominion origin. Campbell boasted of the heritage and praised the virulence, the energy, of his new land, contrasting this with the gray despair and senility he claimed to find in England. In this he indicated that denigration of Europe was one way of establishing the significance of the culture of South Africa. In fact, Campbell himself was well-read in the European classics, yet—in a way a little Hemingway—he pretended that the physical experience of his life was the major spur to his writing. He chose to scorn the litterateurs of London:

> Far be the bookish Muses! Let them find
> Poets more spruce, and with pale fingers wind
> The bays in garlands for their northern kind.
> My task demands a virgin muse to string
> A lyre of savage thunder as I sing.

But the "savage thunder" was to be directed as much towards his own land as towards those threatening foreigners in whose company he was to spend the major part of his life in self-chosen exile; and before he left he attempted the publication of a new literary journal called *Voorslag* (Whiplash) in company with William Plomer. Its title was perhaps more indicative of Campbell's personal attitude than of a more general statement about South African culture. In fact, it is probably true to say that the culture had to be "whipped" from its apathy and smug parochialism that was the truer measure of the country's literary situation at this time. His famous, scathing lines that open the "Wayzgoose" make a double statement, for if there is this moribund culture that Campbell sees all around him, there is also a South African to excoriate its flatulence:

> Attend my fable if your ears be clean,
> In fair Banana Land we lay our scene—
> South Africa, renowned both far and wide
> For politics and little else beside:
> Where, having torn the land with shot and shell,
> Our sturdy pioneers as farmers dwell,
> And, 'twixt the hours of strenuous sleep, relax
> To shear the fleeces or to fleece the blacks.

This satiric mode was an important one, and many of the most articulate and concerned South Africans have adopted its scathing force. Antony Delius (b. 1916) in later decades was to employ similar devices, echoing Campbell's tone but attacking more recent attitudes.

But in spite of his sardonic attacks, it is important to indicate that Campbell loved South Africa, loved his country as only a poet knows how, and that nobody has more expressively brought the beauty of this land into literary form than he. His most famous poems have been much anthologized, yet they have not lost their exquisite passion for being often repeated and well-known.

"The Zebras," "Zulu Girl," "The Serf," are equally the works of a major talent that simultaneously fed upon South African geography and the South African scene at the same time it was inhibited by it. For Campbell, although he loved South Africa, was driven into exasperated exile by its restrictions, by its narrow racial philosophies.

William Plomer (b. 1903), perhaps a more capable though less flamboyant poet than Campbell, also left South Africa in the late twenties and has not returned. His recently reprinted novel *Turbott Wolfe* (1926) is a significant work and reminds us that Plomer is an underrated writer, perhaps because of his very lack of ostentation, of which Campbell had an excess. Yet in his years of exile abroad he has seemed to lose the sense of origins, the sense of connection he had. His subsequent works, although most able, seem far removed from the stream one seeks to trace as evidence of the culture of South Africa.

The Second World War brought South Africans again into the international scene. Until this war, the analogy between both the living conditions and the literature of South Africa and that of Australia or Canada could be seen as close: pioneer settlers forging farms against marauding indigenous people, seeking a new nationality in an alien geography: among them this similarity of experience can be demonstrated. But the political situation changed markedly after the war, and from this point the differences rather than the similarities between South Africa and other English-speaking dominions was most apparent. In fact, in a simplistic way it could be said that this is where, in the expectations of most newspaper readers, South African culture really begins. This postwar period marks the point where race, racial antagonism, political segregation and all its attendant tensions, become the central fact of the South African way of life, and it happens that a large number of brilliant writers in this post-war period were ready to reflect this tempestuous political and racial situation in a sudden efflorescence of a literature.

Whereas previously South Africa could count upon the security of a series of colonially controlled countries, now independent territories began to press their policies of equality and independence towards the boundaries of the one major white-settler nation on the African continent. Only the weak authority of Portugal supported the South African position. Political and intellectual thought increasingly singled out South Africa as anathema to liberal, democratic ideology. Increasingly South Africa was isolated both by design and by circumstance into a separate, narrow and reactionary world.

To be fair to that unhappy country, no other land had quite such a complex racial situation, and it was perfectly possible to remark speciously and ingenuously on the fact that other countries could be accused of unequal and cruel treatment for their racial and cultural minorities. None of this altered the essential fact that South Africa was becoming a pariah amongst world nations, its problems less discussed than totally condemned.

It is a significant fact that from this point all serious South African writing is concerned with race and racial attitudes. It is hard to find another topic advanced in any major writing, even though the usual plethora of popular magazine stories and novels manage to avoid dealing with any realistic special situation at all. From this point, to speak of South African literature becomes synonymous with the discussion of race and politics. As Nadine Gordimer wryly remarked, such novels are "like oranges—major South African exports."

It should be recognized that although South Africa does have a substantial printing industry, and a whole range of magazines and books are published in the country, London remains the major publishing center—as it does for most other African countries. The great significance that this has for South African literature is that it permits a far greater degree of freedom for the writer to criticize the policies of the government, even when this criticism is simply implicit in factual statement. It is true that there can be pressures and assaults on the writer's person in his country, particularly if he is a non-European. But the books do get published, and though the official government censorship bureau keeps rigid check on what is permitted to be imported and read in the country through the ominous and extensive "banned" list, South African literature, like many of its practitioners, continues abroad. Thus it is a curious fact that much of the most essential evidence of South African cultural and social attitudes (as represented through the works of its literary figures) ceases in a functional sense to be indigenous. The significance that this fact of foreign influence has for the writer needs to be considered in much greater detail, for it is in fact a unique situation in the history of letters. There have been exoduses and expulsions before, but not quite this consistent and voluntary departure even by those who are not technically at odds with the restrictive threats of the complex racial laws.

From the late 1940's, then, South African literature concerns itself with race and racial attitudes, and two early works, one by a White and one by an African, typify this movement: *Cry, the Beloved Country* (1948) by Alan Paton (b. 1903) and *Mine Boy* (1946) by Peter Abrahams (b. 1920) also exemplify the tone that was to breed such an extensive progeny in the country. It is not their fault that they both now appear somewhat dated in the present political context. Their idealized sense of mutual compassion and obligation is still a noble and valid concept. Perhaps it is we who have lost our morality in anticipating a violent disaster. They are both tender and effective books, and the characters are only unrealistic to the extent that we now doubt that so much courage exists in the world. Then one thinks of Alan Paton himself and sees that it is beautifully possible.

The story of *Cry, the Beloved Country* is well-known. It celebrates the great beauty of the Natal that Paton himself knows so well. Paton uses a newly-forged stylistic lyricism that avoids being merely excessive by the Biblical structure that stands behind it and the Zulu effects he attempts. Notwithstanding, the tale has its melodramatic moments, with the sad old preacher's son murdering the crusading liberal son of the generous white benefactor. Yet the sense of the beauty of South Africa and the passion that it engenders are to be seen from the first lyric, evocative lines of this novel. This is an impressive example of the intensity of affection that the South African landscape imposes on its residents and which becomes a common observation in the lines of many poets.

This lyric intensity moves beyond the landscape to Paton's similar enormous emotional affection for people. The old priest, his generosity, his anxiety, his trust, is a noble and impressive creation. This novel is perhaps the supreme example of the philosophy of the liberal South African transferred into literary terms. Paton's second novel, *Too Late the Phalerope* (1953), has more strength in its construction. It portrays the white dilemma, this time within the context of sexual temptation and the appalling consequences that come when race and sex are set in opposition. But if this is a better novel, it does not touch so close to the quick of the South African attitude as *Cry, the Beloved Country*, and in spite of the quality of this book it may well be that his short stories, *Tales from a Troubled Land* (1961), still make the best of Paton. They have wit, tenderness, concern, and a kind of tough integrity that prevents them from being merely sentimental. *Spomono* (1967) exemplifies this attitude and indicates the way the South African situation makes its day-to-day demands on human compassion.

A similar moral position is taken by Peter Abrahams in his first novel, *Mine Boy*, but his view is more that of the "inside," for he is an African. The plot, with the innocent, honest country boy, Xuma, coming to town to seek work has become fairly commonplace, and this novel has been stigmatized as being the first of the South African "Jim goes to the city" tales. Innocence must cope with the violence and immorality of the city. And yet, although there is a yearning for the innocence of the country in the manner of the Reverend Kumalo in *Cry, the Beloved Country*, and an admission of the town's corrupting force, the city is also in this case alluring, warm, and vibrant. It is exciting and challenging, and the filth and the excitement seem to be perceived as interwoven: "The street was alive. People moved up and down. Children played in the gutters, and picked up dirty orange peels and ate them. The pulsating motion of Malay Camp at night was everywhere. Warm and intense and throbbing."

The characters also reflect this division: if many are weak, ratty creatures battening on the poor with violence, there is also the enormous courage of old Leah and the constant tenderness of Maisie. But this is a South African novel; and although it would be possible in other countries to match the problems of too rapid and uncontrolled urbanization, in South Africa it is always compounded by race. Abrahams makes it clear that even where there is charity and goodwill, race brings its insidious poison. Most of the whites in *Mine Boy* are generous-hearted and sympathetic. The young white miner, Paddy, is particularly well-intentioned and finally willing to risk his entire career in joining a strike on behalf of the Africans. And yet, when he says, "I am a man like you, and afterwards I am a white man," Xuma answers vehemently: "You say you understand, but how can you? You are a white man. You do not carry a pass. You do not know how it feels to be stopped by a policeman in the street. You go where you like. You do not know how it feels when they way 'Get out! White people only!'"

Thus, from the earliest stages and from the most humane and understanding of men there is already the admission of the totality of the color issue that it appears cannot be bridged by any mutual sympathies or understanding. Abrahams left South Africa, lived for a time in Ghana, and subsequently in the West Indies. Although he wrote several more novels, only one of them concerned South Africa; the rest, although of interest, seem curiously rootless in dealing with the exile theme. *A Night of Their Own* (1965), which is set in South Africa, concerns a rather James Bond-type situation. A young African lands on the coast of Natal from an unidentified submarine, bringing money to support the guerrillas of the coming insurrection. The stereotyped racial characters give no extra strength to this melodramatic piece, and it would appear that Abrahams for all his birth no longer expresses the cultural concerns of his country.

If Paton and Abrahams share a certain kind of humane liberalism, a compassion which is perhaps the inevitable component of any writing, they are perhaps also the first stage of a split in literary attitude which can regrettably enough be seen primarily in racial terms. In saying this, perhaps one is merely adding evidence that everything in South Africa is seen in racial terms. From Paton stems a line of development, not necessarily direct in its influence, but following the same stream: the attitudes of white liberals—concerned, tender, and often despairing. From Abrahams, although his own vehemence is relatively mild, stems the stream of black writing with its necessary indignation and sense of grievance. This is not to say that these two streams are always completely separate. There obviously can be violently angry white writers such as Harry Bloom (b. 1920) in his *Episode in the Transvaal* (1956). There can be immense compassion and tolerance in the novels of black writers. Nor could one honestly insist that it is regularly possible to distinguish literature on a color basis without knowledge of the biography which exposes race. Nevertheless, as a literary device that allows us to pursue consideration of significant South African attitudes, such a division has a partial validity. It is a distinction that might well be anticipated from the expected attitudes. After all, white concern is a somewhat different emotion than the African's response to what amounts to persecution. For the Whites it is often am intellectual sympathy, although they too may suffer from government edicts. No matter how deeply they are moved by African suffering, it is in the final analysis an intellectual and emotional reaction from which in many cases they can withdraw. It is a voluntary and therefore temporary attitude, an intellectually willed sharing of suffering, for they do not suffer all the specific persecutions and detractions that impose upon every aspect of the day-to-day life of an African. The "sleg vir blankes" (whites only) edicts which enforce color separation on social amenities, the pass laws which control the free movement of Africans within their country, the separate but unequal status of social welfare services inevitably impose directly on the African most painfully. The African is permanently doomed to this situation by his color. This knowledge lends a note of exasperation and extra indignation to the situation, making the African writing often violent and angry where the white author's may often be wry, ironic, and sad.

Few white writers now seem overtly political; rather, they express directly or implicitly through their tales the emotional deprivation, the stultifying of the normal humane impulses which their national situation imposes. There are a number of such writers, indicating the extraordinary virility and wealth of South African writing—even granted the fiercely difficult political circumstances. There is the work of Gerald Gordon, the well-known Cape Town attorney; the concerned and generous-hearted Jack Cope (b. 1913), whose novel *Albino* (1968) makes the irony of pigment deficiency into a kind of extended metaphor of South Africa's color situation. The two best-known may perhaps be used to exemplify the attitudes of white South African writers, the more so in that one, Dan Jacobson, lives abroad while the other, Nadine Gordimer, remains to write in South Africa—although her last novel has in fact been banned.

It is difficult to know whether, while living abroad, Dan Jacobson (b. 1929) will continue to draw upon the South African situation for his work. Earlier writing—*The Price of Diamonds* (1955), *A Dance in the Sun* (1956)—was closely involved with the incidents of contemporary South Africa. But the color issue is most expressly developed in his later novel, *Evidence of Love* (1961). In it he argues what marks the evidence of human love in South Africa. Within its pessimistic plot his conclusion appears to be that one must be prepared to be jailed for that love; that the measure of emotion is the willingness to be persecuted for it. The plot of his story concerns a young man of mixed race whose color is sufficiently light that in England he can "pass." Sent to England to study, and freed of the pressure of the color bar, he develops all those human potentials specifically denied to him because of his race. When he meets a South African white girl he falls in love with her. Then they face the decision of where they shall live and to what purpose. They choose to return to South Africa—not because it can be useful, but because the gesture has to be made to demonstrate commitment. On their return, they are arrested for contravening the laws against miscegenation and dealt harsh sentences, for mixed marriages are expressly forbidden. The situation is seen in its bitter absurdity and in its cruel implications. The declaration of the young hero, Kenneth, before the court, articulates the whole problem:

> By arresting and bringing us to this court, the State has made my love for my wife, and her love for me, a public and political act. For this reason we cannot be punished by the court, but only released by it—released from the public and political hatreds, the public and political guilts which make ugly the most private and secret lives of everyone who lives in this country.

No doubt Nadine Gordimer (b. 1923) would sympathize with this point of view, and yet her treatment of such events is more subtle, more dispassionately ironic, though certainly no less sharply critical. As would be expected from any good writer, her work stretches more broadly than the narrow limits of a national culture, if that is simplistically considered to mean only the specific localized context of a society; her work touches upon the universals of human experience. Although firmly linked to South African residence, her characters are often not specifically concerned with immediate racial issues but carry on their marital wrestlings, fall in love, grow up, undertake those things which are simultaneously the most obvious and the most profound of human events. She is perhaps the finest short-story writer of this generation, and as such she touches chords which are shared by people everywhere. Nadine Gordimer's stories are the type that makes a tiny event into the microcosm, making innocent incident press to the very heart of experience, developing a sense of the identities within the human heart rather than the national distinctions.

But in the short stories of Nadine Gordimer the incident which provokes the moment of emotional revelation—which is at the heart of any short story—is regularly African. In "The

Train from Rhodesia," for example, it might be any event that exposes to a young wife the insensitivity and harshness of her husband. It happens that the incident concerns the man's tough negotiation with an African over a small carving. In "The Catch," with its description of an Indian fishing in Natal, the minor event becomes cross-colored by the embarrassment of racial expectations.

When she writes about the South African condition, as she does in her novels such as *Occasion for Loving* (1963), Gordimer touches deeper than most, because her subtlety searches with exquisite skill into the deepest consequences of the human act. The best example of her work may well be the story "Which New Era Would That Be?" On the surface it is a slender description of a young white girl and her escort who go to visit an African and attempt to carry on a simple friendship in a situation where everything is to be complicated by the unnaturalness of the racial awareness that interrupts all innocent interaction. The irony of the story rests in the distinction between what she thinks she is and what the African thinks of her. She considers herself intellectually beyond racial attitudes, and yet she exemplifies them. Cleverly, Nadine Gordimer describes her arty dress, "earrings that seem to be made by a blacksmith out of bits of scrap iron. On her feet she had sandals whose narrow thongs wound between her toes, and the nails of the toes were painted plum color." She exposes a bright innocence which is, in the final painful analysis, the worst kind of crass insensitivity. Cleverly, Gordimer has given greater prominence to the African point of view. Jake, the hero, knows the progressive Whites well:

> These women—oh, Christ!—these women felt as *you* did. They were sure of it. They thought they understood the humiliation of the pure-blooded black African.... Yes, breathless with stout sensitivity, they insisted on walking the whole teeter-totter of the color line. There was no escaping their understanding. They even insisted on feeling the resentment *you* must feel at their identifying themselves with your feelings.

Here is a complex and subtle series of emotional interactions; but above all it indicates that nothing can exist in natural innocence when the whole aura is conditioned by race. Even the girl's decision that she would like to eat curry at an Indian restaurant becomes redolent of racial attitude. As Jake remarks again, "A woman like that would want to be taken to eat at an Indian place, even though she was white and free to eat at the best hotel in town." The description of poor Jennifer is at one level a sardonically cruel performance; at another, it exposes a much deeper corrosion, for in other circumstances she would have achieved her own kind of ease.

For the Africans, the source of ease is much harder to find. They express their despair and dismay often through the form of the autobiography. Perhaps the autobiography for them is equivalent of a kind of journal. This form intersperses the structure of art most minimally between experience and writing. Perhaps it is for this reason it is selected, for beside the desire to create art there is the need to make a record. Many are well known: Bloke Modisane's *Blame Me on History* (1963), Alfred Hutchinson's *Road to Ghana* (1960) are two that are widely read abroad, but undoubtedly the best is Ezekiel Mphahlele's *Down Second Avenue* (1959).

Ezekiel Mphahlele (b. 1919) is a major African writer whose intelligence and humanity have made him a significant spokesman for the Africans. His book records his childhood when he was brought from the village to be reared in the slums of Pretoria's Second Avenue. Conditions in the ghetto were hard, the struggle for survival provoked cruelty and violence, and yet at the same time it made for tenderness and self-denial. Through all the impositions of police and the whole repressive circumstance of his life, there is also a humanity and a sense of family community, no matter the difficulties. In particular, he records lovingly his Aunt Dora and her struggle to give him the education that would permit him to escape from this condition.

No one has better caught the atmosphere of this community because the account is not a propagandist tract; it does not focus only on pain and oppression: there is the fun of the old silent films, the natural child games, and the adventures of schooling. Nevertheless, he is not a sentimentalist; he does not minimize the humiliation that such conditions bring to a sensitive man. In fact, Mphahlele recognizes better than any other writer the great dilemma of the South African author of conscience. If you wish to voice your anger and resentment, you risk forfeiting that detachment which makes art and thus gives your writing other than mere polemic force. Anger is a natural enough response to the South African situation, but unless it is transmuted by the "distancing" structure of art, it remains the dross of mere propaganda. The writer's task only begins with his own emotional experience; he has to go forward and force his reader to respond with an equivalent intensity. When Mphahlele thought of leaving the country, a friend said to him, "You've got all the material you want here and the spur is always there." He answered, in a way that applies to all South African writing concerning the political situation:

> That's the trouble: it's a paralyzing spur; you must keep moving, writing at white heat, everything full of vitriol; hardly a moment to think of human beings as human beings and not as victims of political circumstances. But one must crack up somewhere. Maybe this is it for me. I'm sick of protest creative writing, and our South African situation has become a terrible cliché as literary material.

Here he puts his finger on the problem. No one in South Africa can ignore the racial tension, yet to write about it becomes quite literally monotonous, for description of these events is the role of the sociologist, not the artist. The artist must see the complexity within people and not the simplicity demanded by color interpretation, which makes inevitably for mere melodrama if race and color alone decide virtue and vice, the hero and the villain. Once the stereotypes are broken and the muddled and misguided people exposed with all their human foibles, there can be no political tract. There might rather develop the material of the profound tragedy that marks the human condition. Yet it is no easier simply to turn away from South African events, because then the vitality of conscience, which is an urgent part of a writer's nature, is lost. Mphahlele observes again:

> If you tried to go away somewhere and ceased to care, you'd still be in the larger denomination of the world which required man to care; you'd become a more bitter cynic; and while you shrivelled up in the acid of your cynicism, the world wouldn't be at all worse off after your exit.

Notwithstanding, he chose exile. It is revealing that his sense of loss, of division from his true cultural links, preoccupies his writing. During his many travels, which have taken him to residence in East and West Africa, in England and in the United States, he constantly returns to thoughts of his country: "Countless times I have dreamt about the deep valleys and craggy mountains of Pietersburg. I've revisited them in my dreams, never in my flesh."

Other writers have been less successful than Mphahlele in controlling their indignation and bitterness. To this extent they have been trapped into a single tone, for anger becomes the motivation of their writing. Partially, this is true even of such an impressive writer as Alex La Guma (b. 1924). His bitter short novel *A Walk in the Night* (1962), concerning the notorious District Six of Cape Town, is saved from being merely polemic only by the honest vehemence of its tone and a sense of pointless tragedy that pervades the inevitability of its tawdry events. La Guma's is an ugly world, a world of dirt and sweat and violence and poverty. His characters take on a kind of low-level heroism as they make their rough deal with social circumstance. The following description is typical of La Guma's setting, the shabby backdrop against which his pathetic characters struggle:

> It was cooler under the sagging roof, with the pile of assorted junk in one corner; an ancient motor tyre, sundry split and warped boxes, and old enamel display sign with patches like maps of continents on another planet where the enamelling had cracked away, and the dusty footboard of a bed. There was also the smell of dust and chicken droppings and urine in the lean-to.

Yet within this depressing environment his characters make an heroic swagger to conceal the bitter social impotence that they must feel. They find in simple but inescapable brutality the assuaging of the pent-up frustrations of legal restrictions on their acts. There are beatings and kicks and blood, but this is not all. In a story such as "Nocturne" there is an unexpectedly tender, if tentative, approach towards the beauty of Chopin being played so feelingly by a girl at the piano, as though La Guma himself wishes to touch another dimension of feeling. But La Guma's most intense response is implicit in the most remarkable metaphor yet devised for the South African situation: "Deep down inside him the feeling of rage, frustration, and violence swelled like a boil, knotted with pain." La Guma's prose could act as the surgical lance to release this poison.

Richard Rive (b. 1931) stands somewhere between Mphahlele and La Guma in his attitude. His view may be a bleaker interpretation of circumstance than Mphahlele's, yet there is a greater sense of potential heroism, of human triumph amongst the despair than La Guma's cynical violence. Rive's short story "Strike," though ostensibly a factual account of the attempt to form a national strike, touches the humanity of the situation. "Rain" makes the simple pathos of lost love into something near tragic in the racial circumstance. Perhaps his best short story is "The Bench," in which the small and doomed decision of the African to sit upon a "Europeans Only" bench soon ends in his violent removal. The last lines are indicative of the new heroics that are possible after the gesture has been made:

> Now it was his turn to smile. He had challenged and he felt he had won. Who cared at the result? "Come on, you swine," said the policeman, forcing Karlie through the crowd. "Certainly!" said Karlie for the first time, and stared at the policeman with the arrogance of one who dared sit on a EUROPEANS ONLY bench.

There has been a kind of heroism expressed that is nonetheless a sign of significant dignity, because it is on the surface the consequence of such a minor event. This issue becomes perhaps the basis for all African writers, of whom I have discussed only a few: how to find human dignity within a situation that is expressly contrived to deny it to an African. If this is at one level a social and political fight, this does not prevent it being the basis of a literature, as the concerns of human expression are necessarily the same.

Perhaps a writer who most beautifully attempts to expose this sense of determined though embattled humanity is the poet Dennis Brutus (b. 1920). He can be seen in the most direct line of present-day South African elements discussed above. He has the anger of La Guma and yet he has the compassion of Paton. If he is prepared occasionally to write with the angry urgency that approaches propaganda, he is aware of the significance of art, as he creates a tender lyric poetry to express his impassioned dismay. He recognizes that he lives in a world of violence:

> Investigating searchlights rake
> our naked unprotected contours;
> boots club our peeling door.
> Patrols along the asphalt dark
> hissing their menace to our lives...

This environment is not only an immediately personal and political thing but also the material for a literary statement. But Brutus is too sensitive a man to describe this only in social terms. As a poet must, he finds in love possible alternatives to his situation. His *Sirens, Knuckles, Boots* (1964), contains a poem to his wife in which he wrote:

> and answering, you pressed my face against your womb
> and drew me to a safe and still oblivion,
> shut out the knives and teeth; boots bayonets and knuckles...

But these escapes can only be temporary within the particular culture which Brutus, as other South African writers, has inherited. How does either life or art put up its thin humane defenses against this harsh society? Brutus seems beautifully assured, yet his feeling is at such an instinctive poetic level that it does not permit an entirely rational explanation. It has the unqualified certainty of the unconquered spirit. In a moving poem he remarks.

> Somehow we survive
> and tenderness frustrated, does not wither....

That "Somehow" is indicative, for it seems to indicate the inability of the poet to define more specifically the apparently impossible continuance of charity. Yet it makes quite clear that in South Africa tenderness can and must survive. It is the most essential role of the writer to make this eternal statement.

Within the restrictions and tensions of South Africa the impassioned assertion is still made in many guises. Athol Fugard (b. 1930), in his popular international dramatic success, *The Blood Knot* (1965), sets out this situation in theatrical terms, making his theme a parable in which brothers divided by color must fight out their cruel destiny. Subsequent plays by this distinguished young dramatist, including *Lena and Boesman*, which received its premiere in South Africa in 1969, investigate the same appalling sense of deprivation and loss. The fact that he writes in South Africa and can produce his works suggests perhaps there are still chinks in the armor of a society that endeavors to insulate itself against the jabs of its literary tradition.

From the arrival of Jan van Riebeeck in 1652 until the arrival of Lord Charles Somerset, as governor of the Cape settlement in 1806, Dutch had been the official language of court, education, and government and Malay-Portuguese the language of the seaports and commerce. Throughout the eighteenth century Afrikaans, a spoken language based on the dialects of Zeeland, Utrecht, and South Holland and modified by African languages, developed rapidly and widely and became the primary language of the Cape Coloreds, then of the Orange Free State and the Transvaal. English superseded Dutch in government and polite society, but in 1875 a movement began in the Cape to replace Dutch entirely with Afrikaans: its journal, *Die Patriot*, was for twenty years quite influential.

After the 1899-1902 war, literature in Afrikaans suddenly flowered—first, as might be expected, in poetry of considerable lyric quality celebrating the people and places of their country, the war and its cruelties, the field and the farm. C. Louis Leipoldt, J. D. de Toit, and Eugene Marais (whose "Winternag" is especially noteworthy) quickly gained wide fame, even on the Continent.

The poets were soon followed by the prose writers C. J. Langenhoven—perhaps the most venerated of this early group—a humorist and satirist of a gentle disposition and unusual insight whose poem "Die Stem van Suid-Afrika/The Call of South Africa" became the national anthem, and D. F. Malherbe, the first university professor of Afrikaans, who encouraged a fresh generation of writers and wrote with skill and sympathy of the Cape vineyards in the past. His ministerial profession influenced his attitudes and allusions. But in prose little of lasting value was produced.

The publication in 1934 of the Bible in Afrikaans (by the British and Foreign Bible Society) was a great fillip to the use of that language for literary endeavors; and as in Australia, New Zealand, Canada, and the West Indies, "the poets of the thirties" challenged established ideas about the content and form of verse and poetry, though they maintained the political views of Afrikaners.

The principal poets of this group were W. E. G. Louw and his brother N. P. van Wyk Louw, author of *Raka*, a dramatic poem set in Africa, and other works that departed from traditionalist religious ideas, established the poet as a prophet, and proposed that reason was normally subservient to brute force. In "Die Hond van God" (The Hound of God), which is often almost opaque, the poet deals with the universal theme of the conflict between human and divine love. Others of the "digters van dertig" (poets of '30) were Elizabeth Eybers, a plangent poet concerned with women's experiences, and D. J. Opperman, who might well be described as an intellectual poet. Eybers describes, with rare insight, a woman's experience during the months of pregnancy in what many critics hail as her most successful poem, "Die Stil Awontuur" (The Quiet Adventure); yet her other poems, such as "Sleep-walking Child" and "Snail," included in *The Penguin Book of South African Verse*, and which were translated by herself, are equally beautiful.

Opperman's verse, which includes many brief lyrics, is generally a reflection of contemporary life with its industrial and commercial, scientific and urban problems. It tackles national and universal themes, and the seriousness is in clear contrast to the work of Uys Krige, an associate of Roy Campbell, whose work is generally light and positive, though he was an exponent of the social and political consciousness of the Depression years. His "The Song of the Fascist Bombers" and "Swallows Over the Camp" are more than "war poems," for they capture with great poignancy the inner conflicts of the participants. Take, for example, these lines from "Swallows Over the Camp":

> The swallows glide
> above the gate,
> and all the world
> is warped with hate...
> The swallows come,
> the swallows soar.
> And we, shall we
> find love once more?

Randolph Vigne, a Cape Town literary critic, has observed that "Krige's war book, *The Way Out* (1946), and some of his English short stories are among the body of English South African writing that will live": it is equally certain that his Afrikaans compositions and translations into that language of the work of such poets as García Lorca will survive.

Quality fiction in Afrikaans has been slow to develop, though popular novels have proliferated. Part of the problem, of course, is the small educated population to whom anything more than "a good story" appeals. Notwithstanding, F. A. Venter's *Die Swart Pelgrim* (1952), Englished as *Dark Pilgrim* (1959), another novel on the theme of the villager coming to the alien city, has some merit. Other fictionists, such as Jan Rabie, Etienne le Roux, and W. A. de Klerk and André P. Brink show promise and may yet develop into prolific, quality novelists.

Now in Afrikaans literature there are the beginnings of a kind of thaw. Previously this writing was at the service of the beliefs of the conservative church, which makes the basis of the Afrikaaner racial ethic. Etienne Le Roux and the so-called Group of Six are writing ambitious works which, if not by international standards dramatically adventurous, nevertheless—granted the monolithic traditionalism of the Afrikaner *Volk*—constitute a significant minor revolution. But the future of Afrikans writing is severely constrained by the small number of those who can read it.

Nevertheless, the expectation of revolution must at present be considered a dream in the yearnings of the exiles. It is said that revolution happens when a government grows more lenient: there is no evidence that this is happening at present in South Africa. With the exception of certain white liberal South African writers of the quality of Gordimer, Cope, and Paton, South African writing at present is an exile writing. Brutus, Plomer, La Guma, Mphahlele, Nkosi, Modisane, and numerous others are all found abroad, writing within a cultural environment foreign to their antecedents within their native country.

To what extent, then, can the writing within the country reflect the contemporary social culture? The meretricious tales that form a large proportion of the works at present published in the country make their own pertinent and depressing comment on the state of the national culture by their very popularity. To the extent that writing is a direct criticism of the government, it can perhaps reflect nothing vital at all.

South African censorship is all the more severe because it is so miserably self-imposed. There is evidence that booksellers and publishers check devoutly with the government bureau before accepting consignments of books rather than face a loss. To this extent they give evidence that they are not prepared to press the possibilities even to the limits of the restrictive South African censorship laws which, by banning a writer, make certain that his works are neither read nor quoted within the country. They act as the anxious watchdogs of the government. Yet writing does not have to be wholly political to make its critical statement. Writing can make a social assertion obliquely by its very existence in the situation. Since such literature insists, as must all art, on human integrity and compassion and generosity, it is implicitly critical of a regime where those vital and instinctive feelings are seen only in terms of the inconsequent issue of race.

If we seek a contemporary South African writing that best reflects the present situation in that country, we may find it in the "little" magazines. Perhaps they enjoy some extra freedom just because the government does not feel challenged by the minority audience that they reach. The legendary *Drum* continues. It exerts an important influence on African writers in the country as one of the few markets available to them. Its demand for a particular type of light, tough story written in glib though vigorous prose has been claimed to have been the basis for the prominence of the short story in South Africa. But except for some courageous journalistic exposés it touches literature only peripherally.

At a more serious level, there are four publications that struggle in South Africa. They battle, as do small magazines everywhere, with limited subscriptions, with a national audience which—though not exactly hostile—is basically indifferent to experimental writing. In this case, their difficulties are compounded by the political situation. The most professional is the journal *Contrast* (Cape Town), and this is matched by the Johannesburg journal *The Purple Renoster*. Although both of these are impeccably liberal, *Contrast* seems to find it possible to write literature without making too overt a political statement. The Johannesburg magazine is more open in this regard because of the vehement integrity of its editor, Lionel Abrahams.

Guy Butler has introduced a new journal, *New Coin*, which (in an intriguing broad-sheet format) has published the poetry of some of South Africa's young, experimental poets. But the major journal, which struggles from number to number, is published in Johannesburg and is called *Classic*. This remains the sole opening for serious publication of African writing in South Africa. Its editorial board is distinguished; its pages, though of varied quality, have been the outlet for much of the initial work of Africans now regarded as the most distinguished exponents of writing among South Africans. Its problems are distressingly compounded by the unreasonable attitude of some that it should cease to exist as a gesture against government restrictions upon it. This argument is that since it cannot take the stand of publishing whatever writers it might wish, it should die with its principles intact.

The early literature of South Africa may be compared to that of Australia, but whereas in Australia the absorption of the sense of national identity into a literature continued in a direct stream—the river moving from the initial convict settlements towards the prime sense of national destiny—in South Africa it went from that early settlement to the ultimate catastrophe of a political and racial impasse.

It is for this reason that when one attempts to define South African culture through its literature, one comes up against the culture of race. One comes up against the fact of exile. One comes up against the necessity of propaganda, which militates against substantial writing. One comes up against the attitude that to avoid race is to abdicate from the responsibility of a humane intellectual even when this intrusion disturbs, even destroys, the natural bent of a writer.

One thing is clear in South African literature: it is boxed in by the political implications of race. The impact of this theme on the national literature will be apparent in many ways: it will be controlled by government legislation and its continuing indigenous culture will be distorted by the dreams of the exile who publishes abroad. The kind of international writing that is possible in Canada—simultaneously Canadian yet freed from the dictates of a very specific cultural situation—is not possible for the South African, because only the meretricious writer of escape novels can avoid the painful dilemma to which his country has made him the reluctant and yet committed heir.

Bibliography

Beeton, D. R., and W. D. Maxwell-Mahon, eds. *South African Poetry: A Critical Anthology*, 1966.

Butler, Guy, ed. *A Book of South African Verse*, 1959.

Callan, Edward. *Alan Paton*, 1968.

Cope, Jack, and Uys Krige, eds. *The Penguin Book of South African Verse*, 1968.

Friedman, Marion V., *Olive Schreiner: A Study in Latent Meanings*, 1955.

Gordimer, Nadine, and Lionel Abrahams, eds. *South African Writing Today*, 1967.

Hobman, D. L. *Olive Schreiner: Her Friends and Times*, 1955.

Hooper, A. G., ed. *Short Stories from Southern Africa*, 1965.

McNab, Roy. *Poets in South Africa*, 1966.

Miller, G. M., and H. Sergeant. *A Critical Survey of South African Poetry in English*, 1964.

Slater, Francis C., ed. *The New Centenary Book of South African Verse*, 1946.

Snyman, J. F. L. *The Works of S. G. Millin*, 1955.

Wright, David, ed. *South African Stories*, 1960.

lg2

Science

G. G. Cillié

𝓘t seems appropriate that the first scientific observation that was recorded in South Africa was in astronomy, the most ancient of all the natural sciences. The first commander at the Cape, Jan van Riebeeck, the founder of Western civilization on the southern tip of Africa, records the following in his diary on 17 December 1652, only eight months after coming ashore: "In the evening between 9 and 10 o'clock saw E.S.E., and southward from the head of the giant (Orion), about 80 degrees above the horizon, a strange star with a tail, the tail extending northwards right on the knees of the giant, and the head mostly to the south, about 10 degrees away."

Van Riebeeck records the position and appearance of this comet for several subsequent dates, and it is interesting to note that his first record predates its discovery by the famous Danzig astronomer Hevelius (1611-1687), a contemporary of Newton and Halley, by three days.

When the Lords Directors of the Dutch East India Company appointed van Riebeeck as commander of the first settlement at the Cape of Good Hope, their main idea was to establish a halfway refreshment station where their trading vessels to the East Indies would at all times be able to obtain water, fresh vegetables, and meat. For about two centuries after 1652 the people who settled in South Africa found themselves so much preoccupied with the struggle for survival that there remained little time for the investigation of scientific principles. The beauty of the night sky, with its strange constellations around the South Pole, must have attracted the attention of many of the inhabitants from time to time. But they had neither the inclination nor the opportunity to study natural phenomena.

Early maps put the Cape five degrees too far east, a fact that must have caused considerable confusion to navigators attempting to find it. Governor Simon van der Stel extended great hospitality to a group of French missionaries on their way to the East when one of them, Father Gui Tachard, declared himself willing and able to measure the longitude of the Cape by means of the eclipses of Jupiter's satellites. In addition to reducing the error of five degrees to two degrees, Tachard at this very early stage heralded the important contribution that South Africa was to make two-and-a-half centuries later to double-star astronomy by his discovery of the duplicity of the bright star Alpha Crucis.

The first person to make a really significant contribution in South Africa to our knowledge of the far southern skies was another French priest, Abbé de Lacaille (1713-1762), who worked at the Cape for about two years, 1751-1753. Lacaille, among other things, had measured an arc of the meridian in France, and was chosen by the French Academy of Sciences to do the same in the Southern Hemisphere in order to confirm the spheroidal—as opposed to spherical—shape of the earth. In spite of his being a very careful observer, Lacaille's arc, extending to about 100 miles north of Cape Town, gave discordant results that indicated a shape of the Southern Hemisphere significantly different from that of the Northern Hemisphere. It was only seventy years afterwards that Colonel (later Sir) George Everest—of Mount Everest fame—carefully inspected the tract of country over which Lacaille measured his arc and pointed out that the discordance was occasioned by the gravitational attraction of the mountain masses in the neighborhood of the two terminal stations, causing Lacaille's plumb lines to deviate from the true vertical.

From his Cape observations of the Moon and Mars, Lacaille managed to calculate the most accurate values for the distances of the Sun and the Moon then available. He also produced a very valuable star-catalog, which contains accurate positions of 9766 southern stars; in addition, he did quite an amount of surveying for the government around Cape Town. Lacaille introduced and named the following southern constellations: Fornax, Horologium, Reticulus, Sculptor, Pictor, Pyxis, Antlia, Octanis, Circinus, Norma, Telescopium, Microscopium, and Mensa—the last named after well-known Table Mountain, which he must have admired frequently during his stay at the Cape.

The oldest scientific institution in South Africa is the Royal Observatory of the Cape of Good Hope, established in 1820 "for the improvement of astronomy and navigation." Not until 1828 did the first appointee as Her Majesty's Astronomer at the Cape, the Reverend Fearon Fallows, begin proper astronomical observations at the site which the observatory still occupies on a slight rise a few miles from Table Bay docks. Fallow's successor, Thomas Henderson, during a brief stay of little over a year made enough observations for a catalog of southern stars as accurate as the best northern catalogs. His most outstanding contribution was the discovery of the first reliable evidence of a measurable parallax for a fixed star, that of Alpha Centauri. Astronomy books usually do not credit Henderson with this "first," because he delayed the publication of his result for Alpha Centauri for so long that Bessel, whose observations were made several years later, got his determination for the distance of the star 61 Cygni in print first.

Thomas Maclear succeeded Henderson in 1834, and for nearly forty years he pursued the task of measuring southern stellar positions, proper motions, and the positions of the Sun, Moon, and planets with great energy. He was a close friend of the famous explorer David Livingstone, whom he helped considerably in many ways. Just after Maclear's arrival at the Cape the most famous astronomer of his day, Sir John Herschel, came ashore with his own instruments to set up a temporary observatory only a few miles from the Cape Observatory. During his stay Sir John completed a task begun by his distinguished father, Sir William Herschel, to catalog the nebulae and the double stars.

The person who accomplished more than any one else in South Africa for the promotion of astronomy was Sir David Gill, Her Majesty's Astronomer at the Cape for the period 1879-1907. He encouraged astronomers from northern observatories to visit the country and was responsible for the eventual establishment of a number of oversea observatories in South Africa; he took a keen interest in geodetic work and helped to plan the triangulation system for the country. Under his supervision an arc along the thirtieth meridian was measured from the Natal coast as far as Zambia.

While photographing a bright comet in 1882 with an ordinary camera attached to one of his telescopes, Gill introduced photography for the determination of accurate stellar positions on a very large scale. This led to the eventual publication of the well-known *Cape Photographic Durchmusterung*, which gives accurate places and magnitudes of 454,875 stars, thus supplying the complement for a similar catalog for the Northern Hemisphere. It also gave rise to an even more ambitious international undertaking, the so-called Carte du Ciel, in which different observatories were given the task of measuring the positions and brightnesses of the stars down to a certain magnitude in different zones of declination. The Cape's own contribution to this program contained around 800,000 stars.

The Republic Observatory, in Johannesburg, developed out of the old Transvaal Observatory, a provincial meteorological establishment, largely as a result of a petition from the South African Association for the Advancement of Science after the visit of the British Association to South Africa in 1905. This observatory, with its 26½-inch refracting telescope, became a leading institution for all matters relating to double-star astronomy; its directors were indefatigable and careful observers of double stars, and through their observations at the telescope and subsequent reductions they made very important contributions to our knowledge of these stars. R. T. A. Innes discovered the fixed star nearest to us in space and appropriately called it Proxima Centauri.

Several observatories in the Northern Hemisphere have established southern branches in South Africa, and amongst them the earliest one was the Leiden Observatory in Holland, which has had close associations with the Republic Observatory since 1923 and has carried out extensive programs in the photometry of southern variable stars. Yale University Observatory erected a 26-inch refractor on the grounds of the University of the Witwatersrand, Johannesburg, in 1925; before its removal to Australia it contributed more than half the total of the trigonometrical parallaxes from all observatories in the world.

The Boyden Station of the Harvard Observatory, originally sited in Arequipa, Peru, in 1889 was moved to Mazelspoort, fifteen miles out of Bloemfontein, in 1927. With its 60-inch reflector and a range of smaller telescopes it contributed significantly to our knowledge in such different astronomical fields as comets, meteorites, variable stars, galactic structure, and external galaxies. Since 1955 the Boyden Observatory, as it is known today, has become a joint project a number of institutions and is run by a council in which the following are represented: the Smithsonian Astrophysical Observatory, Armagh Observatory, Hamburg Observatory, Uccle Observatory (Belgium), and the University of the Orange Free State.

On the flat-topped Naval Hill in the middle of Bloemfontein there is another American observatory, the Lamont Hussey Observatory of the University of Michigan. With its 27-inch refractor, put up in 1928, it has been making valuable contributions to our knowledge of visible double stars. When the planet Mars makes its closest approaches to Earth it is best seen from South African latitudes: the best earth-based photographs of the planet that we possess today were made by the Flagstaff (Arizona) astronomer V. M. Slipher, on Naval Hill and by W. Finsen at the Republic Observatory in Johannesburg.

The Radcliffe Observatory, established in Oxford, England, in 1772, was moved to Pretoria in 1937. Its main instrument, a 74-inch reflector, which was the biggest telescope in the southern hemisphere for a number of years, was completed in 1948; since that time it has made very significant contributions to our knowledge of the constitution of our galaxy and the Magellanic clouds.

No doubt the picture given above of astronomy in South Africa will undergo important changes in the not too distant future. The observatories are having stringent economy measures applied to them, and their localities, as well as those of the Republic Observatory and the Boyden Observatory, are suffering from city encroachment. All four of these institutions will soon be compelled to consider moving at least their more sensitive instruments.

While navigators during the seventeenth and earlier centuries produced more or less inaccurate maps of the coastline of southern African, reliable knowledge of the geography of the region could only result from scientific measurements like those of Lacaille, Maclear, and Gill, which were mentioned above. A system of geodetic triangulation according to Gill's plans was carried out for Cape Province and Natal between 1882 and 1893 and for the Orange Free State and Transvaal in 1906. Systems of primary and secondary triangulations covering the areas between the geodetic arcs for all of South Africa have been completed. The Trigonometrical Survey Office, a government agency founded in 1919, started using aerial photography in 1936 for the correction of existing maps and for the construction of new maps in conjunction with careful ground-control surveys. The whole country is covered by a map of 1:500,000, while maps on the scale 1:250,000, both topographic and topo-cadastral, have been published for most of the country. Larger scale maps are available for special regions.

Almost the whole of South Africa consists of a plateau between 3,000 and 5,000 feet above sea level, bordered by a coastal belt which is broad in the east and narrow in the west. The two regions are separated by an almost continuous escarpment, prominent and up to heights of 10,000 feet and more in the east (Drakensberg Range) and consisting of fold ranges in the south. Owing to anticyclones over the Indian and South Atlantic Oceans in summer, areas of relatively low pressure develop over the central plateau, causing rain, which is frequently accompanied by thunderstorms and less often by high wind and hail. The winters are dry, with plenty of sunshine and cool, clear nights. The generally low rainfall over most of the country—on the west coast it is less than 100mm. per year in parts—and the frequent occurrences of droughts, as well as frost and hailstorms, makes farming in most parts a very hazardous business. Ever since they moved inland farmers have stood in need of a good meteorological service.

Scientific meteorology began with Lacaille, who kept the first continuous instrumental weather records for a year during his visit. At the instigation of Sir John Hershel, regular meteorological observations were made at the Royal Cape Observatory from 1841 onwards. J. G. Sutton is regarded as the true pioneer of meteorological research in South Africa because of his work in this field done at a fully-equipped meteorological station at Kimberley, which was financed by the De Beers Company. G. W. Cox initiated studies of the upper atmosphere by means of balloons in 1918. Nowadays daily records of the weather from many stations all over the country—as well as a few outside it, like Tristan da Cunha, some 1,700 miles west of Cape Town, and Marion Island, some 1,100 south-east of Port Elizabeth—are correlated by the Weather Bureau in Pretoria with a view to weather predictions. Accurate short-range weather forecasts are broadcast daily, and local forecasts are available to aviators and others. But in spite of using the most modern methods—including radio, radar, the United States weather satellites, and a high-speed computer—no dependable long-range weather forecasts, which are so important for South African farming, can yet be given.

Apart from the Weather Bureau, significant contributions to our knowledge of lightning have been made by the Bernard Price Institute for Geophysical Research in Johannesburg, especially under Sir Basil Schonland, who became the head of the Harwell Institute for Nuclear Research after leaving South Africa. By means of high-speed photography, the "life history" of a lightning flash from cloud to ground was discovered: a leader stroke emanates from the cloud and this triggers a bright return stroke one hundredth of a second later.

Because of the low rainfall, which is generally erratic in its nature and distribution, and the high run-off, there is a paucity of ground-water supplies on the plateau in South Africa. A great deal of scientific work has gone into the tracing of underground water supplies and into methods of checking run-off as well as the re-use of water. The Department of Irrigation undertakes systematic hydrological research concerned with the measurement of run-off. Forest hydrological work is carried out by the Department of Forestry and the faculty of forestry at the University of Stellenbosch. The Council for Scientific and Industrial Research has pioneered modern methods for finding underground water by making use of the vertical force magnetic variometer and measurements of electrical resistivity. After intensive work by the National Institute for Water Research of the C.S.I.R. in Pretoria an extensive plant for the purification of effluent has been set up at Windhoek in Southwest Africa (Namibia), and the purified water is re-used.

Copper, tin, and gold were mined in southern Africa before the arrival of the white man. Governor Simon van der Stel became interested when Hottentots showed him some copper ore that they brought from Namaqualand. In 1685 he himself led an expedition to the north along the west coast. This lasted for six months and took him to the so-called Koperberg (Copper Mountain), where plenty of evidence for the presence of copper was discovered. Van der Stel decided at the time that it would be too difficult to work it, and only 170 years later serious mining started in the vicinity of Okiep. Even today the American-owned Okiep Copper Company experiences serious problems in its mining operations due to lack of water and fuel locally.

During the eighteenth century a number of travellers with scientific leanings mentioned the rock types they observed during their travels. It is a great pity that Charles Darwin spent only eighteen days during 1836 in South Africa. A trip through the Drakenstein and Hottentotsholland mountains, north of the Cape Peninsula, aroused his interest in the local geology. If he had gone further afield, he would doubtless have seen interesting fossils around Clanwilliam and in the Karroo, which would have stimulated their scientific study at an early date.

The man who became known as the "father of South African geology" was Andrew Geddes Bain (1797-1864), who came to South Africa with the British settlers in 1820 and is to this day remembered by travellers in the Cape Province as the builder of Bain's Kloof Pass and Michell's Pass between Wellington and Ceres as well as the Queen's Road, leading northwards over Botha's Hill from Grahamstown to the valley of the Great Fish River and past Fort Beaufort to the Winterberg. It was while working on the latter project that he read Lyell's *Principles of Geology* and became so enthralled that the pursuit of this science became his ruling passion for the rest of his life. While roadmaking he came upon the fossils of the Permian reptiles of the Karroo, of which he made an extensive collection. He offered this collection to Grahamstown as the start of a local museum and, when it was refused, sent it to England.

Whilst Bain is credited with the discovery of the enormous fossil wealth of the Karroo beds, a surgeon friend of his, W. G. Atherstone, who worked with Bain in geology, is remembered especially for the fact that in 1867 he identified the first diamond that had been picked up by children playing with an attractive little stone that they had picked up on the bank of the Orange River. Lorenzo Boyes, Clerk of the Peace at Colesberg, knowing that Atherstone had some knowledge of minerals, sent the stone, enclosed in an ordinary envelope, to Grahamstown by mail on 15 March 1867. After determining its density, hardness, and behavior in polarized light, Atherstone decided that it was indeed a diamond. It was eventually sold for 500 pounds to the governor at the Cape, Sir Philip Wodehouse. This was the beginning of the diamond industry in South Africa: in 1966 the total value of diamonds sold amounted to almost $55,000,000.

Atherstone advised that a search be made for diamonds along the Orange and Vaal rivers, and the discovery of the "Star of Africa" of 82½ carats by a Griqua herd-boy led to the first mineral rush in South Africa. The first diamond pipes were discovered in 1871, and from then onward proper mining operations replaced the unsystematic alluvial digging. Kimberley, with its giant open mines from which millions of carats of diamonds have been taken, has for long periods during the past century been synonymous with diamond production.

Gold in workable deposits was first found in the eastern Transvaal between 1870 and 1873 in the Murchison Range near Pietersburg and in the Pilgrim's Rest area. In 1882 the Barberton goldfields produced a gold-rush, but this was nothing compared to the rush that resulted after the discovery of the gold-bearing deposits of the Witwatersrand in 1884. In the more than 80 years of its activity the gold mining industry of the Rand has influenced the development of South Africa in many ways, including the advancement of science. Some of the problems that had to be solved were those of mining at depths beyond 10,000 feet; of finding the best methods of extracting the gold, and more recently uranium, from the ore; and of applying modern scientific methods of prospecting. Applications since 1930 of geophysical gravimetric, magnetic, and seismic methods led to the extension of the gold-producing area to eastern and western Transvaal, as well as to the gold-producing area to eastern and western Transvaal, as well as to the more recent discovery and development of the Orange Free State goldfields. With South Africa producing (according to some estimates) 60 percent of the total world output, it is authoritatively stated that gold production in the country is at its peak today. In 1966 about 31 million fine ounces of gold were produced in the Republic.

The discovery of gold on the Rand led to the institution of the Transvaal Geological Department with G. A. F. Molengraaf as state geologist, and under him the first systematic geological survey was begun. A Geological Survey Division for the whole country came into being after Union in 1910, and with a trained staff it has been carrying on the work of making geological maps of the country. Through the efforts of individual geologists, as well as systematic work by the Geological Survey,

Science

South Africa has been shown to be a country rich in most of the important minerals. Apart from deposits of gold in Transvaal and the Orange Free State and of diamonds in the northern Cape and near the mouth of the Orange River, there are deposits of copper in the Cape, in South-West Africa and in Transvaal; coal in the northern Free State, southern Transvaal, and Natal; manganese and asbestos in northern Cape; nickel, chromium, platinum, tin, and phosphates in Transvaal. The most recent discovery (1969) was that of natural gas on the continental shelf off the south coast of Cape Province.

To the end of the nineteenth century the study of geology in the Republic was in the hands of individuals who published their results in oversees journals, but the Geological Society of South Africa, formed in 1895, has since done much for the science, especially through its journal. Practically every university in the country has a department of geology where students are trained to advanced levels.

It was mentioned above that Bain's interest in geology was stimulated by his discovery of fossils in the eastern Cape. Today we know that South Africa is rich not only in minerals but also in fossils. The well-known paleontologist Robert Broom in 1932 made an estimate of the number of reptile fossils in the so-called Beaufort Beds of the Karroo. From his field studies in his favorite districts of Beaufort West and Victoria West he estimated that on an average five creatures lie exposed for every square mile. For every fossil lying in view there would be about one thousand lying under dust or boulders or covered by vegetation. The fossil beds cover an area of 200,000 square miles and reach to a depth of 5,000 feet (average: 2,000 feet). With these dimensions, Broom claimed that the whole of the Karroo formation may contain the staggering number of 400,000 million fossils. Up to that time only about 350 different species of reptiles and reptile-like mammals had been recovered, and Broom concluded that probably millions of new species remained to be discovered. He estimated that at any time around one million specimens lie on the surface, of which thousands are weathered into dust and thousands more become exposed by further weathering of the land surface.

Broom, who came to South Africa at the age of 30 in 1897, was an enthusiastic zoologist and a practicing physician. Shortly after his arrival he published his first paper on the fossils that were at that time entrusted to the safe-keeping of the South African Museum in Cape Town. In due course more than 300 papers on South African fossils came from his pen. The first dinosaur discovered by Bain was sent to London for study, and so were some others found during the nineteenth century. The remains were fragmentary, and little could be learned from them, especially as they had no skulls. Further dinosaurs have been described; but the study of dinosaurs has been neglected in South Africa because it takes months to excavate one of these prehistoric animals and a correspondingly long time to prepare it for study. Besides, although they are an interesting reptile order, they are only an exploratory off-shoot of the evolutionary line. One learns far more of the evolution of the mammals by a study of the transition stages between the reptiles and the mammals, and the history of the mammal-like reptiles (*Theropsida*) is locked up in the Beaufort beds. By now a fairly good picture has emerged of the land-dwellers of the African section of the ancient southern continent, Gondwanaland.

The mammal-like reptiles of the Karroo form a vast group of related reptilian orders that developed through a period of fifty to sixty million years, covering practically the entire range of the vast structural gap between primitive ancestral reptiles and the earliest mammals. The overall sizes of these animals varied from that of a rat to more than twelve feet in length, some herbivorous and some carnivorous. Some lived on dry land, while others lived in swamps and marshes; some were adapted for swimming and were presumably amphibious. Apart from specialization, lines of descent from reptile to mammal and from reptile to bird can be traced.

Besides the up-to-now still incompletely studied mammal-like reptiles, South Africa has given to the scientific world a series of highly interesting fossil skulls of so-called ape-men. In 1924 R. A. Dart of Johannesburg received a small fossil skull that was found in a lime deposit at Taungs, north of Kimberley. He concluded that it belonged to a child of about five years old and represented a new kind of primate, intermediate between man and the living apes. The press at the time hailed the discovery of *Australopithecus Africanus* as that of the "missing link," but many scientists at the time dismissed the specimen as that of an ape, although they were prepared to admit that it was an unusual specimen. In 1936 Broom discovered an adult ape-man of similar type in hard limestone cave breccia at Sterkfontein, about thirty miles west of Johannesburg and confirmed many human characteristics of the Australopithecine family. Broom's specimen is known as *Plesanthropus Transvaalensis*, while another genus and species, *Paranthropus robustus* is based on a good specimen from Kromdraai, not far from Sterkfontein. At Swartkrans, in the same vicinity, imperfect specimens of *Paranthropus crassidens* were found in 1948 and 1949. In the Makapan Valley near Potgietersrust more ape-man material has come to light and Dart described it as *Australopithecus prometheus*. These Australopithecinae possess many human characteristics, and Dart thinks they may have had the faculty of speech; yet their brain sizes and prominent brow-ridges give them an ape-like appearance. Being too recent in geological time, these beings cannot be real ancestors of man but may be slightly modified survivors of an ancestral type from which man came.

Stone implements were systematically collected in South Africa by T. H. Bowker in the eastern Cape Province about 1955. Because of the widespread occurrence of these implements, Bowker was soon followed by other pioneers. J. C. Richard attempted a classification of the stone-age cultures in 1880, but the first comprehensive work on the subject, *The Stone Ages of South Africa* (1910) was written by L. Peringuey, director of the South African Museum. Only in 1929 were the foundations for a scientific study of South African archaeology laid by the publication of *The Stone Age Cultures of South Africa* by A. J. H. Goodwin and C. van Riet Lowe.

The promotion of archaeology in South Africa has been stimulated by its introduction as a degree subject at several universities and by the establishment of the Archaeological Survey in 1935, the formation of the South African

Archaeological Society in 1947, and by the work of the Bernard Price Foundation for Paleontological Research.

South Africa is particularly rich in prehistoric rock engravings and paintings, the so-called "Bushman paintings," the number of sites having passed the two-thousand mark many years ago. The work of the famous French pre-historian Abbé Breuil in South-West Africa, indicates that many sites remain to be discovered there: he found no less than sixty new sites in the course of one month. The abbé concluded from his studies that rock painting is an art of considerable age in South Africa: coloring materials were used as long ago as the Middle Stone Age. Series of paintings in several styles, belonging to distinct periods of the development of the art, are often found in the same cave. Only the latest phases of the art can be attributed to the Bushmen, who roamed the country when Van Riebeeck landed at the Cape and are today found in out-of-the-way corners of South-West Africa.

The Bushmen live a hunter's life similar to that of the Old Stone Age men of Europe; the Hottentots whom Van Riebeeck found around the Cape in 1652 and with whom he traded cattle, were pastoralists and fishermen on a stage of development about the same as the New Stone Age.

Not until 1913 was the first pre-Bushman human fossil discovered near Boskop in the Transvaal. The remains consist of a cranium of enormous size (1750 cc.), a few limb bones, and a piece of the lower jaw. Haughton in his original description of this important find compared it with the big-headed Cromagnon race of Europe, whereas Elliot Smith pointed out affinities with Neanderthal man. From Boskopoid material that has been found in other places it is believed that Boskop Man and probably related types were fairly widespread over the continent of Africa, and inhabited South Africa before both the Bushmen and the Hottentots. Kenya is now generally believed to be the place of origin of mankind.

The rich flora around the Cape attracted attention from the beginning of European settlement, and visitors took great pains to convey some of the plants to Europe for cultivation. Linnaeus' *Hortus Cliffortianus* (1727) mentions quite a number of these; it was he who named the national flower, the *Protea*, because of the many and varied forms in which it is found. The country of origin of some indigenous South African plants was completely forgotten by the middle of the eighteenth century; *Nerine sarniensis* became known as the Jersey Lily, and the real home at the Cape of the *Aloe Soccotrina* was only rediscovered at the end of the nineteenth century. Up to the middle of the eighteenth century all accounts of South African plants were written in Europe and were based on somewhat incomplete collections and on cultivated specimens.

The real study of Cape flora began when interested travellers and botanists started their collecting and studying of the plants in South Africa. The Swede Karl Thunberg, who came to the Cape in 1772 for the first time, is known as the "father of South African botany"; his *Flora Capensis* gives fairly precise localities for about 3,000 plants. He was followed by other collectors: Burchell with 8,700 items; Drege with 200,000 items divided into 8,000 varieties; Ecklon and Zeyher.

The first South African to do systematic botanical work was Ludwig Pappé, Colonial Botanist and first professor of botany at the South African College, subsequently the University of Cape Town. He collected extensively early in the nineteenth century and his collection, together with that of Zeyher, formed the nucleus of the Cape Government Herbarium. A full account of the Cape flora in several volumes, *Flora Capensis*, was started by W. H. Harvey, for some time resident at the Cape, and the first three volumes appeared between 1859 and 1865. The work was later continued in London and completed only in 1933.

A new period in the development of botanical science in South Africa began towards the end of the previous century with the work of H. Bolus, P. MacOwen, and R. Marloth at the Cape, S. Schonland at the Albany Museum Herbarium in Grahamstown, J. Medley-Wood in Natal, and Burtt Davy and I. B. Pole-Evans in Transvaal. The most important herbarium in the Republic is now the National Herbarium in Pretoria, for which Davy's collection became the nucleus; but almost every university and museum in the country has its own herbarium. Important works on South African plants, apart from the *Flora*

Capensis (published through the Royal Botanical Gardens at Kew), have been *Flora*, by R. Marloth; *The Orchids*, by H. Bolus; *The Flowering Plants of South Africa*, by Pole Evans; *The Genera of South African Flowering Plants*, by E. B. Philips; and *Lithops*, by G. C. Nel. Two important journals in South Africa are wholly devoted to botany: *Bothalia*, issued by the National Herbarium at Pretoria, and the *Journal of South African Botany*, published by the Botanical Society of South Africa.

Owing to the lack of a sufficient number of suitably trained botanists, scientific studies of South African plants have lagged behind the studies undertaken for economic considerations. Studies of grasses have been made at the universities of Natal, Potchestroom, and Pretoria, largely with a view to their value as fodder and the possibility of cultivating them under semi-arid conditions on the high veld.

The gladiolus is perhaps the best-known product of South African cultivated flora. Hybridization and selection over a period of two hundred years have yielded a wide variety of attractive flowers derived originally from local wild forms, though the unique collection of succulents has claimed the interest of botanists and collectors throughout the world and proteas and ericas are becoming widely known, especially through specimens that are displayed at flower shows and by florists overseas.

The first organized efforts in plant pathology in South Africa started when the Transvaal government appointed a mycologist, I. B. Pole-Evans, in 1905. He was joined by Miss E. M. Doidge some years later, and together they became a vigorous nucleus of a plant pathology section of the Department of Agriculture after Union in 1910. Miss Doidge recorded and discussed five out of the hundred or so well-recognized bacterial plant pathogens known the world over. She and Pole-Evans succeeded in eradicating citrus canker, a bacterial disease previously well-established in the country.

Ecological studies in connection with South African plants began when early travellers made their records. Griesbach in 1823 expressed the view that the flora of the south-western Cape probably constitute a distinct unit in world plant geography. This has been confirmed by further investigations. Maps of South African vegetation have been drawn since 1886.

Veld burning, which is widely practiced in the Republic, results in the large-scale destruction of vegetable matter instead of its being returned to the soil. This gives rise to deficiencies of humus. South African soils are now known to be seriously deficient in humus, phosphorus, and nitrogen. Until the establishment of the Department of Agriculture, with its numerous experimental stations, each one devoted to the study of local farming problems, and the faculties of agriculture at the universities of Stellenbosch, Pretoria, Natal, and the Orange Free State, South African farmers had to use their own intuition or hit-and-miss methods to combat their many problems. Agriculture has been a major industry in South Africa ever since the first so-called "free burghers" were granted land in 1657 on which they could farm for their own account. Conditions of soil, rainfall, and vegetation at the Cape differ so vastly from those in the countries of origin of the first settlers that the farmers had to adapt themselves completely to their new environment. As the eighteenth and nineteenth centuries progressed and farmers settled further inland, they found that they had to adapt their methods once again to new circumstances.

With the closer settling of the country, overgrazing and cultivation led to serious erosion of the topsoil. A large amount of effort is devoted today to the combating of two of the most pressing problems of the farmers: the general scarcity of water and soil erosion. The latter is carried out mainly through the National Soil Conservation Board, which was established by act of parliament in 1946. Since most of the Republic is unsuitable for arable farming, a large portion of the land contributes to agricultural production only in the form of natural grazing. By keeping unadapted animals and using wrong methods, much of the natural pastorage has been destroyed and erosion has taken over in many places. As a result of research at a number of different field stations, methods have been devised for the maintenance of the veld in a highly productive state as well as for its improvement under badly overgrazed conditions. Research on the nutritive value of natural fodders is carried out by the Division of Veterinary Services and at the Nutrition Research Institute at Potchefstroom.

Maize is the main crop of the Republic, being the staple food of the Bantu as well as having the production of dairy products, eggs, and pork dependent upon it. By far most of it is produced within the so-called "maize triangle," which covers the northern Free State, and southern and south-western Transvaal. Owing to erratic rainfall in this area, production varies considerably from year to year. From a bumper crop of ten million tons in the 1967 season it fell to about half that amount the next year. Successful research has been carried out at Potchefstroom for the developing of new varieties of maize as well as Kaffir corn which are more drought - as well as disease-resistant than the old varieties.

Wheat, oats, barley, and rye are grown particularly in the drier areas of the south-western Cape; and as a result of research at Stellenbosch, hybrid types have been found which give an adequate return, are disease-resistant, have a suitable straw length and—in the case of wheat—have good baking qualities.

Among many other crops on which research is being done, special attention is devoted to sugar cane, tobacco, and tea.

The first sugar-cane plant was introduced into Natal by the pioneer botanist Medley Wood. The sugar industry of Natal and Transvaal produces upward of one million tons of sugar a year. The producers have an experimental station at Mount Edgecombe, in Natal, where cultivation methods are studied and a Sugar Milling Research Institute in Durban is supported jointly by the South African sugar industry and the C.S.I.R.; since its establishment in 1948 it has contributed greatly to the improvement of methods of refining. Research for the improvement as well as the protection of the South African tobacco crop is carried out at the Tobacco Research Institute near Rustenburg in the Transvaal.

South Africa still imports most of its tea from Ceylon. Although imported tea plants were first grown locally in the botanical gardens at Durban as long ago as 1851, serious production of tea began only in 1880. At present an attempt is being made to make the country self-sufficient, as there are evidently suitable areas here for the cultivation of tea. An indigenous tea, called *rooibos* (red bush), was discovered many years ago in the Cedarberg Mountains near Clanwilliam in the Cape Province. Through patient research a local medical practitioner, P. le F. Nortier, discovered how to cultivate the plants, and this has given rise to a "red tea" industry in that area.

There were times in the past when farmers in the northern Cape, Orange Free State, and Transvaal had to watch powerless while vast swarms of locusts devoured every green blade on their farms. Scientific inquiry provided the answer to this problem, too. J. C. Faure, like his Russian colleague B. P. Uvarov, observed that a locust takes on a different form and coloring when it roams by itself than when it travels in a swarm. The hoppers of the brown locust (*Locustana pardalina*) are gray or green when it is living singly, but orange and black when in a swarm. The solitary phase permanently inhabits the areas from which outbreaks originate. Armed with this knowledge, it became possible to trace the breeding areas of the two kinds of locust, the brown and the red (*Nomadacris septemfasciata*), which cause so much havoc when they swarm out of them. For the brown locust this area covers the middle Karroo, and for the red locust it lies in Zambia. Control methods consist of keeping the two kinds of locust confined to their breeding areas.

Much research is done all the time in South African faculties of agriculture, in the agricultural colleges, and on experimental farms on insects and other pests. The most successful method of avoiding losses due to virus diseases in vegetables and wheat consists in developing hybrid varieties. In this way blight disease in potatoes, spotted wilt disease in tomatoes, and root-rot and take-all in wheat are being held in check. The maize-stalk borer was a serious threat to the maize crop until it was discovered that it could be effectively combated by the timely application of DDT powder. Citrus production, which is an important industry in parts of the Cape Province and Transvaal, would have been impossible if it had not been for the insecticides parathion and malathion. In eastern Cape Province more than one-and-a-half million acres became useless as a result of very dense prickly pear. Special insects—the cactoblastis moth, the cochineal insect, a borer and a weevil—were introduced to destroy the prickly pear.

Van Riebeeck himself laid out vegetable and fruit gardens soon after his arrival, planted the first grape vines, and made some wine. With the arrival of the French Huguenots in 1688, some of the best available know-how in respect of the culture of grapes and the making of wine was introduced. Because of its Mediterranean type of climate, characterized by cool, rainy winters and hot, dry summers, the western Cape Province proved eminently suitable for wine production. Early South African wines, associated with the Constantia area on the north side of the Cape Peninsula mountain range, became world famous. But at the end of the nineteenth century the wine industry at the Cape almost came to an end as a result of the destruction of thousands of vines by *phylloxera*. Research showed that certain American varieties were immune to this disease, and these were used as root stock. In time the wine industry recovered, so that red and white wines, as well as sherries, of excellent quality have been produced on a big scale during the last few decades. Scientific research assisted in selecting the right types of vine for the different wines, as well as finding the best methods of controlling fermentation and of aging. This work is done mainly at the university, the Western Province Fruit Research Station, and the National Institute for Wine Research—all three at Stellenbosch—and by the big K.W.V. (Farmers' Wine Co-operative) at Paarl.

Farmers in the south-western Cape produce vast quantities of summer fruit for the local and export markets. These are made up of peaches, plums, apricots, melons, watermelons, pears, and apples. The Western Province Fruit Research Station and its twelve substations are continually trying to develop new varieties of fruit trees through selective breeding, as well as studying the influence on the crop of climatic and soil conditions. A successful fruit crop today is more often than not the result of a strict scientific program carried out by the farmer on the instructions of the appropriate agricultural agency. It begins with the selection of the proper tree variety, remedying soil deficiencies, combating insects and pests at the appropriate times, and the proper method and time for harvesting and handling the product afterwards.

The most important of the insect pests in the orchards and vineyards of the western Cape are the codling moth (*Carpopsa capitata*) in apples and pears, the Mediterranean fruit fly (*Ceratitis capitata*) in all deciduous fruits, and the Argentine ant (*Iridomyrmix humilis*), which promotes the increase of pests like mealy-bugs, aphids, and scale insects. A spray program of DDT has brought the codling moth under effective control; ants are being controlled by effective poisons like dieldrin.

Of the tropical fruits produced in Transvaal and parts of Natal the most important are mangoes, avocados, and pawpaws. Valuable research on them, as well as on citrus products, is being done at the Sub-tropical Horticultural Research Station at Nelspruit, in Transvaal, where (among other things) pawpaw strains of superior quality have been developed.

The deep ravines (kloofs) in the mountains along the south coast of South Africa, where the rainfall is fairly high, are the home of several kinds of valuable indigenous hardwoods, of stink wood, and yellow wood. The indigenous forests, whose remnants are still to be found in the area around Knysna in southern Cape Province, cover only about one per cent of the area of the Republic. Through the last three centuries they have become depleted because they provided most of the building timber for the early settlers. Nowadays these forests are strictly protected, and a program of forest management has been introduced to encourage regeneration. Indigenous woods are suitable for furniture and other specialized uses only; as a result, extensive afforestation has been undertaken with fast-growing exotic trees like wattles, eucalypts, and pines. These plantations cover more than a million and a half acres in Cape Province, Natal, and eastern Transvaal, and it is estimated that the Republic will be self-sufficient in timber in 1975.

Exotic trees in South Africa are in a dangerous position because indigenous insects are acquiring a taste for them in the extensive plantations. The pine emperor moth (*Nudaurelia cytherea*) is controlled by keeping pigs in infested plantations; the pine thrip (*Heliothrips haemorrhoidalis*) is kept under control by suitable spacing and thinning of the trees; and the Tachinid parasite (*Compsilura concinnata*) has been introduced to attack the pine brown-tail moth (*Euproctis terminalis*). Valuable bluegum plantations have been saved by the introduction of the Mymarid parasite (*Anaphoidea nitens*), which keeps the eucalyptus snout beetle (*Gonipterus scutellatus*) under control. In Natal the wattle bagworm has received considerable attention, and it is possible to predict and control outbreaks. Wood-boring beetles—in particular *Hylotrupes bajulus*, the European house borer—have become established along the coast, and it has been found that wood can be effectively protected against them by treatment with pentachlorophenol. Similar treatment of wood and wooden floors has proved effective against dry rot (*Cryptotermes brevis*) and termites.

Two species of trees known in South Africa as Port Jackson and Rooikrans, originally imported from Australia to tie down the sandy soil of the Cape Flats between the Cape Peninsula and the rest of the mainland, have now multiplied to such an extent along the south coastal region as far as East London that they have become a serious menace to the rich floral wealth in this area. Two other importations from Australia, the Australian myrtle and hakea, have likewise multiplied profusely in the coastal areas. Of the four, hakea is undoubtedly the biggest menace for our indigenous flora, as it is no longer confined to the sandy coastal region but has spread to the ravines of the coastal mountains. An ambitious program is being carried out for the finding of effective methods to control hakea.

The first settlers at the Cape found big game in plenty in the immediate vicinity of the Cape Peninsula: hippopotami, rhinoceroses, hartebeest, eland, and kudu, with lions and elephants not very far away. Hunters drove these animals further inland as the permanent settlement expanded, and naturalists from Europe who came to the Cape to collect specimens for scientific study had to travel further inland in order to meet game in considerable numbers. In 1799 the German traveller Lichtenstein had to go as far as the Sundays and Great Fish Rivers in the eastern Cape to encounter elephant, rhinoceros, eland, and lion. By the early nineteenth century wild animal herds had migrated as far as the Orange River.

A great naturalist who travelled extensively in South Africa, making careful notes about the habitat and mode of life of the animals he encountered, was William Burchell, who came early in the nineteenth century and took back to England large collections of mammals, birds, insects, and plants.

The first scientific institution in South Africa that included the study of animals and plants in its objects, was the South African Museum, established in Cape Town in 1825. The governor, Lord Charles Somerset, appointed Andrew Smith (1797-1872) as its initial superintendent. Smith was a medical doctor, holding the position of Deputy Inspector-General of Army Hospitals, and a good friend of Charles Darwin, whom he met here. Smith's wide interests included the animal life of the country. Between 1834 and 1836 he undertook various expeditions into the interior and made extensive collections. His outstanding contribution was four large volumes describing the mammals, birds, reptiles, fishes, and invertebrates of South Africa.

Little research has been done on animal problems connected with the wild life of southern Africa, which is unique for its splendid variety, especially of antelopes. Efforts to conserve the fast-disappearing herds resulted in the establishment of game reserves; the best-known is the Kruger National Park, begun as the Sabie Game Reserve in 1878 through the farsightedness of President Paul Kruger of the Transvaal Republic. The park today covers an area of 8,600 square miles, and with its immense wealth of large and small game is a great tourist attraction, because the animals in their natural habitat—even the lions and elephants—can be viewed from close quarters. Since 1931 several other game parks have been established: the Etosha Game Reserve in northern South-West Africa, where big herds of springbock can be seen; the Kalahari

Gemsbok National Park, where the oryx, South Africa's most beautiful antelope, is protected; the Addo Elephant National Park near Port Elizabeth, established for the preservation of the last remaining herd of Cape elephant; the Mountain Zebra National Park near Cradock, in the Cape Province; the Bontebok Game Park near Swellendam, in Cape Province; a number of smaller parks in Orange Free State and in Natal, where, in addition to other animals, rhinoceros (also the rare white rhinoceros) can be seen.

Unfortunately, the game reserves came too late to save a kind of zebra called Kwagga and the Cape Blue Buck from total extinction. Scientific work on the wild life of South Africa, which is being started in connection with the game reserves, is very much in its infant stage. It has been known for a long time, however, that wild animals are the carriers of a number of dangerous diseases like nagana, snotdisease, foot-and-mouth disease, African swine fever, rinderpest, and rabies, all of which affect domestic animals.

Research on local mammals has been done chiefly by the South African Museum, the Transvaal Museum, and the Kaffrarian Museum in King Williams Town. Reptiles have been studied in the Albany Museum and at Port Elizabeth, where F. W. FitzSimons established a snake park. From the Transvaal Museum has come the authoritative *Lizards of South Africa* (1943), the first systematic treatise on this group, while the study of marine biology is being carried on at the University of Cape Town and at the South African Museum. Protozoology, parasitology, and embryology have become the special fields of the department of zoology of the University of the Witwatersrand. Functional zoology and fishes are the special fields at Rhodes University in Grahamstown, zoo-geography at the University of Natal, and freshwater snails and mites at Potchefstroom University.

In 1938 a very exciting discovery was made off the East London coast when a specimen, *Latimeria chalumnae Smith*, a living example of the coelocanth group, presumed extinct for over seventy million years, was brought ashore. Unfortunately, the specimen was incomplete—its entrails having been removed before it came into the hands of J. L. B. Smith at Grahamstown—but Smith afterwards recovered further specimens that were caught near the Seychelles Islands.

The cold Benguella current along the west coast of South Africa, with its rich supply of plankton, contains relatively few species, but fish are present in vast schools. By contrast, the warmer waters along the east coast contain a much greater variety, but fewer fish. It is estimated that the fishing grounds around the South African coast cover something like 150,000 square miles, most lying off the west coast and some along the Agulhas Bank, between Cape Agulhas and Port Elizabeth. Because of the great economic importance of these grounds, intensive research has been done on them by the Division of Fisheries through its research vessels and aquarium at Sea Point, near Cape Town.

Merino sheep were first introduced into the country by Colonel Jacob Gordon in the late eighteenth century. Since then wool has become one of the nation's chief exports. From the earliest times the inhabitants found that the domestic animals—horses, cattle, and sheep—which they brought with them from Europe, were prone to local diseases and parasites. When the Voortrekkers moved out of the Cape Province into the Orange Free State, Natal, and Transvaal around 1838, they found that their trek-oxen were attacked by diseases carried by ticks and the tsetse-fly.

Cattle raising had scarcely become established in South Africa when it was threatened with total extinction in the 1890's by rinderpest and contagious pleuro-pneumonia, which had entered from the territories on the north. A young Swiss veterinarian, Arnold Theiler (1867-1936), was given the task of finding means to curb the scourge of rinderpest. With the help of others he developed a suitable vaccine, and by applying further stringent measures the disease was eradicated. Unfortunately, measures to combat foot-and-mouth disease have not been quite as successful, and local outbreaks occur from time to time. After the Anglo-Boer War, Theiler continued his investigations into a variety of stock diseases, and this led eventually to the establishment of the well-known Onderstepoort Veterinary Research Institute near Pretoria in 1908.

Theiler made invaluable contributions to the knowledge of different animal diseases and found the remedies in some cases. He showed that gall-sickness in sheep is transmitted by the blue tick, *Boophilus decoloratus*, and is due to a blood parasite, *Anaplasma marginale*. Although he succeeded in developing successful methods to combat this disease by a suitable vaccine, he found no similar method to fight another tick-borne disease, East Coast fever, which entered the country from the north. Two further tick-borne diseases—redwater in cattle and heartwater in cattle, sheep, and goats—are controlled by dipping in order to destroy the ticks. Theiler also devoted attention to the virus diseases horse-sickness and blue-tongue in sheep. He found that both were transmitted by a small species of gnat (*Culicoides*). Suitable vaccines were developed at Onderstepoort for both these diseases, and in view of the prevalence of blue-tongue, it is no exaggeration to say that without the vaccine from Onderstepoort profitable sheep-farming in southern Africa would have been impossible. Another virus disease, prevalent especially among small rodents in the Orange Free State, is rabies; this is almost invariably spread here by the bite of rodents of the family *Viverridae*, known popularly as meercats. In this way human beings and domestic animals become infected and die unless vaccinated very soon after the bite.

The bacterial diseases in animals for which successful combat methods have been worked out include glanders, botulism ("lamsiekte"), bloedpens, contagious abortion, and anthrax (at one time the most widespread). Since anthrax can affect human beings when infected meat is eaten (or by means of the wool, hides, and skins of infected animals), the successful control of anthrax was a major achievement.

When the Europeans landed at the Cape in 1652 they encountered small yellow-skinned peoples: the Bushmen, a nomadic race who stalked their game with bows and poisoned arrows and spoke a strange tongue full of clicks; and the Hottentots, who were nomads as well, but with cattle. They also spoke a click language, and could be recognized most easily by the large, fatty posteriors (*steatopygia*) of their women. There were, in addition, the "Strandlopers" (beachcomers) and the Korannas. Together with the Australian aborigines and a few small groups of black people discovered fairly recently in the mountainous regions in the north of South-West Africa, these small yellow people are regarded as living remnants of Stone Age man.

About the time of the European settlement in the south-west Cape, the Bantu (black people) moved downward from the north, mainly along the east coast, driving the yellow races before them. Being threatened on two sides and having to fight against fearful odds, the Bushmen were drastically reduced in numbers and lost their identity by being absorbed into the Bantu and the so-called Colored people of the south-western Cape. Bushman and Hottentot traits can often be recognized in individuals of these groups. The surviving groups of more or less pure-bred Bushmen and Hottentots migrated northward along the west coast, and their remnants today are found in out-of-the-way parts of the Kalahari, where especially the Bushmen surprise one with their capability to survive under extreme desert conditions. Anthropological and archeological research devoted to these indigenes continues.

South Africa has been called a paradise for medical research because of the varied composition of its population, who have so many feeding habits and social backgrounds all living under the same climatic conditions. Marked differences, for example, in the incidence of heart disease between Whites and Bantu occur and have been found to be related to eating habits. Similarly, the widespread occurrence of *kwashiorkor* among the Bantu is thought to be due to deficiencies in their diet.

There are occasional accounts of the outbreak of epidemics during the early history of the settlement at the Cape, and especially smallpox took a heavy toll. The government was held responsible both for dealing with outbreaks of infectious diseases and for public health generally, and did this by providing hospitals and health officers. The enormous loss of life that resulted from an epidemic of influenza in 1918 acted as an important stimulus for the creation of the Union Department of Health. In the meantime the large concentration of Bantu around the gold mines of the Witwatersrand, where working conditions were so totally different from those in the home environments, resulted in the deterioration of public health. This led to the establishment of the South African Institute for Medical Research in Johannesburg, and through the researches carried out at this institution the effects of diseases like pneumonia, tuberculosis, and silicosis have been drastically curbed.

Together with the faculties of medicine at the universities of the Witwatersrand, Cape Town, Pretoria, Natal, and Stellenbosch, the South African Institute for Medical Research has done much research in pure and applied bacteriology, pathology, parasitology, and pharmacology. Since 1947 medical research at the universities has been stimulated further by the establishment of research units supported by the C.S.I.R. These units deal with specific problems and cover such widely different fields as amoebiasis, bilharziasis, heart diseases, dental decay, human physiology, and social medicine.

Surgery has been very much in the limelight since Dr. Christiaan Barnard completed a successful heart transplant in the Groote Schuur Hospital, Cape Town, during the night of 2 - 3 December 1967. By this "first" Barnard and his team brought great honor to the University of Cape Town and the Republic.

On Saturday, 2 December 1967, Denise Darvall was admitted to Groote Schuur Hospital with severe injuries from an accident shortly before. Intensive resuscitation was commenced immediately, but a neuro-surgeon declared her to have inevitably fatal brain damage. Intensive resuscitation was continued and permission was obtained from the girl's father to remove her heart and kidneys after death for use in transplant operations. The heart team was alerted and the blood of the injured girl, both red and white cells, was found to be almost perfectly compatible with that of a patient in the hospital, Louis Washkansky, suffering from an incurable condition of the heart. Within half an hour of the beginning of an open-heart operation on Washkansky—when his body had been cooled to protect his vital organs—the injured girl died. The electro-cardiograph showed complete paralysis of her heart.

The girl's heart was exposed and connected to a heart-lung machine, which began cooling her blood. When sufficiently cooled, her heart was removed and transferred to a second heart-lung machine and fed with cold blood. Washkansky's aorta was clamped to isolate his heart, and his severely damaged heart was removed, leaving portions of both chambers to serve as stems onto which the new heart could be grafted. While the rest of his body continued to be fed by the heart-lung machine, the new heart was sewn in. The clamp on his aorta was released, and the new heart was fed with blood from the heart-lung machine while re-warming of the blood began. When the correct temperature had been reached the new heart was given an electric shock, and some two-and-a-quarter hours after it had stopped it started to beat once more. The heart was gradually allowed to take over from the machine and this process was completed half-an-hour later.

Thirty-six hours after the operation Washkansky's blood pressure, pulse, and temperature were reported quite normal, and when he could speak for the first time he said he was feeling fine. The condition of the patient, who at one stage seemed to have made a remarkable recovery, suddenly started to deteriorate after about a fortnight, and when he died after eighteen days, the whole country mourned his passing.

Since then Barnard and his team have done four more successful heart transplants. The patient who has lived longest with his new heart, Dr. Philip Blaiberg, had his operation on 2 January 1968, a month after Washkansky's. Recently a second hospital, Wentworth Hospital in Durban, completed South Africa's sixth operation of this kind.

Meanwhile, the medical faculty at the University of Stellenbosch is carrying out an extensive program of research on organ transplantation in conjunction with Johns Hopkins University Hospital in Baltimore. For this purpose baboons from the primate colony of the university are extensively used.

When Van Riebeeck landed at the Cape, Isaac Newton was a youngster of six years, and those who settled at the Cape during the seventeenth and eighteenth centuries came from a Europe that was only beginning to appreciate the value of the natural sciences. They had left their countries of origin without experiencing the power of the scientific approach. The British who came during the early part of the nineteenth century had been exposed to science to a greater extent, because by now the scientific revolution in Europe was further advanced. These immigrants settled largely in the eastern province of the Cape and later in Natal; therefore, it does not come as a surprise to note that the early South African natural scientists mostly had English names, and that many of them came from the eastern parts of the country. The very obvious disparity between the scientific achievements of the English-speaking South Africans as opposed to Afrikaans-speaking inhabitants in the past has gradually levelled off as a result of the establishment of universities where scientists of both language groups are today being trained in ever-increasing numbers. The following are known as "English" universities, because they use English as medium of instruction: The University of Cape Town; Rhodes University, in Grahamstown; Natal University of Pietermaritzburg and Durban; The University of the Witwatersrand in Johannesburg. The Afrikaans-medium universities are The University of Stellenbosch, The University of the Orange Free State, The University of Pretoria, Potchefstroom University for Christian Higher Education, The Rand Afrikaans University, in Johannesburg. And there are two double-medium universities: The University of South Africa, in Pretoria, which carries on most of its instruction by correspondence, and The University of Port Elizabeth.

All these institutions have faculties of science, but only Cape Town, Natal, Witwatersrand, Stellenbosch, and Pretoria at present have faculties of medicine and engineering. Natal, Stellenbosch, Orange Free State, and Pretoria have faculties of agriculture, and only Stellenbosch has a faculty of forestry.

The few Bantu universities, severely underfunded and catering to generally less well-prepared students, do not have noteworthy graduate programs; the best-qualified Bantu have traditionally attended Cape Town and Durban Universities.

Much of the research done in the fields of physics, chemistry, and the mathematical sciences is undertaken as a background to studies in other sciences or to industrial development rather as an end in itself. An important reason for this is that because of the high rate of industrial expansion, science graduates, without research training, are being absorbed into employment immediately after graduation. The universities are finding it progressively more difficult to obtain adequately trained staff in the sciences, because of the much more lucrative careers for scientists in industry. Furthermore, the available scientists are scattered among so many institutions that it has not been possible to form research teams at the universities except in a few isolated cases.

There are a number of research institutes that have grown out of work done in university departments. The Leather Research Institute arose out of work done at Rhodes University; the Fishing Industry Research Institute of the C.S.I.R. and the Magnetic Observatory at Hermanus developed from work done at the University of Cape Town; the Bernard Price Institute of Geophysical Research and its origin at the University of the Witwatersrand. South African physicists, chemists, and mathematicians have not contributed significantly to fundamental research for the reasons given above and because of the lack of adequate facilities for research in the pure sciences.

Perhaps the most important step forward for the promotion of science since World War II was the founding of the C.S.I.R. at Pretoria in 1945. The activities of the C.S.I.R. cover most of the sectors of science and its applications, and it operates under an independent council, made up of leaders in science and industry.

The most important part of the physical plant of the C.S.I.R. consists of a number of large buildings on a campus near Pretoria. These buildings house the different institutes, such as the National Chemical Research Laboratory, the National Research Institute for Mathematical Sciences, the National Physical Research Laboratory, and several others. A number of the institutes and research units are situated in other localities.

The development of standardization and the preparation of codes of practice in the Republic is entrusted to the South African Standards Council, whose executive agency is the South African Bureau of Standards. Its chemical division deals with chemicals, foodstuffs, textiles, timber, fuel, metals, leather goods, paints, oils, and insecticides, while other divisions cover metrology and all phases of civil, mechanical, and electrical engineering.

The Atomic Energy Board is responsible for research into peaceful uses of the atom. Work connected with the extraction and processing of uranium and other restricted and essential materials has been done by the Board, which also seeks to expand the existing uses and the development of new uses for radio isotopes, to control the importation of radio isotopes, and to study nuclear power developments. Its major facility is the National Nuclear Research Center at Pelindaba, near Pretoria, where its reactor, Safari I, is operated at 20 MW. The Board has its own Van de Graaff particle accelerator and support the accelerator of the Southern Universities' Nuclear Institute near Faure, in Cape Province.

In view of the importance of pure and applied science to the development of the Republic, a Scientific Advisory Council to the prime minister made up of a number of leading scientists in different fields, was recently instituted. The function of the Council is to investigate and make recommendations to the prime minister in regard to all scientific matters.

The latest available list gives about 150 scientific and technical societies in South Africa, many of which are country-wide and some regional; but not all of them are exclusively concerned with scientific research. Those that are include the

Astronomical Society of Southern Africa, the Botanical Society of Southern Africa, the Geological Society of South Africa, the Medical Association of South Africa, the Royal Society of South Africa, the South African Association for the Advancement of Science, the South African Chemical Institute, the South African Geographical Society, the South African Institute of Electrical Engineers, the South African Institute of Physics, and the South African Mathematical Society. A similar list gives the titles of about 350 South African periodicals at least partly devoted to the dissemination of scientific knowledge.

It is a far cry from the day when Van Riebeeck recorded his first observation of a comet in 1652. Scientific activity in the Republic of South Africa has increased by leaps and bounds, especially during the last twenty-five years. Up to the present scientists in the Republic have grappled more with problems specific to the country, and the tendency to do this will no doubt continue for some time. On the other hand, as scientific activity increases, scientists will begin to make more important contributions to our basic knowledge.

Bibliography

Crocker, H. J., and John McRae, eds. *South Africa and Science*, 1929.

Flint, William, and J. D. F. Gilchrist, eds. *Science in South Africa*, 1905.

McIntyre, Donald. *An Astronomical Bi-Centenary: The Abbé de Lacaille's Visit to the Cape: 1751-1753*, 1951.

____. *Comets in Old Cape Records*, 1949.

Science in South Africa. Council for Scientific and Industrial Research, 1949.

Thom, H. B., ed. *Jan van Riebeeck's Journal*, 1952.

3

Religion

Anna L. Conradie

Theological and ecclesiastical controversies and problems have played an important role in the cultural patterns of South Africa and even partly determined the political theory and practice of its various governments. In the second half of the nineteenth century and in the twentieth century the three Dutch Calvinist churches have not only exerted a powerful influence on the molding of the Afrikaans culture but have also—at least in synodical pronouncements—canonized the political theory of separate development. Aspects of its theology have also determined the general philosophy and especially the political philosophy taught at some South African universities. Contrary pronouncements by eminent churchmen of other denominations, as well as the creation of the Christian Institute as an interdenominational and ecumenical area of encounter between Christians, have again evoked repercussions in almost every aspect of South African culture; and these developments cannot be understood without some reference to the history of the various churches and religious movements in South Africa in the past three centuries.

Historically and numerically, the Dutch Reformed Church is the most important extant religious denomination, claiming about three million adherents—about one million of whom are Bantu or Colored.

When the station established by the Dutch East India Company at the Cape in 1652 developed into a settlement and the settlement into a colony, it became necessary to import Dutch Reformed ministers from the mother church in the Netherlands to provide for the spiritual needs of the growing population. Until 1795 the Cape consistory was under the control of the Dutch Reformed ministers from the Netherlands to provide for the spiritual needs of the growing population. Until 1795 the Cape consistory was under the control of the Dutch East India Company and the Amsterdam *classis*, or presbytery. Yet various factors, among which were the decline of the Company and internal dissensions in the church in the Netherlands, retarded the expansion and consolidation of the Dutch Reformed Church in the colony, so that by 1795 only seven congregations had been established, missionary activity was sporadic, and it was confined to the slave population and Hottentot families in the service of farmers.

When the colony passed into British control the connection between the Cape church and the Amsterdam classis was severed, as the latter was now situated in a hostile republic. In 1824 the first synod of the independent Dutch Reformed Church in South Africa met. Yet almost immediately the political situation presented problems which would affect this church closely and lead to the establishment of two new Calvinist churches independent of the Dutch Reformed Church: the Hervormde Kerk and the Gereformeerde Kerk.

In the course of the eighteenth and early nineteenth centuries the trekkers had moved steadily east and north and eventually clashed with African tribes moving south. The grievances of the trekkers, which centered on British race policies on the frontier, resulted in the Great Trek of the 1830's, when the Voortrekkers moved beyond the political boundaries of the Cape Colony into the interior.

On the whole the Voortrekkers were devout Christians. But as they gained new territories and proclaimed new republics—which were in turn annexed by the British government—attempts by the Dutch Reformed Church to establish communication with them were viewed with suspicion. The colonial ordinance of 1843 had defined the Dutch Reformed Church as the Church *in the Cape Colony*. The problem was thus whether the Voortrekkers could submit themselves to the Cape Synod while remaining politically independent. Moreover, Dutch Reformed ministers were appointed and paid by the British government, which also exercised some authority in the administration of the Church. In 1820 the governor, Lord Somerset, had even sent Dr. George Thom to Scotland to persuade clergymen of the Scottish Presbyterian Church to fill vacancies in the Dutch Reformed Church. It is therefore not difficult to understand that the congregation in the new territories preferred to look to the Netherlands for ministers. In 1852 the Reverend Dirk van der Hoff arrived in the Transvaal and established the Hervormde Kerk, which had no connection with the Cape presbytery and became the State church of the Zuid-Afrikaansche Republiek in the Transvaal.

Soon a third Dutch church was established. In the nineteenth century the mother church in the Netherlands was split by schisms between "liberal" (or "rationalist") elements and an evangelical and pietistic movement that claimed to have remained faithful to the spirit of the Synod of Dordt in 1619. A minister of this latter Christelijke Afgescheiden Kerken in Holland, the Reverend D. Postma, arrived in the Transvaal in 1858, where he found that some congregations were dissatisfied with the close connection between state and church in the Hervormde Kerk; they were also opposed to the practice of hymn-singing in church, and they considered that both the Hervormde Kerk and the Dutch Reformed Church had deviated from pure Calvinist doctrine. These issues led to the formation, by Postma, of the Gereformeerde Kerk (sometimes called the dopper Church) in 1859.

The numerically strong Dutch Reformed Church had in the meantime also established congregations in the northern republics, and after 1907 the four provinces each had its own synod. In spite of various attempts to unite the Dutch Reformed Church—a fifth synod had by 1957 been established in South-West Africa—the first meeting of the General Synod of the united Dutch Reformed Church under one moderator took place only in 1962.

Although the Dutch Reformed Church represents 42.9 percent of the White population, as against 6.2 percent of the Hervormde Kerk and 3.3 percent of the Gereformeerde Kerk, all three Calvinist churches accept, as regards doctrinal and confessional standards, the Heidelberg Catechism (1563), the Confessio Belgica (1561) and the Canons of the Synod of Dordt (1619). The greater mass of Afrikaans-speaking South Africans belong to these churches and the language used in church services is almost exclusively Afrikaans, although there is a movement in the Dutch Reformed Church to introduce occasional English services.

Of these churches the Dutch Reformed Church has been most active in the mission field. Apart from missions in Nyasaland, Nigeria, Rhodesia, and Zambia, it controls three mission churches within South Africa itself. Of these, the Dutch Reformed Sendingkerk works among the colored population. In 1961 it became a fully autonomous body, with its own synod, although the final discipline of white ministers working in the daughter church still rests with the synod of the mother church, which contributes considerable financial support to the Sendingkerk.

The Nederduitse Gereformeerde Kerk in Africa is the African mission and is organized along the same lines as the mother church, with a general synod and four provincial synods—six in all, if we take into account that the Cape and Transvaal synods have each divided into two.

The Indian Reformed Church works among Indians in the Cape, Natal, and the Transvaal (there are almost no Indians in the Orange Free State). This mission Church is controlled by the General Synod of the Dutch Reformed Church via the Commission for Mission Work, and there is no institution for the training of Indian evangelists, who are at present trained by white missionaries.

White candidates for the ministry in the Dutch Reformed Church are trained in the faculties of theology of the universities of Stellenbosch and Pretoria; the latter also trains Hervormde candidates, while the faculty of theology of the University of Potchefstroom provides for Gereformeerde candidates. Colored candidates attend the Dutch Reformed Mission School at Wellington, and there are theological schools for the training of African ministers at Pietersburg, Witsieshoek, Decoligny, and Dingaanstat. At Hammanskraal, outside Pretoria, there is a theological school for African candidates of the Gereformeerde Kerk.

In the long annals of the Dutch Reformed Church and its sister churches in South Africa there were many dedicated and outstanding personalities, such as Andrew Murray (1828-1917), whose statue stands outside the Groote Kerk in Cape Town. With his elder brother, John, he was sent to be educated in Scotland and at Utrecht, and after an absence of eleven years he was in 1848 appointed minister at Bloemfontein, with a congregation scattered over an area of 50,000 square miles. His achievements in this period included the founding of Grey College, of which he became the rector and which later developed into the University of the Orange Free State. In spite of his flock's initial opposition to him on the grounds of his Scots ancestry and his connection with the Cape Church, he gained their confidence to such an extent that he served as intermediary between the Boers in the Transvaal and the British government and was also sent to England as a delegate to dissuade the British government from abandoning the Orange River sovereignty.

In 1860 Murray accepted a call to Worcester, in the Western Cape. His evangelical fervor led to an immense revival, which spread throughout the entire country and at least fifty young men were directly inspired by Murray to present themselves as candidates for the ministry at the new theological seminary established at Stellenbosch in 1859. Four years later he was called to most important pulpit in the whole of South Africa: the Groote Kerk in Cape Town.

Andrew Murray had a flair for organization and practical detail. In 1862 he was elected moderator of the Cape Synod for the first of seven times; he became the first President of the

Y.M.C.A. in Cape Town; he established the Normal College in Cape Town, and when he became minister in Wellington in 1871 he founded the Huguenot Seminary, a training college for teachers and an institution for the higher education of women after the model of Mount Holyoke College. (It later became known as the Huguenot University College for Women.) His urgent sense of the need for missionary work led to the founding of the Wellington Missionary Training Institute in 1877. Largely as a result of his enthusiasm, Dutch Reformed missions were established as far afield as central and east Africa.

However, Andrew Murray is famous primarily for the great many devotional books which he wrote in the seclusion of Clairvaux, his home at Wellington. These were translated into almost all European languages as well as into Russian, Japanese, Chinese, three Indian languages (Hindi, Urdu, and Telegu) and several Bantu languages. Strictly orthodox in his teaching, he was yet profoundly influenced by the English mystic William Law, and among his most beloved books he counted the autobiography of Saint Theresa of Avila, the works of Ruysbroeck, and the *Theologica Germanica*. His visits to Britain and to America, where he preached before large audiences, established his reputation as a great spiritual leader.

Professor J. du Plessis, the biographer of the Murray family, was appointed in 1915 to the chair of theology at Stellenbosch University. The Dutch Reformed Church had had its fair share of doctrinal controversies and heresy charges, but the du Plessis case inflamed the public interest in an unprecedented manner and led to a polemic which came to an end only in 1932. The formal charges against du Plessis concerned his teaching (1) that the Bible was not in every part infallibly inspired; (2) that the modern reconstruction of the history of Israel was correct; (3) that Christ, when he became man, relinquished His divine characteristics and was not omniscient; and (4) that a minister may hold views contrary to the doctrine of his church without informing the synod. This polemic stimulated theologians to re-examine entrenched orthodox views and influenced many outstanding scholars of divinity in the next generation.

The Anglican Church came to South Africa in the wake of the first and second British occupations of the Cape, but took root with the coming of the British settlers in 1820. Initially only naval and military chaplains were allowed, but after 1810 colonial chaplains were introduced to care for the growing number of Anglican settlers and civil servants. In 1847 Dr. Robert Gray (1809-1872) was consecrated as the first bishop of Cape Town. Gray's interest in education—he established the Diocesan College for Boys at Cape Town (known as Bishops) as well as St. Cyprian's School for Girls—had to take second place in view of the immense task of organizing the Anglican Church in South Africa. One of his first tasks was to divide the dioceses and to obtain clarity with respect to the legal and ecclesiastical position of his Church of the Province as against the erastianism of the Church of England in South Africa. Separate bishoprics were established in Grahamstown and Natal in 1853. Bishop Colenso of Natal (1814-1883) was deeply interested in missionary work and in particular sparked off a controversy by not insisting on the divorce of wives in polygamist African converts. The chief controversy, however, was due to Colenso's *Commentaries on St. Paul's Epistle to the Romans* (1861) and *The Pentateuch and the Book of Joshua Critically Examined* (1863), which were considered to be rationalist and influenced by the new "liberal" theology. Today most of Colenso's views are no longer considered heretical by the Anglican Church.

The furor over the theology expressed in these works resulted in the problem of authority in the colonial sees that had already on several occasions caused tensions in the see of Cape Town. When Colenso was summoned by Gray on charges of heresy he was found guilty. Gray deprived him of the bishopric of Natal and prohibited him from exercising any divine office. But Colenso, as Gray had done, appealed to the Privy Council and was re-instated. However, the anti-Colenso group in Natal refused to accept him, and a new bishop, Macrorie, was appointed in 1868. A small part of Colenso's diocese sided with him and has maintained its independent position as the Church of England in South Africa to this day, although not recognized by the larger Church of the Province of South Africa, which claims 1,500,000 members.

As a result of the Gray-Colenso controversy the position of the Anglican Church in South Africa was clarified. It was to be regarded as a voluntary society, dependent on a common faith and a common loyalty. South Africa, then, forms a separate self-governing province of the Anglican Church in communion with all other provinces and with the archbishop of Canterbury. It is divided into fourteen dioceses, each under the care of its bishop and with its own diocesan synod, which is composed of all the clergy in the dioceses and lay representatives of all races.

The Church of the Province of South Africa has no separate mission church. Each diocese is divided into parishes, and it is the responsibility of the priest in charge of each parish to care not only for his own people, but also for those persons who are not cared for by other Christian workers, irrespective of race of color. Non-white persons may be appointed to positions of authority in the church, though Bishop Zulu is at present the only African bishop: his ministry is not confined to people of his own race, and he in fact ordained a white priest in 1963. Non-white archdeacons and canons have jurisdiction over white clergy and lay members.

White candidates for the ministry are trained at St. Paul's Theological College in Grahamstown; African candidates are trained at the interdenominational Federal Theological Seminary of Southern Africa at Alice; at St. Bede's College, Umtata; at St. Augustine's Ordination Test School, Modderpoort, and diocesan colleges at Lebombo and Damaraland in South-West Africa.

There are records of Roman Catholic missionary activity in Africa as far south as the Zambesi as early as the fifteenth century. Bartholomew Diaz, on his journey round the Cape, had planted crosses at several points along the coast, and in 1501 the first church in South Africa was built by Joao da Nova in Mosselbay. In 1635 shipwrecked Catholic sailors built another church at the mouth of the Umzimkulu River in Natal. However, the Dutch and French settlers were exclusively Protestant and the Catholic Church obtained its first firm foothold in South Africa only in 1837 with the consecration of Rayjond Griffith as first Vicar Apostolic for South Africa. Although a small mission station was established at Malmesbury in the western Cape in the 1840's, Bishop Griffith himself was primarily concerned with making contact with Roman Catholics in remote areas. This was the purpose of his many visitations to inhospitable parts of the country. His diaries tell of his vicissitudes and adventures in a manner typical of his rather irascible personality; in spite of ill health, Griffith established the first Catholic school and managed to raise funds for the building of St. Mary's Cathedral in Cape Town. In the next century Roman Catholics succeeded in establishing a chain of mission stations across South Africa, one result of which was the ordination of African clergy and bishops. In 1923 the first apostolic delegate to South Africa was appointed, and now there are four ecclesiastical provinces (each with a metropolitan archbishop) and sixteen dioceses, each with its own bishop, ministering to about one million communicants.

Candidates for the priesthood are trained in the two national seminaries: St. John Vianney in Pretoria and St. Peter's at Hammanskraal—which is reserved for African students. Some of the larger religious congregations have their own seminaries and novitiates.

The expansion of Catholic missionary work has been offset by a marked lack of success among Afrikaans-speaking South Africans. This is caused not only by the deeprooted Calvinist traditions of the Afrikaner, but also by the linguistic barrier. Even today an Afrikaans-speaking Catholic experiences great difficulty in finding a priest to whom he can confess in his own language, and it is a rare event to hear Afrikaans in Roman Catholic services. A few Dutch and Flemish priests were introduced in the nineteenth century, but as the Afrikaner had by then achieved his national identity and no longer considered himself as Dutch, this step did not really allay the suspicion that the Catholic church was a "foreign church." Since 1952 an

Afrikaans quarterly, *Die Brug*, has been published by the Dutch Dominicans at Kroonstad. It caters for the few Afrikaans converts and has brought to the notice of Afrikaners the Catholic origin of many of their Dutch ancestors, has contradicted uninformed and sometimes slanderous accounts of the "Roomse Gevaar" (Roman danger), and has discussed cultural and political issues closely touching the Afrikaner within the context of Catholic thought. An English-language weekly, the *Southern Cross*, is published in Cape Town.

It is a curious feature of the second half of the nineteenth century that three remarkable men, each at the head of a different church, were closely associated with each other. Andrew Murray and Bishop Gray were at one in their fight against erastianism. The Anglicans had actually used the Groote Kerk for twenty-seven years before their own cathedral was built, and Murray and Gray had at one stage considered a union of the Anglican and Dutch Reformed Churches. But Andrew Murray was also the friend of a younger contemporary, Frederick Kolbe, who was to become one of the greatest of South African Catholics.

Frederick Charles Kolbe (1854-1936), the son of a Rhenish missionary, was born in Paarl, near Cape Town, of an old Cape family. He studied at the University of Cape Town and at the University of London, then for some time lived with the Murrays in Cape Town. He always remembered Andrew Murray with the greatest affection and admiration. His decision to become Catholic, which soon became a desire to enter the priesthood, took him to Rome, where he was present when his friend, John Henry Newman, received his cardinal's hat. He obtained the degree of doctor of divinity with distinction at the Gregorian University but renounced a scholastic career in Europe to return as priest to St. Mary's Cathedral in Cape Town. His autobiography, *Up the Slopes of Mount Sion* (1920), describes his intellectual and spiritual development during the first period of his life. Later he wrote many books on various subjects, of which the most famous are perhaps *The Art of Life* (1924) and *The Four Mysteries of the Faith* (1926).

Kolbe's ecclesiastical duties did not deter him from pursuing a wide range of interests. He was appointed examiner in literature and philosophy at the University of Cape Town; his interest in art contributed to the founding of the Michaelis School of Art of the university; he devoted himself enthusiastically to the improvement of choral music in the church; his *Shakespeare's Way* (1929) was acknowledged as a remarkable contribution to the interpretation of Shakespeare; he was a keen mountaineer and botanist.

For eighteen years Kolbe was editor of the *South African Catholic Magazine*, to which he was also the chief contributor. His lack of sympathy with the English during the Anglo-Boer War and his protests against the concentration camps at Worcester cost him the editorship of the *South African Catholic Magazine*. He did not hesitate to declare, "I am not pro-Boer. I *am* a Boer," and he prophesied the development of an indigenous and brilliant Afrikaans poetic tradition. His love for the Afrikaner was equalled by his love for the African; he unequivocally condemned the rule of the majority by a minority and emphasized his faith in the future of the African as an integral part of South African life.

When Kolbe died in 1936 his chief mourner was General Jan Christiaan Smuts, whose *Holism and Evolution* (1926) he had criticized as naturalism in *A Catholic View of Holism* (1928). This friend of Hertzog, Smuts, the poet Louis Leipoldt, and President Steyn left an indelible mark on South African culture in general, and in particular on South African Catholicism. At most English universities in South African there is a Kolbe Society, and at the Kolbe Winter Schools priests and laymen participate in discussions on philosophical, theological, and social problems. No less a person than Dr. Louis Leipoldt remarked that Kolbe was "the greatest of all South Africans."

There were some Methodists in the British occupation garrison, but the new Wesleyan denomination was not readily tolerated; the first Methodist minister to arrive at the Cape, Barnabas Shaw, was even refused permission to hold divine service; but since he was primarily a missionary, he obtained the reluctant permission of Lord Somerset to work among the

Namaqua people along the west coast of the colony. Like many other missionaries of the nineteenth century, Shaw did not know the language of the aboriginal peoples and knew nothing of their religion and mythology; yet by 1826 he had established a thriving Christian community in Namaqualand.

To the east Methodism was also soon to establish itself. A young Methodist minister, William Shaw (1798-1872), came to South Africa with the 1820 settlers as the chaplain of some Wesleyan families and settled near Grahamstown. He was the only clergyman at the frontier at the time, and he served both Boers and Britons. His ideal, however, was to establish a chain of mission stations in the African interior, and this he proceeded to do with zeal; it is mainly due to Shaw's influence that the Methodist Church of South Africa has more African members than any other mission church. The story of his struggles, disappointments, and triumphs are related in his book *The Story of My Mission to South-East Africa* (1860).

While Barnabus Shaw had devoted himself mainly to Namaqualand and William Shaw to the extension of the church in an easterly prong to Natal, a third famous missionary, Robert Moffat (1795-1883), settled in Kuruman to the north, in what is today known as Botswana. With his wife, Mary, he developed the station at Kuruman into a flourishing Christian settlement. He translated the Bible into Sechuana, built a church to seat five hundred people, and was himself an explorer and pioneer of note. In order to obtain wood for his building, he travelled through seven hundred miles of unexplored territory and also visited Mzilikazi, the feared chief of the Matabele. His book, *Missionary Labours and Scenes in Southern Africa* (1842), rightly made him famous. One of his greatest ideals was to abolish the slave trade in central Africa and to take Christianity and commerce to the African interior. It was Moffat who brought David Livingstone to South Africa as a missionary, though Livingstone was to achieve fame primarily as an explorer.

Until 1883 the Methodist Church of South Africa was under the direct control of the Missionary Society of the Wesleyan Missionary Church in England. In that year the first South African conference took place, and all missions and churches south of the Transvaal were placed under its jurisdiction. By private act of the South African government the South African Methodist Church became an independent, autonomous body in 1927, and in 1932 all Methodist churches in Southern Africa came under the jurisdiction of the South African Conference, the supreme body of the church.

The Methodist church has a missionary department that incorporates the South African Missionary Society (founded in 1887) and the Missionary Extension Fund (founded in 1904). The Nzondelelo is an African Methodist organization in Natal, established for the financial support of missionary work. White candidates for the ministry are trained at Rhodes University and non-Whites at the Federal Theological Seminary at Alice.

The Reverend George Thom, who had been sent by Lord Somerset to find ministers of the Scottish Presbyterian Church to fill vacancies in the Dutch Reformed Church, in 1814 formed the first Presbyterian church in South Africa, a congregation consisting mainly of members of a Highland regiment and people from other denominations. It was not until 1824 that a distinctively Presbyterian church was established in Cape Town, and Presbyterian churches were subsequently established in the other colonies and Rhodesia. The first General Assembly of the Presbyterian Church of South Africa was held in 1897 in Durban. The formal constitution of this church embraces the General Assembly (the highest ecclesiastical body), the presbytery, and the session. Each of these bodies consists of clergy and laymen, both White and non-White. Although for many years there were two Presbyteries in the Orange Free State, one for Whites and one for Africans, they were united in 1955, and today there are about 200,000 African Presbyterians—twice the number of white Presbyterians. Most congregations are segregated by race.

The former African, Colored, and Indian Presbyterian extension (or mission) churches are now united in one Church Extension and Aid Committee. It provides financial aid and guidance with the aim of eventually integrating these churches and with the white congregations. The United Free Church of

Scotland and the Swiss Presbyterian Church, in particular, have achieved much among the Bantu and Tsongo peoples.

The Presbyterian church will always be remembered for its close connections with Lovedale College in the Eastern Cape. One of the founders of the London Missionary Society was Thomas Love, a Scot who was a Presbyterian minister in London and who later became secretary of the Glasgow Missionary Society. In spite of the ensuing dissension between the established Presbyterian Church of Scotland and the Free (evangelical) Presbyterian Church, several missionaries were sent out to Chumie, north-east of Grahamstown. In 1824 John Bennie and John Ross established a station called Lovedale in honor of Thomas Love. Lovedale was primarily a seminary, and its first principal, William Govan, offered educational facilities to members of all denominations and races. Following the Moravian example, pupils were also trained as blacksmiths, carpenters, printers, and bookbinders as well as teachers and missionaries. The educational standard was very high. In 1870 James Stewart succeeded Govan as principal. He believed in a two-stream educational system that would provide moderately well-equipped Africans for pastoral work and also highly educated Africans as leaders and educators of the next generation. The teaching of trades and crafts continued, a hospital was added, and Lovedale became the first training school in the country for African nurses. This institution eventually developed into the first institution of higher education for Africans, Fort Hare University College, which was founded in 1916.

The Lutheran Church now claims about 50,000 White and 600,000 non-White members in South Africa.

The first Lutheran to come here was a Moravian missionary, Georg Schmidt, who in 1737 undertook to convert the Cape Hottentots and the Bushmen. With the permission of the Dutch East India Company and the Dutch Reformed Church, Schmidt established the origins of the later famous Moravian mission station at Genadendal. However, as the Dutch Reformed Church refused to allow him to baptize his converts, Schmidt returned to Europe in 1744. Thereafter, for more than forty years, little was done in this direction until in 1787 the Moravians once again attempted to reopen Genadendal. This time the brethren were allowed to administer the sacraments and to preach to the Hottentots—provided they did so in areas not already occupied by congregations of the official church. It is an undisputed if remarkable fact that many of the Hottentots at Genadendal had retained their faith and were still able to say the prayers taught to them by Schmidt. The mission developed rapidly and, not always to the joy of the brethren, involved the teaching of trades, schooling, and administration. When Commissioner-General de Mist in 1803 granted protection to all forms of worship at the Cape, there was one Lutheran Church serving the White community at the Cape; eventually, three kinds of Lutheran churches were established: White, non-White, and mission societies, which are linked in the Council of Churches on Lutheran Foundation in South Africa.

Among the mainly Wesleyan settlers of 1820, there was a small number of Baptists; one of them, William Miller, was the founder of the Baptist Church in South Africa. With the arrival of additional ministers from England the Church grew slowly but steadily, and by 1872 the Baptist Union of South Africa, a voluntary federation of Baptist churches, was formed and was followed in 1892 by the South African Baptist Missionary Society and in 1927 by the Bantu Baptist Church.

The Baptist Theological College of Southern Africa in Johannesburg trains White candidates for the ministry, and until the project of a training center for Colored students is realized, such candidates are required to take a four-year correspondence course in theology through the Ministerial Education Committee of the Baptist Union. African candidates are trained at the Baptist Bible Institute at Debe Nek in the Cape Province, while those candidates who have obtained their matriculation certificate are encouraged to take a degree in theology at the University of South Africa.

The Apostolic Faith Mission of South Africa was begun in 1908 by an American, John G. Lake, who five years later registered the Mission as a company and in 1961, by private act of parliament, had it recognized as a church.

The Apostolic Church in South Africa has Colored, Indian, and African daughter churches, for it considers that the interests of the faith are best served by separate churches corresponding to different racial groups. Its total membership is about 500,000. White candidates for the ministry are trained at the Apostolic Bible College in Johannesburg, Colored candidates at the Bible College in Cape Town, and African candidates in Pretoria.

As a result of the evangelical revival in England in the late eighteenth century, a new interest developed in missionary work among the so-called heathen. Of the various missionary societies established at this time, the London Missionary Society was perhaps the most famous. It was a non-denominational body, but the majority of the missionaries it sent to South Africa were Congregationalists. These later established Congregational churches, which formed the Congregational Union in 1877 and the United Congregational Church of Southern Africa in 1963 (with present membership of 300,000). White candidates for the ministry are trained at Rhodes University, where they follow the same courses as Presbyterian students.

Most of these Christian churches in South Africa run organizations for both Whites and non-Whites, such as womens' and mothers' associations, student Christian societies, youth camps, homes for unmarried mothers, orphanages, old people's homes, and voluntary associations to help the underprivileged. The Roman Catholic Church, in particular, is well known for its excellent hospitals and maternity homes throughout the country.

The Jewish religion, comprising 3.8 percent of the population of South Africa, has synagogues in most of the larger towns, runs orphanages, offers bursaries to students, and assists the needy through its various organizations. Apart from its 116,000 White members, it has about 100 Colored adherents.

The mythologies of the "Khoi-Khoi" (Hottentot) peoples found at the Cape have had no influence on religious patterns in South Africa. The few surviving Bushmen in the Kalahari have retained vestiges of their mythology, but their self-chosen isolation, shrinking numbers, and reluctance to communicate with other peoples make it difficult even for the anthropologist to establish with certainty their religious beliefs. Yet these diffident people, on the verge of extinction, have in many parts of South Africa left cave and rock paintings which throw some light on their religious beliefs in past centuries.

Of the indigenous peoples of South Africa, numbering perhaps twelve million, who do not belong to any of the Christian churches or Asiatic religions and who have retained their traditional mythologies, are usually classified as animists, but from the anthropological point of view this naming is not correct. African religions often vary from tribe to tribe in spite of a common acceptance of ancestor-worship and medicine men.

Occasionally certain practices of some tribes (for example, ritual murder) come into conflict with the law of the country; more often than not such events are concealed from the authorities and continue to be practiced in more remote areas.

It is from the heathen Africans that the independent African churches draw most of their 2,500,000 members. As these Africans feel that their way of life is threatened by Christianity—which is identified with White civilization—they prefer to accept a form of Christianity developed from within their own situation, and one of the most important projects in the religious life of South Africa at present is to provide preachers of the independent African churches with a theological education that will meet their needs without distorting the fundamental tenets of Christianity.

There are more than two thousand African sects in South Africa today, which may be divided into three streams:

(1) *The Ethiopian Churches*. These churches originally seceded from Christian mission churches on racial grounds. The Ethiopian Church was founded in 1892 by an African minister, Mangena M. Mokene, who resigned from the Wesleyan Church. His slogan, "Africa for the Africans," was intended to be applied also in the ecclesiastical field. In 1896 another African minister, James M. Dwane, resigned from the

Wesleyan church to join the Ethiopians. He became the leader of the African Methodist Episcopal Church of South Africa, which was the outcome of an affiliation between the Ethiopian Church and the African Methodist Episcopal Church in the United States of America. Later the Anglican church founded the Order of Ethiopia (of which Dwane became the head) in order to meet the problems presented by the independent African churches in the mission field. The Order of Ethiopia is in full communion with the Church of the Province and works chiefly among the Xhosa people. Not all of the members of the Ethiopian Church followed Dwane, and the remainder splintered into various factions and sects.

(2) *The Zionist Churches*. Zionism was introduced to South Africa by Daniel Bryant, an American missionary of the Christian Catholic Apostolic Church in Zion, who in 1914 baptized the first African converts in Johannesburg. Thus was formed the Zion Church, which was later named the Zion Apostolic Church. This church has since splintered into hundreds of Zionist churches, the members of which are almost entirely heathen converts. The American Zionist Church's emphasis on divine healing, triune immersion in baptism, and the second coming of Christ have, in the African context, led to a syncretism with African customs in which purificatory rites, taboos, healing, and speaking in tongues have become an integral part of their religion.

While Ethiopianism stresses the importance of a racially pure African Christianity under a strong African leader, symbolized by the Lion of Judah, King of Kings, King of Ethiopia, Zionism wishes to secure a supernational bond with the Holy Land by means of the power residing in names. For example, the Apostolic Jerusalem Church in Zion of South Africa, by incorporating the names "Apostolic," "Jerusalem" and "Zion" secures in a special way the spiritual strength of the church.

(3) *Messianic Churches*. These churches have developed fairly recently. They preach a secularized eschatology in which hope of the imminent transformation of all things consumes the faithful. An inspired prophet is also considered a political

leader: he promises liberation from suffering and slavery, political freedom, material prosperity, and health. The figure of Christ fades more and more into the background, and the faithful await the coming of the New Messiah, the Black Christ.

The last twenty years have seen a phenomenal growth of the African independent churches: B. G. M. Sundkler, in his authoritative book *Bantu Prophets of South Africa*, observes that in 1913 there were some 30 churches, in 1918 about 76; in 1932 the number had grown to 320, and in 1948 to about 880. In 1955 a total of 1,286 churches had applied for state recognition and in 1960 the number was 2,200.

The membership of the movement grew to 761,000 or 9.6 percent of the total African population in 1960. During the same period the African membership of the Methodist Church, the largest mission church, dropped from 12.9 percent of the total African population in 1946 to 12.1 percent.

With the exception of a few hundred Buddhists, Zoroastrians, and Confucians, the main Asiatic religions represented in South Africa are Hinduism and Islam; of these, Hinduism has by far the greater number of adherents (311,000 as against 192,000 Muslims).

Islam made its appearance in South Africa two centuries before the first Hindus arrived in 1860; Muslim slaves from Java and Ceylon were shipped to the Cape in the first years of the Dutch settlement. In 1694 Sheik Yusuf, who had protested against the Dutch authorities in the East Indies, was exiled to the Cape together with an entourage of forty-nine relatives and attendants. It was mainly due to him that Islam was consolidated at the Cape among the Malay population. (Near Cape Town is his tomb, built high above Macassar beach on the dunes: this impressive building is one of the most popular Muslim shrines in South Africa.)

Since the end of the seventeenth century the Cape Muslims, or Malays, have become a permanent part of the Cape community and many of them live in restored old Dutch houses in the Malay quarter of Cape Town. There was some danger that they would be absorbed into the larger Hindu community, but the first South African Indian missionary, Safi Sahib, helped them to regain their identity as Muslims. Today Indian and Malay Muslims are about equally divided: 98,500 Indians and 93,250 Malays, amounting to a little over one percent of the total South African population. In addition to Indian and Malay Muslims there are about 5,000 African and 300 White Muslims.

The first South African mosque was built by the Malays in Cape Town in 1850. Today there are over a hundred mosques in South Africa, more than half of which are in the Cape. The Juma Musjid Mosque in Grey Street, Durban, is the largest mosque in the southern hemisphere. Although there have been many holy men in the Muslim community, Muslims reserve their greatest respect and reverence for two Muslim saints: Badsha Pir, a mystic whose shrine is in Durban, and Sufi Sahib, who established many Islamic mission stations, teacher-training centers, madrassas (Islamic schools), mosques, and orphanages. These two men came in the wake of the 1860 indentured Indians, and many striking and moving legends are recorded concerning the miracles performed by them.

There are many Muslim associations concerned with charity, education, and welfare work and benefit the entire Indian community. Muslim organizations for the propagation of Islam are to be found in most cities, and much successful evangelical work has been done among Africans.

With the exception of a few hundred White and Colored converts, Hinduism is confined to the Indian community and thus mainly to Natal, where most Indians have settled; with few exceptions they all embrace orthodox Hinduism. The increasing lack of interest in their faith among Hindu youth is ascribed by the Hindu community to the growth of materialism, the decadent influence of American and English films, and the Western way of life prevalent in the large urban centers.

South African Hinduism has been influenced by reform movements that originated in India to meet the encroachment of other religions and to counteract entrenched social customs, such as the caste system and inequality among the sexes. Of these the most important are the Ramakrishna Centre, established in 1947, the Divine Life Society (1949), and the Parmahansa Yogananda (1960). These movements attempt to overcome divisions among Hindus in South Africa caused by language barriers and by different religious cults and rites. The universal character of Hinduism and those elements that it has in common with Christianity and Islam are stressed. Special attention is paid to the practice of yoga, the teaching of religious philosophy, and social work; ashrams have been founded to which members may retreat for meditation and guidance. Yet in South Africa Hinduism remains very much a closed religious community for, with the exception of the Arya Samaj movement, there is very little prozelytizing on the part of the Hindus.

The standard of living of the average Hindu family is very low, and over sixty percent of the men are unskilled and semi-skilled workers; nevertheless, the twenty-four major temples in South Africa are large and ornate. The Pietermaritzburg temple, although smaller, is situated in spacious grounds where annual fire-walking ceremonies take place. In the poorer areas small corrugated-iron sheds are often used as temples.

All the major churches in South Africa—with the exception of the Dutch Reformed Church and the Hervormde Kerk (these two churches withdrew in 1961) and the Gereformeerde Kerk (which was never a member)—belong to the World Council of Churches. The Roman Catholic Church does not belong officially to any ecumenical body but sends observers to conferences and discussions and participates unofficially in ecumenical activity.

About twenty-eight churches and mission societies belong to the Christian Council of Churches in South Africa, with the exception of the Afrikaner churches (they withdrew in 1961) and the Roman Catholic Church. To the World Alliance of Reformed Churches, or Presbyterian Alliance, belong the Presbyterian Church, the Dutch Reformed Church, the Hervormde Kerk, the Bantu Presbyterian Church, and the Tsonga Presbyterian Church. (These last two independent churches are at present negotiating to effect a unity.)

The Reformed Ecumenical Synod consists of the following churches in South Africa: the Dutch Reformed Church, the Gereformeerde Kerk: the Nederduitse Gereformeerde Kerk van

Afrika; the Nederduitse Gereformeerde Sendingkerk; and the Church of England. The three Afrikaner churches commune in an inter-church committee. The Federal Missionary Council of the Dutch Reformed Churches encompasses the mother and daughter mission churches.

Bearing in mind the history and missionary policy of the various churches in South Africa, we must now consider the challenge that the policy of apartheid has presented to these churches in the middle of the twentieth century. We must see it especially in the light of the fact that the Nationalist Party, which explicitly proclaimed and enforced this policy, was brought into power in 1948 by voters who were not only predominantly Afrikaans-speaking but predominantly members of the three Dutch or Afrikaner churches.

It should be remembered that the Dutch colonists had transformed a wilderness inhabited by nomadic Hottentot and Bushman tribes into vineyards, grain lands, and pastures. On the eastern frontier they had sacrificed lives and property to keep at bay the marauding African cattle rustlers who had never been indigenous to the territory occupied by the settlers. Their isolation and their common faith, of which the Dutch Reformed Church was the symbol, contributed more than any other factor to their growing sense of self-identity.

When Lord Somerset decreed that English should henceforth be the only medium of instruction in state schools, he experienced unexpected resistance; the Dutch Reformed Church became an active force in the unification of the Afrikaner. For half a century it was this church that had saved the Dutch language from extinction by establishing schools and a teachers college. With the establishment of the Voortrekker republics, considerable attention was again devoted to education in the mother tongue under the supervision of the church; and in the period of reconstruction after the Anglo-Boer War all three Dutch churches supported the Christian National Education movement. In the Transvaal the Gereformeerde Kerk established the first theological school in 1869 at Burgersdorp; it was transferred in 1905 to Potchefstroom, where it has developed into the Theological

School of the Potchefstroom University for Christian Higher Education. In 1917 theological training of candidates of the Hervormde Kerk commenced at the Transvaal University College, which developed into the University of Pretoria.

The struggle of the Dutch Reformed Church against compulsory instruction through the medium of English was of far greater significance than would appear at first sight, for the Dutch language had almost imperceptibly developed into a new language, Afrikaans. Even before the acknowledgement of Afrikaans as one of the official languages of the country, the translation of the Bible became an urgent question. Supported by all three Dutch churches, the first Afrikaans translation was published in 1933. This was followed by the rhyming of the psalms by the poet "Totius" (J. D. du Toit, 1877-1953) and by the rhyming of the hymns, which were set to music by Professor F. W. Jannasch and other South African composers. The Dutch churches thus contributed to the Afrikaner national identity in the sphere of religion, education, and language.

This self-identity had been achieved at great cost, and it was natural that it should be defended against continued efforts of the British to subjugate and absorb the Afrikaner, both politically and culturally. The isolation of the Afrikaner was thus a conscious defensive attitude that also involved a policy of segregation with respect to non-Whites. This policy was never presented as a doctrine of the church, but it was the attitude of most colonial peoples. In South Africa it was intensified by some members of the London Missionary Society on the eastern frontier.

The Reverend Vanderkemp's mission station at Bethelsdorp was accused of being a den of vice and laziness, and it is certain that he was regarded by frontiersmen as a sentimental ideologue. Since the slave trade had been abolished, Hottentot labor was in great demand. Hottentots charged farmers with cruelty, while the farmers (who were compelled to support an entire Hottentot family if they employed the father) accused Hottentots of vagrancy, vice, and laziness.

In 1820 Dr. John Philip (1775-1851) took charge of mission work in the colony. His main ideal was to obtain just treatment for both Hottentot and African, and this quite soon involved him in politics.

Philip took it upon himself to make a thorough study of the Hottentot problem, which resulted in an ordinance giving Coloreds the same legal rights as white colonists. In *Researches in South Africa* (1828) Philip perhaps exaggerated the cruelties and injustices perpetrated against the Hottentots, and the libel action that followed almost ruined him financially and endangered his standing. But his influence on Lord Glenelg was certainly such that it seemed as if colonial policy was in the hands of the missionaries, and this was one of the reasons for the Great Trek.

Henceforth, missionaries and liberal churchmen were often suspected of being agitators and troublemakers.

It is common, though inaccurate, to represent British South Africanism as liberal and Afrikaans South Africanism as pro-apartheid. Both are traditionally pro-apartheid, and in both groups there are many people who oppose this policy. The difference today is that the majority of English-speaking churchmen condemn segregation while the synods of the three Afrikaner churches support the Nationalist Party policy on scriptural grounds. Similar segregation in Australia and New Zealand has escaped condemnation.

The exigencies of Afrikaner history certainly led to a certain possessiveness with respect to their own culture, but it should be emphasized that this does not imply that the white mother church considers itself superior to the non-white mission churches. The attitude of the Afrikaner churches has always been that mother and mission churches represent legitimate differences of cultures and that each church should best serve its own people. It was not the church but the state that in the Transvaal explicitly rejected equality. Article 9 of the Transvaal Constitution of 1858 declared: "Het vok wil geene gelykstelling van gekleurden met blande ingezetenen toestaan in Kerk noch Staat" (The people will not grant equality of non-Whites to Whites in either Church or State). This was certainly a different attitude from that of the Cape Synod of 1857, which spoke of separate "gestichten" for white and non-white members of the church. It was clearly stated that separate services should be permitted, not because it was justified by Scripture, but in view of the "weakness" of some members of the congregations. Nevertheless, what was a concession to weakness in 1857 became a fixed pattern a century later, and this pattern is reflected most clearly in the legislation of the Nationalist government since 1948, specifically in the Group Areas Act (1950) and in the Bantu Education Act (1953).

Apart from the creation of rural reserves for Africans after 1913, which later developed into Bantustans, residential segregation—the restriction of Africans to locations outside cities and towns—had been in effect for more than twenty-five years prior to the passing of the Group Areas Act. This Act, however, involved large-scale removal of African, Colored, and Indian people to separate zones. The often large distances between white and non-white areas made it virtually impossible for non-Whites to attend churches, and vice versa. Moreover, while some church property became redundant, new churches and other amenities had to be built in the areas to which non-white members of congregations had been removed. Separate institutions also had to be provided in non-white areas for the theological training of non-white candidates for the ministry.

Although there is no law prohibiting a person of any race from worshipping in any church, this freedom is severely qualified and curtailed in the Native Laws Amendment Act, No. 36 of 1957. According to this act, the government may direct that the attendance by Africans at any church or other religious service or church function on premises situated within any urban area outside an African residential area shall cease from a date specified, if in its opinion: (a) the presence of Africans on such premises or in any area traversed by them for the purpose of attending at such premises is causing a nuisance to residents in the vicinity of those premises or in such areas; or (b) having regard to the locality in which the premises are situated, Africans should be present on such premises in the numbers in which they ordinarily attend a service or function. Any African who contravenes this direction by attending a church or other religious service or church function shall be guilty of an offence and liable to the penalties prescribed in the act.

With the Bantu Education Act of 1953, control of African education was transferred from provincial departments to the Department of Native Affairs of the central government, and in 1958 the new Department of Bantu Education took over all African education.

Up to 1954 missions and churches had controlled about ninety percent of state-aided Bantu schools. In that year the government decided that subsidies to teachers colleges and to mission-run primary and secondary schools would be progressively reduced and terminated in 1957; churches could either close their schools or rent or sell them to the department. They could retain their institutions on an unsubsidized basis if these were registered as private schools, but such registration would be permitted by the minister of Bantu education at his own discretion.

The handing over of African education to the central government met with strong opposition, especially from the Anglican, Catholic, and Methodist churches which, in the course of a century and a half, had built up many famous educational institutions. They considered that the direct influence of Christianity was necessary in African education in order to combat secularization and national extremism. However, all mission bodies handed over their institutions to the state, with the exception of the Church of the Province of South Africa (which surrendered only some of its institutions and closed others) and the Catholic Church (which resolved to run its schools on an unsubsidized basis and immediately set about amassing large funds to continue with its educational work). One important result of the Bantu Education Act was the closing down by the government, contrary to the alternatives it had itself offered, of Adams College in Natal, founded in 1853 by the American Board of Missions, Boston. This college had trained many leading Africans of South Africa and adjacent territories and had counted among its teachers Chief Albert Luthuli, Dr. D. G. S. M'Timkulu, Sir Seretse

Khama, Mr. Joshua Nkomo, Chief Gasha Buthelezi, and Dr. Z. K. Matthews (headmaster of the high school at Adams College for a short while and subsequently professor of law and Bantu studies, later vice-principal of Fort Hare University College). When Fort Hare, too, became a state institution, Dr. Matthews resigned. After an interval he was appointed by the government of Botswana as its minister to the United States and permanent delegate to the United Nations. He died in office in Washington in 1968.

The Population Registration Act of 1950, the Prohibition of Mixed Marriages Act (1949) and the Amendment to the Immorality Act (1950), as well as the social and religious implications of the doctrine of separate development as a whole, evoked strong condemnation on the part of church leaders such as the Anglican Archbishops Joost de Blank and Geoffrey Clayton and the Catholic Archbishop Denis Hurley of Durban. The Apostolic and Afrikaner church leaders did not protest.

In 1955 the Federal Council of the Dutch Reformed Churches in South Africa drew up a statement for publication overseas that represented the policy of its synods with respect to race relations. It stressed the following points: that the development of indigenous churches was in accordance with our understanding of Scripture; that if the development of indigenous churches had led to unchristian exclusivism on the part of Whites, the reason should be sought not in any ill will towards non-Whites, nor in the official policy of the church, but in uncontrollable circumstances and human weakness; that the mother and mission churches reserved the right to regulate their membership according to the realistic demand of circumstances, without willfully neglecting their duty to participate in the communion of believers. In a 1956 addendum the following statement occurs: "We accept the existence of separate churches according to each indigenous group. As a matter of principle no person will be excluded from corporate worship solely on the grounds of race or colour."

The various conferences organized by the Dutch Reformed Church and its sister and mission churches as well as interdenominational conferences concerning the implications of Nationalist legislation in a multi-racial country culminated in the famous Cottesloe Consultation. As a result of events at Sharpeville and the Langa disturbances in Cape Town, the Anglican archbishop of Cape Town appealed to the World Council of Churches to convene an inter-racial and interdenominational consultation, which took place at the Cottesloe residence of the University of the Witwatersrand during December 1960. It was attended by the eight member churches of the World Council in South Africa: the Anglican Church, the Dutch Reformed Church (Transvaal), the Methodist Church, the Presbyterian and Bantu Presbyterian Churches, the Congregational Union, the Dutch Reformed Church (Cape), and the Hervormde Kerk. The World Council's delegation consisted of six men headed by Dr. Franklin Fry of its Central Committee.

The consensus of the Cottesloe Consultation was that no Christian should be excluded from any church on grounds of race and color; that the state should make provision for adequate facilities for non-Whites to worship in urban areas; that the possibility for effective consultation between the government and the leaders of non-White peoples should be created; that no Scriptural grounds existed for the prohibition of mixed marriages (although social, legal, and cultural factors should make such marriages inadvisable); that the disintegrating effects of migrant labor on African family life and the low wages of the vast majority of Africans should receive serious consideration; that job reservations should be done away with. It was further recommended that a South African conference of World Council members should be created to deal with local problems.

Immediately after the Consultation representatives of the Hervormde Kerk dissociated themselves from these resolutions, claiming that they had not had sufficient support to defeat any of them. They reaffirmed their faith in racial segregation as being both scripturally justifiable and practically expedient. The prime minister, supported by the Nationalist press, criticized those delegates of the Dutch Reformed churches who had accepted the Cottesloe resolutions as not representing the views of their synods; and in the course of 1961 the synods of the Hervormde Kerk and of the Dutch Reformed churches of the Cape and Transvaal condemned the Cottesloe resolutions and withdrew from the World Council of Churches.

The tense situation was aggravated by the publication of the book *Vertraagde Aksie* (1960), translated and published as *Delayed Action*, almost simultaneously with the Cottesloe Consultation. *Vertraagde Aksie* consisted of essays by eleven theologians from all three Afrikaner churches, severely criticizing the attitude of the government and synods on race relations and rejecting racial discrimination and segregation as unscriptural. A charge of heresy was laid by the Hervormde Kerk against one of the contributors, Professor A. S. Geyser, head of the department of New Testament theology at the University of Pretoria. The Synodical Commission of the Hervormde Kerk found Professor Geyser guilty, and he was deposed as minister of the Hervormde Kerk. (Two weeks after the verdict Professor Geyser accepted the chair of divinity at the University of the Witwatersrand.) In 1963 the hearing of Professor Geyser's case began in the Supreme Court; but as the parties reached an agreement, it was terminated before the evidence was completed. The Synodical Commission undertook to pay all legal costs, re-instated Professor Geyser as minister, and acknowledged a bona fide mistaken interpretation of his views.

Ministers of the three Afrikaner churches who could not accept the ruling of their synods had in the meantime launched a Christian monthly magazine, *Pro Veritate*, with the aim of discussing South African social and ecclesiastical problems in the light of Scripture. This publication, which has an interdenominational and inter-racial editorial board, now has a circulation of over 5,000. It is violently opposed by the synods of the Afrikaner churches and also by the government as an integrationist and propagandist magazine.

One of the most important results of the Cottesloe Consultation was the establishment of the Christian Institute in 1963 by some 280 foundation members representing the majority of the Christian churches in South Africa, and including the three Afrikaner churches. However, it was not only the Cottesloe Consultation and the disappointing reaction of the synods of the Afrikaner churches that led to the founding of the institute. Long before Cottesloe ecumenical study groups concerned with the social implications of the gospel had been active in Johannesburg, Pretoria, Cape Town, Stellenbosch, Kroonstad, East London, and the Transkei—largely as a result of the initiative of Afrikaans church leaders. An awareness of deteriorating race relations, especially after Sharpeville, and of the necessity of an ecumenical approach to the divisions between churches and Christians in South Africa were other contributing factors.

The Christian Institute is open to members of all churches, irrespective of their denominational commitments. It does not pretend to be more than a fellowship of individual Christians and does not attempt to fulfill the function of any church. Nor does it overlap with the Christian Council of South Africa, although the closest cooperation exists between the two bodies.

At present its financial resources are derived from contributions by South African supporters, membership fees, and donations by churches and Christian organizations overseas. Donations from overseas constitute some forty percent of the institute's income, and this is used mainly for work among the African independent churches.

Almost all church leaders in South Africa, as well as professors and lecturers of the theological faculty at the Free University of Amsterdam (a stronghold of Reformed Calvinism) and of the Theologische Hogeschool at Kampen have expressed their appreciation for the work of the Christian Institute. Many theologians, ministers, and laymen of the Afrikaner churches also actively support the institute in spite of the fact that it continues to be denounced as an antigovernment propaganda device.

The director of the institute is the Reverend C. F. Beyers Naude. Although his defense of the Cottesloe resolutions and his editorship of *Pro Veritate* had been frowned upon, he had nevertheless been elected moderator of the Southern Transvaal

Synod in 1963. When he sought permission to accept the post of director of the institute, the Northern and Southern Transvaal synods refused his application; he therefore relinquished his status as a minister and accepted the directorship of the institute.

The Christian Institute continues to be heavily attacked in the Afrikaans press and in the official organs of the Afrikaner churches. In 1965 *Die Kerkbode* objected to the fact that there was a Roman Catholic on the board of the Christian Institute. In the same year Professor A. D. Pont addressed a student body of the University of Pretoria, stating: "It is not far-fetched to allege that the Christian Institute and the journal *Pro Veritate* are nothing but liberalist stepping-stones from which propaganda which suits communism admirably are carried into our churches," and at a Volkskongres on Communism the Christian Institute was accused of "playing the Communist game." Pressure was exerted on church members who had joined the Christian Institute to resign from it, and security police began to watch and question some of its members.

As a result of allegations made in articles published under Professor Pont's name in *Die Hervormer*, an official organ of the Hervormde Kerk, the Reverend Beyers Naude and Professor Geyser (chairman of the Christian Institute) instituted an action for defamation against Professor Pont. One of the innuendos, according to the plaintiffs, was that they were communists, mainly as a result of their participation in the Mindola Conference in Zambia in 1964. Mr. Justice Trollop awarded the plaintiffs the highest amount ever awarded for libel in a South African court, namely 10,000 rand each. He stated that he hoped the amount awarded would vindicate the right of Mr. Naude and Professor Geyser, who were prominent theologians, to advocate and declare their views in public and to continue to support and establish bodies and publications like the Christian Institute and *Pro Veritate*.

As a result of continued action by the Hervormde Kerk against the Christian Institute, some ministers resigned and some were deprived of their status. Professor A. van Selms and the Reverend Dr. C. J. Labuschagne had been compelled at the time of the Geyser heresy trial to relinquish their posts in the faculty of theology at the University of Pretoria but had remained in the department of Semitic languages, which was not subsidized by the Hervormde Kerk. These men became ministers of the Presbyterian Church, and many members of their congregations followed them, so that the Presbyterian Church thereupon decided to conduct some services in Afrikaans.

Attempts to assess social situations in terms of the spirit of the gospel are criticized also by some English-speaking theologians who consider that the church should not become involved in politics. This was also the line taken by Prime Minister John Vorster when, in reply to a *Message to the People of South Africa* by the interdenominational Theological Commission set up by the South African Council of Churches, he is reported to have said that the task of ministers was not to turn their pulpits into "political platforms... to do the work of the Progressive Party, the United Party, the Liberal Party." A few days later he was reported to have added, with reference to ministers who wished to follow the example of Martin Luther King Jr: "The cloth you are wearing will not protect you if you try to do this in South Africa." In reply to an open letter to the prime minister by the Council of Churches and the Christian Institute, in which they protested against this interpretation of their standpoint, the prime minister replied that they were in fact attacking the government from the pulpit under the cloak of religion.

In all fairness to the prime minister, it should be said that leaders of the English-speaking churches have all too often used the universe of discourse of party politics in the pulpit instead of the universe of discourse of the gospel, which enjoins the Christian to testify in the world as witness of Christ, in the spirit of supernatural charity. It was in this spirit of charity that Archbishop Hurley offered practical help and food to the Africans removed to Limehill in 1968. Christianity, inasmuch as it involves the whole man, also enjoins the Christian to procure social justice—whatever the cost may be; but this does not mean that the Gospel should be exploited as a textbook for anti-government or pro-government propaganda.

But this also holds for many Dutch Reformed ministers who preach Nationalist ideology under the cloak of religion from the pulpit, over the radio, and on national festivals such as the Day of the Covenant. Professor D. J. Kotze's "volksfilosofie" in his *Positiewe Nasionalisme* (1968) lists the criteria of sound Afrikanerdom, of which the most important are acceptance of the policy of the Nationalist Party, the use of the Afrikaans language, and membership of one of the Afrikaner Calvinist churches. Another example of the confusion of different universes of discourse was Dr. Hertzog, a deposed cabinet minister and leader of Calvinist nationalist conservatives, who stated that the leader of the fight for white civilization in South Africa must necessarily be the bearer of "Calvinist principles," where "Afrikaner Calvinism" is identified with "Afrikaner nationalism." According to Hertzog, English-speaking South Africans do not measure up to the strict qualifications of Calvinism and are therefore vulnerable to the onslaughts of liberalism and communism. Only the Calvinist Afrikaner is fit to rule the country.

Dr. Hertzog's irresponsible statements were repudiated by the prime minister, and he has been ridiculed by almost all sections of the community, including Afrikaner Calvinists. Professor André Hugo of the University of Cape Town, himself a Calvinist, has declared that Calvin himself would have been painfully surprised at most of the political views justified as Calvinist principles. Others have pointed out that many English-speaking South Africans and Afrikaners are Calvinists without necessarily supporting the government; that Calvinism is not a political party; that "Calvinism," "White Civilization" and "Afrikaner Calvinism" are not synonymous.

These differences of opinion reflect aspects of the current controversy between *verkramptes* (conservatives) and *verligtes* (enlightened ones) in South Africa. The verkramptes form an ever-hardening core of political Calvinists who wish to perpetuate the idea of the Afrikaner nation as a chosen people with a special historical vocation. The increasing numbers of verligtes among Afrikaners, many of whom accept Nationalism not on religious grounds but as an interim sociological program, are skeptical with respect to ex cathedra pronouncements concerning the will of God in South Africa and spurn the infallibility of the new Calvinist papacy. They are prepared to relax their traditional exclusivism and to support ecumenical endeavor. The struggle between verligtes and verkramptes has even affected the literary life of South Africa. In the South African Academy verkrampte pressure groups are attempting to make the awarding of the highest literary prize, the J. B. M. Hertzog Prize, instituted in 1907, conditional upon the soundness of the national and religious (Calvinist) sentiments of the writer. The verkramptes, together with the *Broederbond*, or society of "hard" nationalist Calvinists, also at times influence appointments at some universities, where a candidate may be appointed for his sound political and Calvinist commitments. The verkrampte-verligte controversy is also waged on the campuses of universities and in student Christian organizations.

All these phenomena indicate a profound re-assessment in South Africa, particularly among Afrikaner Calvinists, of the meaning and implications of Christianity as a historical and incarnational religion. It should not be overlooked that the Calvinist Afrikaner churches themselves are perturbed at the political implications ascribed to their theology. They are increasingly anxious to vindicate their goodwill, to refute unjust accusations that they are the puppets of party politicians, and to lessen tension between racial and linguistic groups. This is true especially of the Gereformeerde Kerk, which has been most careful and moderate in its official pronouncements.

Bibliography

Brown, W. E. *The Catholic Church in South Africa*, 1960.
Cawood, L. *The Churches and Race Relations in South Africa*, 1964.
Conradie, A. L. *The Neo-Calvinist Concept of Philosophy*, 1960.

Cottesloe Consultation. *The Report of the Consultation among South African Member Churches of the World Council of Churches 7-14 December, 1960,* 1961.

Davis, H. *Great South African Christians,* 1951.

Du Plessis, J. *The Life of Andrew Murray,* n.d.

Hinchliff, P. *The Anglican Church in South Africa,* 1963.

— *The Church in South Africa,* 1968.

Sundkler, B. G. M. *Bantu Prophets in South Africa,* 1948.

4

Art and Architecture

Heather Martiennsen

If Table Bay has not been praised so often as the Bay of Naples it is probably because it has not been seen by so many people, especially by the eulogizing and poeticizing generations. In fact, it must have had an almost overpowering impact on the navigators of the fifteenth and sixteenth centuries; but these men turned their admiration in the first place to the soil, climate, and supply of fresh water. The easy growth of trees or plants invited settlement; the crowding mountain ranges afforded watersheds, protection, and soil deposits; the bay, with its almost total surround of coastline, was the safe harbor they needed to break their long voyage to the Far East. But the pattern of South African art follows the pattern of settlement, and this has its inevitable beginning in the grand setting of the western Cape Province.

In the seventeenth and eighteenth centuries the problems were those of harnessing nature, not preserving it. The indigenous growth of fertile valley and sunny slopes was pushed back by the formal patterns of vineyards and orchards and the even texture of grain. Presiding over this orderly scene were the simple sturdy farmhouses, surveying their acres of land against the protective backing of the mountains. Between the fields and vineyards ran the straight line of the drive, bordered by oaks and chestnuts and ending before the house in a tidily walled enclosure. Such houses as these are still among our most treasured architecture: they are certainly our oldest, and their protection is the concern of both state and privately sponsored organizations, and also, it is to be supposed, those privileged individuals who still retain ownership of them. It is greatly to our advantage that these first buildings were so fine. It was to be a long time before their architectural equal appeared anywhere else in the land.

The eighteenth century Cape farmhouse is essentially a very simple structure. Once the type had been evolved it was used again and again with slight modifications. The professional architect played little part in the early settlement, and with few exceptions building at the Cape was the work of Malay craftsmen using local materials. The plan waits upon the structural limitations. Shortage of matured timber and difficulties of transport called for roof trusses limited in size and the use where possible of other materials. Poor local bricks and the arduous voyage to Holland for fine tiles and bricks necessitated buildings of limited height and protective eaves. Spacious sites encouraged broad zoning, ample courts, terraces, and spreading wings. These take shape as a simple L, U, or H, or sometimes even h plan. The broadcast stretch of wall faces the approach, backs a deep, uncovered terrace (or "stoep"), and has at its center a wide and elaborate entrance door surmounted by a stretch of wall breaking into a gable where it passes the eaves level; it is flanked symmetrically with rows of tall sash windows with shutters to cover the lower halves in the Dutch manner. The houses are of one story only.

The gable is the characteristic feature of the building style. Gables terminate each wing, the steep thatched roofs abutting against them at the end. The largest and most important gable, however, is always the one over the entrance door. It is often elaborately silhouetted, accentuates the main frontage, and distributes to each side of the entrance the dripping of water from the eaves, thus acting in lieu of a canopy. Though gables were much in use before the eighteenth century in Holland and Germany, and even in England, their placing on the Cape farmhouses follows the plan, and therefore attains a certain uniqueness.

The pattern of the scrollwork is a delayed and provincial version of European fashion: rococo or baroque in the earlier examples, becoming neo-classical towards the end of the eighteenth century. They are rarely of any architectural pretensions and show the limited variations in the vocabulary of Malay plasterers. Plaster is the characteristic finish. The porous walls needed a generous coating, which thereafter was subjected to layer after layer of seasonal whitewashing until a characteristic patina was evolved of hand-drawn surfaces, catching the sun and shadow in slight modulations and glinting with the iridescence of small salt and lime particles in the light.

The town itself developed with a simple formality. Cape Town is spread on a slight slope between a protective curve of mountains and its bay. From the sea up to the houses of government officials ran the short straight Heerengracht, with streets branching off to right and left, flanked by houses and buildings of importance. At the end the street continued in an avenue of oak trees on either side of which were developed, in due course, the present houses of parliament and the botanical gardens. This avenue still forms the delicate spine of the city, almost the only palpable survival of the simple elegance of its foundation.

The town houses that survive from the eighteenth century are provincial—or colonial—classicist, usually two stories high, with a flat roof sometimes graced with a "dak-kamer," or roofroom, from which the bay, with its incoming or outgoing shipping, could be seen. In Cape Town itself little remains of the old buildings. The Castle, erected for defense in the seventeenth century to replace the earlier fort, is the oldest remaining structure. Of public buildings, the old Supreme Court and the Groote Kerk were at least partly the work of two of the few trained artists or architects of whom there is any record, Thibault and Schutte.

The one-time Burgher Watch House, built in 1755, is now adapted as an art gallery to house the valuable Michaelis collection of Dutch paintings of the seventeenth and eighteenth centuries. These hang very aptly in the spacious rooms with their shuttered windows and tiled floors, and what the gallery lacks in modern lighting it makes up in charm of setting. Another museum, this time of old furniture, is the Koopmans de Wet House, one of the best-preserved of eighteenth-century buildings, first built in 1701 and later remodeled. Again the setting and the exhibits form an harmonious whole. On the opposite side of Strand Street stand three more historic buildings: the old Lutheran Church (1770) in "Cape Gothic" style flanked by its parsonage (wrongly called the Martin Melk House) and the Sexton's House, both in the characteristic eighteenth-century town house style. Best known of the farmhouses of the eighteenth century in the vicinity of Cape Town is Groot Constantia, first built as the home of Simon van der Stel, the Commander of the Cape Settlement. After his death in 1712 the house was re-built in its present form, an irregular U-plan embracing a courtyard, with a gable of mixed style completed about the middle of the century. Another early edifice is the Wine-cellar, attributed to Anton Anreith, with a scene of wine-treading featuring Ganymede and generous baroque swags hanging over the cornice. At a little distance from the house and its subsidiary buildings is a charming oval bath, again showing the hand of the local monumental plasterers, and all around the vines grow. From the broad terrace in front of the house one looks across a low white wall over the straight flat vineyards to the narrow blue stripe of sea.

Inland from the Cape Peninsula the fertile valleys of the Western Province provided mile after mile of vineyards, and here on the slopes the serene houses appeared, whose names, recalling old nostalgias, are so often associated with the finest wines of the country: La Provence, Vergelegen, Morgenster, La Gratitude, Meerlust, Rhone.

Of quality and historic interest equal to that of the buildings is the furniture of the time, of which a considerable quantity survives, most of it preserved in private houses, but a great deal in museums throughout the country. It is, of course, most happily seen in buildings of the period, now protected by the Historic Monuments Commission, or by municipal and private enterprise. This sturdy furniture is of a surprisingly high quality, especially if compared with "colonial" furniture in other parts of the world. It was made of exceptionally beautiful woods, chiefly stinkwood, yellow-wood, or imported oak and mahogany. In style it reflects Dutch, English, and French influence, the last stimulated by the settlement of French Huguenots after the revocation of the Edict of Nantes (1685). Fortunately for the development of the Cape, many of these immigrants (apart from having the country skills so useful for fruit- and wine-farming) were trained handymen, carpenters, and cabinet makers. The other important source of skills was among the Malay slaves imported in the middle of the seventeenth century by Jan van Riebeeck to serve the Dutch East India Company at the Cape. Many of them, too, had been carpenters and masons, and had brought with them Eastern methods of furniture construction and design, almost anticipating the "chinoiserie" that was to become such a fashionable taste in western Europe.

Cape furniture is heavier in appearance and construction than contemporary work in France and England and lacks its extreme elegance, its fashionable and often frippery decoration. The range of types is understandably smaller, most of the pieces being for storage: cupboards, wardrobes, and the characteristic *kist* (or *kas*), which varied from a large chest to a chest of drawers. Strong and simple, finished with fine brass fittings, these were evidently inspired by the stout, beautifully wrought sea-chests that arrived at the Cape and sometimes served similar function as "wagon-kists" in the service of country settlers. Also made in great numbers, of course, were chairs, settees, and tables—again heavier and plainer than their European counterparts, but perhaps not necessarily less handsome for that reason, and possibly more generally useful. The finest and most delicate touches of European craftsmanship are inevitably not to be found. The seats are sometimes of cane or rattan, suggesting an Eastern influence, or are formed by the lacing of *riemples*, or thongs of partly cured hide, a sound form of seat still much used on chairs and benches made in craftsmen's workshops.

Also surviving from the eighteenth century are a number of churches, some (like those at Tulbagh and Graaf Reinet) converted to museums. Both of these are T-shaped in plan, a good way of providing the maximum accommodation (for there was seating in all three arms) without having to increase the span of the roof trusses beyond what current resources of material and skill could manage.

By the middle of the nineteenth century the settlers had penetrated deep into the country, often following the missionaries, founding towns throughout the eastern Cape Province and up the coast to Natal, and as far as the Limpopo River, which was to be South Africa's northern boundary. A manner of building accompanied them, which slowly left behind in time and place the Cape tradition, no longer appropriate to requirements and means.

The nineteenth century produced everywhere buildings that while often charming, could not compete in quality with those of the old Cape settlement. There was neither leisure for their construction nor the same kind of labor available. For work in the more desolate and arid regions, materials had to be conveyed long distances, and they were often imported to ensure their suitability for this purpose. At this stage the chief influence was naturally England, and the style of building is a reflection of style as it changed there: Georgian, through Regency, to Victorian Gothic—especially for domestic buildings—with a heavy-handed version of the Classical for buildings of civic importance. The occasional flashes of charm during this time, arising from the playfulness of cast iron and timber filigree, jaunty roofed verandas and high rooms with ceilings stamped in metal relief, were thus chiefly found in buildings whose function and basic structure were too impermanent to outlast the century, while stout but dingy town halls, banks, and government buildings persisted drearily into the twentieth century, accompanied decade after decade by the construction of more and more different buildings in the same or similar style.

In 1892 Herbert Baker (1862-1946) arrived in the country to join Cecil Rhodes's circle, and a second important architectural injection stimulated the South African building scene. Baker had been trained in the Arts and Crafts tradition, which emanated in England from the William Morris movement, and together with Edwin Lutyens (1869-1944) had developed a strong feeling for sound materials and workmanship that was so dearly needed then in South Africa after a period of rapid development that saw the inevitable accompaniment of shoddy building. Limited as his vision might ultimately appear, he had an important influence on architecture throughout the country: directly through his own vast practice and indirectly through the group of younger architects who followed him passionately.

Conversant with the sound methods and sturdy traditions of the Kentish vernacular, and of English country building in general, Baker saw at once that the best of the South African background lay in the old manners and methods of building at the Cape, and particularly in the Cape Dutch farmhouse. He was himself a staunch product of latter-day Romanticism, and it is to his credit—perhaps through the more alert perceptivity of his friend Lutyens—that he came to appreciate the greater dignity and monumentality of the Classical approach, though he never used it rigidly. He was, in fact, typically eclectic, which provided perhaps the most flexible background against which a creative attitude to architecture might at this stage emerge. His hundreds of charming whitewashed and often gabled houses, his many simple and sturdy churches reflecting old traditions of the English countryside, his two or three public buildings (he even did a small railway station in the Cape), the most distinguished of their kind in the first decade of this century, were widely enough spread to make an indelible mark, particularly in the Transvaal, where Johannesburg was becoming the commercial center of the country, and therefore the most demanding center for building enterprise and development.

Among his best-known and most important works at the Cape is Groote Schuur, the house built for Rhodes, and the residence since then of all South African prime ministers. The design of this house was hampered by the fact that it was partly the remodeling of an existing structure: the plan is a modification of the traditional U-type, but the final appearance cannot be said to follow the eighteenth-century tradition with any clarity. This is not, of course, in itself a criticism; but the house does not emerge as entirely satisfactory on any level. Many of his later houses, often less pretentious and healthily eclectic, are more meaningful in the architectural sense. He found the gable-ended roof attractive and justifiable and approved of features such as the broad stoep, the courtyards, paved floors, and whitewashed walls. He appreciated the fine woodwork of doors, windows, furniture; he married the features of quality of the Cape Dutch buildings to well-remembered features from his own country (such as timber roof-trusses) and developed in particular the garden settings of the house in the informal manner so successfully developed in England by people like Gertrude Jekyll, with whom he was on close terms. The cultivation of indigenous shrubs and plants helped to relate the house to its South African setting and provided a stimulus to architectural horticulture.

Baker came to the Transvaal just after the turn of the century, and immediately impressed his architectural personality on the young and developing environment. His houses are today status-symbols in the residential suburbs of Johannesburg. His biggest work in the Transvaal, and in the country as a whole, was undoubtedly the Union Buildings in Pretoria, administrative capital of the newly-proclaimed Union of South Africa. Shortly after the Act of Union of 1910 one-and-a-half million pounds was voted to the construction of this work, and Herbert Baker was appointed its architect. A commanding site on one of the koppies surrounding the city permitted a long extension of two great blocks, enclosing courtyards and linked by a semicircular building embracing an amphitheater. On the flanks and below the buildings terraced gardens are laid out with flowers and shrubs: behind, trees mount the slopes and form a background to the site. The material used was stone, and the style as a whole is Classical, carrying two domed baroque towers and transmitting echoes of Christopher Wren and the later Italians, but also fragments of the Cape tradition. It is not perhaps great architecture, but it was the most considerable thing Baker had done up to that date, and it marks the debut of a kind of Imperial-Colonial architecture that was to appear in various forms in the capitals of the British Empire, most notably in New Delhi, where Baker joined Lutyens in 1913 on the design of the new city.

Though the Union Buildings remained Baker's largest work in South Africa, perhaps his most distinguished one is the South African Institute for Medical Research, built in Johannesburg in 1912. Here his planning and treatment are almost Palladian in effect. The plan leads through a series of courts flanked by wings. A domed tower emphasizes the central axis. The balustraded blocks are white (which Baker always felt to be the color most appropriate to South Africa) and are set among lawns and trees.

While Baker was busy on the Union Buildings, Lutyens was appointed to design the Johannesburg Art Gallery. He visited South Africa for this purpose in 1910, and while in Johannesburg he was invited to design a war memorial for the Rand Regiment, which was erected in 1911 in Eckstein Park, adjacent to the Zoological Gardens. It has the form of a triumphal arch, very mannerist in style, with an arch intruding into a pediment and the figure of Victory on a dome over the whole. The Art Gallery, in Joubert Park, again reflects his somewhat wayward Classicism: like so many art galleries of the time and later it is more concerned with monumental disposition of solids than an interior space with a special function. However, it takes its place among the more important buildings in the Transvaal.

These were probably the two most eminent architects to contribute to the developing pattern of building in South Africa. It was not until the 1930's that the next important influence was to be seen: that of the so-called International Style of the twentieth century. It was introduced in the first place as a result of the enthusiasm of a group of young Johannesburg architects led by Rex Martienssen, first a student and later a teacher in the School of Architecture of the University of the

Witwatersrand in Johannesburg and energetic and dynamic co-editor of the *South African Architectural Record*. Le Corbusier was the architect most admired by this group, and he came in time to know some of them. It was always their hope that he might one day come to South Africa and leave some mark, but although he himself spoke of it in letters as a possibility, he never visited South Africa. Perhaps the war broke the decision: by the time it was over Martienssen had died, and the links had to a great extent been severed. However, contemporary architectural design made considerable strides, first in the Transvaal and then throughout the country. It is difficult to say that there are any buildings of international importance or aesthetic magnitude, but there is a great deal of good work about, and Johannesburg, for example, is an almost totally twentieth-century city. Having its beginnings as late as the 1980's in what was not much more than a mining camp, it had few buildings from early years of a quality to warrant preservation. Even the few examples of Edwardian charm were for the most part demolished because of the rising value of land and the desire for buildings that would earn their keep.

Baker's followers had provided a nucleus of architects working with integrity in a sound style of domestic design, which gradually gave way to the character of the mid-century. Perhaps it is mostly in domestic building that any flavor characteristically South African emerges. Many influences have shaped the small but comfortable house of the average prosperous citizen. The ranch-style house popularized in the United States has had a lot to do with determining a type of house found in the outer suburbs on anything from one to three acres, while the way of life of the community—an out-of-doors living involving terraces, enclosed and partly enclosed courtyards, swimming pools, and an easy transition from house to garden—has become characteristic. Houses of a lower income group, or those confined by the smaller lots of inner suburbs, tend to be a pocket version of the more elaborate "country-living" style, for the suburban pattern of residence is very much a South African thing. The large blocks of apartments in and near a city like Johannesburg tend to be populated by the large group of latter-day immigrants or by unmarried and younger persons in transit to the inevitable suburban destiny. Local influences on the design of domestic buildings are the outdoor living invited by the climate, and then the stoep, terrace, and courtyard (the *lapa* of the tribal Bantu), which are called forth to tender to this and provide the privacy for it. The single-story house, first acclimatized at the Cape, continues to be the norm in house construction. Particularly in the last decade a type of house has emerged at the hands of young architects which combines the easy arrangement of a Mediterranean type of vernacular with what has been found useful or graceful in the local. Commercial and industrial buildings tend today to be more "international" in general character, though here and there, perhaps in the use of materials or a grouping of shapes, the better architects produce something of a more personal nature. In the main one finds much that recalls the range of urban types of the United States, from closely grouped tall buildings in the bigger centers to the flatter appearance of the isolated dorp. At present the fast development of the suburban or neighborhood shopping center is evolving—often in a clumsy way—its own functional aesthetic. In general, however, South Africa looks architecturally younger than the United States—except in a few early towns of the Cape province, where some of the old work still stands.

The relationship to architectural work in the United States has been enormously fostered by the fact that rapid economic and industrial development in South Africa since the Second World War has turned eyes towards the technological advances in the United States. Large projects are often in the hands of American or European firms that find it convenient to establish branches here. Architectural education in this country is entirely in the hands of the universities of Cape Town, the Witwatersrand, Pretoria, Durban, and the Orange Free State. Postgraduate studies, once almost inevitably pursued in Europe, are now more often than not undertaken in the universities and technological institutes of America. The new tendencies to expand architectural schools by adding departments of town and regional planning and of building science, are contributing to the planning of new towns and to technological advances everywhere.

The influence of the university background, moreover, operates in keeping the young architect intellectually conscious of his place in history. The study and awareness of his own heritage, for instance, has produced refreshing work by some of the more sensitive, which (without constituting anything like revivalism) evokes and keeps alive a kind of continuance of the vernacular tradition that has developed in the past.

Although descriptive drawings—and, of course, maps—had been made from time to time by visitors and officials connected with the Cape, it was not until the first British settlement of 1795 (and particularly from 1806 onwards when the Cape came into the hands of the British for the second and longer period) that drawings and painting began to appear in the country in any numbers. There are literally hundreds of names associated with pictorial art in South Africa before 1895, of whom the greater number were English. Very few of these were professional artists—probably not many more than fifty—and even these were not artists of any great standing. Their paintings, and particularly their drawings, were for the most part descriptions of the country, its people, flora, and fauna, made during sojourn or travel, whether for military, prospecting, or missionary purposes. The intention was primarily to record, and the *rapportage*, though often charming, is technically naive or merely pedestrian.

The period during which these artists worked (the first three-quarters of the century) was that in which the Romantic movement grew and flourished in Europe. In France the main emphasis was perhaps on the exotic; in England, on the sentimental. Everywhere wild nature, wild passions, the horrific or melodramatic, infused paintings. At the turn of the century the leading artists in England were Joseph Wright, Henry Fuseli, William Blake, Thomas Lawrence, and the young Turner (Constable did not exhibit his famous "The Haywain" until 1822), and it was the period of the great watercolorists like Gilpin, Crome, Girtin, Cotman, and Cox. For the educated, some training in drawing and painting ("taking a view") was commonplace. Despite the Romantic winds rising behind and before them, most of the artists working in South Africa were interested largely in recording, not interpreting, what they saw. This was, however, necessarily biased by their own background experience in seeing and understanding.

Among the more important of these traveller artists (or topographical artists as they are sometimes called) one of the earliest was Samuel Daniell (1755-1811) who—with his elder brother, William, and his uncle, Thomas—traveled and made sketches from which engravings were afterwards produced. The two elder Daniells traveled to the east; Samuel visited the Cape and served as secretary-draughtsman to a mission to Bechuanaland (now Botswana) in 1801. In 1806 he left for Ceylon, where he died. Some of his studies of South African peoples and animals were engraved by himself; others were done by his brother. Undoubtedly his work is valuable primarily as Africana and takes its place among other records of the time. Apart from its naive charm, however, his oeuvre (and that of his contemporaries in South Africa) has an important bearing on the professional painting that was to succeed it: for more than a hundred years the pre-occupation of the painter working in South Africa has been the description of his environment, and the differences in style have resulted from the problems and their solutions that have concerned each generation; the kind of training they have had, and of course their individual vision. Samuel Daniell saw the countryside and its inhabitants through the eyes of a nineteenth-century Englishman and recorded what he saw in the mode of his day. The farm laborer, the hunter, and the tribal African all appear as versions of the elegant personages who may be found in English illustration. The landscape and flora do not to the same extent reflect the current fashion in delineation, since there was less precedent for these. Here naivete replaces convention, and the strangeness of the artist's experience is reflected in the strangeness and often gaucherie of his drawings. In no case do we find anything like a realistic or photographic portrayal: the painters were simply not equipped for it. Only in the delicate drawings of town streets and buildings do we find something of the direct and unemotional perspective of actual observation; and these are, of course, extremely important as records of the early appearance of the towns or settlements in question.

Of all these early painters the one who perhaps identified himself most closely with South Africa was Thomas Bowler (1813-1869). He started off in 1833 in a clerical capacity at the Observatory, having been sent out with references from England for that purpose; but by 1839 he had left government service and set up as a teacher of drawing in Cape Town. There he settled for the rest of his life, except for visits to other parts of the country and trips to England during the second of which he died. He was closely connected with the earliest efforts to promote and exhibit art in Cape Town and published a great number of prints taken from his drawings and sketches, which were almost all topographical in character. Among his paintings some of the most attractive are studies of Table Bay in calm and storm, sometimes recording shipwrecks, and seldom solely aesthetic in intention.

Another important, because characteristic, artist of this group is Thomas Baines (1820-1875). Unlike Bowler, he never actually adopted South Africa as his home but made several lengthy sorties out to the country, usually as a member of prospecting expeditions. He arrived first in Cape Town in 1842, perhaps intending to settle, and early in 1848 he journeyed up the coast, probing with expeditionary travelers for some distance inland, visiting Port Elizabeth, Grahamstown, and Colesburg. Altogether this adventure, which included military service, took about five years, and he returned to London in 1853. His next voyage was to Australia, but he came back to South Africa and was in Cape Town again in 1859. By 1865 he was once more in England, but returned to Cape Town two years later. He died in Durban in 1875 in the midst of preparations for a further expedition inland.

The major interest of men like this was clearly not painting, which seems to have been a hobby, or a means of livelihood, rather than a vocation. When the professional artist began at last to emerge he combined the technique of the trained stylist with description of what continued to fascinate, and thus the tradition of landscape was carried on into the stream of South African painting. Certainly there is very little of any other sort of painting to be seen in the country in the early part of the twentieth century. It must be realized, of course, that especially at this time—but in fact all through the years of South African development—an important part has been played in the art scene by the settler, the artist born and trained in one of the older centers, or perhaps returning to that center for a while. Even artists born in South Africa usually trained in Europe; they continued to do so after the establishment of art schools in South Africa itself, so that the South African environment was always seen through a vision controlled to some extent by its development abroad.

Among the professional artists to settle in the country at the end of the nineteenth century was Gwelo Goodman (1871-1939) who, having come to South Africa in 1886 to work on the railways, returned to study in Paris in 1895 and finally settled in South Africa in 1915. He is an exemplar of the trained painter of some taste and technique but no considerable vision, whose end in painting was purely, if competently, descriptive. Of the same generation were Frans Oerder (1867-1944), who came to South Africa in 1890, a painter of rather more quality, trained in the solid tradition of Dutch craftsmanship; Erich Mayer (1876-1960), in South Africa from 1898, whose sentimental descriptions of the colorful land became enormously popular; and the sculptor Anton van Wouw (1862-1945), who arrived in South Africa in the same year as Oerder and enjoyed a precarious livelihood until he began to be recognized as a competent portraitist and monumental sculptor. All these men worked in the academic traditions of England, Holland, and Germany, and it was—strangely enough—two South African-born painters who first showed some departure from academic naturalism.

The name of Hugo Naude (1869-1941) is the first that can be inscribed on the roll of South African artists of any significance. He cannot be said to have been of anything like international stature, and many men of his generation and ability are hardly noticed today in countries that had flourishing schools of painting at the time, but in South Africa he was so undoubtedly *primus inter pares* that he virtually stands alone. He was born in Worcester in the Cape Province and after some years spent at the Slade School in London and in Europe returned to South Africa as the first post-impressionist painter of his country. Never so advanced in vision as his contemporaries in France and Germany, his style is more English in character and shows little more than a loosening up of descriptive technique, a fresh and impromptu use of color not quite daring enough in its escape from the dominance of the subject to be considered Fauve, but different enough from academic veracity to set a trend in painting that is retained today in the country as a whole in still-life, landscape, and portraiture. Now, instead of seeing the South African scene through the eyes of the callow nineteenth-century reporter, wondering at everything he sees but too biased in his experience to see it fully, we find the more sophisticated techniques of the latter-day Impressionist whose style dominates his subject to such an extent that he observes nothing that cannot be rendered in terms of those techniques. Impressionism gives us a minimum of rapportage, because the painter is so excited by his manner of translating his seeing into pigment that *what* he sees becomes irrelevant: it is *how* he sees that matters.

Close to Naude in age and training, though working and teaching in the Transvaal, was Bertha Everard (born in 1873 in Durban), a product of the Slade and Westminster schools. Her landscapes are formalized, not reflecting so much of the Impressionist influence as one might have expected, but showing perhaps more affinity with the decorative schools that emerge from Purvis de Chavannes and the Nabis. Together with her elder sister Edith King (a watercolorist), her daughters Ruth Everard-Haden and Rosamund Everard-Steenkamp, and granddaughter Leonora Everard-Haden, she represents a family of women painters and teachers highly regarded for their pioneering work.

Throughout the first half of the present century painters continued to be interested primarily in landscape. As the Impressionist and related styles became more widely accepted and eventually "academic," so the easily taught manner of painterly, selective description became the norm for South African painters. From the landscapes of the south of France it was an easy translation to the landscapes of the Cape—largely Mediterranean in character—and it was at the Cape that most painters chose to work and where painting first flourished. A whole school of landscapists and painters of street scenes held sway, varying from the witty and delicate to the merely pedestrian, but usually with a sensitivity to the quality of paint more English than French, and by the same token lacking to a large extent that importance that calls for a certain ruthlessness of vision. It was perhaps not entirely by chance that styles of painting that could properly be regarded as being of the twentieth century were first developed in the Transvaal, where the landscape made little appeal to those looking for subjects that could be treated in the accepted French or English way. Walter Battiss (b. 1906) and Alexis Preller (b. 1911) are easily the most distinguished artists of this new development.

Battiss learned his early techniques in Johannesburg and found his first inspiration in the lively work of the indigenous rock-artists of southern Africa, which as a young man he helped to record. Later visits to Europe and contact with contemporary artists there provided stimulus to his creative vision, which has remained intensely personal all his life. Africa continues to supply his motifs, which he combines and alternates with complete abstraction. His work is colorful, painterly, various, happy, and always instantly recognizable. His canvases have tended to be small, and never pretentious or bombastic. Nevertheless, he is one of the two or three painters of importance in the country.

Alexis Preller traveled to London and then to Paris for periods of training but has not identified himself at all clearly with any current art styles. His manner of painting—grave, precise, often with Surrealist overtones and relations—has maintained through all the vicissitudes of style about him an output of paintings, large and small, of a strongly hieratic character. Again his motifs are often drawn from the African image, reflecting the solemnity of ritual and magic, but sometimes non-figurative. He always displays an immaculate technique, which has never yielded to the current of recent expressionistic styles. He stands in the forefront of South African painting today.

Though there are many painters of this generation in the South African scene, few can really be said to have made any large contribution to the development of style. Perhaps mention should be made of Gregoire Boonzaier, leader of the landscape school of the Cape, and May Hillhouse, also of the Cape, whose work reflects a kind of abstract intimism.

In the years preceding the Second World War several painters of quality came out to South Africa: Georgina Ormiston, a fey and delicate abstractionist; Wolf Kibel, whose expressionist style might have made more impact if it had not been for his early death; Jean Welz, an architect turning first to abstraction and later to a more descriptive technique with echoes of Cézanne; Maurice van Essche, an expressionist embracing with energetic appreciation the African environment. To South-west Africa came Adolph Jentsch, exploring with patience and with complete disregard for the clamorous styles of the twentieth century the arid reaches in the midst of which he now dwelt.

Since then the scene has changed. Another generation has grown up and is taking over. The wave of abstract expressionism that washed over America, England, and western Europe could hardly fail to make its impact upon a group of young painters, traveled, eager, and aware. This has recently been followed by the arrival of Op and Pop ideas, and these have had considerable effect, particularly on students who are emerging with an orientation quite different from that of their predecessors. The South African scene at this point therefore reflects the imposition of ideas currently occupying artists everywhere upon the slower and more remote essays of the past. Distance from the source is bound to affect the final statement. The young artists travel abroad when they can, but they must rely to a great extent on reproductions, and are therefore influenced by no impact of actual scale or paint handling. In spite of this, South African painters were strongly influenced after the Second World War by the schools of painting which involved, almost as their *raison d'être*, heavy and purposeful use of textures. So completely, in fact, did South African painters respond to abstract expressionism and tachism—perhaps in its less extreme forms—that by the 1960's it was the characteristic genre, and it is almost by a painful effort that painters are realizing that other methods may produce less dead-end results.

It is hard to say whether a definite South African genre has ever existed. The population from which the artists are drawn is relatively small and scattered. The African community has produced some significant artists, but in general there is not at present the economical or educational climate to foster their emergence in any great numbers.

Of the post-war generation of artists there are a few names that should be mentioned. Cecil Skotnes has won international notice for his very personal development in wood-cutting; Cecily Sash is working on optical relations of colors in a "hard-edge" style of flexible line very much her own; Guiseppe Cattaneo, who settled here shortly after the war, has applied his Italian feeling for texture and form to abstractions in various materials; Gunther van der Reis moves from two to three-dimensional compositions of greater or lesser abstraction; Helmut Starcke has emerged as a distinguished protagonist in the field of Pop art.

There are a number of competent artists who work still in the abstract-expressionist manner; there are some who continue to wrestle with the problem of rendering landscape and still-life in terms of twentieth-century abstraction. The relation between two- and three-dimensional design is beginning to be felt here as it is overseas, and sculpture becomes a difficult term to define.

More traditional is the sculpture of a small number of non-white artists of distinction. Traditional, that is, in a European rather than an African sense, as there is no tradition of sculpture among the Bantu-speaking tribes of southern Africa. Young artists such as Lucas Sithole or Sydney Kumalo work in wood or clay, using animal and figure subjects. Their inspiration comes from twentieth-century European sculpture, with a local idiom resulting from imperfect contact with the foreign works. Educational facilities in art are limited for the Africans, and their awareness is fostered usually by private teaching. Their plastic imagination is often quickly caught by the primitive idea in contemporary sculpture and almost translated back into vivid forms, suggesting magic. The sculptures are lively and interesting: development to greater stature is difficult, as there is an even smaller body of distinguished sculpture in the South African scene than of painters.

South African painters have not on the whole shown much interest in representing the human figure—the sculptor's traditional subject. The greater number of sculptors who have worked here have been settlers. One of the earliest of these was F. W. Armstrong (b. 1875), who came out in 1904 to teach art in Grahamstown and brought with him those English academic principles that have formed the basis of all art schools in this country. Ivan Mitford-Barberton (b. 1896), a South African trained at the Royal College, was later to embed the same principles into the educational pattern of the Michaelis Art School in Cape Town. Working in more advanced styles was his contemporary, Moses Kottler, who came to South Africa during the First World War and speedily became acknowledged as one of the major artists resident here in the years between the wars. He is known especially for some fine figures in wood, gently stylized, of African subjects. Lippy Lipshitz (b. 1903) has lived in the Cape since childhood and has become probably our most distinguished senior sculptor. Working chiefly in wood and stone, with a poetic vision, he is difficult to classify, but very much of his generation everywhere who avoided the excessively formal, preferring to emphasize a vibrancy and tension peculiar to whatever material they handle. Coert Steynberg, of the same generation, is a South African who has experimented with a variety of styles and is known for his many memorial sculptures. Still, some of the most exciting sculpture of today is that of the younger men, such as the Bantu artists referred to earlier, Richard Wake, and Else Dziomba, Gerard de Leeuw, Eduardo Villa, George Joholkowsky and Solly Disner. Of course, the advance of younger artists is due to some extent to the development of the art schools. Technical colleges continue to offer courses in art education, commercial art, crafts, and—tentatively—industrial design. From the beginning, however, art departments were attached to the universities and university colleges, some of the oldest and best known being at Cape Town, which is most distinguished, perhaps, in sculpture and graphic art; Rhodes University in Grahamstown; and the University of Natal. Among the newer departments are those of the University of the Witwatersrand at Johannesburg (with teaching emphasis on painting and art history and theory), and Stellenbosch University, which specializes in crafts such as jewelry. Most of the younger artists in the country are graduates of these schools, which thus form an important factor in the artistic background of South Africa today.

If the heritage of the South African artist is inevitably that of Western Europe, there is no doubt that special factors in his present environment are bound to influence his imaginative equipment. In this generation he takes for granted and responds with unaffected enthusiasm to current trends in Europe and America. On the other hand, there is now no strangeness in his physical environment, nor any drive to "report back" on his visual experiences. The flora and fauna, climate, and geological setting become gradually more commonplace as the generations of artists follow one another, and are for the most part ignored. Even the generations who reacted creatively to the stimuli of the African setting have passed.

The African peoples south of the Limpopo have never produced any very important art forms, and although for a while their tribal way of life intrigued white painters and afforded considerable subject matter for pictorial art, they themselves, when they emerge today as artists, take their place among their white colleagues simply as contemporary artists, sharing to a greater degree than might be expected the sources of style and subject.

The only indigenous art form of any great aesthetic value to have appeared in this area is the rock painting and engraving of those nomadic people, now virtually extinct, whose latest surviving representatives were called by white settlers the Bushmen. The works themselves were first observed in stony areas of the Cape Province, particularly where the formation of the mountain rocks provided overhanging ledges that contributed to the preservation of the "galleries" of drawings, and correspond, as has now been generally observed, very closely in style to the paleolithic work familiar to us in caves of the Dordogne area in France and in the northern and eastern regions of Spain. It is patently clear from even the most superficial observation that the drawings of the two areas are so similar in character and intention that we can infer a corresponding similarity in the way of life of the people who produced them. Though there is some controversy as to the exact dating of the South African rock pictures, it would seem that they are of relatively recent date, and this must inevitably be of archaeological and anthropological interest. To the artist and discriminating spectator, however, they are sufficiently interesting as works of art, and as such should be regarded as among our most important artistic possessions: yet many of them are fading now, owing to recent exposure, or disappearing as the result of irresponsible interference. Some examples, and especially stones on which the characteristic pitted engravings appear, have been moved to museums in various parts of the country, but most of the sites are in a precarious condition.

The style is the closely observed and delicately executed profile of animals, especially antelope, and of processions of human figures showing a characteristic steatopygy and brandishing spears and sticks, or bows and arrows, familiar to all who have visited or seen illustrations of the caves of western Europe. The pigment used is red or yellow ochre and black and white, mixed apparently with any available liquid or semi-liquid medium (a favorite seems to have been the urine of the rock-rabbit, or hyrax) and applied with a type of spatula.

These enchanting little drawings are familiar to all South African artists, though it is not easy to estimate to what degree they might have stimulated creativity, except insofar as the artist in South Africa is always aware of Africa. Indeed, he has not a great opportunity to be aware of much else. I have referred to the improving efficiency of travel and reproductions, and of the always increasing range and possibility of visual awareness, but the artist here has to work quite hard at keeping in contact with what is "going on." As for the past, he has his libraries, both public and private; but he has a very limited access to original world—or even European—art of either present or past. The South African collections seem to reflect the story of settlement: seventeenth- and eighteenth-century Dutch art; eighteenth- and nineteenth-century English art; nineteenth- and twentieth-century French art. These may all be seen, but nothing in profusion, and, for the most part, not the greatest artists. Cape Town's Michaelis Gallery (referred to earlier) boasts a Frans Hals portrait and a Ruisdael landscape. The South African National Gallery, in the Gardens at Cape Town, has a good collection of South African art, of paintings of the English school (including Reynolds, Stubbs, Sickert, and Steer) and sculptures of Dalou, Rodin, and Epstein. Johannesburg (in the gallery designed by Lutyens) has an el Greco "Apostle Thomas," some French Impressionists, and a small collection of early moderns, including Derain, Gleizes, Gromaire, Herbin, Leger, Lurcat, Metzinger, and the slightly younger group of Manessier, Pignon, Singier, and Soulages. The Johannesburg Gallery was originally founded as a museum for contemporary art, and is probably the most important of the general collections; it has a small but representative collection of Dutch paintings, a larger collection of English paintings (including Pre-Raphaelite and other nineteenth-century works) and a fairly extensive collection of prints. The sculpture includes two Rodin portraits and works by Borrdelle, Dalou, Daumier, Despiau, Epstein, Maillol, and Henry Moore.

Here and there in different parts of the country smaller collections contain interesting items: several Sickerts at Pietermaritzburg and the celebrated portrait of T. S. Eliot by

Wyndham Lewis in Durban. There are also, of course, collections of South African painting and sculpture, though nowhere so systematically built up as might be supposed. Cape Town takes the lead here at present, but there is a great need for the showing of works of art everywhere in the land. It is now unfortunately too late to acquire important works of the past, but a country so rich should see that some of those riches are deviated to the importation of great works of later days.

Private collections, however, are growing rapidly. The Rembrandt Corporation has bought a very comprehensive collection of Op and Kinetic art works by internationally known artists, some good Italian and French contemporary sculpture, modern French tapestries, and a large collection of South African art. The South African Breweries, the Schlesinger Organization, and several of the universities are also assembling collections of South African art, while the Egon Geunther Collection of African Art should also be mentioned. Many private citizens have shown their collections recently, and among well-known collectors in the country are Mrs. Mary McEwen (the Gioris Collection), Dr. W. L. Chaskelson, and Mr. Ivan Katzen. All of the above are in the Transvaal: at the Cape there are several small but quite distinguished private collections.

Perhaps a new professionalism is at last emerging in South African art, wherein the young painter or sculptor will find himself regarded, with the architect, as an educated and responsible member of the community rather than the more or less gifted product of a casual Bohemia: the next decades should provide a definitive answer.

Bibliography

Alexander, F. L. *Art in South Africa Since 1900*, 1962.
Atmore, M. G. *Cape Furniture*, 1965.
Bouman, A. C. *Painters of South Africa*, 1961.
Bradlow, Edna and Frank. *Thomas Bowler of the Cape of Good Hope; His Life and Works, with a Catalogue of Extant Paintings*, 1955.
De Bosdari, C. *Cape Dutch Homes and Farms*, 1953.

Gordon-Brown, A. *Pictorial Arts in South Africa During Three Centuries to 1875*, 1952.

Greig, Doreen. *A Guide to Architecture in the Republic of South Africa*, 1969.

Jeppe, Harold. *South African Artists: 1900-1962*, 1963.

Lewcock, Ronald. *Early Nineteenth-Century Architecture in South Africa*, 1963.

Martienssen, Heather. *South African Art of the Twentieth Century*, 1967.

Wallis, J. P. R. *Thomas Baines, Artist and Explorer: 1820-75*, 1941.

5

Law

Ellison Kahn

One of the most cherished of the cultural inheritances of South Africa is its Roman-Dutch system of law, the issue of the marriage of the law of Holland and Roman law; it is systematic yet flexible, infused with equitable notions, and developed by jurists of outstanding ability.

In the Netherlands the first Roman law influences were felt in the thirteenth century, and there followed a steady infiltration of Roman law in the next century, which thereafter accelerated, leading to a wholesome reception in the sixteenth century, to be followed by a long period of bloom, which was summarily cut short by the French invasion. The Roman-Dutch law was eventually deposed in 1809, to be replaced initially by the *Code Napoleon* and finally by a Dutch code based on that of France.

Roman law in the formative years was applied technically as a subsidiary common law, but its influence was nonetheless great. The Netherlands joined the great civil-law family of legal systems (which included France, Germany, and Italy) that had a wholesale reception of Roman law. They never belonged to the less systematic and more casuistic common-law family sired by English law, which spread to the United States (save for Louisiana), Canada (save for Quebec), Australia, New Zealand, and elsewhere in the one-time Empire and Commonwealth.

When the Republic of the United Netherlands (through the Dutch East India Company) occupied the Cape of Good Hope in 1652, Roman-Dutch law began its life in the southern tip of the dark continent; and Roman-Dutch law meant, in the final resort, the law of the province of Holland, because of its predominance in the administration of the company. Yet, after the permanent British occupation of the Cape commenced in 1806, the conquerors left intact the local system of law. The inhabitants were guaranteed the rights and privileges that they had enjoyed hitherto, which were understood to include the Roman-Dutch law. As white occupation spread, whether under the British or not, so advanced the Roman-Dutch law: to the final boundaries of the colony of the Cape of Good Hope, to Natal, to the independent republics of the Transvaal and the Orange Free State, to Southern Rhodesia, to Basutoland, Bechuanaland Protectorate, Swaziland, and finally to South-West Africa.

So the Roman-Dutch legal system has continued in southern Africa (and nowhere else, except in a somewhat attenuated form in Ceylon) despite its demise in the land of its birth. It may be thought, then, that the Republic of South Africa belongs to the civil-law world. But there are those who would classify her system rather as hybrid, as they would also classify the systems of Scotland, Louisiana, and Quebec, because of the pervasive influence English law has had in the past century and a half. Herein lies the source of much heart-searching that is not yet stilled.

In the early days the British government contemplated the gradual assimilation of Roman-Dutch and English law through legislative process: in 1828 in the Cape criminal procedure was remodeled on English lines; civil procedure, though not to such a marked degree, was similarly refashioned; in 1830 the English law of evidence was introduced, and practice and procedure took on an anglicized appearance that has never been lost.

In the law of succession the English system of executorship supplanted the Roman-Dutch rule of universal succession of heirs in 1833; the English underhand form of will was introduced in 1845; and in 1873 and 1874 the legitimate portion and other restrictions on the freedom of testation were removed; but otherwise this field remained the domain of Roman-Dutch law.

In mercantile law English influences were very strong. In 1843 a Cape ordinance set the basis of the insolvency law of the future, with a nice mixture of English and Roman-Dutch legal principles; from 1861 the companies legislation was framed on that of the United Kingdom, as was the law of negotiable instruments, merchant shipping, patents, trade marks, and copyright. In the nineteenth century the expansion of commerce, it was found, could not always be catered for by a legal system that had died in the land of its birth.

Natal and the independent republics of the Transvaal and Orange Free State soon followed the lead of Cape Province in the amalgamation of the two legal systems by legislation, but it was not only by the direct road of legislation that English law marched into the legal systems of southern Africa. It also crept in, often hardly observed, along bypaths, through decisions of the courts and through legal practice. There were many reasons for this phenomenon, so reminiscent of the reception of Roman law into the Netherlands centuries before: the training in England of a large number of the judges and practitioners, especially in the early days; the adoption of English as the official language of the Cape and Natal; the easy access to English text books and judicial decisions and the difficulty in obtaining copies of and reading the "musty manuals of the Middle Ages" written in Latin or Dutch; the availability of English precedents of contracts, wills, and other legal documents; the influence of the Judicial Committee of the Privy council, the ultimate court of appeal. Small wonder that where the Roman-Dutch authorities were silent, difficult to comprehend, or contradictory, recourse was frequently had to the rules of English law. There were areas where such reference was infrequent, as in the law of persons and family relations, succession, property, sale, and lease; but other areas where it was constant, as in the law of delict (tort), parts of the general principles of contract, mercantile law, criminal law (particularly with some of the special offences), the law of agency, and constitutional and administrative law. Nor, unlike most civil-law countries, was there a code that could provide a bulwark against the ceaseless onslaught of the alien law.

There were great nineteenth-century judges who in large measure succeeded in giving expression where possible to the admonition *petere fontes*—men such as the Scot, Menzies; and Sir Henry de Villiers in the Cape; Sir Henry Connor in Natal; and Kotze in the Transvaal. Nevertheless, by the time the four colonies united in 1910, there was a substantial overlay of English law on the original Roman-Dutch base, fastened fairly tightly by a system of judicial precedent patterned on, though not as strict as, that of England, and of a type unknown to the Netherlands of the old authorities.

Since Union there has been a swing back to consultation of the old authorities as the primary source of the common law. This has undoubtedly been caused by a resurgence of national pride in the historic legal system, which has as been accentuated by the work of the university schools of law, though recourse to English precedents has become avowedly only for persuasive purposes. Naturally, in those few branches where South African law is by legislation virtually the same as that of England— notably the law of evidence—English decisions may even attain at times the status of binding authority. And where the court is interpreting a statute framed on an English model, such as the Companies Act, 1926, or the Bills of Exchange Act, 1964, the conclusions of the highest courts of England will have great persuasive power. But elsewhere reference is made to them simply as illustrations of correct reasoning. In the past two decades in particular, a number of South African judges, and especially the judges of appeal, have been stressing the duty of the courts to give expression to the rules of Roman-Dutch law. In a recent *cri de coeur* the chief justice, Mr. Justice L. C. Steyn, pronounced his *credo* in unmistakable terms. In *Trust Bank van Africa, Bpk.* v. *Eksteen*, 1964 (3) S.A. 402 (A.D.) the case raised the question whether the South African law of estoppel is to be found in the decisions of the English courts. No court, he stated, has the power to replace our common law with that of another country. The same would hold true even where there is identity of legal principle in the two countries. But reference to, or consideration of, the principles of a related legal system is perfectly in order, and indeed of great service in obtaining clarity on the best application, adaptation, and development of our own principles. Having regard to other systems in this way, however, is quite a different thing from absorbing them. The chief justice mentioned reference to a related legal system: there are those who consider that the close relations and European laws, with their civil-law background, are not English law. In practice, however, hitherto it has been rare for persuasive material to be sought outside England, the United States, and Scotland. The reasons are the ease in reading material in English, the accessibility of material in English, the accessibility of text books on the Anglo-American legal systems, and the presence of codes in Continental systems. A judgement on a specific provision of a code is of less persuasive force than one on an abstract principle of common law.

On the importation of English law, the late Mr. Justice F. P. Van den Heever, a renowned legal scholar, was wont to draw the parallel of the cuckoo in the nest. Some similarity, he said, is seen between a rule of the Roman-Dutch law and that of English law, then "With pleasure, if indeed not with joy, it is stated that there is no difference," and then the entire body of Roman-Dutch rules is replaced by that of England.

That this has happened on a number of occasions is not to be denied—not indeed was Mr. Justice Van den Heever himself entirely guiltless of supplanting Roman-Dutch law by English law.[1] But in several instances the highest court has rectified the situation. The law of contract can be used for illustrative purposes: the identification of the Roman-Dutch requirement of a *justa causa* for a contract with the English requirement of valuable consideration, on which Lord De Villiers C. J. insisted to his dying day, was rejected by the Appellate Division in 1919. Again, the tendency of the courts to apply the English law to the problem of impossibility of performance discharging a contract was bluntly declared wrong by the same court in the same year. On the other hand, the rules restricting contracts in restraint of trade, admittedly taken from the English law, have continued to be applied by the courts. There has been an occasional question whether we should be so prone to absorb every detail of the foreign rules, but no one has yet suggested a return to the Roman-Dutch law, which, it seems clear, found nothing offensive in such contracts. Manifestly, there are at least odd pockets of the law where the rules stated by the institutional writers do not work well in modern conditions or do not square with present-day notions of right. How far, then, can the judiciary move in adapting the Roman-Dutch system to contemporaneous needs and values?

The courts find they have a limited area of maneuver; beyond this they feel compelled to abide by the old legal rules and leave it to the legislature to effect the necessary changes. The boundaries are dictated by intuitive feeling, the product of judicial experience, and loyalty to the legal tradition. Occasionally a court will go an appreciable distance. So it was in *Blower* v. *Van Noorden* (1909 T. S. 890), which decided that the liability of an agent who exceeds his authority is not on the contract itself, as the Roman-Dutch writers said, but upon a breach of implied warranty of authority, as in English law. "During the two hundred years which have passed since Voet," explained Chief Justice Innes, one of the greatest of South African judges, "the doctrine of commercial agency has been developed along lines then already recognized, though not fully explored, with the result that an agent is now regarded as one to whom no contractual liability in respect of agreements entered into in the name of his principal can possibly attach. He is simply and solely the representative of another." This decision may perhaps be explained as the logical conclusion of a trend already manifest in the Roman-Dutch law, a line of approach that has recently been adopted by the Appellate Division in certain cases. The judges have from time to time said that the Roman-Dutch law is a living system, not one petrified at the time it ceased to obtain in Holland. Another process is to transpose Roman-Dutch rules to a modern South African setting, with the necessary modifications, as shown in *Robert Construction Co. Ltd.* V. *Willcox Bros. (Pty.) Ltd.* (1962 (4) S.A. 326(A.D.).) where the Appellate Division resurrected the *causae continentia* doctrine of jurisdiction and fitted it into the present structure of the Supreme Court.

The principle of abrogation by disuse is also available to the courts. It applies both to enactments passed before British occupation (provided desuetude took place before 1910) and the common law. The particular rule must have been out of use for a considerable time and must be discordant with present-day sentiments. In 1914 it was held that adultery had for these reasons ceased to be a crime, and five years later the subsidiary penalties, such as the inability of the parties to marry or inherit from each other, were found, too, to have come to an end. It is not an easy matter, however, to establish that a Roman-Dutch rule has fallen into disuse.

Where the ambit of a Roman-Dutch rule is clear, it will not often happen that a court will deny, limit, or extend it. The court may question its fairness, and may even urge legislative intervention, but it will almost always say *judicis est jus dicere sed non dare*. Recently, for instance a provincial court was faced with a question that had come up twice for decision before, but in which the Roman-Dutch authorities had not been examined, the judges following English law: if A pays B's creditor, not on B's instructions, nor as his agent, nor in order to save B's affairs from loss (i.e., as *negotiorum gestor*), but simply to benefit himself, has A a claim against B founded on unjust enrichment? Aided by certain academic studies, the court went fully into the old writings and concluded that according to them A had such a claim. It was unhappy at having to reach this conclusion, but felt that it had no option.

But say a rule that has been expounded and applied by the courts for many years is now challenged as not truly reflecting the Roman-Dutch law. The reaction of the judges is not uniform. There are pronouncements that "if the decisions had disregarded fundamental principles of our law, we might have to reassert those principles even at the cost of reversing judgments of long standing." The Appellate Division recently has been giving these sentiments practical force. Eighty-one years after the English law of nuisance had been adopted in South Africa, the Appellate Division in 1963 declared that it was not identical to the Roman-Dutch law, which must be applied. The result has not been entirely happy, for the legal profession is not at all clear what the Roman-Dutch law is. This is one of the spheres where, contrary to the adage so frequently on the lips of South African academics, English law is rich in principle and Roman-Dutch law poor. Another activity of the Appellate Division that has met with a mixed reception is its insistence on *animus injuriandi* as an essential requirement for liability for defamation. In 1931 a leading academic wrote that "when jurists or judges say that *animus injuriandi* is part of the connotation of the wrong of defamation, as Charles Lamb said of Coleridge's metaphysics, it is only their fun." But in a catena of decisions commencing in 1962, the highest court has come down with all the force at its command in favor of the element of *animus injuriandi*. This has been applauded by some writers as an admirable reassertion of the true Roman-Dutch principle; others have been perplexed at the precise meaning the Appellate Division is giving to the expression. Though the details may be worked out in the future, and the present struggles of pleaders abate, there remains a fundamental objection that the passage of time will not eliminate: that the ultimate court has overlooked the changed nature of the wrong of defamation. "It is," as an eminent judge of appeal, Mr. Justice Schreiner, put it over twenty years ago, "no longer regarded primarily as an insulting incident occurring between the plaintiff and the defendant personally, with publicity only as an element of aggravation.... The delict of defamation has come to be limited to the harming of the plaintiff by statements which damage his good name." In short, not the use but the publication of the words in question is the core of the defamation action today. The result, says Professor R. G. McKerron, is that often liability depends not on whether there was *animus injuriandi*, but on whether the defendant was negligent in publishing the words; and thus it cannot be said that *animus injuriandi* is an essential element of defamation.

In marked contrast to the Appellate Division's insistence on turning the clock back in the law of nuisance and defamation is its blunt rejection of pleas to restore the old law of certain of the special crimes. Frequently it has categorically stated that a particular legal rule may not be in conformity with Roman-Dutch authority, but it has now become settled by curial practice. For instance, the court has said that the inclusion of obstructing or impeding the administration of justice within the scope of contempt of court came originally via the English law and is now part of South African law. Again, while the court has agreed that the crime of housebreaking with intent to commit a crime is not in accord with the old authorities, it has pointed out that the crime has been tried daily by the courts for years and held that the position must be left as it is. In the sphere of special crimes the Appellate Division has indeed been a disappointment to the legal fundamentalists.

The movement to rid the stream of alien waters is thus checked by the desire not to impede its free flow in the day-to-day task of the administration of justice. Where the judiciary, in carrying into effect its laudable aim of applying Roman-Dutch legal principles, falls somewhat short of the ideal today is its hesitancy in molding them to modern circumstances. Occasionally the impression is left, after reading a judgment in which the old authorities are reviewed in depth, that a greater awareness of the social purposes of the law in promoting justice in the society of the present day is called for. In the fullness of time, when there is broad satisfaction that the judiciary has preserved the Roman-Dutch inheritance from all danger of being sullied, the courts may feel themselves freer to move in a policy-oriented direction.

The same impression of distaste with interfering with the rules of Roman-Dutch law is yielded by an inspection of the statute book. This is best illustrated with reference to the law of husband and wife. At a time when many countries of the western world have been making bold legal changes to enhance the economic and social status of married women and have been tending to widen the ground of divorce, South Africa has been treading with an ultra-cautious step. At common law, unless the intending spouses entered into an antenuptial contract, marriage results in community of property and of profit and loss, and the vesting of the marital power in the husband. The matrimonial proprietary regime is one of co-ownership of a joint estate in undivided shares, of which the husband is the sold administrator. He is head of the family and has the predominant say in matters concerning the common life and the minor children. The one advantage of the rule—and it is a considerable one—is that the wife ultimately participates in the increased fortunes of the family. But in return she loses legal capacity, so that she is little better than a minor under her husband's guardianship. The alternative is for her to marry by antenuptial contract, whereby each spouse keeps a separate estate, though still the husband retains predominant control over matters regarding the common life. The great disadvantage is that the wife does not share, as rightly she should, in the family's fortunes that are immediately attributable to the husband's efforts. In practice marriage settlements simply do not make good this loss. The solution seems to be the introduction of some system of community of acquests during the marriage, possibly coupled with equality of each spouse in their administration, as in the Netherlands and West Germany. But the legislature seems unwilling to take any such radical step. It has given a wife subject to the marital power various capacities in relation to building societies, insurance policies, banking accounts, and the like. In 1953 it passed a statute called the Matrimonial Affairs Act, which restricts the husband's marital power in minor respects by preventing him from dealing with certain property without his wife's written consent, gives a married woman capacity to be a party to certain lawsuits, requires the mother's as well as the father's consent for a minor to marry, and empowers a divorce court to grant maintenance to the innocent spouse.

As for divorce, the two common-law grounds of adultery and malicious desertion have been supplemented by the Divorce Laws Amendment Act, 1935, by only two further grounds of relative insignificance: the first, that the other spouse has been insane for a continuous period of seven years; the second, that the defendant has been declared an habitual criminal and been subsequently detained in prison for at least five years. Suggestions for additional bases for divorce suits (that go nowhere near the controversial territory of the marriage breakdown principle), for instance, the basis of cruelty, hit the hard and stony surface of South African legal, social, and religious conservatism. If both spouses desire a divorce, the generous scope of malicious desertion in practice makes it easy to obtain; but if only one desires it, it may be found that South African law is not very accommodating.

It is not always a disinclination to break with the past that restrains the hand of the lawmaker. The reason may lie in a sense of gallantry to females. Nowhere is this more clearly shown than in the preservation of two Roman rules, the *senatusconsultum Velleianum* and the *authentica si qua mulier*, designed to protect woman against "feminine weakness." The *senatusconsultum* prevented women from interceding in respect of another's obligation, intercession being the assumption of an alien debt, of which the most important instance is suretyship. The *authentica* specifically imposed the prohibition on intercession by a wife on behalf of her husband. The modern construction is to render the transaction voidable, not void as the Romans regarded it. The woman foregoes the benefits if she makes express renunciation with full knowledge, and even where she does not, if the intercession is to her advantage. The tendency of the courts has been to expand the meaning of advantage, though a recent case has interpreted the exception to the assertion of the *authentica* as limited to an intercession which is clearly to the benefit of the wife herself. The legislature has contented itself with abolishing the benefits only in a few circumstances, one being where a woman borrows money from a building society or stands surety for or takes over the debt of someone else to a building society; another is where a woman accepts or endorses a bill of exchange or makes or endorses a promissory note. But though Henry IV abolished the benefits *holus bolus* in France in 1660, and Ceylon followed suit in 1924 and Rhodesia in 1959, so far the South African legislature has stood immovable. Not even the oft-cited words of Mr. Justice Van den Heever have made an impression: "One of the incongruities of this inconsequent age is the fact that women, while enjoying full rights of citizenship, including that of making or marring policies of State as effectively as any male, are able in their private affairs to invoke a defense based on their innate fecklessness and incapacity and so avoid liability in respect of obligations which they have deliberately assumed."

In 1962 the Law Revision Committee reported that the reasons advanced for abolition of the benefits were not altogether convincing, and because the members of the committee were divided on the matter, it was decided to make no recommendation. It is a matter of common knowledge that opposition in professional circles to the repeal comes from those who feel that it would be wrong to deprive a woman of benefits protecting her from the consequences of her altruistic acts, and in particular, those acts in favor of her husband.

Traditionally, South African policy has been one of separation of the accepted racial groups, each of which is regarded as having its own national (i.e., blood-bond) and cultural identity. Little attention is paid to the controversial meaning of the word "race." The broadest division, and the one most significant for legal purposes, is into Whites, Bantu (Africans, or Natives in former parlance), Asians ("Asiatics" is the word actually used) and Coloreds. Political control is firmly in the hands of the Whites, who take the attitude that the undeniable lesson of history is that the creation of a multi-racial integrated state will inevitably lead to the dominance of the largest group, the Bantu, and the loss of collective identity and absorption of the Whites.

The present governmental policy is that the days when the non-Whites were regarded as the children of Ham—the hewers of wood and the drawers of water—are gone. Each racial group is to be allowed free rein for the expression of its inherent characteristics. The Whites must no longer be party to ethnocentrism. On the one hand, they are entitled to preserve their own culture; on the other hand, they must protect and advance the separate cultures and legitimate national aspirations of the other racial groups. Since assimilation at any point of contact leads to absorption, as far as feasible (an important limitation in practice) there must be separation politically, socially, culturally, biologically, economically, and territorially. This is the philosophy of what used to be called "segregation," then (for some years after 1948) *apartheid* ("apartness") and now, to bring out fully the positive, dynamic nature of the intended self-determination, "separate development." It does not contemplate partitioning of the country between the racial groups, however; the utmost that present policy envisages is the ultimate settlement of a significant part of the Bantu population in national homelands, comprising at most 13 percent of the whole country, which might achieve independence. The larger portion of the African population will have to remain as "temporary sojourners" in white South Africa. For the Coloreds and Indians, no separate homelands are intended: they are to be given a limited form of self-government in their own group areas in white South Africa. This holds out the prospect of opportunities for them to attain governmental positions hitherto out of reach of the non-Whites. But there is no intention of surrendering an iota of ultimate white control. And this political horizontal stratification must surely, if to a lesser extent, be reflected in economic life, the Whites occupying the higher strata.

The Constitution of South Africa does not contain a Bill of Rights. There is no fundamental law that ensures equality of treatment of different classes and races, though there is no provision, as there was in the Constitution of the old Transvaal Republic, which expressly states that there is to be no equality between White and Black. Parliament, a supreme legislature and representative only of Whites, can pass by ordinary procedure an act that is partial or unequal in operation as between races and classes; and so, within the limits of its legislative competency, can a provincial council pass a discriminatory ordinance. But where there is no empowering act of parliament or provincial ordinance the courts will strike down as invalid for unreasonableness any by-law, regulation, or administrative action that results in substantial inequality between sections of the population; for, in the words of Chief Justice Centlivres, "it is the duty of the courts to hold the scales evenly between the different classes of the community."

In the cases where it has the capacity to pronounce on the validity of enactments or administrative acts, the judiciary does not insist on identical treatment being afforded to all groups. It does not even require exact equality of different treatment. But it draws the line at substantial inequality of different treatment. If that is what parliament or a provincial council wishes to permit, it must say so in unmistakable terms in an act or ordinance. The seminal decision in the affirmation of this "separate but not substantially unequal" test was that of the Appellate Division in *Minister of Posts and Telegraphs* v. *Rasool*, (1934 A.D. 167). The postmaster-general had statutory power to establish and control post offices, including issuing instructions for this purpose to subordinates. On his orders the post office at a certain town was divided into two parts, one for Whites and the other for non-Whites. Hitherto Indians had been served at the white counter, there being a separate counter for Africans. R, an Indian, asked for an order compelling termination of the new division. For the purpose of the case, R admitted that the services rendered at the two counters was equal. By a majority the Appellate Division held that the instruction was not void for being partial as between different classes. In its view an administrative act or piece of delegated legislation was not invalid merely because it divided the community into Whites and non-Whites for administrative purposes. Differentiation based on race or language might indeed be advantageous, enabling the various sections to be served by officials acquainted with their customs, requirements, and languages.

There has never been a suggestion of approval by the South African courts of the United States Supreme Court's view that separate facilities are inherently unequal. Differentiation, however, must not become discrimination. For instance, a local authority that has power to regulate the use of the seashore and sea-bathing may not give the Whites all the rock-free beaches with good access by road, and the rock-strewn, dangerous beaches, difficult of access by road, to the non-Whites. Again, a licensing body may not take a man's race into account in deciding whether to grant a license. But, of course, the common-law rule is at the mercy of the omnipotent legislature. When a judicial decision proves unwelcome to the government, it may decide to introduce permissive legislation. Thus, in 1955 the Motor Carrier Transportation Act, 1930, was amended to allow transportation boards, in deciding on applications for motor-carrier certificates, to give preference to applicants who belong to the same class as the majority of persons to be catered for by the particular transportation service. Most far-reaching in this direction is the Reservation of Separate Amenities Act, 1953. A person in charge or control of any public premises or public vehicle may make a reservation for a particular class or race, and his action cannot be invalidated simply because no amenity has been demarcated for another race or class or such amenity as has been demarcated for it is inferior.

In determining whether differentiation has trespassed into the forbidden ground of substantial inequality, the courts use a yardstick of common sense. They would not, for example, concern themselves with the fact that the railway concourse of non-Whites in Johannesburg is not a attractive as that for Whites.

Nor does the judiciary turn a blind eye to the country's social history and structure. If an enactment distinguishes between different races without defining them, the courts will apply the tests of origin or "blood," of physical appearance, of mode of life and associations, of general acceptance and repute. The predominant factor is physical appearance. In one case a man with an African great-grandmother but otherwise of white descent, appearance, mode of life, and associations was held to be White and not Colored.

Not only in the interpretation of legislation does the judiciary take account of the racial pattern of the country. Thus, in construing restrictive conditions in title deeds to land, it has assumed knowledge of the fact that it is common practice to employ Africans as domestic servants and that such employment of Whites is rare. But acquaintance with social conditions is not allowed to justify discriminatory treatment because of race, such as lower damages to a Bantu than to a

White man for pain and suffering flowing from an assault, or heavier punishment to an offender simply because he is a person of color. Every now and then allegations are made that criminal sentences are unequal, to the disadvantage of non-Whites, but though there may be instances of this, it has no legislative sanction and is against the common law as frequently pronounced by the Supreme Court.

Since the National Party came to power in 1948 on the *apartheid* platform, separation of the races has become less and less a matter of social convention and more and more a product of legislation.

The keystone to the implementation of government policy was the racial classification of all inhabitants. This difficult problem, fraught with tragic consequences for thousands of persons, was tackled by the passing of the Population Registration Act, 1950, in terms of which every one was to have his race settled and given an identity card reflecting it. Numerous troublesome questions have arisen in the administration of the statute, which has had to be amended on several occasions.

Biological segregation received increased support from parliament. The Immorality Act of 1927 had forbidden carnal intercourse outside marriage between White and Bantu. In 1950 the prohibition was extended from Bantu to any non-White, and in 1957 the new Immorality Act prohibited any indecent or immoral act between White and non-White. Marriages between them, which had been infrequent and contrary to conventional morality, were banned by the Prohibition of Mixed Marriages Act, 1949. But the two statutes did not and still do not apply as between the different non-white groups.

In the political field the process of removing non-white participation in central government was taken to its conclusion. When the Union of South Africa was formed, the constitution was framed to meet the demands of the northern provinces, the Transvaal and Orange Free State, that the non-white vote should not be extended to them and only Whites be allowed to sit in parliament. The entrenchment of the Cape non-white vote on the common roll by the requirement of a two-thirds majority vote for change did not prevent the removal of the Bantu voter from the common roll through an act passed with the requisite majority in 1936, the compensatory separate representation of Africans by white members of the two houses of parliament. Twenty years later the same fate befell the Cape Colored voter, though this time the government had to pack the senate to secure its two-thirds majority. At the same time the entrenchment of the non-white vote was ended. Subsequently this separate representation was ended for the Bantu by legislation passed in 1959, and for the Coloreds by legislation passed in 1968.

This deprivation was justified by the concurrent granting of separate political institutions to the two groups. The Bantu Authorities Act, 1951, envisaged three grades of Bantu authorities—tribal, regional, and territorial—based on the chief and a form of tribal organization consistent with traditional Bantu democracy. Further to facilitate the advance of the eight prospective Bantu national units, the Promotion of Bantu Self-government Act was passed in 1959. The only self-governing territory to be created in South Africa has been the Transkei—in 1963. The self-government it enjoys is of a restricted character. (In the associated territory of South-West Africa there is a further self-governing territory, Ovamboland, created in 1968 under the Development of Self-government for Native Nations in South-West Africa Act of that year.) The preliminary steps towards the emergence of the remaining self-governing territories are now being taken.

For the Coloreds there is the Colored Persons Representative Council, which is to have certain executive and legislative powers over Coloreds, subject to cabinet control. Ultimately the Indian Council, at present with only advisory functions, may attain a similar status.

Apartheid in political matters is fostered by the Prohibition of Political Interference Act, 1968, in terms of which a political party can have members of only one of the four racial groups and no one of another racial group may assist a political party or one of its candidates.

Political expression for Coloreds and Indians is also to be granted through their own local authorities. This contemplates further territorial separation. The principal means of attainment is the Group Areas Act, the original version of which was passed in 1950. It aims at the division of the country into areas for exclusive occupation and, to a considerable degree, ownership by the different racial groups other than the Bantu. Inevitably the large-scale population shifts and deprivation of rights in land involved in the implementation of this measure have produced hardship. The government contends that this has been kept to a minimum and that it is engaged in positive community development through a state department by that name created in 1961.

The administrative machine has also been geared to the policy of separate development, resulting in greater centralization of the affairs of Africans, Indians, and Coloreds. School education of these three groups has been taken away from the provincial councils and vested in the new central government departments of Bantu Education, Colored Affairs, and Indian Affairs.

Educational apartheid, traditional in lower education, was made mandatory in higher education in terms of the Extension of University Education Act, 1959, which at the same time sponsored the creation of separate university colleges for Coloreds, Indians, and Africans.

Economic segregation also shows the familiar negative and positive faces. There are measures to uplift the economic status of the African, Colored, and Indian groups, such as the Promotion of the Economic Development of Colored Development of Bantu Homelands Act, 1968, the Rural Colored Areas Act, 1963, and the Colored Development Corporation Act, 1962. There are the acts that have led to community development of Africans in white urban areas, through housing programs and subsidized transportation. On the other hand, there are the numerous laws passed to curtail the influx of Bantu to towns or to facilitate their removal or relocation; that prohibit strikes by Bantu (and also lockouts by their employers), providing for compulsory arbitration in their stead; that aim at breaking up trade unions with members belonging to different racial groups; that prohibit employment of Bantu in certain skilled work; and that allow for the reservation of certain types of work or a percentage of them for employees of a particular race (called familiarly "job reservation").

In these and other ways the government has endeavored to strengthen those conventional and psychological rules that make birds of a feather flock together and produce what has been termed "natural apartheid." Total economic separation, however, is acknowledged as beyond the bounds of practical politics, so social contact between the races cannot be shut off.

The opponent of the apartheid philosophy contends that it holds out greater peril for white survival than the policy of a non-racial integrated society. (The most optimistic forecast will not yield a white population of more than 25 percent of the total outside the Bantu national homelands.) How can the bulk of the Africans and all the Asians and Coloreds be expected to rest content with a society in which political rights and most of the economic opportunities are confined to Whites? But the answer of the champion of apartheid is that each racial group is made up of persons of common traditions, sentiments, and ideals, which must be preserved and fostered. Different races cannot live harmoniously in an integrated society; polarization is essential.

The problems thrust up by efforts to preserve the cultural distinctiveness of the various races are graphically illustrated by the story of the recognition of African law and the creation of African courts. The African law that the Europeans first encountered differed from tribe to tribe in details, but agreed in the principal institutions. It was fairly advanced for a primitive system. In its absence of written law (the Bantu did not know of writing before the coming of the white man) and legislation it was similar to the system of tribal laws of the early Germanic period of European history that ended about the fifth century A. D.; but it also had certain attributes of the following Franco-Germanic period, of the feudal era, and even of the early Middle Ages, for there was little of self-help, private vengeance or the judicial duel to be found and the distinction between crime and civil wrong was seen, even if rather dimly. Family relations and succession were the most developed branches of law. Marriage was polygynous, on the agnatic principle. Testamentary succession was unknown. The rules of intestate succession normally were on the basis of primogeniture. Collective family responsibility for the wrongs of individuals was a hallmark of tribal law. The tribe had a system of courts, coming into operation if the village or family head could not settle the dispute. Normally there was a two-tier system of tribunals, the lower manned by the headman or sub-chief, from which appeal lay to the chief. The procedure was innocent of professional lawyers: the participants were the adult tribesmen, and the process was arbitrational, seeking to find an acceptable solution to the parties and the community.

The tribal legal process sought to create equilibrium in a static society. The unwritten law was the heart of the tribal system, absorbed by the members unconsciously as part of communal life. The attachment, being personal and not religious, proved unable to withstand large-scale contact with the economy, culture, and religion of the Whites. Increased mobility of Africans and their settling-down on white-owned farms or in white-controlled towns resulted in the severance of tribal links and the loss of popular knowledge of indigenous law.

The early attitude of the white governors of indigenous African law varied from place to place and time to time. In the Cape Colony in the great reserve of the Transkei it was recognized generally, but with no special African courts of original jurisdiction; in British Bechuanaland such general recognition was coupled with exclusive civil jurisdiction and considerable criminal jurisdiction vested in tribal chiefs; in British Kaffraria only tribal rules of succession were officially recognized, though magistrates *sub rosa* applied African law generally where public policy was not affected; and elsewhere in the colony only tribal rules of succession were applied.

Natal for long expounded Shepstone's policy of control, not civilization, of the native, whose laws were not to be abrogated unless contrary to the principles of humanity. Chiefs were allowed to retain much of their civil and criminal jurisdiction. The third quarter of the nineteenth century, however, saw a partial relaxation of these principles; and to some extent native law was codified, in the event being somewhat altered and becoming more rigid.

The Transvaal initially subjected the Africans to "the laws of the land." From 1881 provision was made for the application of native law by native commissioners' courts where it was consistent with "the general principles of civilization." The Orange Free State afforded no general recognition to native law.

Order was finally achieved in 1927 when the Native (now Bantu) Administration Act was passed. The time had come, it was said, to bolster up the decaying power and status of the chiefs and to allow for the country-wide application of African laws through a series of special courts. In essence the structure created by this statute obtains to the present day; all that has happened is a slight intensification of the policy of separation that it initiated.

At the lowest level are the chiefs' and headmen's courts, with jurisdiction in civil claims arising out of African law and which may be entrusted with limited jurisdiction in criminal offenses. Such a court is not one of record, and legal practitioners may not appear before it. Traditional tribal usage is to be observed. Appeal lies to the Bantu affairs commissioner's court, which has to rehear the matter. Critics contend that the chiefs' and headmen's courts are anachronisms. African society is no longer homogeneous, and it poses problems with which it is beyond the capacity of a tribal court to cope.

The courts at the higher levels are at present manned by Whites. The court of original jurisdiction is that of the Bantu affairs commissioner, which resembles the ordinary magistrate's court in that the judicial officer has the same legal training as a magistrate and the limitation of jurisdiction as to civil causes of action is the same. But there are several major differences: there is unlimited jurisdiction as to the amount in dispute in civil cases, and the court hears all disputes between Bantu, magistrates' courts being incompetent (though not the Supreme Court). Where questions of Bantu law are involved the court may apply that law, provided that it is not opposed to the principles of public policy or natural justice. Appeals lie to one of three Bantu appeal courts. Further appeal to the Appellate Division of the Supreme Court requires leave of the Bantu appeal court and the Appellate Division. These Bantu appeal courts are staffed by Bantu affairs commissioners elevated to the position.

To reduce legal costs, in 1929 Bantu divorce courts were established to hear suits for nullity, divorce, and separation in respect of civil marriages between Bantu, without derogation from the jurisdiction of the Supreme Court. Of course, these tribunals apply the ordinary law of the land.

The avowed objects of the new dispensation were a lowering of costs of litigation, the application of African law in appropriate circumstances without incurring expense in proving it, and a simplified form of procedure. Grave doubts have been expressed whether all these aims have been achieved. While the tariff of costs in the Bantu affairs commissioner's court is lower than that in the magistrate's court and far lower than that in the Supreme Court, private agreements between litigants and their legal advisers to pay costs at a higher level are commonplace. Nor have the hopes that Africans would conduct their cases themselves on a large scale been realized. Lower costs in practice appear to be the rule only in the Bantu divorce courts.

As for judicial cognizance of Bantu law, while this is frequently assumed by the presiding officer, it has been queried whether he has been adequately trained to justify this.

Finally, while the rules of procedure in the Bantu affairs commissioner's court are somewhat simpler than those in the magistrate's court, they are beyond the understanding of the tribal African—indeed, of the average law White. The Bantu affairs commissioner's court is not the counterpart of the chief's court of old; its procedure is far more formalistic, rigid, and technical.

The partial recognition of Bantu law has also brought problems in its train. It is only where it is applied by the Bantu affairs commissioner or is recognized by legislation that it achieves the status of a personal law; otherwise, it is simply disregarded by the courts as not being portion of the law of the land. Common law rules, for instance, have not been adapted to take cognizance of customary (i.e., polygamous) unions between Bantu. Thus, while Bantu affairs commissioners' and appeal courts in actions between Africans were always prepared to grant damages to an African female for the wrongful causing of the death of her partner in the customary union, the Appellate Division in *Suid-Afrikaanse Nasionale Trust en Assuransie Maatskappy* v. *Fondo* (1960 (2) S.A. 467 (A.D.).) denied such relief where the defendant was not a Bantu, on the ground that the defendant's action is confined to the wife whom the deceased was obliged to support at common law—which means the wife who is party to a civil marriage. Fortunately, this intolerable state of affairs was ended by remedial legislation.

The question of recognition of customary unions shows in a most interesting way the clash between two disparate ideals: the upholding on the one hand of the traditional rules of the Bantu and on the other of the Christian concept of monogamy. By the end of the nineteenth century the early liberal attitude of certain courts allowing for recognition of customary unions which, while potentially polygamous, were de facto monogamous, had hardened into complete refusal of recognition. African polygamous marriages were regarded as contrary to public policy; but the authorities through legislation in various ways did take cognizance of them in order to do justice to the female partners. Finally, the Bantu Administration Act, 1927, made provision for the protection of the innocent partner to and offspring of such a union, both as regards material property rights and succession claims. And the Workmen's Compensation Act, 1941, gave benefits to the woman left a widow, provided neither she nor the deceased was a party to a subsisting civil marriage.

At the present there are two schools of thought on the recognition of Bantu law and the special Bantu courts. The one holds that each ethnic group among the Bantu has its own pattern of culture, the uniqueness of which does not disappear simply with education and civilization. It is wrong to perpetuate the nineteenth-century denigration of the Bantu's law as primitive and inferior, incapable of adaptation to modern conditions. Customary law, in those large fields where it can fill a role, should be allowed as much play as feasible. The other school contends that tribal law should be confined to apposite circumstances, where traditional rules are in fact obeyed. A realistic attitude should be taken, which has regard to the breakdown of the subsistence economy, to migratory laborers bringing back to the reserves the mores of town life, and to the detribalization and urbanization of so many of the Africans. Commercial transactions of today, it is urged, cannot be adequately catered for by tribal law. Nor would it be right to distort Bantu traditional rules to cope with situations that are adequately and effectively cared for by the common law. The adherents of this approach question the wisdom of continuing with the parallel set of Bantu courts.

The constitution of South Africa, as embodied in the Republic of South Africa Constitution Act, 1961, reproduces many of the principles of the constitutions of the United Kingdom and the Commonwealth countries, though admittedly it has its own unique principle of discrimination on grounds of color. The creation of the Republic, which brought in its train the departure of South Africa from the Commonwealth, effected no fundamental change save the State President (elected by the two houses of parliament) for the queen, with the governor-general as her representative, as the head of state. No attempt was made in 1961 to return to the non-parliamentary executive, with the state president as its head as well as head of the state, that had existed in the nineteenth-century republics of the Transvaal and Orange Free State. The advantages of the system of cabinet government were only too clear. It ensured that the government, while by convention nominally dependent for its existence on the confidence of the House of Assembly (the lower parliamentary chamber) in fact through strict party discipline controlled parliament. Public sentiment did not even call for an effort to assert a local root for the constitution. The appeal of constitutional autarky or autochthony was small. The statute creating the republican constitution was passed in the ordinary way, "by the Queen's Most Excellent Majesty, the Senate and the House of Assembly of the Union of South Africa."

There remain the traditional two houses of parliament. The lower one, the House of Assembly, with 166 members, is directly elected by Whites, male and female, who have attained the age of 18: there are no franchise qualifications to be satisfied. Election is, as it has always been, in single-member constituencies, with the majority vote prevailing, a system that has at times (as elsewhere) resulted in a government being returned with a majority of the seats by a minority of the electorate. The upper house, the Senate, approximately one-third the size of the Assembly, is partly nominated and partly elected—by proportional representation and by electoral colleges in each province composed of its members of the Assembly and its provincial councilors. The composition of the Senate, the various methods of dissolving it, and the loss of seats of nominated senators on a change of government ensure that normally its party political make-up is a reflection of that of the lower house, but even if the opposition has a majority in the upper house, the government can carry on. Should a bill passed by the House of Assembly be rejected by the Senate, it nevertheless goes to the Senate president for signature in the same session if it is a taxation or appropriation bill; otherwise, it goes for such signature if it is passed in a succeeding session not in the same calendar year. Naturally, this method of resolving deadlocks, taken over from the Parliament Act of Great Britain, does not apply to a bill that has to be passed by the two-thirds majority entrenched procedure. Not that this is of any significance today, for the only entrenched section left is that guaranteeing the equality of the official languages, and the constitutional struggle of the 1950s showed how a government can artificially create a two-thirds majority by altering the constitution of one of the legislative chambers. The issue of entrenchment belongs to "old, unhappy, far-off things, / And battles long ago." Very likely the scene of constitutional problems will one day shift to the Bantu self-governing territories.

There is another area which ever since 1910 has threatened to be stormy and yet which, probably because it has never been the center of party political controversy, has remained relatively tranquil. It concerns the constitutional position of the four provinces.

The founding fathers of the Union of South Africa, while determined to create a unitary and not a federal constitution, were prepared to make concessions to the local sentiments of the four colonies. One way of accomplishing this was by converting the colonies, without change of boundaries, into regional areas of a status superior to that of mere local authorities, although not coordinate with the central authority, as would be provinces in a federation. The provinces that emerged were something unique in constitutional experience. Over the years harsh things have been said of them, such as "unclassifiable monstrosities" and "hybrid conglomerations." But though within six years of their creation the Jagger Commission recommended their replacement by smaller divisional councils, true local authorities, or federal units, the hold of the provinces on to life has proved remarkably tenacious. There have been small changes in their constitutional structure, but their essential character has remained unchanged.

The chief executive officer, the administrator, is appointed for five years by the cabinet, which alone can dismiss him. The post is non-political, though naturally governments in the vast majority of cases appoint their own supporters. The administrator has certain personal powers, such as fixing the time of provincial council sessions, and he controls finance, for an appropriation ordinance requires his recommendation. On the other hand, the general administration of provincial affairs is vested not in him but in the executive committee of five, of which he is a member. The other four members up to 1962 were elected by the provincial council by proportional representation. This frequently led to executives being divided on party lines, sometimes with the administrator holding the balance of power. The original hopes of a non-party, "best-man" executive, like a company's board of directors, were never realized. The change in 1962 has resulted in the election of the four members of the executive committee other than the administrator by simple majority vote, the party in power making a clean sweep. This does not eliminate all problems in the committee, for the administrator may not be sympathetic to the political outlook of the others, and it denies the opposition the possibility of acting as a watchdog on the executive. As long as a system of responsible government is denied the provinces, clashes between the administrator or executive committee and the provincial council—which can remove neither—remain possible.

A provincial council has the same number of members as the province has members of the House of Assembly, with a minimum of twenty-five, which has always meant a special delimitation for the smaller provinces, Natal and the Orange Free State. In the Cape and Transvaal electoral boundaries for central and provincial elections coincide. Election is by the white parliamentary voters, each of whom is qualified to stand for election. The council has a fixed life of five years. From the start councils have been constituted on party political lines.

The legislative powers conceded to the provincial councils, with a few exceptions, are on topics of little importance. Of the four major powers, only direct taxation has been drastically whittled down by central legislation because of abuse by the councils. The result has been increasing dependence of the provinces on assignment of revenue by parliament—today half of their income comes from central subsidies—and the increasing unhappiness of the treasury at its inability to control provincial expenditure. Another power, over education, has through successive acts of parliament been confined to that of Whites, and even here a measure of governmental control is now being exercised. Roads and local institutions are the other two important legislative powers, and into both of these inroads have been made by parliament.

In 1914, in the case of *Middelburg Municipality* v. *Gertzen*, the Appellate Division of the Supreme Court decided that provincial councils exercise original legislative capacity, so that provincial ordinances are classified as statutes and not mere by-laws or regulations. Thus they escape the judicial tests of reasonableness and certainty imposed on the legislation of bodies, such as the executive and local authorities, clothed only with delegated legislative powers. But parliament remains supreme. It may by ordinary legislative process eat into the legislative powers of provincial councils; it may legislate on any topic assigned to a council; and an ordinance repugnant to an act of parliament is to that extent of no effect. Furthermore, a provincial council is restricted territorially, its legislative powers being confined to its boundaries. Finally, to ensure that provincial councils do not contravene fundamental governmental policy, cabinet approval is required before an ordinance comes into force. It is a form of control admittedly very seldom employed, but there is no convention that it should be restricted to cases where the government considers that the proposed ordinance will be *ultra vires*.

Complaints about the workings of the provincial system are perennial. It has been said that it yields all of the evils of party politics and none of the advantages. The sessions of the provincial councils are brief and uninspiring. Though they sport capital cities, the provinces are bereft of a proper civil service. Cooperation and coordination between the provincial administrations and between them and the central government, it is frequently claimed, is not close enough. What justification can there be, for instance, for infectious diseases being the responsibility of local authorities, ordinary diseases that of provincial administrations, and mental diseases that of the central department of health? Other alleged defects of the present provincial structure are unhealthy overlapping of services with central and local authorities and inter-provincial jealousies leading to wasteful capital expenditure. But any major change in the system is beyond the reach of practical politics.

Pre-Union influences still make themselves felt, too, in the structure of the Supreme Court of South Africa. It is composed of the Appellate Division at the apex, a tribunal that hears only appeals from the other divisions (soon to be increased to seven), some with satellite local divisions (including circuit local divisions). If it be asked how there can be six provincial divisions in a country that rejoices in only four provinces, the answer is that the concept is notional only, for jurisdictional purposes, and that in addition to the Cape, Natal, Orange Free State, and Transvaal provincial divisions, there are those called the South-West Africa Division and the Eastern Cape Division, which is carved out of the eastern areas of the Cape Province. (The proposed seventh provincial division is that of the Northern Cape, taking the place of the Griqualand West local division.) Every division is absolutely bound by the decisions of the Appellate Division; but each provincial division (with its local divisions) is otherwise an enclave of its own, not bound by the decisions of any other division. While there are provisions enabling a law suit to be moved from one division to another, and there are now uniform Rules of Court for the whole country, it is not much of an exaggeration to say that the Supreme Court exists in name only, for the provincial divisions are bound to one another by little more than a common allegiance to the Appellate Division.

The judges of the Supreme Court are appointed and elevated to higher positions by the cabinet. Though in strict law there is practically no restriction on the cabinet's choice, in practice appointments are almost always made from among the ranks of the senior practicing advocates (S.C.'s, or senior counsel). The rare exceptions are those who previously were in the public service, such as law advisers or attorneys-general. Since 1910 there have been seven such appointments, among them the present chief justice and one of the judges of appeal. In the great majority of cases judges of a division have been chosen from among the advocates practicing in that division.

A judge retires at the age of 70. He can be removed by the State President on address from both houses of parliament on the ground of misbehavior or incapacity, but no such address has ever been made.

It would be idle to pretend that in the selection of judges extraneous considerations such as political sympathies, friendship, and relationship have never played a part. South Africa is no more immune to occasional influences of this sort than most other countries where judicial appointments are made by the executive. And it can hardly be expected of the present government to choose an advocate who has been vociferously opposed to the admittedly stringent security legislation that the government has sponsored—assuming that such a person would be prepared to go on to the bench, which is most unlikely. There is also a general requirement of complete bilingualism of a prospective judge. But by and large, allowing for the occasional exceptions, cabinets (if not always picking on the best possible incumbent for a vacancy) have limited their choice to those in the ranks of the successful counsel, where, as it were, the public has already made the initial screening of eligibility.

Judges have rarely had political careers before their elevation to the bench. This is not because it is felt that this would be a disqualifying factor, though politics are played hard. Probably there would be general agreement that it could be an additional qualification, aiding, as J. B. S. Haldane once put it, "in checking the danger of abstractness in mental outlook." It is because politics and practice at the bar do not mix well. An advocate must devote his entire attention to his work if he is to reach the top. It has happened that a politician with only a part-time practice or one who left active life in the law to become a prominent member of parliament—in the government or chairman of an important committee or a parliamentary officer—has been found a seat on the judiciary, but such cases are few and far between. And the Bar Association has from time to time openly stated its disapproval of the step that was taken.

An offer of a seat on the bench, though frequently it means a financial sacrifice, is rarely refused. It would be going too far to say that advocates as a whole feel it their moral obligation to accept, though in the past there have been some who have thought so, and no doubt today there are those who are of the same view. There are other, perhaps weightier, considerations too. It is a position that enjoys great public esteem. The judiciary has a striking reputation for probity, ability, and fairness. Becoming one of the seventy-five or so distinguished men (there has never been a female judge) who fill the posts in the various divisions of the Supreme Court to most advocates marks the culmination of a successful career.

Accusations of political bias on the part of the judges are never made; but there have been occasional suggestions that judges have acted wrongly in sitting mute when administering the drastic statues that, in the interests of the security of the state, have invaded the citizen's liberty of person, movement, association, and assembly. Where are the ringing denunciations of an Atkin?, it has been asked. Indeed, one or two critics have gone even further, and pointed to cases where, they contend, the courts have had such regard to the circumstances that obtained when the act was passed and its general policy and nature that they have departed from the traditional strict construction of legislation invading fundamental civil rights. In occasional extra-curial statements judges have indignantly denied the validity of these criticisms and stressed the judiciary's duty to apply the law that parliament saw fit to enact. Certainly, there have been more recent decisions in which the leaning of the courts in favor of liberty when interpreting legislation has been clearly manifested.

There is nothing in the law to prevent a non-White being raised to the bench; in fact, it has never happened in the history of the country or the preceding colonies and states. Membership of the bar by non-Whites has been so rare as to be almost nonexistent. Even were an Indian, Colored, or Bantu to acquire a leading practice as an advocate, in the present social milieu it is unimaginable that he would be made a judge of the Supreme Court of South Africa. In a Bantu national home, however, the possibility of an African judge in the distant future cannot be dismissed. Under the Transkei Constitution Act, 1963, for instance, the republican cabinet may constitute a Transkei High Court to replace the existing division of the Supreme Court and Bantu appeal and divorce courts in the territory. The status of the High Court is to be as far as practicable that of a provincial or local division. Appeals will lie to the Appellate Division in the ordinary way. So far the cabinet has not constituted such a High Court.

The principal lower court is that of the magistrate. Unlike judges, magistrates are civil servants. Only in the larger centers can they be found engaged exclusively in judicial work; otherwise, they perform a mixture of judicial and administrative functions. This system, an inheritance from the colonial past, has been found impossible to replace by one of a lower judiciary recruited from among practicing advocates and attorneys. Though by standards of private practice the position of magistrate is not well remunerated, it is still one of the plums of the public service, and without it as an attraction recruitment to the department of justice would be even more difficult. Rather has the tide of events brought an enlargement of the scope of magisterial jurisdiction. This has been in the form of the establishment, since 1952, of regional magistrates' courts, vested only with criminal jurisdiction, but of such dimensions (three years' imprisonment, a fine of R600, ten strokes) as to elevate them to the status of intermediate courts. The ordinary magistrate's court (that of one of the 260-odd districts) has a general civil jurisdiction of R1,000 and a criminal jurisdiction of six months' imprisonment, a fine of R200 and ten strokes.

The public service has been sensitive to criticism of the qualifications of the magistrates. The lowest academic qualification is roughly of the level of the lowest academic qualification of attorneys, though the latter will very likely soon be raised substantially. About a third of the magistrates are more highly qualified, and appointment to the rank of regional magistrate is confined to these. Of recent years strenuous efforts have been made to encourage prospective magistrates to embark on more advanced study and to give them systematic academic and practical tuition through a special training division of the department of justice. But admirable though these attempts are, they cannot entirely overcome two major difficulties: one is to secure sufficient competent men in competition with the calls of private practice with its prospects of higher rewards; the other is to provide magistrates adequately equipped to decide on civil matters, the vast bulk of which come before the lower courts. Normally, before appointment a magistrate will have acted a public prosecutor, but he will not have participated directly in civil trial work—though he may have had some experience of its workings as a junior clerk.

Recently the first non-Whites have been appointed to the magistracy, as Africans serving in African areas. They do not try cases involving Whites.

It will already have become apparent that the private legal practitioners are divided into two branches, those of the advocate (the English barrister) and of the attorney (the English solicitor). The advocates are known collectively as the bar; the attorneys, for a reason that has never been satisfactorily explained, the side-bar. There are over 400 practicing advocates and some 3,500 practicing attorneys. The advocate alone is entitled to audience in the Supreme Court. His work, which comes to him on brief from an attorney, consists principally of appearing in court and giving advice on opinion. He is, of necessity if not by choice, a lone wolf, for partnerships are not permitted. The general practitioners of the law, who are in direct contact with the public, are the attorneys. While the academic qualification for the bar is the LL.B. degree, the attorney can have a lesser qualification, such as a B.Juris degree or a diploma in law. As already indicated, the attorneys' profession seems set on raising the minimum academic qualifications for its members. Ideally, or course, the LL.B. should be required of all professing the law, whether as judicial officers or private practitioners. Possibly, in the fullness of time the ideal will be attained by the attorneys. Then the claim of many of them that the two branches of the profession should be fused will be strengthened.

The proposal of fuse is a hardy annual. The attorneys who argue for it claim that many of them are more competent at conducting cases in court and more skilled lawyers than a goodly proportion of the junior advocates. Fusion, they contend, by preventing wasted efforts through using the services of two men where one would do, will reduce legal costs. The answer of the supporters of the present division is that the saving in cost will not be great and will not be worth the price—the loss of the dispassionate and objective approach of counsel to a legal case and the disappearance of a closely knit body of advocates, bound by strict disciplinary rules and steeped in legal traditions, specialists in legal research and the presentation of legal argument, from whom the judiciary has so successfully been drawn. And if heed be paid to the history of Natal, which up to 1932 allowed dual practice, fusion will result in inferior pleading and a weakening of the caliber of the bench.

Surveying the criminal law and its administration, of such importance and interest to the man in the street, the dispassionate observer of the South African scene will be struck by the strange mixture of conservation and experimentation before him. There is an admirable scheme of treatment of offenders in gaol, aimed at their rehabilitation. But it can hardly work well while the number of short-term prisoners remains so high. At present each year over 162,000 persons (about 133,000 being Bantu and 25,000 Coloreds) go to prison for a period of up to one month, and another 142,000 (124,000 being Bantu and 5,000 being Coloreds) for a period of between one and six months. In a large proportion of cases, the crime in question was a non-serious statutory one, such as breach of curfew regulations or failure to produce registration documents. Mr. Justice J. H. Steyn of the Cape bench has frequently drawn attention to the impossibility of doing rehabilitative work among these prisoners who are incarcerated for so short a time, and the danger of creating real criminals out of them through contamination with incorrigibles in prisons. The answer, he suggests, is more fining, probation, and suspended sentences with fines. The aggregate in gaols each day, however, continues to rise, and at present is about 74,000.

Another aspect of the criminal scene that gives constant cause for concern is the growing prevalence of crimes of violence and sexual offences. The reaction has been two-fold. The first has been to alter the rules of criminal procedure to assist the prosecution, which has led to some inroads into the accusatorial system of criminal procedure by the inquisitorial system. Thus the authorities have been vested with greater power to detain an accused awaiting trial and a witness—an attorney-general (the public servant in control of prosecutions in the area of a provincial division of the Supreme Court) may prohibit the release of an arrested person on bail—in the interests of public safety, or order, or the administration of justice—and has considerable capacity to detain witnesses likely to give material evidence. In addition, an attorney-general has been given a wide discretion to dispense with a preparatory examination in the magistrate's court and to order summary trial in the Supreme Court. (These powers, and certain additional ones, such as detention of suspected terrorists for interrogation, are also intended to be used to secure convictions in what some call "political crimes," and that the government refers to as "crimes against the State.") The second reaction has been to make criminal punishment more drastic. In 1952, for instance, the legislature laid down compulsory whipping for certain serious offences; the result was that the number of strokes imposed increased from 32,000 in 1952 to 73,000 in 1953, and to 94,000 in 1958, though by 1965 it had dropped to 79,000. In that year, however, the courts were revested with their discretionary powers. Another striking way in which the severity of punishment has been increased has been the extension of the number of crimes for which the death sentence may be imposed. As this trend is in the opposite direction to that of most Western countries, it calls for examination.

The movement for repeal of capital punishment has always been weak in South Africa. Prominent abolitionists have been few and have largely been confined to the thin ranks of academics, penal reformers, and clergymen. It caused a minor sensation when in 1966 Mr. Justice J. D. Cloete of the Eastern Cape Division stated in an address that he was convinced that the death sentence did not act as a deterrent to anyone, that even the most experienced judges could err imposing it, and that it should be ended. The important Penal and Prison Reform Commission, 1947, under the chairmanship of a judge distinguished for his great experience in and legal writings on the criminal law and its processes, Mr. Justice C. W. H. Lansdown, concluded that the case against capital punishment had not been made out. Care, it said, must be taken in applying the experience of other lands to South Africa, "in which the bulk of 80 percent of its population has not yet emerged from a state of barbarism." Because of the numerous safeguards against error, the risk that an innocent man might be hanged was not a real one. There was one dissentient voice, that of Dr. Agnes Hoernle, a social anthropologist, who stated the basic arguments of abolitionists that the death penalty was not an effective deterrent, that the guiltless might be executed, that the punishment was indefensibly vindictive in peacetime, and that it debased those who carried it into effect.

Public opinion, too, felt the majority of the commissioners, was not ripe for sweeping away capital punishment. Among the very few present-day vocal supporters of repeal of the death sentence, some contend that Whites generally believe that the threat of execution acts as a deterrent to non-Whites, and, naturally, that if it stays for them it must stay for Whites.

There is agreement that the incidence of crimes of violence is horrifying. The most recently published data, those for 1965-6, reflect 6,043 cases of murder reported, resulting in 3,940 sent for trial and 1,456 convicted (1,255 being Africans)—as compared with 850 four years earlier. In sum, 8,640 persons lost their lives through crimes of violence. A total of 25,449 cases of robbery were reported, 2,663 being accompanied by aggravating circumstances. There were 8,562 cases of rape or attempted rape reported, with 2,356 convictions. The number of executions rose to 124.

In the past quinquennium the average number of persons hanged each year has been around 100. Twenty-five years ago only 17 persons were executed. (The population meantime has risen 60 percent.) In the intervening period 1,300 executions have taken place. If United Nations published figures are reliable, it would appear that South Africa has the unenviable record of being responsible for nearly half the world's capital punishment. But if regard be had to the fact that seven-eighths of the executions are for murder, and that the number of convicted murderers is now nearing 1,500 a year, the picture is not as appalling as it appears at first sight.

The history of the capital sentence in South Africa is of interest. Interpreting the unclear writings in Roman-Dutch law, the judges a century ago had confined it to murder, treason, and rape, discretionary with the latter two crimes, possibly mandatory with murder—a disputed question until 1917, when the first Criminal Procedure Act made it so, save with a woman convicted of the murder of her newly born child or an offender under 16 (raised to 18 in 1959). Up to 1935 the prerogative of mercy was exercised in about three-quarters of the cases. Then the law was changed to allow for a finding of extenuating circumstances in a murder conviction, which the judge could accept and then impose a sentence other than that of death. This power has been extensively used. Concurrently commutations have diminished, taking place in only a quarter of the cases nowadays.

Since 1958 several additional crimes have been made to carry the discretionary death sentence, some of these being of a common-law and others of a statutory nature: robbery with the infliction of grievous bodily harm, or the threat of it, (1958); housebreaking with possession of a dangerous weapon or assault, or the threat of it, (1958); sabotage, a widely defined crime (1962); a resident undergoing training or obtaining information that could further an object of communism or an unlawful organization (1963); a resident advocating abroad economic, political, or social change in South Africa by violent means through aid of a foreign government or institution (1963); kidnapping and child-stealing (1965); participation in terroristic activities (1967). There is some Roman-Dutch authority for the sentence with the crimes to which it was applied in 1958 and 1965.

Some of the capital offences are directed at protecting the state against communism and subversion, others at reducing the incidence of certain serious crimes against person and property—though when it promoted the measure that made kidnapping and child-stealing an offence that could attract the death sentence the government must have been actuated by prescience only, for no serious case of such a crime had yet taken place—this was to happen the following year.

How effective the stiffening of penalties for crime has been in reducing offences it is impossible to say. There is a school of thought that holds that little can be achieved until the conditions of life of most Africans and Coloreds are improved. Among the urbanized Bantu traditional forms of social control are disappearing, and there is a lack of respect for life, property, and order among numerous members of the impoverished detribalized townsmen: in the words of one of South Africa's leading authors, Alan Paton, such "men find no sense of purpose in living, no sense of joy in serving, no sense of fulfillment in dying." The colored population is struggling with the problem of alcoholism, poor housing, and low incomes, and the government is intent on uplifting all the poorer communities, but progress is slow.

If regard be had to the numerous crimes that carry the death sentence and the shocking prevalence of violence among Africans and Coloreds, it is not the high number of executions that calls for comment but rather the low number. Particularly is this a consequence of the extensive use made by the courts of the finding of extenuating circumstances in murder and the tendency to bring in a return of culpable homicide (manslaughter) rather than murder if in an intra-racial non-White killing there is evidence of an absence of premeditation and the presence of drink. One or two sociologists have attempted to explain this phenomenon on the lines of Gunnar Myrdal's analysis of the position of the Negro in *An American Dilemma*: the dominant white group adopts a tolerant attitude to crimes of violence among Blacks, for they lack self-restraint and have a low standard of morality. But this explanation seems superficial. In appropriate cases exemplary sentences are imposed. There would, however, appear to be an understanding by the bench of the disorganized state of urban African and Colored society.

Similarly, it is sometimes said of cross-racial crimes that the tendency is to be severe on the non-White and lenient on the White, which is reflected in the execution figures. This is one of those allegations that in the nature of things is very difficult to substantiate. If it has any truth in it, the position is contrary to the stated policy of the courts and the government. While the execution of a White for the murder of a non-White is rare, there are at least five recorded cases of it. And the courts utter periodical warnings that crimes of violence by Whites on non-Whites will be visited with condign punishment.

Note

[1] The classic occasion was in *Aronson* v. *Estate Hart*, 1950 (1) S.A. 539 (A.D.), in which the Appellate Division had to pronounce on the validity of a "Jewish faith" clause in a will that aims at ensuring that descendants will profess the Jewish faith and marry persons adhering to it. To ensure observance, a forfeiture clause penalizes the beneficiary who breaks the condition by depriving him of his inheritance or legacy. Van den Heever J. A., siding with the majority of the court, held that such clauses were not void for uncertainty, nor were they void as being contrary to public policy. He purported to survey the Roman-Dutch legal authors (many of whom he found, to his dismay, considered such clauses to be contrary to public policy), and eventually rested his conclusion largely on the English case of *In re Besant* (1879) 11 Ch.D. 508. In a recent brilliant piece of research, Dr. C. P. Joubert ("Jewish Faith and Race Clauses in Roman-Dutch Law" (1968) 85 *S.A.L.J.* (402) has shown that Van den Heever J. A.'s investigation of the Roman-Dutch authorities was far from exhaustive and that on proper analysis they will be found to have condemned such clauses as being against public policy, since they conflict with the fundamental principle of freedom of religion.

6

Language

D. R. Beeton

South Africa provides occasion not only for linguistic confusion, but for linguistic exploration, since verbal color and colloquial expressiveness are often summoned from several languages (as disparate as English and Malay or Afrikaans and Zulu) to achieve a particular succinctness or tone. Though I shall be dealing specifically with English in South Africa, I shall in the process be pointing to words and expressions that are common to both the English and Afrikaans language groups in this country.

Educated South Africans are highly conscious of their languages, and English-speaking South Africans, so long accused of indifference to everything that suggests a standard of performance, are becoming increasingly aware of the English they use. An English Academy of Southern Africa was established in 1961, and is active on various fronts in promoting good speech and good writing. It is taking up much the same role in protecting English that its counterpart, the Suid-Afrikaanse Akademie vir Wetenskap en Kuns (South African Academy for Science and Art), so effectively took up six decades ago in assisting the establishment of Afrikaans as a language of clarity and discrimination.

Not that we should for a moment pretend that our English is not different from that of England. To show something of this difference I shall start off by giving two examples of what I mean.

The following conversations could well take place between English-speaking South Africans (and not necessarily uneducated people):

Driving on a country track:
"Oh, do drive more carefully!"
"Why?"
"This road has such a terrible middelmannetjie."

Investigating a case of assault:
"How did he manage to hurt him so badly?"
"He hit him with a knobkerrie."

The translation of these terms makes interesting reading. *Middelmannetjie* means literally "middle little man," and is used to describe the continuous grass ridge that divides so many country roads into two-tire tracks. Try to deprive the English-speaking South African of this word and you would be trying to take from him an important word in his vocabulary. The second word, *knobkerrie*, is perhaps a more explicit, and logical, element in our vocabulary, but a less essential word. *Kierie* (kerrie) is the Afrikaans (originally Hottentot) word for "stick," while "knob" is a word perfectly explicit in English; they come together, to mean approximately "club," and the composite word is used by most people in South Africa, whether Afrikaans, English-speaking, or African. "Club" might well do, and yet local color, force, and expressiveness may well have been lost in the process.

The position of English in South Africa is largely different from the position of English in Australia, for instance. Many of the innovations in Australian English seem to me to have occurred mainly at what may be described, unpejoratively, as a local slang level: words common in English have been adapted to serve a particular raciness. This is a generalization, but it points, I believe, to a characteristic tendency. In South Africa many words previously new to English have very soon become much more than slang and have made a contribution to acceptable English wherever it is used. For the moment I don't want to labor this point, but words such as *trek* and *veld* will indicate what I am getting at.

This different attitude to the level at which innovation occurs has several causes. One is that in Australia a community almost exclusively English-speaking had to accommodate to an indigenous people who in a very short time became an inconsiderable element in the country, certainly in its culture and civilization (although I do not dispute the presence of aboriginal nouns and place names, for example). In South Africa, however, English followed a century and a half after another advanced European language, Dutch, which for over 150 years went through the dynamic birth-pains of producing the locally vital language we know as Afrikaans. That English had to exist beside this forceful, unsettling partner and borrow nothing from it would have been to defy all the rules of linguistic development. Beside this the indigenous African, or Bantu, languages—Zulu, North and South Sotho, Tswana, and several others—are spoken by people far more numerous than the Europeans, and who are spread throughout the country, through town and city, on farm and in industry, in commerce and in domestic service. There is not an aspect of South African daily life that they do not touch, and their vocabulary—direct, colorful, ever-pervasive—has left a pronounced imprint on our English. Indians have brought their contribution, and so have the Cape Coloreds—those people descended largely from Hottentots, Asians, and Europeans. The effect of the now almost-extinct Hottentot and Bushman races has been as distinctive as that of the aboriginals in Australia; possibly less limited, if only because so many of their words, playing as they did an important part in the establishment of Afrikaans, came to English through this most accessible medium.

The impact of South Africa on English vocabulary long preceded Britain's occupation of the Cape of Good Hope, and at the time of her assuming responsibility a great many South African words were already in use, however tenuously. Even before permanent European settlement in this sub-continent, the Cape had been visited by English navigators, including Sir

Francis Drake in 1580. And about twenty years after Van Riebeeck's arrival in 1652 characteristically South African words had found their way into an English book: in 1670 in John Ogilby's *Africa* there appeared words such as *buchu, dagga,* and *Namaqua* (though the manner of their spelling was markedly different).

The establishment of a Dutch settlement at the Cape encouraged a wide assortment of visitors: historians, geographers, botanists, zoologists, adventurers—all of them people who wanted to explore some part or aspect of the country. It was inevitable that this would have a striking linguistic effect. Thomas Herbert's *Some Years' Travels into Diverse Parts of Africa* (1677) made use of words such as *Hottentot* and *assagai* (the second not really a word of South African origin, but given currency and expressiveness by its use in this country). In 1731 Medley's translation of Peter Kolben's *The Present State of the Cape of Good Hope* included, among others, *dubbeltjie, kabeljou, kaross, kierie, kloof, korhaan, kraal, landdros, stinkwood,* and *velskoen.* A book published in 1775, Masson's *Botanical Travels,* added words such as *bontebok, kokerboom, kudu, rheebok,* and *steenbok.* The list grew by the addition in the late eighteenth century of *baas, bloubok, bosbok, grysbok, kaffir-corn, krantzi, quagga, eland, hartebees, tamboekie,* and several other words still current.

The official beginning of European languages in South Africa dates, of course, from 1652, when Jan van Riebeeck and his group of pioneers landed at the Cape. These were people of Dutch origin appointed by the Dutch East India Company to begin and maintain a refreshment station half way on the sea route from Europe to India. The colonists mingled with the surrounding Bushmen, Hottentots, and Africans, and though their language may, at the beginning, not have been much affected, gradually a new idiom—in large measure a new Dutch idiom—began to arise, which in the twentieth century would gather force and result in the already sophisticated language that is Afrikaans.

The first British occupation of the Cape took place in 1795 and lasted for seven years. The Cape was reoccupied in 1806, this time permanently, and English, by now accustomed to colonial climates, put down its tenacious roots. The British, like the Dutch settlers before them, showed their ability to assimilate local coloring, but they were fortunate in that they were able to draw on the adapted vocabulary of their Dutch predecessors as well as on the vocabulary of the surrounding indigenous people.

There were all the problems of adaptation; of adjusting an imported overseas language and cultural background to a local setting. There were the problems of finding suitably assimilable local words that would convey a new experience and project a new insight.

Thomas Pringle shows in his poetry some of these problems; for example, in the opening stanza of *The Emigrants*, where he tries to marry the vales of Scotland with the climes of Amakosa:

> Sweet Teviot, fare thee well! Less gentle themes
> Far distant call me from thy pastoral dale,
> To climes where Amakosa's woods and streams
> Invite, in the fair South, my venturous sail.

Some of the words Pringle has chosen to adapt to South African conditions could not serve his purpose. "Clime" itself is a word that seems curiously unable to reflect the heat and ruggedness the writer encountered. "Woods and streams" points to a similar limitation.

But already in Pringle we are seeing the acceptance of local words. Here we have the beginning of the second stanza of *The Emigrants*:

> From Keissi's meads, from Chumi's hoary woods,
> Bleak Tarka's dens, and Stormberg's rugged fells,
> To where Gareep pours down his sounding floods
> Through regions where the hunted Bushman dwells....

This at times becomes little more than a parade of proper nouns, and in subsequent poems Pringle would give us "The Hottentot," "The Bushman," "The Kaffir," "The Bechuana

Boy," so that it can be seen that the catalogue of our races was, very early on, crossing into the lines of popular poetry. The names we have taken to specify our geography and ethnology have become words we require as part of English, an English that for a century and a half has served South Africa as an official language and, despite the clamor of pessimists, has continually sought to interpret the country as expansively, as specifically, and as dynamically as possible. To find words such as *klipspringer* and *wildebeest* in the *Oxford English Dictionary* is to see how well English has, in fact, adapted itself. Volumes of South African English writing are to the lexicographer minor treasure-houses of expressive vocabulary; it is noteworthy how much is genuinely descriptive, how little superfluous, decorative, or redundant.

A by-no-means unusual example (I chose it specifically for its modest dimension) is *Gold Dust from South African Poetry* (1917), compiled by E. H. Crouch and published in London. The first poem in the collection is entitled "The Song of the Ox-Wagon," which in its initial stanza declares that it was inspired by "The creaking croon of the disselboom." *Disselboom* probably deserves to be indexed (if only among its more dubious fellows) in the *Oxford Dictionary*. *Ox-wagon* was given its vividness, if not its linguistic elements, by that South African odyssey, the Great Trek. In "The Song of the Ox-wagon," among such obvious English colleagues as "fawn," "thicket," and "thorn," we have *kameel*, *vley* (now spelled *vlei*), and *pan*. Both *vlei* and *pan* denote shallow expanses of water; the first a part of a river, the second a pond-like depression more often dust-bitten than water-logged. Several of these words may have seemed picturesquely ephemeral when they were introduced into far-from-deathless ditty, but—so great, it seems, is the need for suitable local descriptives—they have survived.

A later poem in the collection is called "The Voorlopers." *Voorlopers* has a quality that "pioneers" lacks, and therefore, for its local quaintness, claims a place in our vocabulary. The title of the next poem indicates a word that has gone beyond local definition: the reference to "The Voortrekker" would, I think, be understood by most speakers of English in the world.

Yet another poem is called "Ou-ma" (*ouma*), and yet another "The Veldt" (*veld*). "The Kaffir" and "The Bushman" by Thomas Pringle are both anthologized, but an even more interesting title is "The Chief," by Cullen Gouldsbury. *Chief* is a word that has acquired in its African setting a very individual color and has undergone a slight, but subtle, change of concept. Apart from the few titles I have listed, the volume is riddled with indigenes proper nouns. The following titles are indicative: "Stellenbosch," "Komani," "Mashona," "Shumba," "Bongwi." Trees such as *blue-gums* and *mimosas* also occur from time to time.

In 1886 Olive Schreiner in *The Story of an African Farm* gave wide overseas currency to words such as *karroo* (now generally spelt *karoo*), and *kraal* (a word so enriched that it has at least two specifically identifiable meanings: first, a native *stat*—another term completely lucid to the South African English speaker in its sense of "African village"—and, second, an enclosure for domestic animals, particularly cattle and sheep). Oliver Schreiner also made use of the word *kaffir* (which, for example, had found its place in the translation, by Medley, of Kolben's *The Present State of the Cape of Good Hope* as *caffre*, a spelling that has remained completely alien to South Africans): the word has disappeared from polite (though not from vivid colloquial) usage by its identification with "nigger." Another word she uses is *kopje* (now spelt *koppie*), a descriptive which simply cannot, by virtue of its very local physical characteristics, be translated back into "hill." These words are all taken from the opening paragraphs of Olive Schreiner's novel and are little more than an indication of what was by then a growing and necessary vocabulary.

Boer (South African Dutchman, or *Afrikaner*, originally simply meaning "farmer") was a word that Olive Schreiner would rely on again and again; for example, in her great polemic *Thoughts on South Africa*; this was an indication of how widely used the word was towards the turn of the century. Today it has largely been replaced by *Afrikaner*. She would use *oom* and *tante* with a growing lack of self-consciousness, but except in the picturesque and deliberately evocative, these words have not replaced "uncle" and "aunt," though they are perfectly explicit to all English-speaking South Africans. *Tannie*, the diminutive of *tante*, has survived in Afrikaans as a term of affection and intimacy, and, curiously enough, in local colloquial English as a term of mild derision. Olive Schreiner would also talk of the *smous*, a hawker who went from village to village and farm to farm. The sophistication of our age has seen the antiquation of this term, which may otherwise well have survived.

Pauline Smith, very much in the manner of international writers such as Sarah Gertrude Millin and Roy Campbell, would continue the process of giving currency in English to characteristically South African words. *Bijwoner*, which occurs both in her short story collection *The Little Karoo* and in her novel *The Beadle*, relates to a late nineteenth- and twentieth-century system of economic serfdom (of white by white), a system it would take sentences to describe outside this country; yet it remains explicit to those who know our milieu, in spite of the fact that industrialization and urbanization are making South Africa much less rural. A *poor white* (the equivalent of the American South's "white trash," though possibly a little less unkind in its reference) was one of the products of the *bywoner* (an accepted modern spelling). Vehicles, in Pauline Smith's pages, if they were not *ox-wagons* were *Cape-carts*, a pointer to the prevailing South African style of conveyance and nomenclature.

We could go on indefinitely picking out unusual words; some that have found currency and acceptable definition and status, and others—such as C. Louis Leipoldt's coinage of *skerms* (rough shelters)—that in English have fallen by the wayside. What follows is no more than a glimpse of our linguistic plunder.

Deneys Reitz took a word such as *commando*, used it as the title of a well-known book (which has appeared in the widely distributed Penguin series since it was first published in 1929), and the terms of warfare would now be the poorer without it. Herman Charles Bosman in *Mafeking Road* called one of his stories "The Rooinek" (literally the "red neck"), and what was a word of derision for the Englishman in this country could well become a term of affection. As an English-speaking South African I find the savoring of Bosman's titles irresistible: "Starlight on the Veld," "Ox-wagons on Trek," "Mafeking Road," "Makapan's Caves," "Yellow Moepels," "Bechuana Interlude," "Brown Mamba," "Dream by the Blue-Gums," "Drieka and the Moon," "Mampoer," "Splendours from Ramoutsa." Most of the South African words are, of course, geographical place names, but they are used with a familiarity and affection that was quite beyond an early writer such as Pringle. Some of the words in Bosman's list will by now already be familiar, others will be touched on in the discussion that follows.

An examination of a typical glossary to South African English poetry could be a highly valid means of attacking the problem of our linguistic possibilities. Interestingly enough, anthologists subsequent to Francis Carey Slater in his 1945 *New Centenary Book of South African Verse* (from which my selection has been taken) have found it unnecessary to supply a glossary; such, one assumes, is the acceptance they have found of South Africanisms. The following is a brief selection from Slater's list, but shows something of its variety and range:

Amaxhosa, Bechuana, Bushbuck, Bushman, Cape Canary, Duiker, Gnu, Hartebeest, Impi, Induna, Kaffir-boom, Kappie, Karoo, Kloof, Koppie, Korhaan, Krans, Loerie, Mealies, Mimosa, Namaqualand, Oribi, Outspan, Pan, Predikant, Protea, Quagga, Rhenoster, Singsingertjie, Trekker, Utywala.

These words have very different origins, and very different ranges of acceptance, and a discussion of their qualities would, in part, be to provide an interesting historical, scientific, geographic, and social record of this country:

Amaxhosa In current South African usage shortened to *Xhosa* (also *Xosa*), indicating both a tribe and a language. Used by all language groups in this country.

Bechuana	Also nowadays Tswana; the same usage as for *Xhosa*.
Bushbuck	A small antelope; a necessary term to all English-speaking South Africans who wish to describe animals specifically and correctly. Probably a translation of the Afrikaans *bosbok*.
Bushman	Pygmy hunters, who survive in the Kalahari. They were indigenous to the Cape Province, as were the Hottentots. Afrikaans equivalent: *Boesman*.
Cape Canary	Necessary to non-ornithologists for indicating a species of bird specific to South Africa.
Duiker	A word of Dutch or Afrikaans origin, most necessary to describe a particular species of small antelope.
Gnu	An antelope; a word of Hottentot origin.
Impi	Still used in English in this country to denote a Bantu regiment; of Zulu origin.
Induna	Zulu for warrior; well-known to English-speaking South Africans.
Kaffir-boom	Used by all South Africans to denote a particular (and beautiful) type of tree.
Kappie	A sun-bonnet, Voortrekker style; a word that has become acceptable in South African English. Of Dutch/Afrikaans origin.
Karoo	A particular part of South Africa; to English-speaking South Africans it is highly evocative of a particular type of South African scenery; of Hottentot origin.
Kloof	A wooded ravine; of Dutch/Afrikaans origin, and accepted in English.
Koppie	A small hill; of Dutch/Afrikaans origin, and irreplaceable in South African English in

	evoking a particular type of South African scene.
Korhaan (Koran)	A species of bird, belonging to the family of bustards.
Krans	A rocky precipice; widely used by English-speaking South Africans.
Loerie (Lory)	The South African word for the Turaco (Musophagidae), a bird peculiar to Africa. Like several other words, such as *mealies* and mimosa, it is used in other parts of the world, but with a different denotation.
Mealies	The Dutch/Afrikaans word for "maize"; widely used in South African English.
Mimosa	Used to denote a species of acacia; equivalent to "wattle" in Australia.
Namaqualand	Also an indigenous tribe, Namaqua; now used to denote a particular area of South Africa, famous for the flowers that spring up after rain, "Namaqualand daisies."
(Inkosekazi)	Sometimes used, but not generally accepted as part of English. (It is interesting to note that the male equivalent, *inkos*, probably appeared in its first English form as "encoss" in 1625 in a translation, included in *Purchas His Pilgrims*, of Dos Santos's *Ethiopia Oriental*.)
Oribi	A small antelope; of Hottentot origin.
Outspan	The unyoking of oxen, or unharnessing of horses.
Pan	A type of lakelet characteristic of South Africa.
Predikant	Afrikaans for a minister of religion; never accepted as part of English.
Protea	A word of Latin origin, but describing a species of plant almost peculiar to, and widespread in, South Africa.

Quagga	A species of Zebra; used by English-speaking South Africans, though not frequently.
Rhenoster	Afrikaans for rhinoceros; also used to signify a particular type of bush.
Singsingertjie	A cicada; the word has a genuine place in South African English in evoking the South African veld.
Trekker	A nomadic Boer; an abbreviation of voortrekker, but now signifies the nomadic rather than the heroic spirit.
Utywala	Xhosa for strong drink, particularly Kaffir beer. *Kaffir beer* is a widely understood and accepted compound in South African English.

I have examined this list in some detail because several important facts about South African English emerge from it. Though some overlapping is unavoidable, lexical grouping becomes both necessary and interesting.

By far the biggest contribution to South African English has been made by Dutch/Afrikaans. Many of the words are accepted and have general currency in denoting a type of phenomenon rather than a particular species. Many of these words (*veld, trek,* and *commando* are outstanding examples) have found their way into universal English.

The following, which appear in Slater's full glossary, seem to me permanent additions: *kappie, kloof, koppie, kraal, krans, mealie, outspan* (a translation, in part, of *uitspan*), *trekker, vlei,* and *voortrekker*. To this list could be added *dorp* (village), *apartheid, boer, boerewors* (a type of sausage), *braaivleis* (barbecue), *inspan, laager* (originally, to denote Voortrekker wagons drawn up in a circle of defense; now also used adjectivally to denote a conservative, fear-ridden attitude), and *platteland* (country districts). Most of these words are now to be found in the *Oxford English Dictionary*. *Rand*, meaning also "ridge," is a word officially instituted for the South African unit of money and must, because of this, achieve wide linguistic currency. It will be noticed that Afrikaans has also given names to specific types of creature and plant in this country; examples are *eland, springbok, klipspringer,* and *wildebeest,* all firmly indexed in the *Oxford English Dictionary.*

Indigenous birds, animals, fish, reptiles, and plants that can be described in South African English by common names from other languages locally active include *dikkop* (Afrikaans), *gnu* (Hottentot), *kudu* (Xhosa), and *protea* (Latin), all show something of the range of acquisition. *Loerie* (or *lory*), it is interesting to note, was used as early as 1797 by Lady Anne Barnard in her *Journal of a Residence at the Cape of Good Hope.*

The effect of indigenous African languages on South African English has been limited, particularly when compared with that of Afrikaans. It will be noticed from the list that a great many African words are introduced to provide what I have chosen to call, rather contemptuously, Local Coloring, but have by no means become inherent elements in the vocabulary of English. To denote languages and races there has been widespread acceptance, for *Swazi* and *Venda* could certainly be added to *Zulu* and the other languages and tribes recorded above. Impi (from the Zulu) and Karoo (from the Hottentot) have become highly acceptable general words, as have many of the words for denoting plant and animal life. Bantu (people) is the official designation (and a label accepted in linguistic research) for those people who very often now choose to call themselves Africans.

From Afrikaans we have acquired a host of colloquially accepted words. The following is a selection: *baas* (master), *bakkie* (dish), *brak* (mongrel), *gogga* (insect), *opsit* (an Afrikaans version of wooing), *pap* (porridge), *sloot* (ditch), and *stompie* (cigarette butt).

Afrikaans has unfortunately also produced barbarisms in South African English. Among these are: *deurmekaar* (mixed up), *finish and klaar* (usually for "that's settled"), *lappie* (rag), *lekker* (nice; the favorite adjective of schoolboys), *se voet* (literally: "his foot," meaning "nonsense"), *vadoek* (dishcloth), *waslap* (flannel; although *face cloth* has perhaps greater currency than either in South African English).

From my list it will be seen that *pan* (probably as a result of translation from the Afrikaans) has acquired wide currency as the equivalent of a marshy or dried-up lakelet. The following survivals in South African English are composed solely of English elements and enjoy a singular interpretation in this country: *bioscope* (cinema), *ducktail* (teddy-boy), *Greek-shop* (café). Ordinary English words have also been transformed by local usage: in South Africa a traffic light is almost invariably a *robot*, a cooker a *stove*, an electric radiator a *heater*, a pharmacist a *chemist*, and tubing is *piping*. It is difficult to search out the precise cause of these adaptations. They were probably the result of a long period of association, and to those new to this country they sometimes lead to a temporary confusion of meaning. Our worst sins, however, are not the result of new words and coinages, but of corrupted idiom.

It will be noticed that I have dismissed several words as examples of rather self-conscious local coloring. Africa, like most other countries, is very rich in picturesque words which local authors and flamboyant visitors are eager to press into their writings. These words have, however, made little impression, and the best of the writers I have listed have generally incorporated words widely used, and genuinely necessary to the force of the writing.

To South Africans "just now" never means "at once" and seldom means "a little while ago"; it usually means some time within the next few minutes or hours. This widespread habit encourages confusion. *Staying*, as an indication of permanence, has led to a similar confusion.

Direct translation from the Afrikaans has sometimes had much to do with this. *Stay*, for example, is quite clearly a translation of *bly*, which in Afrikaans could also denote *live*, and *just now* comes from *net nou*. *Is it?* for "Is that so?", *make breakfast* for "prepare breakfast," *make a plan* for "do something about it," *make a fire* for "light a fire," *off-load* for "unload," *sick* for "ill," *stand up* for "get up," *come there* for "arrive"—the list, again, is endless. While most cultivated speakers try to avoid these quaintnesses, all of them fall into at least a few of the local habits.

To moan and squeal (for "complain") and to call your home *my place* point to an ugly laxity on the part of some South African English speakers.

Some of the idiomatic corruptions with which we wage continual warfare are no doubt fairly common to most English-speaking countries; *he aggravates* me (for "irritates") and the incorrect use of *disinterested* (for "uninterested") are possibly far more common in the United States than in South Africa. The use of two or more negatives, as in "he doesn't know nothing," hardly occurs in this country, except among immigrants and those Africans using English as a totally foreign medium; that even our semi-literates have resisted this temptation in the face of a compulsory double negative Afrikaans deserves credit.

But Afrikaans has sometimes led us into curious linguistic paths. Few people will speak of anything but *swimming* in the sea (for "bathing"), even when they intend nothing more than a splash. *Shame!* for "What a pity!" (or "I'm so sorry about it!") owes its existence to a very colorful Afrikaans exclamation of sympathy, *siestog*. When on long drives we wish to stop for a picnic or for a rest, we would look for a *rest(ing)place*, where the Englishman in England would be on the look-out for a "lay-by." I cannot pretend that "lay-by" is all that much better than *resting place*, nor that the explicit and American *traffic circle* is weaker than "roundabout." And here we come as South Africans to the problem of deciding where a language is enriched by local adaptation and where it is impoverished. There does seem to me a fairly accessible, though by no means always easy, rule to apply. It is this: if the word is expressive, retain it; where it blurs a valuable distinction, dismiss it.

Shame, to most English speakers, relates to the quality of "guilt and disgrace," and to confuse it with "pity" debilitates the language. To call a "traffic light" a *robot* is to move from the explicit to a term that has an altogether different reference in other parts of the English-speaking world. (The Afrikaans *verkeersein* cannot be held to blame here.) *Bioscope* (which retains much of its currency because of the presence of an Afrikaans equivalent, *bioskoop*) cannot be found guilty on the same charge:

picturesque it may be, but it has a legitimate enough origin, going back as it does to the introduction of moving pictures. An interesting linguistic shift is evident here: *bioscope* almost certainly produced *bioskoop* in Afrikaans; the Afrikaans word is now largely responsible for the retention of the English equivalent. I would defend *resting* place and *bioscope* on the ground of explicitness, but I do not know whether I could make the same defense for *swim* (when I have "bathe" in mind) and *robot* (when I am thinking of a traffic light).

Afrikaans has been responsible for several terms widely acceptable at all social levels. "Must I phone him?" asks the South African company director ("Moet ek hom bel?" in Afrikaans), where in this case the more explicit Englishman would ask "Does he want me to phone him?" *Must I?* does not indicate, to the South African, compulsion, and therefore he has lost a little of the emphasis of good expression. "Are you going to lead water in your lands?" one farmer might well ask of another; he has, albeit unconsciously, the Afrikaans *water lei* in mind, and not the English "irrigate."

There are a few expressions, derived from Afrikaans, that are quite emphatically illiteracies, mainly because they are totally inexplicit, bad in picturing, or simply bad in syntax. I have pointed already to *come there* for "arrive"—but even more widespread is *come with* (or *go with*) used without a succeeding noun: "Are you coming with?" a mother might quite innocently ask her child; "kom jy saam?" in the Afrikaans would be quite acceptable.

"I'm not at all sure about it," an Englishman might venture. "How come?" his South African questioner might surprise him by asking. A simple question; but a big sin, for the South African is asking no more and no less than "Why?". He is—though he may not know it—speaking Afrikaans in translation.

"I want to lend it from you," a child might ask, not having been told that English, unlike Afrikaans, has two words for the process of borrowing and lending. And, in a clear case of direct translation, we have "He threw him with a stone" (for "He threw a stone at him") and "You lie!" (for "You are not telling the truth"): I rather like this expression, because it evidences so much direct feeling. Many of these phrases coming under the eye of an ever more linguistically conscious people are gradually being confined to the very young and the very untutored.

The young and the untutored do not require the presence of Afrikaans to perpetrate linguistic crimes. In fact, minor crime has the same schoolboy attraction in this country as it has anywhere in the world, and schoolboys delight in manufacturing their self-conscious, though assertive and demanding, linguistic offenses. "It smaaks lekker" is almost totally Afrikaans, but also schoolboy English. "It taste nice" (for this is what is meant) is an entirely uninteresting way of saying the same thing. Perhaps one should not be too afraid of allowing color at a young, experimental age, provided that color doesn't become confusion and freedom doesn't change into confinement. "It was this *ou* who said it," is widespread and unselfconscious. (*ou*, from the Afrikaans, is the equivalent of the English "chap" or the American "guy.") A *cool drink* (soft drink) to a South African schoolboy may well be a *coolie* and he may well intend having it with a *sarmi* (a "sandwich")—in an unavoidably clumsy ellipsis—*sarvi* (this afternoon), like the Australian expression "this arvo."

The force of group slang, of which this is a mild indication, makes itself felt in many South African situations; for example, in jail argot and the colloquial terminology coined by mine workers.

"I am finished" (when something has been completed) occurs in most English-speaking countries, but it is probably because of the Afrikaans equivalent "Ek is klaar" that it is used in this country at so many social levels. I cannot, however, find the Afrikaans culpable when an English speaker uses *anticipate* in the sense of "expect" or insists that he wants "to grow his hair," or when he thinks that someone with a fine character is "a lovely person," or when he insists that he "never took the pie," or when, on looking at a painting, he says that he likes the way the artist "has painted Mr. Jones."

But, are we so very wrong when we call a bill or an invoice an *account*; a "wine merchant" or an "off license" a *bottle store*; when we call our "holiday bungalows" *cottages*, and say we are going to the *coast*, where the American would say "shore," the Australian would say "beach," and the Englishman would say "sea-side"?

The effect of Afrikaans, or simply of South Africa, is apparent in numerous other examples, which still hesitate bewilderingly between acceptance and reject.

Our crossroads are *intersections*, our bungalows *houses*, to "go on vacation" or "go on holiday" is to *go on leave* (or to *take leave*), and often to say *excuse me* is to mean "I beg your pardon." To ride a bicycle, as we do, is to take so many more words than necessary to describe the act of "(bi)cycling." (In fact, it is usually necessary to define riding proper as *horse riding*.) We have *flower girls* in attendance at our weddings, *stop-streets* where we don't have robots, and we *write* or *take* examinations rather than "sit for" them. We have, linguistically, *sand* where England is blessed with "soil" (here again, sand proper must be over-carefully defined as *white sand* or *sea sand*). Our fishmongers rather misleading are referred to as *fisheries* and we say *second last* when we mean penultimate. "Monday week" has become very firmly *next Monday*, "abroad" has become almost exclusively *overseas*, and a "flannel" a *face cloth*. A "swim suit" or "bathing suit," very interestingly (see the previous discussion of *swimming* and *bathing*), is in South Africa often a *swimming costume* (a *cossie* to schoolboys). A "tarpaulin" is a *bucksail*, possibly the result of pioneer hunting and camping days (Sir Percy Fitzpatrick's *Jock of the Bushveld* is a highly relevant text here). A *cup* of ice-cream provides for one person; a "tub" in South Africa would be sufficient for a party. And to go back to the beginning: "the Cape" in South Africa is not *any* headland, but our own affectionate and widely-accepted abbreviation of "Cape of Good Hope" or "Cape Province (or Colony)," and for many of us a signal of our geographic origin on this continent.

Language

Some years ago a popular South African musical, *Wait a Minim*, featured the following moods:

Ag (very near to the Scottish "loch") pleez Deddy, won't ya take me to the dr(r)ive-in?

Though this "Southern Suburbs" accent is an extreme dialectal form, it points to characteristic elements in South African English pronunciation. Velar fricatives (in typically South African words such as *ag*), fricative *r*'s, loss of aspiration (in *p*, *t* and *k*), and, in particular, exaggerated and distorted vowel sounds are all to be found in South African English. But possibly because of the presence of so many languages, South African English speakers (particularly among the educated) are very conscious of the sounds they make when speaking English and keep an ear firmly on the "Received Pronunciation" of the British Broadcasting Commission. Even where sounds are imperfectly imitated, the result is often clear speech, and not unpleasing.

There seem, then, to be several classes speaking several broadly differing types of English; the distinctions, as we progress from group to group and region to region, apparently more and more blurred, and yet changing until we arrive at the Southern Suburbs English of Johannesburg, illustrated above. University people, teachers, actors, broadcasters, and some professional people speak an English that owes much to the Southern Standard speech of England. There follows the middle professional group: the accents of bankers and farmers, insurance agents, and civil servants, on the whole are more characteristic of this sub-continent: there is a strong reliance on "spelling pronunciations," e.g., wâist-côat (double emphasis), uncommunicâtive, respîte, decâdes. And the third group, consisting as it does mainly of manual workers, technicians, and traders, produces a badly articulated language. Now, clearly, I have drawn an invidious and crudely tentative distinction between these groups, and though L. W. Lanham's broad classification of Standard, Typical, and Extreme South African speech has some force, there is much more pronunciation (and class) overlapping than one would have in England, where the difference between Oxford and Cockney English, for example, is immense, and signals sharply defined class differences. The picture is further blurred in this country because most South Africans speak English only as a second (and sometimes a third) language: not only Afrikaners, but also Africans, Indians, and Coloreds. For the most part the non-Europeans comprise the lower-class groups, and have, accordingly, a limited sphere of influence. But the Afrikaners, like their English-speaking compatriots, penetrate to all strata of society, and accents far from that of the Received Standard must perforce find acceptance. The effect of Afrikaans, and other languages, on the accents of English speakers has been marked.

Moving from region to region one finds intriguing differences, for example, between the Eastern Cape Province (claiming its descendants largely from the farmer and artisan 1820 Settlers) and the Western Cape Province (where a governing class began to emerge much more than a century and a half ago). Johannesburg will yield up differences as striking as those between the wealthy, superspoken Northern Suburbs (again Jeremy Taylor of *Wait a Minim* gives the clue: "Oh please, Daddy, won't you take me to Inanda?" with a deliberate, refined articulation) and its largely impoverished, shoddily-spoken Southern Suburbs opposite. There are more subtle characteristics: for example, of the largely Jewish Yeoville area, and the polyglot Hillbrow. But this whole matter of regional differences has, as far as I know, been insufficiently investigated.

Few South Africans would be as guilty as Australians of pronouncing *tike* (for "take") and *plice* (for "place"), but we have our own sins in the formation of vowels that need watching at every level—and watching not because to speak "correctly" (whatever that is) has snob value but simply because clear speech is pleasing, and clear. Vowel shortening has the effect of distorting the sound and producing, sometimes, a disconcerting phonemic blurring. Many South Africans tend to pronounce "park" as *pok* or even *pork* (thus confusing a sense

Language

distinction between garden and meat which context must clear up); "car" becomes *co* or *cor;* "garden" becomes *goden* or *gorden.* The vowel in "pin" and "wind" is often identical with that in "sit," and to exaggerate sounds slightly, "fact" often becomes *fect,* "Daddy" becomes *Deddy,* "kettle" approximates *kittle,* "get" sounds like *git,* and "yesterday" becomes *yisterday.*

There is a tendency to add vowels where they are not called for: "Westminister," *Millin* (for "Milne"), *fillim* (for "film"); and to remove them when they should be present: *famly* (for "family"), *juvnile* (for "juvenile"). Some of these, of course, are class rather than national variants and occur only in extreme speech forms. We tend to lose valuable noun-verb distinctions in words such as "contrast," "conflict," "protest" and "survey"; we tend to throw the emphasis forward in words such as "prescribed," "adult," "replace," and to throw it back in words such as "hostess," "formidable" and "controversy." "A man" is pronounced "â man" by the super-careful, and "the man" is "thee man"; "Saturday" is seldom "Saterdi." We have our own curiously insistent pronunciation: a "café," when it is not a "Greek-shop," is a *caffy,* and a "gala" is almost invariably a *gaala.*

But much of this is phonetic pin-pricking and will not account for an English that is not so very much different from that of the British south. We have adopted little from the United States: "laboratory," for example, finds scant favor here, and "anti-" would be frowned upon.

The indigenous Bantu languages will be dealt with in another chapter of this book, but some space must be given here to what is perhaps the linguistic wonder child of South Africa—Afrikaans. Dutch in this country ostensibly degenerated into crude and garbled Dutch; yet from this apparent mishmash, and in the space virtually of decades, there came a language that was able to carry many of the most sophisticated concepts of our day (although, in my opinion, it has so far only infrequently attained the subtlety of English or the comprehensiveness of German). In its literature it is able to embody some of the finest elements of western culture and to combine this culture with a spirit genuinely that of the African continent.

Much of the character of Afrikaans will have been deduced from the foregoing discussion of its effect on South African English vocabulary and idiom. The genius of the language may be noted, and when one remembers that its main ingredient is Dutch, transformed by English, by Huguenot French, by Portuguese and Malay, by Hottentot and Bantu, much will have been said.

The debates about the origin of Afrikaans have been many and dissonant. Several linguists assert that the movement that led to Afrikaans began long before the establishment of a colony at the Cape, and that the separation and different geographical milieu simply gave the final emphatic impetus to a process much longer under way. That South African settlers came from a particular area of Holland and imported and transformed its vernacular has also been disputed. What is generally not disputed is that early Afrikaans owed much of its vitality—indeed its existence—to the fact that the settlement at the Cape was founded at a strategic time: that is, prior to the large-scale development of Standard Dutch, something that could well have forestalled the emergence of a new language. The settlers brought with them what vernaculars they had, found common ground, and, in large measure, a common vocabulary and idiom, affected as it was by the language of the surrounding Hottentots and by the frequent European travellers and settlers at the Cape who often brought with them not only the languages of Europe, but much of the vocabulary of the East where many of them had been stationed. There are some who have alleged that Afrikaans is no more than a Creole tongue, the mongrel by-blow of a Malay-Portuguese that had largely become the language of trade east of the Atlantic. Some have even seen it as a patois vernacular, deriving its character in great measure from the presence of Hottentot. Few nowadays would seriously dispute its very clear Dutch origin, or even that it has upheld many of the standards of its parent.

There are, I think, staunch defenses for those who allege that the settlement at the Cape was not the beginning of a linguistic process but something in the middle or near the end of it. We have to account for a signal feature of Afrikaans: the extraordinary uniformity of its vocabulary and usage. If the Cape settlement had only begun a process, which continued in the centuries that followed, one would—as the trekkers and other settlers became more dispersed and isolated—have expected to find the growth of degenerate vernaculars, of strong local variants, and of tremendous speech diversification, if only because of this isolation, because of tenuous of non-existent lines of communication between group and group. But this didn't happen, and it seems altogether feasible (there are contemporary documents to bear this out) that the change must have taken place before the settlers began to spread out over the country. Linguistically, therefore, the changes may have begun to take place very soon after the arrival of the first Dutch settlers.

The acceptance, however, of Afrikaans as a *language*, as a cultural force, was a much longer process. When, in 1652, Jan van Riebeeck and officials of the Dutch East India Company came to the Cape, they very soon came into contact with Hottentot, Bushmen, and other local tribes, who settled in great numbers in the vicinity of the original Fort and the Castle that replaced it. There was already a sense of community (as linguists, I think, have convincingly demonstrated), but not yet a sense of permanence or identity. In 1657, with the coming into being of the *vryburgers* (literally, free citizens—in this case, farmers and traders not employed by the Dutch East India Company), we have the beginning of a "national meaning," which was further endorsed by the arrival of other settlers, such as the French Huguenots in 1687 who, among other things, gave a further religious impetus to an independent South African existence. Nowadays their linguistic influence is believed to be very limited, although the effect of French on Afrikaans names such as *du Toit, du Plessis, le Roux,* and *de Villiers* is only too apparent. All this time the colony was spreading out, meeting new environmental (and therefore linguistic) challenges. The officials with whom the settlement began became farmers, and the farmers changed slowly from a settled agrarian community to *trekboere,* itinerant ranchers, who moved from area to area in search of fresh grazing for their cattle and sheep. The Great Trek was by no means a sudden development in national character—the urge to move on had become an ingrained, even endemic, way of life, which still persists wherever it is given scope.

By 1800 there was nothing unusual about hearing this curious language of South Africa denoted by various descriptives, such as Kaapsch-Hollandsch, Cape-Dutch, Boeren-Hollandsch, Boeren-Kaapsch, or simply Kaapsch.

It would take chapters—indeed, volumes—to show where and how Afrikaans differs from its Dutch parent, but the following brief extracts from the Bible will help to make this difference apparent. Like South African English, Afrikaans has a different range of vocabulary, but it is in more than lexical and semantic innovations that it is different from the language of its origin. Potent historical-social forces have transformed words and syntax, and have led to a striking loss of infection.

To achieve as complete a comparison as possible both translations are taken from British and Foreign Bible Society editions.

Dutch

PSALM 23

EEN psalm van David.

De HEERE is mijn Herder; mij zal

niets ontbreken.

2   Hij doet mij nederliggen in grazige

weiden; Hij voert mij zachtjes aan zeer

stille wateren.

3 Hij verkwikt mijne ziel: Hij leidt mij in het spoor der gerechtigheid, om Zijns Naams wil.

4 Al ging ik ook in een dal der schaduwe des doods, ik zou geen kwaad vreezen; want Gij zijt met mij; Uw stok en Uw staf, die vertroosten mij.

5 Gij richt de tafel toe voor mijn aangezicht, tegenover mijne tegenpartijders; Gij maakt mijn hoofd vet met olie; mijn beker is overvloeiende.

6 Immers zullen mij het goede en de weldadigheid volgen al de dagen mijns levens; en ik zal in het huis des HEEREN blijven in lengte van dagen.

Afrikaans

PSALM 23

'N PSALM van Dawid.

Die HERE is my herder; niks sal my ontbreek nie.

2   Hy laat my neerlê in groen weivelde;

na waters waar rus is, lei Hy my heen.

3   Hy verkwik my siel; Hy lei my in die

spore van geregtigheid, om sy Naam ontwil.

4   Al gaan ek ook in 'n dal van dood-

skaduwee, ek sal geen onheil vrees nie;

want U is met my: u stok en u staf die

vertroos my.

5   U Berei die tafel voor my aangesig

teenoor my teëstanders; U maak my hoof vet

met olie; my beker loop oor.

6   Net goedheid en guns sal my volg al

die dae van my lewe; en ek sal in die

huis van die HERE bly in lengte van dae.

In 1806, when the British occupation of the Cape became permanent and all formal ties with Holland were snapped, there began a further growth in national consciousness, an awareness of difference and identity, which came ever increasingly to be realized *linguistically*. The political culmination was the Great Trek that began in 1835, and which resulted in the founding of republics in Natal, the Orange Free State, and the Transvaal. In the Cape the church was largely instrumental in keeping the idea of Afrikaans alive, yet there were always curious anomalies; for example, the Zuid-Afrikaansche Republiek (the Transvaal), early in its existence appointed as its president a Dutch Reformed parson from the

Cape, one Thomas Francois Burgers, a man who chose to conduct all his correspondence in English.

For most of the nineteenth century there had been talk of an Afrikaans *moedertaal* (mother tongue). Under the British in the Cape Colony, and after the Great Trek in the republics, Cape-Dutch steadily developed into what we know today as Afrikaans. This was particularly the case among farming communities where there was little opportunity of writing, or speaking, correct High Dutch. The deviations—or mistakes as some commentators would have them—became more and more an unquestioned feature at least of the colloquial language. The characteristics of this new language, or dialect, were carefully recorded by people such as A. N. E. Changuion, S. Zwaartman, C. E. Boniface, and L. H. Meurant; the last two, in their capacities as editors of local Dutch newspapers, made liberal use of local linguistic coloring. Meurant, and two Englishmen, Bain and Rex (who conceived the immortal indigenous character Kaatjie Kekkelbek), are responsible for some of the first written dialogues in a language approaching present day Afrikaans.

There was, however, great opposition—particularly among Afrikaners—to the replacement, in any form, of Dutch with Afrikaans. Two men from Holland, A. Pannevis and C. P. Hoogenhout, recognized the claims of South African consciousness of Afrikaans and did much to work for its recognition. As Christians they realized that the Bible, if it was to do its evangelizing work properly, would one day also have to make its pilgrimage in this strange new language.

A young Afrikaner, the Reverend S. J. du Toit, writing under the pseudonym Een Ware Afrikaander (A True Afrikaner), with his brother, D. F. du Toit, gave the move towards Afrikanerization impetus from within. Together with Pannevis, Hoogenhout, and other Afrikaners they founded in 1875 the Genootskap van Regte Afrikaners (Society of True Afrikaners), which included among its objectives a Bible in Afrikaans, the founding of a newspaper—duly established as *Die Afrikaanse Patriot* (The Afrikaans Patriot)—a dictionary, and the use of Afrikaans in all their official documents. The newspaper, in particular, made a great appeal because of its simple, easily understood *boeretaal* (simple colloquial language), and this at a time when spelling was in a state of tremendous flux.

In 1879 the Afrikanerbond (Brotherhood of Afrikaners) was founded, with a slightly changed *Patriot* as its official organ. There were lively discussions in the paper whether Afrikaans was a patois and whether to use it as a written form was a retrogressive step. This led to lively debate which, in turn, was good for a language that sought and proclaimed vitality. Various little books on Afrikaans by S. J. du Toit and others were issued (one of the first of these, S. J. du Toit's *Eerste Begin els van die Afrikaanse Taal* (First Principles of the Afrikaans Language), appeared in 1876). Attempts—rather abortive ones—at the translation of parts of the Bible were made, and, more significant in the result, a monthly *Ons Klyntji* (Our Little One) was begun in 1896.

After the South African War of 1899-1902 the future of Afrikaans looked bleak in the face of repeated attempts by Lord Milner and his officials at Anglicizing the nation. However, with the granting of independent government to each of the four colonies (Cape, Transvaal, Orange Free State, and Natal) the move was under way once again for the recognition and improvement of Afrikaans. There was, for example a "Vereenvoudigde Nederlandse Spelling" (Simplified Dutch Spelling) campaign, and for the first time it was firmly recognized that though Dutch in large measure remained the written language (that is, apart from English), most educated Afrikaners were in fact talking Afrikaans to one another.

The newspapers which began to appear (for example, *De Goede Hoop* in the Cape and *De Volkstem* in the Transvaal) gave increasingly space to Afrikaans contributions and in many ways served to strengthen the movement for acceptable and accepted Afrikaans. The *Goede Hoop's* editor gave advice so simple that it had almost the character of genius: "Spell according to pronunciation, without deviating unnecessarily from the spelling rules of High Dutch."

In 1905 the Afrikaanse Taalgenootskap (Afrikaans Language Society) was founded, which had as two of its principal tasks the persuading of Afrikaners that Afrikaans should be accepted as their spoken and written language, and the development of this language as a highly acceptable medium. Its journal, *Die Brandwag*, was a great success. Other movements followed: among them, the Afrikaanse Taalvereniging (Afrikaans Language Association), and Onze Taal (Our Language), more magazines, and stirring arguments on behalf of Afrikaans by public figures such as General J. B. M. Hertzog. There followed student movements, movements by women's organizations, and after the Union of the four provinces in 1910, widespread campaigns for the introduction of Afrikaans in the schools, in the three Dutch Reformed Churches (where only Dutch was still recognized), in the universities, and in parliament and government. Gradually, from 1910 onwards Afrikaans replaced Dutch in all these spheres, reaching the peak of its struggle for recognition with the complete translation in 1934 of the Bible. It was recognized beside English in almost every public sphere well before the beginning of the Second World War in 1939. *Die Suid-Afrikaanse Akademie vir Wetenskap en Kuns* (The South African Academy for Science and Art) has played a dominant role in achieving recognition, and in developing the potentiality of the language.

With the advent to power in 1948 of the National Party government, some will have it that Afrikaans is in the ascendancy and English in a state of eclipse and decline. Yet still today in all our newspapers there is heated debate about which of the languages enjoys the greater favor, surely a healthy (if perhaps too competitive) awareness by white South Africans of their dual linguistic nature.

The chapter on literature suggests how far Afrikaans has come as an expressive language, and in the work of a genius, such as the poet N. P. van Wyk Louw, we see not only the textual color it can achieve, but the profound eloquence of which it is capable. It has become a language preeminently suited to the description of—in fact it seems so much the child of—African indigenous conditions: We see this, for example, in Sangiro's *Uit Oerwoud en Vlakte* (From Forest and Plains), where the animal life of this country is described, and even in that masterly saga of insect life, *Die Siel van die Mier* (The Soul of the White Ant) by Eugene Marais.

Bibliography

Beeton, D. R. *Some Aspects of English Usage in South Africa*, 1968.
Boshoff, S. P. E. and G. S. Nienaber, *Afrikaanse Etimologiee*, 1967.
Du Buisson, M. S. *Die Wonder van Afrikaans*, 1959
Hopwood, D. *South African English Pronunciation*, 1928.
Lanham, L. W. *The Pronunciation of South African English*, 1967.
—. *The Way We Speak*, 1967
McMagh, P. *English for South Africans*, 1965.
Nienaber, G. S. *Die Opkoms van Afrikaans as Kultuurtaal*, 1944.
—. *Taalkundige Belangstelling in Afrikaans tot 1900*, 1950.
Pienaar, E. C. *Die Triomf van Afrikaans*, 1946.
Sabbagha, N. J. G. *South Africa's Contribution to the English Vocabulary*, 1969.
Van der Merwe, H. J. J. M. *Afrikaans*, 1968.
—. *An Introduction to Afrikaans*, 1951.
—. *Inleiding tot die Taalkunde*, 1964.

7

Family Life and Popular Culture

J. B. du Toit

It is said of a previous Secretary-General of the United Nations, the late Dag Hammerskjoeld, that when shown the picturesque French Hoek Valley about thirty miles from Cape Town, he remarked that this scene reminded him more of Europe than Africa.

This observation immediately brings us to the problem of presenting to the distant reader a picture of the so-called popular culture—the family life and some aspects of the general way of life—of South Africans. Physically and geographically South Africa belongs to Africa, and all her population groups have no other homeland; and yet it can with some justification be said that South Africa is not Africa. The dominant population groups, the Afrikaans and English-speaking Whites, have their cultural and political roots in western Europe; they still feel themselves part of the Anglo-Saxon and Germanic cultures.

However, like the gold mines and Johannesburg, Cape Town and its Table Mountain, Highveld thunderstorms and Karoo droughts, or the unique fauna and flora, there are distinctly South African features in the social and cultural life of its people. Inevitably the presence of a variety of non-European peoples and cultures, elements from Africa itself and from the Eastern world, have all contributed to a South African way of life. They all form part of a rather complex, even sometimes confusing, picture.

Cape Town, the mother city and Tavern of the Seas, was founded as a half-way station between East and West, and so it always has been: the city where oceans meet, and where East and West have met. It became the community in which developed the "European way of life" adapted to the new country, South Africa.

But acculturation on the international level is inevitable. This process has not by-passed the Cape. Many of the distinctly South African or Cape-Dutch cultural patterns now clearly belong to the past. The unique and stately Cape Dutch buildings of previous centuries have to be restored and preserved in areas rapidly changing in the process of industrialization and urbanization. The rural and patriarchal family of earlier decades no longer fits in with the modern way of life; thus it is in many ways hardly distinguishable from the family in other parts of the Western world. Traditional clothing of early settlers or Voortrekkers belongs to museums or special festivals (*Volksfeeste*). The younger generation—dressed in the latest fashions from London, Paris, or Rome—are "tuned in" not to traditional folk music or traditional "boeremusiek," but to the latest hits in pop music and modern "folk." Here, at the southern tip of Africa, in a shrinking world, they form part of a teenage culture of universal characteristics.

Yet, in contrast to citizens of many other parts of the world, South Africans still live relatively close to nature. The density of population is only 38.13 per square mile, compared with the Netherlands' 155, and Great Britain's 567. With the exception of the Witwatersrand complex, even urban dwellers are generally not too far from the peaceful quiet of nature, and it is sometimes said that especially the Afrikaans-speaking urban dwellers still have at least some relatives or friends living on a farm. The urge to go back to nature or the soil is still felt by the "Boerevolk" of yesterday; but today only 7 percent of the white population are engaged in agriculture, whereas in 1936 there were 24 percent.

Most young married couples, especially those in the bigger cities and towns, start their own households in apartments. It is still the ideal of the average South African family eventually to own or rent a house on its own plot, but as a result of soaring land prices and increasing building costs, this is an ideal that is becoming increasingly difficult to realize.

In the peri-urban areas it is inevitable that valuable agricultural land will be sub-divided for residential purposes. Even in South Africa, with its traditional wide open spaces, its citizens are also calculating the cost of rapid economic and industrial growth in terms of these changes in their way of life and natural surroundings. The urbanized population will apparently have to change their conception of the traditional "place in the sun"; to a lesser extent it will in future be in their private garden, and more provision will have to be made for public parks and playgrounds. Meanwhile, on its annual holiday or week-end trip the average South African family can still enjoy a hinterland of natural surroundings and a wealth of wild life that is hardly equaled elsewhere.

The younger generation may be "tuned in" for tomorrow and superficially share in a culture of beat music, jeans, and ultramodern fashions, but they have certainly not completely divorced themselves from the rural and agrarian background of their forefathers; in a country that is often drought-stricken they are constantly reminded of man's dependence upon the elements.

The average South African family, especially within the context of the urbanized way of life, has much in common with families in other parts of the world. A close and objective examination by the social scientist would reveal some typical and universal phenomena: a decline in the size of the urban family, a more egalitarian relationship between the older and younger generation, changing conceptions of the role of husband and wife, class consciousness, an increase in the percentage of married women in the open labor market, and concomitant problems of marital adjustment and child rearing in a changing society.

South Africans from all ethnic groups have increasingly come to reside in cities and towns. According to the latest statistics 46.7 percent of the total population of the country is classified as urban. In the case of the white population approximately 85 percent today live in towns and cities.

It is without any doubt the family life of the Bantu that has been most seriously affected by urbanization. In fact, the present scene is that of a whole culture in a phase of transition, with the family life bearing the brunt of all the impacts. It is within the family circle, where tribal norms and values are no longer generally upheld, that the often disrupting effect of rapid change can best be observed. The polygynous tribal family, with its patrilineal and patrifocal basis, could no longer maintain itself within an industrialized socio-economic structure based on the Christian religion, which permits only a monogamous family arrangement. The differentiated economic system of the city and the fact that the legal system of the tribe became subsidiary to the common law of the country were likewise inimical. Further, personal contact with the Whites within the family context, as well as through the popular press, the film, and radio, undoubtedly had a profound influence on the Bantu's conception of romantic love and the status of the woman in marriage and the family.

The system of migrant labor and influx-control measures also directly affected the masculinity ratio in the Bantu population in white areas. According to the 1960 census, the ratio of Bantu men to women in the age group 15 to 49 in urban areas was 172 to 100, indicating a gradual change from the previous decennial census in favor of relatively more women.

From the point of view of the traditional polygynous and extended family system, it is also significant to note the housing arrangements in any modern urban environment. All housing schemes are being planned to provide for the primary family only. Seen from this angle, it is clear that the traditional pattern does not fit into the urban way of life and is disrupted.

In more general terms, one could say that the Bantu family is in a phase of transition. From an assessment in terms of statistics and other empirical evidence, it would be obvious that a fairly high percentage of Bantu have accepted the marriage and family practices of the Western world. An analysis of Bantu marriages between 1937 and 1957 indicates an increase in the number of civil marriages, yet a significant number of Bantu marriage ceremonies consist of a combination of church and tribal customs.

Further evidence of the divergent patterns among Westernized Bantu is provided by an analysis of the major types of families: the nuclear family, consisting of father, mother, and children; multi-generation families, with the husband as head of the household; incomplete multi-generation families, consisting of the mother and children; and incomplete multi-generation families with the wife as head of the household. In all cases, families in the cities quite often include additional members, such as relatives.

Symptomatic of the painful process of cultural evolution and adaptation is the state of anomie that often develops. The lack of an integrating and stabilizing set of values, or the conflicting values of two cultures, is not easily understood. As one of those intangible and yet very real aspects of a people's way of life, it is manifested on the level of individual and family relations. Phenomena such as a lack of parental authority and a high rate of juvenile delinquency also reflect these problems.

It is a universal phenomenon that where people have lost certain traditional moral codes and measures of control there is an increase in premarital and extramarital sexual relations and illegitimate births. The Bantu people in South African cities are no exception: illegitimate births in certain urban communities are often as high as 30 to 40 percent. However, statistics such as these should be qualified. In a discussion of the same phenomenon S. P. Cilliers comments, in *The Coloreds of South Africa*: "Not all these births result from loose and promiscuous relations, since many unions between working-class couples are only solemnized after a considerable period of cohabitation, and often stable and life-long relations are maintained without formal marriage procedure at all."

Empirical surveys of the consumption patterns of the urban Bantu family have also shown to what extent a more Western pattern of life has already been adopted. Statistics provided by Market Research Africa reveal that 62 percent of the total income of the Bantu population of South Africa is currently earned by the 33 percent of the Bantu population who live in white urban areas. Although porridge made of mealie (corn meal) is still the staple food of the Bantu—for 70 to 80 percent of the people this is still the main fare at all meals—they are increasingly changing their eating and other consumption habits. About 84 percent of those in cities drink tea in the mornings, while 15 percent of those in cities have coffee; nearly 80 percent consume soda drinks, while 65 percent regularly buy candy and chocolates. Up to a third of all Bantu women in the cities use some kind of cosmetic. Household articles such as radios are owned by nearly 50 percent. The extent to which the urban Bantu have adapted themselves to the economic system is shown by the fact that while ten years ago only 7 percent had made use of a bank, the figure has now risen to 24 percent.

Naturally, figures such as these should again be seen against the background of the general standard of living of the people. Consumption patterns are always closely related to income level, educational qualifications, and other cultural factors. Furthermore, the material aspects of a new culture are quite often the most readily accepted. The way of life of the Bantu family in South African cities also shows this universal trend. In sharp contrast to the eagerness with which the latest and most modern fashions of Western life are accepted, we often find the complex human relations and spiritual problems of a people in search of a new culture, so that the patterns of family life of the Bantu are perhaps best described as typical of a people at a cultural crossroads. In the words of Colin M. Rip,

> Some are living not far removed from purely Native conditions. Others have changed very considerably, indeed; they have become divorced from tribal rule and tradition and approximate to the Europeans in standard of life, occupations, and outlooks. Between these two extremes are the great majority, who retain many of their old cultural characteristics while participating to an increasing extent in their new civilization.

The present system of influx-control measures have far-reaching implications for the family life of the Bantu, and is one of the controversial matters in South African society. In an article dealing with this G. M. E. Leistner provides the following perspective:

> Most countries at an early stage of development are characterized by a sharp dualism within their social and economic structures. That is, a modern sector and a predominantly traditional sector exist side by side. As soon as the traditional sector is no longer able to satisfy the economic and social requirements of the inhabitants (rapid population growth may be a decisive factor in this regard), the countries concerned experience a heavy pressure of rural population seeking admittance to the urban areas which commonly are their most developed areas. Serious economic, social, and other problems arise from this pressure. In South Africa, where exactly the same problems are encountered, they are strongly accentuated by the ethnic composition of the population. Here, ethnic and related factors are such that the only fundamental solution that can be envisaged to the problem of rural-urban imbalance is through developing the Bantu areas rather than through the full integration of the Bantu into the White urban areas. As long as the serious rural-urban imbalance persists, some form of physical control over townward population movements seems indispensable.

Fundamentally, this is a problem of reconciling the diverse interests of the economic, social, and political institutions of the country.

Generally speaking, the Colored population, a relatively homogeneous group, leads a Western way of life. The vast majority of the Colored people belong to Christian churches; the only exception is the Cape Malays, who are Muslims. The birth rate amongst the Coloreds, which at present stands at approximately 44 per 1,000 of the population, is comparable to that of other developing ethnic groups in the world, yet over the last few years there has been a decline in this rate. Especially the families in the higher socio-economic strata have more generally accepted family planning, and here the average size of the family approximates that of Whites.

Extra-marital and pre-marital sexual relations are relatively prevalent, a practice that contributes to the high incidence of ex-nuptial births. As in the case of the Bantu, approximately one-third of all Colored births are annually registered as ex-nuptial. Although many loose and promiscuous relations do exist, couples from the lower socio-economic strata often cohabit without having their relationship solemnized or sanctioned by a marriage ceremony.

It is interesting to note that these data clearly show that ex-nuptial births most frequently occur among population groups of mixed racial origins and at the lower socio-economic level. In *Contemporary Social Problems* William J. Goode writes: "Illegitimacy occurs primarily in lower class families, which are themselves unstable and have little family honor to lose, so that motivation to control courtship is not high." He also adds that although these "consensual" unions are less stable than legal ones, a stable relationship may emerge. "Eventually, most people do marry," he concludes.

Although the nuclear family is among the Colored people the normal structure, the presence of additional members seems to be a fairly general phenomenon. The following are some of the reasons usually given for this feature of their family life: the prevalence of illegitimate births among young unmarried females who remain with their children in their parents' household; the low earning power of working-class Coloreds who thus augment their income; the shortage of inexpensive housing facilities; the presence of grandparents who can take care of the children while both parents are gainfully employed.

In a study of the roles of the husband and wife in the Colored family it was found that significant differences exist between lower- and higher-class Coloreds. S. P. Cilliers sums it up as follows: "This difference relates in the first instance to the distribution of power and authority. Mother-centered and/or mother-dominated families predominate amongst the lower class in contrast to a more father-dominated and equalitarian family pattern amongst the higher social classes."

This great mother-domination among the lower-class Coloreds and American Negroes constitutes a deviation from the pattern of contemporary Western society. In both cases it could be explained in terms of the history and the subservient position of the men before emancipation from slavery as well as the disorganized social conditions of the working class. The significant factor is that the mother-centered and/or mother-dominated family (where it still exists) is a result of instability and social disorganization.

Strong class distinction exists among the Colored people. In the past, distinctions based on pigment or other racial characteristics dominated the entire status hierarchy: the more closely individuals resembled Whites the higher they were on the social ladder. More recent studies seem to indicate that other criteria, such as achievement, education, occupation, and property have become more significant.

In general terms, the problems of the Colored population are typical of a working-class or underdeveloped people with a low standard of living. During the last few years the results of various projects to improve the socio-economic position of these people have given hope for a brighter future: overriding importance will be the tempo at which more skilled and trained manpower and leaders can be provided from among them.

The Colored population has come a long way with the Whites of South Africa; culturally they have much in common; and yet, in a country struggling with some of the most complex human relations problems in the world, the White-Colored relations are, politically speaking, perhaps the most delicate. Paradoxically, personal relations are nowhere more relaxed and spontaneous than when expressed in terms of the general way of life and the popular "folk" culture at the Cape, where the two groups have for more than three centuries worked shoulder to shoulder.

Turning to the family life of the 3.6 million Whites in South Africa, it would be unrealistic—if not naïve—to think in terms of the typical Afrikaans- or English-speaking family. The Calvinist religion, the isolation of rural families, and the sharp contrasts between White and non-White, have in the course of more than three centuries left a deep imprint on the White family.

The first Dutch settlers brought the convictions of the Reformation, the form of Calvinism practiced in Holland, and the pietistic influence of the Dutch middle class. In their new country a renewed belief in the sovereignty of God and the necessity of obeying His commands arose as a result of their agricultural life and dependence on climatic conditions, as well as a result of the dangers inherent in their situation.

These tendencies were strengthened by the arrival in 1688 of the French Huguenots, who brought with them the strong convictions which had caused them to endure persecution in and virtual banishment from France.

The influence of the British Settlers on the Dutch was generally negligible, from the point of view of family life, but there was considerable influence by Scottish ministers in the Dutch Reformed Church and educational institutions. Although not altogether free from tensions, this close Scottish-Dutch relationship at the level of religion and education had a lasting effect on future cultural patterns.

These men brought with them the history of the struggle against domination of the State over the Church and the strict observance of ethical codes and Sabbath-observance then prevalent in Scotland. Most of them had studied in Holland before coming to South Africa and were there further influenced by the pietistic movement. They laid great stress on personal conversion, religious training in the homes, missionary enterprise, and the need for prayer meetings. The revival of 1862-64, which led to so many personal conversions, and the struggle against the liberalism of the nineteenth century left a lasting impression on the religious life of the Afrikaner.

While family life in South Africa is so often seen as a blend of the Anglo-Saxon and the Germanic—with some typically English forms of etiquette and customs even among the Afrikaners—the role of the earlier educational institutions is perhaps not always appreciated. Under the guidance of the Scottish ministers, especially Dr. Andrew Murray, some of the leading girls' schools were founded. Institutions such as The

Good Hope Seminary in Cape Town, the Huguenot Seminary at Wellington, Bellevue at Somerset East, Bloemhof Girls' High School at Stellenbosch, and the Seminary at Graaff Reinet, all had strong influence on the family life of the Afrikaner. Several of these institutions employed English and American teachers, whose role in the process of acculturation should not be underestimated.

The nature of family life, leisure, and recreation was further strongly influenced by the very strict observation of the Sabbath as a day of rest. Combined with formal and solemn church services and regular church attendance within the patriarchal family circle, this pattern was characteristic of the local community life up to a few decades ago. Even today, however, no commercialized sport or recreation is allowed on Sundays.

And yet the recent unprecedented technological developments, economic growth, and urbanization have brought along many modifications. Still, descriptions such as "basically conservative" or "relatively stable" would be applicable to the majority of South African families. Visitors from overseas have often remarked on the hospitality and relaxed atmosphere encountered in the average South African home. Especially in rural areas, the family has retained its friendly and unsophisticated atmosphere; familialistic terms in the form of address can still be found. Even in the more urban atmosphere, these phenomena reflect some elements of the closely knit patriarchal community, and from a sociological viewpoint it could be said that the South African white family closely resembles British, American, or Western European prototypes.

More than four decades ago a considerable part of the white rural (or originally rural) population was suffering from economic and social retrogression. The investigation of this problem resulted from a visit paid to the country in 1927 by the president and secretary of the Carnegie Corporation of New York. With the corporation's generous financial support and the active participation of two American sociologists, Kenyon L. Butterfield and C. W. Coulter, the so-called Carnegie Commission brought out a comprehensive report on this burning question, *The Poor White Problem in South Africa* (1932).

The findings and recommendations of the Carnegie Commission directly contributed to the establishment of departments of sociology and social work at South African universities. The first chair in sociology was created in 1933 at the University of Stellenbosch and was first occupied by Dr. H. F. Verwoerd. The period 1934 to 1940 saw the extension of this more academic interest in family life in South Africa to all the other universities or university colleges. In line with the recommendations of the Carnegie Commission, the emphasis was mainly on the training of skilled social workers.

It is significant that the Carnegie Commission, while describing the poor white problem as an "acute manifestation of influences and conditions that were generally prevalent in the social structure," also paid special attention to the mother and daughter in the family. This aspect was dealt with by M. E. Rothman, one of the foremost women in the Afrikaans literary and cultural field. The consensus was that the poor white problem could be solved only with due attention to the key role of the woman in the educational and cultural life of the people. In more general terms, the plight of many families was at that time explained in terms of maladjustment to changed conditions, such as the urban way of life and industrialization. It was especially the Afrikaans-speaking families, with their rural background, who were often lifetime "immigrants in a new society."

Economic development, expanded university education, and occupational differentiation have since the 1930's materially changed the picture, yet the emphasis on the role of the woman in the family of the 1970's is equally justified.

Empirical studies that have appeared since the report of the Carnegie Commission have dealt more specifically with family patterns. The Dutch sociologist G. A. Kooy studied one hundred farmer families in the Transvaal and came to the conclusion that in many respects they closely resembled families in the heart of the Netherlands. While partially still subscribing to the values of an agrarian and traditionalistic community, these families were inevitably integrated into the broader urban society. Most significant is the fact that Kooy found two images of family life on the Transvaal Highveld: the family as an isolated rural community and the family as part of the bigger industrial-urban society.

During the last two decades various studies of family life in the urban centers of South Africa have been undertaken. The Commission of Enquiry into Family Life established by the Nederduitse Gereformeerde Kerk investigated in Pretoria in 1948 the relationship between urbanism and family size. A sample of 1551 white families was selected from the voters' roll. The majority of the families (870) were Afrikaans-speaking, but a substantial number (444) spoke English. There were also 191 bilingual families and 46 families speaking one of the other European languages. The major finding in this project was the decline in the size of the urban family. While the respondents in the sample had an average of 3.3 children per family, the parents came from families with an average of just over 7 children per family. The reasons for the reduction in family size are probably the same as those underlying this phenomenon in other parts of the world: economic pressures, housing difficulties in urban communities, social mobility, and mothers working outside the home.

Of great significance, especially in view of the present tempo of urbanization in South Africa, is Beryl Unterhalter's study of marital role conceptions, the socialization of the child, and values and norms pertaining to families living in blocks of flats (apartment buildings). She points out that more South African urban families will in future have to live under these circumstances. (It was estimated that in 1966, some 37 percent of the dwelling units for Whites in Johannesburg were flats in high-rise buildings.)

Some of Unterhalter's main conclusions, derived from her interviews with 198 so-called "Flatland" wives, were: (1) "Flatland families had internalized middle-class norms and aspirations which adequately regulated their behavior. However, if Flatlands are to develop among other ethnic or social classes in the South Africa of the future, it is likely that a wide range of social problems will be created by a failure to provide adequate facilities for family life or community interaction"; (2) that in this most urbanized and densely populated part of South Africa the opinions of housewives "indicated a generalized pattern of conservatism and respect for tradition"; (3) that residents of Flatland were not "adrift in a world of changing values," but that they respected the "traditional integrative forces in family life"; and (4) "That, even in a densely-populated urban milieu, there is no decline in the social significance of the family. Flatland families, like many modern urban families, are not without their difficulties, and irritations...the present study does not show any decline in the essential nature, or importance of the family as a social institution."

A picture of family life in South Africa would be incomplete without a brief reference to the problem of disorganization in marital and family relations. As in most other countries of the Western world, this is a very real problem as reflected in the divorce rate.

The legal grounds for divorce in South Africa are adultery, malicious desertion, imprisonment for five years after having been declared an habitual criminal, and incurable insanity. To obtain a divorce, the parties (or at least one of them) must establish before a court of law the existence of one of the legally recognized grounds for divorce. However, the causes for the breakup of the marriage-relationship, which often lead to adultery or desertion, are usually of a sociological and psychological nature. In studies on divorce in South Africa the most frequently mentioned causes or factors associated with divorce are alcoholism, incompatibility, infidelity, sexual problems, financial problems, and differences on the socio-cultural and spiritual level.

Figures show that divorces in the white population have increased very considerably since 1913, the first year for which details are available. The modified divorce rate, which gives the number of divorces per 1,000 married couples, has increased from 1.13 in 1913 to just over 6.0 in the 1960's. (The same trend is found in countries such as England and Holland, where this divorce rate increased from 0.20 to 1.16 in 1913 to 3.80 and 2.19

in 1956, respectively.) In South Africa, as in most other countries, there was a sharp rise in the incidence of divorce during 1946-47, which was generally attributed to the social instability of the war years, hasty marriages contracted during this period, and the personal adjustment problems of returning soldiers, as an aftermath of the war.

The urban divorce rate is substantially higher than the rural one, the highest divorce rate being found in Johannesburg, the most urbanized center in the republic—and also the most cosmopolitan.

The available crude divorce rate (the rate per 1,000 of the population) for Coloreds and Asiatics is much lower than the corresponding figure for Whites, but this does not mean that there is a smaller proportion: marriages are dissolved *de facto* without recourse to the processes of law and a correspondingly large percentage of couples live together without their marriages being officially solemnized. These trends are also responsible for the relatively lower marriage rate and high rate of illegitimate births in this population group.

As a result of a national conference in 1954, the South African National Council for Marriage Guidance and Family Life was established. In addition, regional and local marriage guidance councils were established in order to combat the problems of family disorganization and lay emphasis on education for marriage and family life. Such bureaus for marriage guidance are functioning in most of the major cities.

In terms of the National Welfare Act, a special Commission for Family Life was appointed in 1968 to make a country-wide inquiry into the nature and extent of broken marriages and the causes and consequences of divorce. Indications are that the main emphasis of this commission will be on an evaluation of the existing measures and services for combating divorce. It is generally felt that the answer to this problem is to be found in educational measures rather than stricter marriage and divorce laws.

A recent investigation based on a representative sample of 1,000 Whites between the ages of 25 and 34 living in cities, towns, and villages revealed some further characteristics of family life in South Africa today. These "Homemakers," the young adults of yesterday and the potential leaders of tomorrow, live in a socio-cultural context within which many penetrating questions about the traditional differences between Afrikaans- and English-speaking South Africans are being asked. In spite of their separate churches, schools, and many other groupings in terms of language, some other alignments are developing across the language barriers. Of significance for the immediate future is the fact that approximately 55 percent of this group have Afrikaans or both Afrikaans and English as their home languages, while 45 percent speak English or another language.

The average family of this younger generation consists of 2.3 children; some 76 percent of the families live in urban areas with a population of 10,000 or more and approximately 80 percent of them live in houses. The relatively smaller family has in South Africa as elsewhere come to stay; the present birth rate is approximately 2.3, a figure which closely corresponds with those of countries such as Australia, Canada, and the United States.

For many generations, then, the family and kinship system had perhaps a somewhat stronger influence on the social and cultural life of the people than in a more heterogeneous and urbanized society. Strong family ties and traditions and a more parochial outlook on life were symptomatic of this situation. However, in the more competitive and materialistic contemporary society the traditional Afrikaner family has lost some of these characteristics. While achievement is emphasized, descent and ascribed status is of less importance. At the economic and professional level the distinctive lines between Afrikaner and English are often rather vague, and marriages across the language barrier are now not exceptional. And yet, in spite of these trends, the impact of history, tradition, religion, and two official languages is still strongly felt in the family life of the country. By and large each language group still has separate churches, schools, and a variety of cultural and charitable organizations. At the same time coordinating bodies provide contact at the higher level.

In general, then, behavior patterns in South African families are a blend of tradition and innovation. If the family is still relatively conservative, this can be attributed to the role of the church and the general spiritual climate in the country. As some indication of the influence of the church and religion, it should be mentioned that recent surveys have shown that 40 to 45 percent of the homemakers in the 25-to-34-year-old group attend church at least once per week. By and large the Sabbath is still a day of rest.

Looking at certain aspects of family life, it would therefore appear as if the moral climate in South Africa is still somewhat different from that in other parts of the world. At the same time South African family life is by no means free from the social and cultural stresses and strains experienced elsewhere. As indicated, the divorce rate is relatively high.

When observing more closely its people at play—the leisure and recreation and mass entertainment of South African society, it will also be clear to what extent it has drifted into the main current of popular world culture.

South African clothing and eating habits stem directly from our ancestors', which gradually changed until the unique pattern that we know today evolved.

With Jan van Riebeeck came a number of tradesmen, soldiers, and laborers, but few women. The clothing of this first group of settlers was simple and functional. Gradually the settlement expanded, the first free burghers (those not in the employ of the Dutch East India Company) were given land, and a permanent way of life started. The fashion of clothing worn at the Cape altered slowly, and what was worn came mainly from the Netherlands. The basic simplicity of garments, accompanied by a particular taste for neatness and correctness, was a manifestation of the Calvinistic philosophy.

Yet one can deduce that fashions at the Cape were not too far from the contemporary European styles, since (despite the distance) the Cape kept in good contact through ships and travelers who continually called there. New fashions took many years before they became acceptable, though, and took even longer to penetrate to the interior. At the distant outposts the clothing had, of necessity, to be adapted to the practical needs of the farmers. For his clothing, the trekker had to rely on a jacket and trousers made from tanned hides, and he had to make his own shoes. The bonnet of the Voortrekker women is of special interest in the history of South African feminine fashion, because it is a reflection of the outdoor life at the frontiers, where women's complexions had to be protected from the hot sun. This bonnet was created by combining the nineteenth-century Poke bonnet and the eighteenth-century cap, which was decorated with embroidery done in carefully stored thread.

With the economic advancement of the nineteenth century, fashion consciousness increased, and women from the newly developed cities and towns of the interior competed in ordering the latest cloth and patterns for best and wedding dresses from Europe. Because no cloth was manufactured in South Africa before the twentieth century, all material was ordered from England or Europe.

The influence of the English on the clothing is decidedly noticeable. In spite of the hot climate, heavy English gabardine and serge were used for working clothes and men's wear, including the dark blue uniform that the South African police and railway personnel wore until recently. English influence was also seen in school uniforms. The English gym tunic was the accepted school uniform for girls since early in the present century. The school blazer and tie were worn with this tunic, and it became such a strong tradition that in spite of the climate, some schools still have this as their compulsory uniform.

With the development of the South African textile and clothing industry, particularly after the Second World War, a tendency to adapt the fashions to suit South African conditions became apparent, and comfortable, less formal dress is preferred today. One result of this is the safari suit, a purely South African fashion for men, which is now ubiquitous as office wear.

Because of the difference in seasons, fashions in South Africa are six months behind Europe, and this interim gives the clothing industry the opportunity to adapt the European fashions that are likely to be popular here.

South African eating habits and food preparation, which originated in Europe and England, have changed to suit the new circumstances.

Certain dishes, which are thought of as typically South African, can be traced back to a specific country, even though the preparation or serving may differ. For example, the South African milktart is known in Europe, but not as in a puff pastry case. The wide use of Eastern spice mixtures, such as curry, is clearly the result of the influence of the Malay slaves who were to be found at the Cape during the time of the Dutch East India Company.

Some local dishes have originated circumstantially. For example, Waterblommetjies is a type of plant that grows only in southern South Africa and a Waterblommetjie-bredie, or stew, is a genuine South African dish.

The way of life of the Trekkers had a great influence on their eating habits: from necessity they dried meat as a method for its preservation. Dishes that are still popular among the Afrikaans-speaking population are salted ribs and biltong: salted ribs are barbequed over coals, while biltong is meat that is well treated with salt and spices and then dried until it needs no cooking.

Other kinds of Afrikaner food are boerbeskuit (a type of rusk baked from unsifted flour with salt-rising yeast), flat bread, and griddle cakes. The Afrikaans-speaking South Africans' pattern of eating can be accepted as typical. One aspect is their love of meat, which is sometimes eaten as often as three times a day—especially on farms. The extreme climatic conditions, which often inhibit the cultivation of vegetables for a great portion of the year, means that much use is made of dried fruit, split beans and peas, and such vegetables as pumpkin and squash, which can be stored for a long time. A result of this is that a meal is often unbalanced as regards starch and protein. The usual Sunday dinner is particularly notable for its large variety of dishes; for example, two or more meat dishes, saffron rice with raisins, sousbone (sweet-sour dried beans), potatoes or sweet potatoes, stewed dried fruit, and a salad such as tomato or beetroot. This meal then ends with a cooked pudding.

As knowledge of nutrition increases, as meat prices rise, and fresh fruit and vegetables are more readily available, eating habits are changing, yet the South African still remains faithful to his love of meat and one of the most favored ways of entertaining is a "braaivleis," or barbeque, with the accent on typical barbeque dishes.

South African wines, such as the Johannesburg Riesling, have gained in favor both throughout the continent and more recently in North America and Europe, as have rock lobsters and Granny Smith apples, originally from Australia.

It is often said that a characteristic of the Englishman is his attachment to his daily newspaper. If this were true, the popularity of the daily—and especially the Sunday—newspaper in South Africa could be another reflection of the English way of life. However, factors such as urbanization of the population and the level of literacy, especially of the developing non-white population groups, should also be considered when interpreting any data on the press.

South Africa has come a long way since one of its first newspapers, the *Commercial Advertiser*, was published by Thomas Pringle in 1824. He and John Fairbairn were two of the pioneers in the field of the press and of journalism in the Cape Colony of those days. Alan F. Hattersley, commenting in *An Illustrated Social History of South Africa* on the freedom of the press in those pioneer days, writes: "Fairbairn was the substantial victor in the struggle of the Twenties for freedom of comment, and his growing influence maintained, through the difficult years of frontier warfare and financial stringency that followed, the cause of colonial self-determination."

In such a vast and sparsely populated country circulation was always a problem, and factors such as education for many years retarded the development of a thriving press. In spite of these problems, the latter half of the nineteenth century witnessed the birth, and death, of several newspapers and journals at the Cape, in both English and Dutch.

Today, after more than a century, the problem of the popular press in South Africa lies at a somewhat different level. Typical of mass media in any modern society, it is often caught up in the vicious circle of mass circulation, sensationalism, and popular taste. Another complicating factor, which is perhaps not generally appreciated, is the racial and cultural composition of the reading public. Large numbers of the potential non-white readers are still in a developing stage. On the other hand, with a relatively small white population, the number of more discerning readers is much smaller than in a larger European society. Consequently, the type of newspaper or journal presenting more sophisticated and less popular reading matter would have a relatively small market. In general, then, most of the popular South African newspapers or journals are at present attempting to strike the happy medium, so that a general feature of most of them—at least those with some provincial or national prestige—is the combination of the "popular" with the "popular-scientific" reading matter.

Another trend with far-reaching implications for the role of the popular press in South African society is the concentration of newspaper power. In November 1968 the country was stirred by a proposed take-over by one of the leading printing and publishing companies in the country of 66 percent of the shares of another major newspaper company. Had this taken place, it would have meant that this group would have obtained control (or a say in) of nine of the nation's thirteen English-language dailies and four of its five weekly newspapers, excluding minor local publications. At that time the prime minister, Mr. B. J. Vorster, warned this company that the government did not believe that their proposed take-over would be in the public interest and that legislation would be introduced to control newspaper consolidation as well as the control of newspapers by overseas interests. This whole issue focused attention upon the problems connected with monopolistic tendencies in the popular press. The matter is no doubt further complicated by politics: up to the present most newspapers published in the Afrikaans language have supported the government, while most of the English-language papers have been more or less in opposition to it.

However, most of the leading newspapers in South Africa, whether Afrikaans or English, seem to be wary of monopoly. In spite of the general pattern of alignment in terms of support of the government, there are still differences in degree. The debate around the proposed takeover has also clearly indicated that most leading newspapers in South Africa are still highly sensitive to their task of independent thinking and criticism. Seen from this angle, it was even suggested that eventually the freedom of the press would be adversely affected by such mergers.

According to the recent *National Readership Survey* (1968) more than one million newspapers are sold in South Africa on week days and approximately 1.38 million on Sundays. In proportion to the total population of approximately 18.7 million, of which a majority of non-Whites are not regular buyers of newspapers, this would represent a comparatively high figure: in Nigeria one newspaper is sold for every 160 inhabitants, and in Rhodesia and Egypt one for every 122 inhabitants.

Within each province the twenty daily newspapers (of which seven are published in Afrikaans and thirteen in English) have a dominating influence in the city of publication and its immediate region. The five Sunday newspapers, of which three are in English and two in Afrikaans, circulate nation-wide. Circulation figures of the Sunday newspapers range from 300,000 to 400,000 copies. The largest daily news circulation is just over 170,000, while the smaller ones are between 7,000 and 10,000. Only 25 percent of the daily newspapers published are in Afrikaans, although nearly 60 percent of the total white population is Afrikaans-speaking. This tendency could be explained in terms of the following factors: relatively more Afrikaans- than English-speaking South Africans read newspapers in both English and Afrikaan; English-speaking South Africans, being relatively more urbanized, more regularly read newspapers; non-white readers still buy more newspapers in English than in Afrikaans. Another significant factor is that most of the older and established evening papers are published in English.

A detailed study of newspaper circulation among Whites over age sixteen showed that newspapers in English were read by 53.3 percent of potential readers, compared with 31.5 percent who read dailies in Afrikaans, and that three out of ten Whites over sixteen years of age do not read daily papers.

The position is notably different as regards the circulation of Sunday papers; although only two are published, their total circulation today nearly equals that of the three older English-language papers. Afrikaans-speaking South Africans have in recent years become in much larger numbers regular readers of Sunday papers; those in Afrikaans are read by approximately 54.5 percent of all Whites over the age of 16, as against 59.1 percent who read Sunday newspapers in English. Only about one out of ten Whites over the age of 16 years does not read any Sunday paper.

As a result of the general nature of the Sunday newspapers—sensational reporting, an overdose of sex and crime—and the interference of this medium with the traditional conception of the atmosphere of the Sabbath in the family, the growth of the circulation of Sunday papers has caused concern in certain circles. Notwithstanding these characteristics, in general the Sunday papers have been quite active in soul-searching about such matters as cultural and ethnic relations in the country. More recently they have feature strongly in the controversy about the cultural and political image of the modern Afrikaner. Where the tendency has been to categorize South Africans in terms of liberal ("verlig") and conservative ("verkramp"), the newspapers were naturally most active in this game. The result of all this is that South Africans have in recent years experienced more intensely the impact that the popular press has on current ways of thinking and acting. The more precise role of any newspaper in this complex process of mass communication would be difficult to sketch; suffice to say that, apart from the element of sensation, the press in South Africa is in general also playing an important role in the process of critical and constructive thinking.

Further, it would appear that the non-Whites read relatively more newspapers in English than other languages. Among the Colored people, of whom over 70 percent in the age group 16 years and over could be classified as literate, about 30 percent read daily newspapers and about 50 percent read weekly or Sunday newspapers. Although nearly 90 percent of the Colored people have Afrikaans as their home language, figures seem to indicate that weekend and Sunday publications in Afrikaans are becoming more popular.

Asiatics and urbanized Bantu, who are predominantly more proficient in English than in Afrikaans, also mostly read newspapers in English. Several daily or weekly newspapers and journals cater specially for the needs and tastes of these non-Whites. A weekly newspaper published in Johannesburg specially for the Bantu has quite a large readership.

In general, the quality of South African newspapers and journals would compare favorably with the more popular American or European papers. The discerning reader might sometimes find them rather provincial or parochial, with insufficient coverage of international news, but there are signs of a more outward movement in recent years. News and feature articles on other parts of Africa are increasingly often published. The contents of South African journals also strongly reflects the current trends in European and American publications.

Besides its own variety of popular magazines published in either English or Afrikaans, a large number are imported from England, the United States, and Germany. Local editions of some weekly American newsmagazines are also printed in South Africa. Popular magazines seem to follow the modern pattern: they are richly illustrated and cater to the interests of the family; those consisting mainly of picture-stories and comic strips enjoy a wide circulation, especially among youth and the less-discerning readers. A few titles chosen from those with the highest circulation suggest their format and content: *Personality, Fair Lady, Femina, Woman's Life, Die Huisgenoot, Sarie Marais, Die Landbouweekblad, Farmer's Weekly, Rooi Rose, Kyk,* and *See.*

It will be clear from what has been said that reading habits have been affected by the modern forms of presentation of material. Censorship and a great deal of public concern about the alleged ill effects of certain paperbacks and comic books have not substantially changed the situation. In this respect South Africa is sharing with the rest of contemporary society the advantages and disadvantages of the revolution in mass communication. And in the absence of sufficient objective knowledge about the effect of reading matter, especially in a multi-cultural society, it is often impossible to provide consistent norms and guidance.

The first library in South Africa was the law library that Van Riebeeck brought out to the country. In 1761 Joachim von Dessin, Master of the Court, bequeathed 3,856 volumes to the Dutch Reformed Church as curators, with the stipulation that this should form the nucleus of a free public library. In 1818 Lord Charles Somerset, Governor of the Cape Colony, established the free South African Public Library, the funds for which were obtained from a tax on wine. Hattersley suggests that as a result of Somerset's initiative "Capetown, after 1818, was in possession of a public library that was certainly the finest collection of books in British territories South of the line." Somerset's successor found that the use of tax money to support a library was unconstitutional, and in 1829 it became a subscription library. Today the South African Library is still one of the most significant cultural assets of the city of Cape Town.

The first century of library history is largely that of the Cape Colony, with its numerous subscription libraries. In 1875 Sir John Molteno, then colonial secretary of the Cape Colony, passed regulations whereby aid was given (on a percentage basis) to all public libraries, a policy that continued to 1955, when the so-called free library service was established.

The development of library services in South Africa during the past three decades can be described as phenomenal. During this period the free library services of the four provinces were founded; school libraries were inaugurated; five library schools were established at universities, and the central government's libraries were consolidated and reorganized. The majority of public libraries, under the auspices of local authorities, have changed from subscription to free libraries. It can safely be stated that during these three decades more has been achieved for South African libraries than during the entire period prior to 1940. There is, in fact, no town or village without its free library service, and even at central points in the country, such as on farms or at lonely police stations, a library depot is served by a mobile unit.

Local authorities are responsible for library buildings and staff, according to standards laid down by the South African Library Association, while the provincial library service provides books and audio-visual material such as films, records, and art prints.

Statistics on library membership, book circulation, and the bookholdings reflect the increasing popularity of this service. It is significant to note that in some rural communities and smaller towns, up to 70 percent of the Colored readers are children. While this is a result of better educational facilities, these statistics also indicate the role of the library service for the developing population groups of the country.

Today, university courses in library science are offered by fourteen universities for the various ethnic groups of the country. The University of South Africa, a correspondence institution, offers both diploma and degree courses to all racial groups.

Relatively little is known about the psycho-social effects of broadcasting in a multi-racial country: countrywide surveys have generally concentrated more on the size of audiences in an attempt to determine the value of radio for advertising purposes. However, indications are that both the government and universities will in the near future launch a more coordinated and comprehensive study of mass communication. The Human Science Research Council in Pretoria has recently created an institute for research on communications.

In the absence of television, radio-listening is without doubt the most popular medium of mass entertainment. In 1968 more than 1.7 million radio licenses were issued, so that with an estimated 5 listeners per radio, the South African Broadcasting Corporation at present claims a potential total of 8.5 million listeners. Surveys on leisure and recreation have shown that listening to the radio is still the most popular way of spending an evening.

The entire broadcasting system in South Africa is under the control of the South Africa Broadcasting Corporation, which is managed by a board of governors consisting of the chairman and eight members appointed by the state president and falling under the jurisdiction of the minister of posts and telegraphs. The revenue of the S.A.B.C. is derived mainly from license fees and the advertising services of its separate commercial stations.

During the 1969 parliamentary session the introduction of television was again discussed, and the minister of posts and telegraphs, Mr. M. C. G. J. van Rensburg, acknowledged that rapid technological developments might soon force the government to introduce television, although this is still a matter of relatively low priority. The minister announced a six-point plan for its introduction: (1) television will be state-controlled; (2) there will be bilingual service for Whites and multi-lingual services for Africans; (3) television will be "no extension of the film industry," nor will it be allowed to have a seriously harmful effect on the press; (4) it will not constitute a continuous independent-parallel service to radio; (5) emphasis will be on cultural and information items and commercials will be strictly controlled; (6) the entire television service will be under the closest possible control and supervision. In the meantime permits for closed-circuit television are now being freely granted.

At present the S.A.B.C. offers three country-wide services: one in Afrikaans, another English, and "Springbokradio," a bilingual service that broadcasts advertisements and in general caters for the more "popular" taste. Regional services are provided on the Witwatersrand, in Natal, and in the West and South-eastern Cape Province.

Radio Bantu is a service specially for Africans, in which seven native languages are used. In the past eight years the Bantu broadcasting time has risen from six hours a day (one-

and-a-half hours on four separate frequencies) to eighty hours a day in Zulu, Southern Sotho, Xhosa, Tswana, Northern Sotho, Venda, and Tsonga.

The Protea Program, directed from the Cape Town studios, is one in which the Colored people have a more prominent share through the active participation of their cultural and social leaders, entertainment groups, and singers.

Seventeen languages are now beamed by the transmitters over a network of 55 FM stations, 12 medium-wave AM stations, and two short-wave stations, so that the "Voice of South Africa" can now be heard by all interested listeners. Today 89.4 percent of the White population, 82.4 percent of the Colored people and 80.8 percent of the Bantu can enjoy FM reception.

The S.A.B.C.'s External Service, with its call sign "Radio R.S.A," began in October 1965 and broadcasts in English to Europe, the United States, Canada, the United Kingdom, Australia, New Zealand, and several states in Africa. In addition, Afrikaans is broadcast to Europe and Central Africa, French and Portuguese to Europe and several states in Africa, Dutch and German to Europe, and several Bantu languages to neighboring African states.

The S.A.B.C. also runs a well-equipped News Film Unit which in 1968 alone produced 175 films, most of them on request from television agencies abroad.

Evaluated in terms of the content of its programs, the general impression is that Radio South Africa is attempting to strike a balance between providing mere entertainment and educational and cultural uplift. Some observers have criticized especially the commercial service and its emphasis upon "pop" or "beat" music. Serials broadcast in the afternoons especially for housewives and children have built up a listenership far in excess of 600,000. South Africans also have their favorite radio personalities, while popular weekly programs for the family have created "characters" reflecting idiosyncrasies and traits typical of the inhabitants, both white and non-white. In a more serious vein, the S.A.B.C. has also introduced panel discussions aimed at a critical analysis of current social or cultural issues.

While the radio as a medium of communication in South Africa is decidedly nationalistic—often to such an extent that it has sometimes been accused of political bias—some popular programs unmistakably reflect cultural trends beyond the borders of the country. Dr. P. J. Meyer, the chairman of the S.A.B.C., in his latest annual report has said that since South Africa forms part of the world-wide process of inter-communications, it will be directly influenced by thoughts and actions emanating from the Western world especially. In particular, he mentioned the task of constantly taking stock of the situation in a sober and objective way and reporting on this to the nation:

> Fortunately, an adult society is not helplessly subjected to the influence of mass media, neither radio nor any other medium. The information and comment provided by mass media are digested by a society and its leaders to become part of them—and this process implies that such information and comment can also be rejected. It is an outmoded theory that mass media are able to indoctrinate or influence society and people at will.

Various studies on leisure and recreation have indicated that South Africans are keen cinema-goers. Since television has not yet been introduced, attendance tends to be fairly high and the drive-in cinema especially seems to be very popular with families. A recent sample survey of young white South Africans in the age group 25 to 34 has shown that during a typical week 25 percent go to a drive-in movie and 27 percent go to an indoor one. Another nationwide study of Whites over the age of 16 has indicated that nearly 85 percent sometimes go to the cinema, of which 24 percent have said that they attend once a week. Attendance rates among non-Whites would naturally be relatively lower. In the case of the more Westernized Colored and Asiatic population groups, similar surveys have revealed that respectively 37 and 83 percent sometimes attend the movies.

Of more significance would be the nature of the material to which South African audiences are exposed. From observations by film experts and critics it would appear that popular tastes in films correspond with those in America. The prevailing pattern in order of preference seems to be sex, action, and hearty laughs. Proof of this is the fact that whenever a film that is rumored or thought to be of an erotic nature is released by the Board of Censors, it breaks box-office records. In South Africa, as elsewhere, the elements of sex, violence, popular taste, and mass audiences go hand in hand. "Westerns" are generally less popular, surprisingly enough, than in other countries, and the public is rather apathetic about horror films, which have a big market in some countries.

On the other hand, audiences are becoming more sophisticated. An indication of this is the kind of criticism leveled at the Board of Censors and the growing interest in the film as an art form. Films purported to be a reflection of the problems of the community have also had large attendance.

As yet South Africa has no film industry of its own. While a number of outstanding documentaries, especially for overseas television use, are produced annually, entertaining films of merit are still scarce, although there has been an upward trend in the standard of this type of film. Several companies are presently obtaining a major share in the importation, distribution, and screening of films.

At present individual producers pioneering the South African film industry are gaining popularity with mass audiences: Jamie Uys, Jans Rautenbach, and Emil Nofal have had remarkable success with low-budget productions. With their creative ability they have indeed used the film as an entertaining medium while also touching on some of the country's controversial problems. One film, *Katrina*, which deals with an inter-racial love relationship, handled with sincerity and integrity, was released in 1969 by the Publications Control Board, and is expected to be shown overseas.

In view of the country's potentially small home market, it would seem that only with overseas cooperation could big feature films be produced. In the words of Emil Nofal, the producer of a most entertaining and challenging film, *The Candidate*,

> There is no substitute for imagination and integrity. This is where our future lies: it lies with the young men of resourcefulness and imagination who are going to use this medium without lashings of money and big staff. They are going to go out into life and film it as it is, not fabricate it in a studio. We must lean more towards a documentary approach, like the Continentals.

South African audiences seem to have discovered that the film as an entertaining and popular culture medium and yet possessed of great merit can be produced without big capital or artificiality.

In a heterogeneous society the censor certainly has no easy task. Recent public comment indicates that the images people have of the censors vary in terms of their own views of the functions of the film. By and large, opinions seem to be that the Board of Censors, a sub-unit of the Publications Control Board, is taking into consideration the general trends in popular taste while still fulfilling their task of guarding the nation's morals.

South African folk music, which is vastly popular, should not be confused with the so-called folk music that became popular in the United States in the 1950's. This latter folk music movement has spread in the last decade among the young English-speaking South Africans, especially in Johannesburg, where Keith Blundell and Des Lindbergh are its chief proponents. Unlike the traditional folk music, which has preserved its original characteristic of spontaneity, in rural districts—in some parts until the 1950's—the "folk-pop" movement is an urban recreation found in coffee bars, where it gradually began to lose its original character of self-activity and has become cabaret and music-hall music. To most Afrikaans-speaking South Africans it remains a foreign recreational pastime which on the one hand attracts young people on account of its "differentness"—its so-called modernity—but on the other hand, on account of the lack of songs in their own Afrikaans language, remains for the moment foreign to their characteristically national and own ("volkseie").

It is possible, however, that nineteenth-century history will be repeated: then many songs of visiting "Christy Minstrels" (as visiting American minstrel groups were called from 1848 to the 1870's) became so popular that the melodies, with either translated or new words, were taken up into Afrikaans folk music and accepted as completely indigenous.

A similar influx took place at the same time in spiritual music, where the hymns of Mooday and Sankey, with Dutch and later Afrikaans words, replaced existing hymns, and, in spite of spirited opposition from professional musicians, are still used in the Calvinist service together with the Psalms and evangelical hymns.

But this early borrowing of American folk songs does not mean that there are no original Afrikaans songs and dance tunes. On the contrary, many folk songs played a functional part at picnics and dances right into the twentieth century, so that these songs, in spite of the incoming Anglo-American dance songs, were still used.

Folk-dancing, which began to disappear with the urbanization of a part of the farming population in the twentieth century, re-appeared in a modified form when the so-called "Volkspele" (folk games) movement was started in 1914 by the educationist Dr. S. H. Pellissier at Boshoff in the Orange Free State, in imitation of the Swedish folk dancing movement. Dr. Pellissier avoided the name folk *dancing*, and replaced it by folk *games*, to avoid opposition from the three Calvinist churches. In contrast to real folk dances, volkspele have strict rules governing steps and movements as well as costumes. These have a greater uniformity, which makes possible spectacular mass effects at national festivals but which prevents the unselfconscious and spontaneous fun of true folk dancing. The display element in the volkspele is also foreign to real folk art.

Family Life and Popular Culture

Up to the end of the nineteenth century the writing down of Afrikaans folk songs was unmethodical and sporadic. The Frenchman Charles Etienne Boniface, who settled in South Africa in 1807, wrote down a few melodies in the 1840s and used them with his own words; and in the 1880s a visitor from the Netherlands, Dr. H. P. N. Muller, wrote down a few as illustrations for his story of travels through the Transvaal. The first spiritual folk songs, the so-called "Liederwysies" (song-melodies) were written down and published in the Transvaal in the nineteenth century by an immigrant teacher from the Netherlands, H. Visscher. But most investigators were folklorists or philologists who were more interested in words than in music and who often had no knowledge of music.

There is little to speak of in the way of English South African folk songs, hence the interest in the contemporary "folk song" movement, which is practically all in English.

The case is different with the Coloreds, among whom folk songs were preserved longest, because they retained their functional significance as dance- and work-songs. However, where the function has died out, the folk songs are dying out. Thus, in the nineteenth century in the wine-farming areas of Paarl and Stellenbosch there were a number of songs sung by Coloreds during the wine-making, when they were treading the grapes barefoot. When these songs were wanted in 1968 for the publication of a book on wine culture, nobody could be found who could still sing them. As mechanical means of grape-pressing were adopted, the songs became superfluous and died out. Only an elderly writer who had grown up on a wine farm remembered a few.

In Colored districts where urban culture is still superficial, the typical four-line songs may survive with the form a-a-b-a:

Die kelkie sonder voet,	The wineglass without base
Ja, die kelkie sonder voet,	Yes, wineglass without base
Toe lag ek oor my lippe,	Then I smile with my lips
Maar ek huil in my gemoed.	But I weep in my heart.

or in the form a-a-a-b:

Hier sit ek onder die hoogte,	I sit here under the hill
Hier sit ek onder die hoogte,	I sit here under the hill
Hier sit ek onder die hoogte,	I sit here under the hill
Met trane in my oë.	With tears in my eyes.

Another example is "O, brandewyn laat my staan (three times), Want ek moet nou huis-toe gaan." (O brandy, leave me alone, for I must go home.)

The Cape Malays were, and still are, partly the preservers of the old Dutch song tradition, although today they sing most of their songs in Afrikaans. This group still have their song associations that devote themselves to the singing of various folk songs, usually with the accompaniment of banjos, guitars, and one or more drums. Their repertoire consists of so-called Duth songs (of which the words are already corrupt), sentimental songs, and "moppies" (Calypso-type), of which the first part of the couplet is sung by a leader (voorsanger) and the refrain by a chorus. Each group has its own name and costume, and each year in January, after Ramadan, a great song festival is held in the Cape Town City Hall.

The radio regularly broadcasts instrumental arrangements or choral performances of folk songs and what is still called "Boeremusiek" (farmers' music, or folk music), but this is to a large extent already commercialized. However, for most people this broadcast folk music is the passive experience of what was once active participation. There are Coloreds who possess guitars, but the songs they sing to the guitar accompaniment are of the widely known international sort.

In a land favored by an equable climate and long hours of sunshine, outdoor activities take up a lot of the average citizen's leisure time, but since the greater part of the population lives inland they are not, as in seaboard countries, able to spend most of their free time on the beaches or in the waves. Yet South Africans have excelled at most of the popular outdoor sports, including swimming, where the very absence of the sea has forced the many young swimmers into pools and hence into competitive swimming.

Physical education advocates have of late been worried by the fact that the increased spectator attendance at most sports has not been counter-balanced by a corresponding increase in the number of active participants. This has been particularly true of rugby football, the country's national sport, where many senior clubs, previously able to field as many as six under-19 sides, now find themselves unable to provide one team. Cricket, on the other hand, seems to attract larger numbers every year. The venture of the Afrikaans-speaking section into cricket, together with the success achieved overseas by national teams, no doubt accounts for this upsurge of interest.

The influence of British sport is still strongly felt; by contrast, efforts to introduce American sports, like baseball and softball, have met with relatively little success. Baseball, in fact, is said to be losing favor fast, and in some areas competition has actually stopped.

There is only one sport which has a purely South African origin; this is the game called Jukskei. Played with two bottle-like "pins," the game, like bowls to a certain extent, has its object the scoring of the nearest number of lies and hits.

Rugby football has been the national sport since the first international tour towards the end of the last century. The main impetus to the game came in 1906 when the first South African team to be called the Springboks (after the indigenous type of buck) toured Great Britain with marked success. From the University of Stellenbosch at the Cape, long regarded as the nursery of the game, students carried rugby to all corners of the country and Southern Africa.

Today international tours to and from France, Great Britain, Argentina, New Zealand, and Australia have become a regular feature. Attendance of 60,000 to 80,000 at rugby marches is common and far larger than in most countries with far bigger populations. In fact, South Africa has been said to be rivaled only by the New Zealanders in rugby fervor. Between tours the inter-provincial competition for the coveted Currie Cup (donated by the late Sir Donald Currie, one-time head of the Union Castle Mailship Company), has become an annual event of national importance. Winning the Currie Cup for rugby is comparable to winning the World Series in baseball, and a tremendous amount of provincial prestige is at stake. Spectator fervor reaches fever pitch and quite often key matches are preceded by weeks of heated and quite often acrimonious controversy in the sports and correspondence columns of the daily and the weekend press.

For a young South African boy not to play rugby is quite often frowned upon as marking of "softness" and boys idolize their rugby heroes even more than they do film stars. To be selected to wear the green and gold rugby jersey for your country still represents the highest achievement in South African sport.

The country's record at "rugger" has been a proud one. Next to New Zealand, South Africa can faithfully regard itself as the strongest rugby-playing country in the world; in fact, from 1937 to 1956 the world crown rested firmly in South Africa, despite a determined attempt by New Zealanders to rest it away in 1949.

Many of the most famous rugby players of all time played for South Africa. The names of Bennie Osler, Paul Roos, Hennie Muller, and Gerhard Morkel are still mentioned from reverence in rugby circles all over the world.

Much to the alarm of the rugby administrators, soccer—and more particularly professional soccer—has of late been drawing bigger and bigger crowds. The main reason for this has been the presentation of the game: mostly at night, with drum majorettes in attendance and supporters' clubs whipping up enthusiasm. The National Football League matches often draw crowds of up to 30,000—as compared with 26,000 at the Currie Cup rugby matches. Most matches held on Saturday afternoons draw smaller crowds.

It can thus be said, after four seasons of professional soccer,

> that the game has come to stay, and but for the expulsion of South Africa on political grounds from the international association, would probably already be the country's national sport; that the family man prefers to watch his sport on Weekday nights so as to be free to take part himself or have his leisure away from sport on Saturday afternoons.

It must also be mentioned that competitive sport is prohibited on Sundays, except in Natal where (on account of a remarkable provincial ordinance withstanding the stresses of time) gate money can still be charged on the Sabbath. Thus the tendency to have midweek sport, either evening or afternoon, is likely to increase with time, leaving more and more free leisure hours over the weekend.

Apart from the fact that golf is the third most popular participation sport (angling comes first, followed by bowls), South Africa has done remarkably well at this sport. Names like Gary Player and Bobby Locke have become synonymous with the best anywhere in the world, and every year the country produces a fresh crop of promising juniors. The slight stoical and often dour African outlook, coupled with the climate, which provides excellent year-round opportunity for practice, has probably been responsible for the golfing successes.

We should have produced top-class tennis players more regularly, considering the climate and the opportunities until now to compete all over the world. A few, such as Eric Sturgess before the war and Cliff Drysdale after the war, have made the international class, but our mixed fortunes in Davis and Federation Cup matches are a pointer to the relatively low standard of the game. The answer here lies perhaps in the social approach: while clubs abound, and there is one to be found in the smallest hamlet, style and technique are of little consequence, the social element being all-important.

Cricket has been played in South Africa since the days of the British administration at the Cape, and international tours to Britain since the turn of the century, and to Australasia since the 1930's, have helped to place the game on a firm footing. Until recently, however, it was frowned upon by the Afrikaans-speaking section as an "English game," and as a result was mainly controlled by a select number of clubs in the main centers. Following the post-war successes in Australia and England (South Africa has now twice in succession won Test matches against England and Australia), the game has mushroomed in popularity among the Afrikaans-speaking section.

Apart from these major sports, the most popular are lawn bowling (numerically very strong but more of social value and with little spectator appeal), hockey (with the women in particular ranking among the best in the world), athletics (in which sport South Africa has produced in relation to the number of competitors perhaps the greatest percentage of top-class swimmers, including world-record holder Karen Muir and Ann Fairlie).

Sport has been, ever since the Boer War and the subsequent years of friction between descendants of British and Afrikaners, a singularly unifying force amongst the white section of the population, political and language barriers being forgotten on the sports fields. And it is often said that Premier John Vorster has greatly enhanced his image with the English-speaking section through his avid enthusiasm for golf. Long-range effects of the present national policy that extends apartheid to sports remain to be seen; already international team sports have curtailed with some countries, and Olympic participation has been denied. The fillip that these meetings with world-rated teams provides could affect both spectator enthusiasm and participators' achievements, but these consequences cannot be judged for some time.

The role of music in the popular culture of South Africa is not at all considerable compared to many other countries: opera in Italy; pipe bands in Scotland; orchestral and chamber music in Germany, Austria, and France; guitar music in Spain; and even the high school marching band in the United States (where the performance standard is notably high) are all notable for their omnipresence in the lives of most citizens. But in South Africa these forms of musical expression are peripheral to the general culture. There are, however, numerous choirs, small orchestras of generally non-professional instrumentalists, and local vocalists of near-international quality who have been trained by competent teachers, many associated with the universities. The South African College of Music, a branch of the University of Cape Town, under the leadership of Professor Gunter Pulvermacher, has provided a stimulus to the widening of music in the general culture.

There is as yet no vibrant recording industry; the local companies focus on African jazz and popular vocal and small-group instrumental music that replicates the popular music of Europe and America.

Likewise, theatrical entertainments tend to be part of the local "high culture," except for performances by visiting overseas artists. There is no permanent professional theater group, though amateur musical theater has successes. Both ballet and modern dance have a following. Again, the universities encourage actors and dramatists but have a small, devoted clientele.

To date perhaps the most well-known South African singer has been Miriam Makeba ("Mama Africa"), the daughter of a Swazi mother and a Xhosa father, born in Johannesburg in 1932. In 1954 she formed a group known as the Skylarks, who specialized in Afrobeat, a blend of jazz and traditional melodies of her country. When she was in Venice for the 1959 film festival, where her anti-apartheid documentary, *Come Back, Africa*, was featured, her passport re revoked; she travelled to London, where she met Harry Belafonte, who facilitated her entry—and subsequent popularity—in the United States. She was one of the entertainers at the 1962 birthday party for President John F. Kennedy, and in 1966 she received the Grammy Award for best folk recording; however, after giving testimony before the United Nations Committee Against Apartheid, her records were banned in South Africa, her citizenship was revoked, and she was denied the right to return to her native country.

Bibliography

Andrews, H. T., ed. *South Africa in the Sixties*, 1962.
Bouws, Jan. *Die Afrikaanse Volkslied*, 1958.
Cilliers, S. P. *The Coloureds of South Africa*, 1963.
De Kiewiet, C. W. *A History of South Africa: Social and Economic*, 1957.
De Rider, Cecile. *Volkspele uit Sonnige Suid Afrika*, 1953.
Du Plessis, I. D. *The Cape Malays*, 1944.
Friis, Theo. *The Public Library in South Africa: An Evaluative Study*, 1969.

Kruger, D. W. *The Making of a Nation—A History of the Union of South Africa, 1910-1961*, 1969.
Morton, H. C. V. *In Search of South Africa*, 1948.
Muller, C. F., ed. *Five Hundred Years: A History of South Africa*, 1969.
Pienaar, P. De. V., ed. *Kultuurgeskiedenis Van Die Afrikaner*, 1968.
Theron, Erika, Ed. *Die Kleurlingbevolking Van Suid-Afrika*, 1958.
Young, F. B. *In South Africa*, 1952.

8

Philosophy

Anna L. Conradie

Philosophy is naturally a late-blooming phenomenon in any culture, its study customarily subordinated to immediate, practical needs (except where it is seen as an important adjunct to theology and thus to the preparation of an educated clergy), its students few, its professors in the universities and seminaries often part-time and overworked, its contribution to the commonwealth often derided, ignored, or—more frequently—not adequately valued. In any era or nation there are few who have contributed to the basic areas of philosophy (logic, aesthetics, ethics, epistemology, politics, and metaphysics) new or significantly adapted and modified ideas, so that critics are found who complain that while the sciences always seem to move forward, philosophy seems to stand still, that it is without justification in an economy where cost-effectiveness is the major consideration.

But as that popularizer of philosophy Will Durant commented many years ago, "Most of us have known some golden days in the June of life when philosophy was in fact what Plato calls it, 'that dear delight'; when the love of a modestly elusive Truth seemed more glorious, incomparably, than the lust for the ways of the flesh and the dross of the world." And that Truth has been revealed to many by just a few memorable modern philosophers: Henri Bergson, Benedetto Croce, and Bertrand Russell in Europe; George

Santayana, William James, and John Dewey in the United States. Major philosophers are as infrequently encountered as major poets, novelists, sculptors, or jurists; however, lesser ones make helpful advances at all times, often by elucidation or extension and through analogy, so that their thinking, teaching, and writing can have significant effect in their national cultures. The challenges to developing a guiding philosophy in a nation in which a numerically small group governs a larger populace are not insignificant.

In discussing particular South African philosophers, we shall confine ourselves to those who have become known through their publications to a wider public, both in South Africa and overseas. As far as possible, we group them according to those philosophical trends or schools that they represent.

H. J. de Vleeschauwer is considered a South African philosopher, although he achieved international fame as possibly the greatest world authority on Kant long before he settled in Pretoria after the Second World War. A student of Pirenne and Collé, he became professor of philosophy at the University of Ghent, Belgium, during which period his magnum opus, *La déduction transcendentale dans l'oeuvre de Kant*, appeared in three volumes. (It was also published in an abridged version as *L'Évolution de la pensée kantienne* in 1939.) Heimsoeth's *Tranzendentale Dialektik* was written over a period of ten years in collaboration with de Vleeschauwer. De Vleeschauwer has also established himself as an authority on the Belgian philosopher Arnold Geulincx, to whom he has devoted about twenty works. His own journal, *Mousaion*, published by the University of South Africa, is devoted chiefly to studies on bibliography and librarianship, but it has also contained interesting material on Luther, the Iberian Jesuits, Roger Bacon, Rousseau, and other major philosophers. It is impossible to list here de Vleeschauwer's prodigious publications, but it may be stated that his forte is the historical development of philosophical movements from the Greeks to Rudolf Eucken, the German philosopher who was awarded the Nobel Prize in Literature in 1908 and who established the philosophy of Activism, which emphasized that experience is the source of all value.

Philosophy in South Africa has benefited immensely from the presence of this master teacher during the past twenty years, and he has presented numerous papers at South African and overseas congresses. At the Leibniz Congress at Hannover, Germany, in November 1966, members were overwhelmed by his magnificent exegetical lecture *Perennis quaedam philosophia*. He received many invitations to chairs at universities in other countries but chose to remain head of the department of philosophy at the University of South Africa. As this university functions by means of correspondence courses, he retained enough leisure to devote himself entirely to scholarship; he is now retired.

The Idealist school of philosophy found its two most influential exponents in South Africa in R. F. A. Hoernlé (1880-1943) and A. H. Murray (b. 1905), the grandson of the famous nineteenth-century theologian and minister.

Hoernlé was born at Bonn, Germany, and received his training at the Protestant Landesschule at Pforte, near Naumburg on the Saale, and at Balliol College, Oxford. He then accepted a lectureship at St. Andrew's University in Scotland under Bernard Bosanquet. The influence of Bosanquet on Hoernlé's thought is evident in the Bosanquet-Hoernlé correspondence, since published. In 1908 he took up his first professorship at the then South African College, now the University of Cape Town. His heavy burden of work—he also acted for a year as professor of education and as vice-chancellor of the senate—left him little time for writing or research. Nevertheless, he produced students of the higher caliber such as Jan Hofmeyr and Mrs. Bertha Solomon, both of whom became distinguished figures on the South African parliamentary scene.

After four years Hoernlé moved on to the University of Durham and thereafter joined the department of philosophy at Harvard University. His six years at Harvard brought him into contact with many of the ablest philosophical thinkers in the United States, such as R. B. Perry and W. E. Hocking. His wife's failing health caused him to return to South Africa as professor of philosophy at the new University of the Witwatersrand, Johannesburg, where he remained until his death in 1943. He had come to the University with an established reputation as a philosopher and he soon attracted some brilliant young men to his department: Ian Douglas MacCrone, who later became head of the department of psychology and is now principal of the University of the Witwatersrand; and Andrew Murray, who lectured under him and in 1937 became head of the department of philosophy at the University of Cape Town.

Hoernlé represented the school of Absolute Idealism. He himself termed his idealism the "synoptic approach," inasmuch as he attempted to cohere the various dimensions of reality in the light of a common principle: the mind is a microcosm in which is focused the whole of reality as nature, man, and God. Yet his attempt at synthesis did not entirely succeed. Aspects of human existence such as religion, science, and social life he treated too much as substantive entities without succeeding in finding a unifying principle that would show their coherence. While he thus began with the search for a synoptic view, he ended with a "Schichtenlehre," a doctrine of degrees or levels of reality.

With the synoptic ideal in mind, he took a special interest in the social and political problems of his adopted country. In *South African Native Policy and the Liberal Spirit* (1940), Hoernlé first gives an account of native policy in the Union, including a history of Black-White relations and a critical account of present-day "techniques of domination" in the political, educational, economic, and social fields; thereafter, he analyses the meaning of liberalism. His main argument is that liberty must always be understood as "liberties" and that the two questions (a) What liberties should we strive for? and (b) Who is to enjoy them? have always been answered in concrete historical contexts in such a way that an absolute claim for unrestricted liberty for all men has, in practice, turned out to be a limited claim for specific liberties for a determinate class or group of human beings. The historical setting in which the classical doctrine of liberalism was evolved did not include the setting of a multi-racial society such as in South Africa, in which a minority racial group is the dominant group; hence, liberal ideas have to be re-examined in their application to a society of this type. Hoernlé presents three such possible applications: thorough-going parallelism, total interracial assimilation, or total racial dissociation (or apartheid). All three are compatible with the liberal spirit; but if they are applied only in half-measures, they become domination-cum-trusteeship. These ideas were also developed in earlier articles published in the journal *Race Relations* (of which he became the president), such as "Peoples in South Africa" and "Present-Day Trends in South African Race Relations."

Since the death of Hoernlé, Professor A. H. Murray is the most important exponent of Idealism in South Africa. He studied at the University of Stellenbosch and as a Rhodes scholar went to Oxford, Geneva, and Paris, where he studied under Henri Bergson. At Oxford he obtained the degrees of D. Phil. and B. Litt. On his return to South Africa he worked under Hoernlé for six years and was then appointed as head of the department of philosophy in the University of Cape Town. Apart from his academic duties, he has served on the Library Commission, the Commission of Native Education, as Advisor to the Government on Communism, as Advisor to the Hague International Court on South-West African problems, and since 1963 has been a member of the South African Board of Censors. Apart from many articles, his main publications are *The Philosophy of James Ward* (1937), *Die Volksraad* (1940), and *The Political Philosophy of J. A. de Mist* (1950). He also edited Professor Gonin's translation of Beza's *De Jure Magistratum* (1956).

Murray has always expounded the idealist point of view, notably that of Bradley and Bosanquet, in his teaching. As he is primarily a political philosopher, his main contribution to philosophy in South Africa has consisted in the application of the idealism that he shared with Hoernlé to problems that have arisen particularly in South African social life. This has taken the form of the development of a concept of liberalism which is in many respects opposed to that of Hoernlé.

According to Murray, true liberalism is to be tested in terms of the quality of the human life that it makes possible in a specific historical situation, in the maintenance of the sovereignty of law, and in the absence of stratification between the members of a society. The observance of the two historic devices of liberalism, rule of law and the international autonomy of the historic community, shows us how to maintain liberalism in a racially plural state. When corporations are entrenched in their own legal rights we may achieve liberalism without recourse to "techniques of domination." Murray considers that the liberal must not be afraid to admit the fact of diversities in the population and to maintain these historic diversities in the state. Their maintenance is one of the principles for which liberalism stands, as also devolution of sovereign power, decentralization of the administrative functions of the state, and a policy of separatism involving a diversity of internal autonomies for historical groups. This conception of liberalism Murray finds in the liberal tradition expounded by thinkers such as Hugo Grotius (1583-1645), John Calvin, and especially in the *Vindiciae contra tyrannos*, which is now generally ascribed to Du Plessis-Mornay and Hubert Languet. In his outstanding study of Commissioner-General J. A. De Mist, he shows how De Mist introduced the notion of political pluralism into South African political thinking during the Batavian period in order to maintain the rights of minorities.

An outstanding representative of the school of contemporary British philosophy was Professor D. J. Costhuizen (1926-1969). Having completed his training at Stellenbosch, he studied linguistic philosophy in Amsterdam under Professor Pos and later in Britain. Costhuizen was known primarily for his application of the analytical methods of British linguistic philosophy to political and religious problems. His most remarkable publication is *Analysis of Nationalism* (1965). In these essays he analyzes concepts such as "Afrikaans," "Afrikanerdom," "Christian," "Christendom," "National," and "the will of God," and explores to role of ideology and metaphor in current religious and political talk in South Africa.

Undoubtedly two of the most gifted philosophers in South Africa at present are Professor M. Versfeld of the University of Cape Town and Professor J. J. Degenaar of the University of Stellenbosch. Both are within the existentialist and phenomenological traditions.

Professor Degenaar studied at the University of Stellenbosch and thereafter at the University of Groningen in the Netherlands under Helmuth Plessner and Gerhard van der Leeuw and at Leiden under C. A. van Peursen. His books are relatively short and consist mainly of essays dealing with aspects of a common theme. They are written in Afrikaans and are therefore inaccessible to a public not conversant with Afrikaans or Dutch. He has encountered considerable opposition from conservative Afrikaner intellectuals, but his influence, both at the University of Stellenbosch and at other Afrikaans universities, is steadily increasing.

Degenaar's works fall into two categories. The first category deals more particularly with the interpretation and assessment of individual thinkers. *Evolusie en Christendom* (1965) is a sympathetic treatment of the French Jesuit and paleontologist Teilhard de Chardin. *Die Wêreld van Albert Camus* (1966) is an introduction to the thought of Albert Camus, with particular emphasis on his treatment of absurdity, revolt, and solidarity. *Exsistensie en Gestalte* (1962) is devoted to an analysis of existentialist traits in the poetry of the greatest Afrikaans poet N. P. van Wyk Louw, who was himself profoundly influenced by contemporary European philosophy.

The second category has a much wider scope. *Die Sterflikheid van die Siel* (1963) is an introduction to phenomenological anthropology. The author rejects the traditional dichotomy between the mortal body and the immortal soul. His emphasis on the "mortality" of the soul in effect underlies the unity of man and his commitment to this world and to his fellow human beings. Within this context Dagenaar is able to reinstate the doctrine of the resurrection and to develop a functional theology.

Op Weg na 'n nuwe politieke lewenshouding (1963) consists of four essays in which he attempts to orientate man in the political realities of the twentieth century. The influence of Kierkegaard,

Buber, Husserl, and Heidegger is clearly evident. The theme of the book is presented by the author as follows: man is man through his relationship with men. This involves a new humanism that rejects the Cartesian conception of man as a being enclosed within himself, a thing that manipulates other things and is in turn manipulated. This new humanism is not a fact but a task: it demands that one should escape from self-created subjectivist and nationalist ghettos and stand open and receptive towards other men and other peoples. Only thus does man become whole and "at home" in the world.

In the important little book *Sekularisasie* (1967) these ideas are further developed within the framework of secularization and solidarity. The author argues that the secularization of Western culture either alienates men from one another and from their world or leads to a growing solidarity and intersubjectivity among men. He is particularly interested in the latter possibility, which involves a theology of encounter. Particular attention is paid to the contribution of political ideologies and theological dogmatism to the dehumanization of man. As in all his works, Degenaar here reveals his ability to present the highly technical concepts of contemporary continental philosophy in an exceptionally clear and stimulating manner. This makes his thinking accessible also to the non-philosophic public.

Professor Martin Versfeld is undoubtedly the most powerful philosophical personality in South Africa. He was educated at the Universities of Cape Town and Glasgow, where he obtained a doctorate in philosophy under Professor A. A. Bowman. In spite of offers of chairs at other universities, he has chosen to remain in Cape Town.

Versfeld is fluent in both English and Afrikaans and publishes in both languages. His most important works are: *An Essay on the Metaphysics of Descartes* (1940), a thomist interpretation of Descartes; *The Perennial Order* (1954), and *The Mirror of Philosophy* (1960), which are collections of essays on philosophers and philosophical problems; *A Guide to the City of God* (1958), a definitive work on St. Augustine; and *Rondom die Middeleeue* (1962), an excellent Afrikaans introduction to the philosophy of the Middle Ages. In South Africa Versfeld is considered to be a "thomist" philosopher, and he is indeed the greatest mediaeval scholar in the country. However, his thomism was always wedded to a personalist philosophy, and of late his keen participation in ecumenical problems—he translated into English A. Hulsbosch's contentious theological work *God's Creation* (1965)—and his growing interest in aspects of existentialism, phenomenology, and Eastern philosophy have caused him to break with many of the concepts, and the vocabulary, of official thomism. His latest publications express a situational philosophy which has caused him to write on many problems of acute topical interest in South Afrika. His brilliant handling of the essay form, combined with a phenomenal erudition, has rightly earned him a reputation not only as a philosopher but as a literary artist.

Apart from his book on the Middle Ages, Versfeld has published in Afrikaans: *Oor Gode en Afgode* (1948) and *Wat is Kontemporêr?* (1953), which are collections of essays on morality and history; *Berge van die Boland* (with W. A. de Klerk, 1947), an account of his experiences as a mountaineer and amateur botanist (like Kolbe he has had a species of Cape wild flowers named after him); and *Klip en Klei* (1968). In this book he describes the building of his cottage for his large family on his farm in the Kouga in the Long Kloof. One of these essays, in which he relates his adventures and thoughts as an angler on the Cape coast, was written while he was a visiting professor at Notre Dame University in the United States and reflects his nostalgia for his own country. The personal details are almost imperceptibly interwoven with philosophical reflections. The theme that he develops throughout these memoirs is that of being at home, a theme that involves an analysis of one's relation to others, to nature, and to God. The last essay, "On Patriotism," in which he also discusses General Christiaan Smuts, the man and the thinker, achieves a scope and power that reveals the author's deep understanding of St. Augustine. In the last analysis the patriot is the man who can only be "at home" in his own country, because he is a citizen of the City of God. A combined publication by Versfeld, Degenaar, Adam

Small, and W. A. de Klerk, in which Versfeld contributed an essay, "Morality and Moralism," appeared in 1969.

The northern provinces of South Africa boast of only one outstanding and original phlosopher, Professor H. G. Stoker, who some years ago retired from the chair of philosophy at the University of Potchefstroom in the Transvaal. He occupies a unique position in the philosophical life of South Africa, as he was the first to develop an indigenous Calvinist philosophy that has influenced not only the entire structure of studies at his university but has also inspired Calvinist thinking in both Europe and America.

Stoker studied as an undergraduate at the University of Potchefstroom; in 1922 he obtained his doctorate in Germany under one of the fathers of modern phenomenology, Max Scheler. His thesis, *Das Gewissen* (1925), is today still an authoritative work. He has lectured at many international philosophical congresses, and he attended the Seventh International Congress at Oxford with Professor Hoernlé. He represented South Africa at the first Ecumenical Synod of the Reformed Churches at Grand Rapids, Michigan, and his lectures during this visit to America and also during former visits earned him a lasting reputation among American Calvinist philosophers.

During his long term of service at Potchefstroom University, and as co-editor of *Philosophia Reformata*, the organ of the Dutch Neo-Calvinist philosophy, Professor Stoker played an important role in the creation of a specifically Calvinist way of thinking and as the author of an original Calvinist school of philosophy. (Calvin himself never developed a philosophy.) The first signs of a Calvinist philosophy emerged in the thought of Abraham Kuyper, who was at one time prime minister of the Netherlands. Kuyper considered that Calvinism was not only a theology but a complete view of life that contained also the principles of science and philosophy. These principles Kuyper found in Scripture. The school of Calvinist philosophy at the Free University of Amsterdam developed Kuyper's views by conceiving of philosophy as an account of the whole of reality. But such an account presupposes an "archimedean point," a standpoint *outside* the cosmos in terms of which the cosmic totality may be interpreted. For Professor Bavinck this archimedean point was Revelation; for Professor Dooyeweerd it was the idea of God as Sovereign and supreme Lawgiver; and for Professor Stoker it is God as Creator, hence his philosophic system is termed the Philosophy of the Idea of Creation (*Wysbegeerte van die Skeppingsidee*).

Stoker differs from Dooyeweerd, the most influential exponent of Calvinist philosophy in the Netherlands, in rejecting Dooyeweerd's philosophy of the cosmonomic idea, derived from the notion of God as Sovereign. Dooyeweerd's philosophy leads to a stratification of modal spheres, each revealing its own laws derived from God's universal law. For Stoker the idea of creation is more supple: it lacks the rigidity of Dooyeweerd's modal structures inasmuch as it emphasizes not only the lawfulness of the cosmos but also its spontaneity, freedom, and creative development. According to Stoker, the idea of creation permits of no single basic idea or archimedean point. He postulates a plurality of perspectives, all compatible with Calvinism, which has the advantage of encompassing a greater number and diversity of phenomena. Stoker's philosophy is consequently far less dogmatic than Dooyeweerd's; nevertheless, Stoker agrees with Dooyeweerd that all philosophy is influenced by religious presuppositions which ultimately depend on the philosopher's commitment to an absolute, whether this absolute is the Christian God or some absolutization of a cosmic aspect. The analysis of the role of religious presuppositions in philosophy is one of the most important contributions of Calvinist philosophy.

Professor Stoker has applied his philosophy to various philosophical problems in many articles and publications, both in South Africa and overseas. His book *Beginsels en Metodes in die Wetenskap* (1961) shows its application especially in the field of university studies. In a much earlier work, *Die Stryd om die Ordes* (1942), Stoker's conception of the unity and diversity of the cosmos leads to a theory of political pluralism. His philosophical position also explains his attitude to ecumenism. Ecumenism, interpreted as an attempt to eradicate bona fide religious commitments in favor of a common religious denominator, is a form of rationalism. For Stoker a more acceptable interpretation of ecumenism is an open dialogue between the churches, not with the intention of obtaining a consensus of opinion but of practicing self-examination with respect to contradictions and antinomies in unacknowledged and uncritically accepted theological assumptions. For the same reason Stoker finds no difficulty in accepting the "Conscience Clause" operating at the Universities of Potchefstroom and Bloemfontein (which demands that their staff members should belong to one of the Calvinist churches) for he considers that a university which is committed to a faith does not retard but promotes the quality of its teaching.

Professor Stoker is not only one of the finest philosophical scholars in South Africa but also one of the most open-minded of Calvinist philosophers. A volume of essays dedicated to him on his seventieth birthday was published in 1969: contributions in English, Afrikaans, and Dutch were made by scholars from within and outside of South Africa. (The publication fittingly coincided with the centenary celebrations of the University of Potchefstroom.)

It is noteworthy that three eminent South African politicians of the twentieth century were, in varying degrees, philosophers. Dr. D. F. Malan, who brought the Nationalist Party into power in 1948, obtained his doctorate at the University of Utrecht with a dissertation entitled *The Objective Idealism of Berkeley*. In his political thinking he applied his objective idealism in asserting that every nation or ethnic entity expresses an idea of God. According to him, nationalism means respect for the order imposed by God on his creation. Dr. H. F. Verwoerd, although primarily a sociologist and psychologist, developed Dr. Malan's political philosophy. But from the point of view of philosophy itself, General J. C. Smuts is undoubtedly the most important figure, both for the formal presentation of his philosophical position in *Holism and Evolution* and for the application of this position as premier, soldier, and statesman.

Jan Christiaan Smuts (1870-1950) studied law at the University of Stellenbosch and at Cambridge. On his return to

South Africa in 1895 he was admitted to the bar and began to take an active interest in politics. During the Anglo-Boer war he commanded a force against Britain, but during the First World War he defended the Allied cause. His first important publication was a pamphlet, *The League of Nations: A Practical Suggestion* (1918), which influenced Woodrow Wilson to a considerable extent. In the intervening period between his two terms of office as prime minister (1919-1924 and 1939-1945) he completed his book *Holism and Evolution* (1926), which brought him worldwide fame and which is still prescribed at some European universities. According to Smuts, the holistic factor is operative already in the formation of elementary physical wholes. Through a series of "creative leaps" it operates also in biological structures and in persons. Smuts's views are of the same climate of thought as those of Henri Bergson and Lloyd Morgan. All three philosophers opposed Darwin's account of evolution and interpreted it rather as "creative evolution," the engendering of novelties that cannot be explained by mechanistic materialism. Nevertheless, Smuts does not agree with Bergson and Morgan that the holistic factor is either a spiritual or a teleological principle. He thus cannot identify his holism wth Bergson's *élan vital* or Morgan's directing activity, and holism remains, according to critics, a somewhat enigmatic principle. Irrespective of its metaphysical validity, his theory of holism did influence his political philosophy in that he believed in the integration of nations into supra-national wholes. It was this idea that was the driving force behind his promotion of the League of Nations, the United Nations, and the Commonwealth. Yet, while Smuts's views were apparently opposed to those of Malan and Verwoerd, all three statesmen were essentially concerned with the same problem: the conditions for the peaceful co-existence of national or ethnic groups. The rise of technology and the implications of universal technological infrastructures for national and cultural patterns, however, demands the introduction of new philosophical categories and methods of analysis. That this challenge is being seriously considered by the present generation of academic philosophers in South Africa augurs well for the continued existence of a critical and constructive tradition of philosophical thinking in South Africa.

The tension between different philosophical perspectives accentuates the need for communication between philosophers representing widely varying schools of thought. In South Africa this need led in 1951 to the first Congress for the Advancement of Philosophy in South Africa, initiated and organized by the department of philosophy at the University of Cape Town. Thereafter, every two years (and of late, every year) congresses have been held at all major universities in South Africa. At these congresses usually at least one member of each department of philosophy in the country reads a paper and the discussions, both formal and informal, have contributed immensely to a better understanding between philosophers often separated by great distances in both the literal and figurative sense. Congresses are conducted in both official languages (English and Afrikaans) and are uniracial, at least with respect to membership. When Professor A. L. Conradie in 1965 invited Mr. Adam Small, the colored Afrikaans poet and philosopher of the University College of Wes-Kaapland (for colored students) to attend the Durban Congress and to read a paper, his university college refused him the usual financial assistance allocated to congress-goers on the ground that non-Whites should participate only in non-White congresses—in spite of the fact that Mr. Small was the only non-White philosopher in South Africa and that a non-White philosophical congress would thus be a one-man show. The then principal of the University of Natal, Dr. E. G. Malherbe, thereupon offered him the necessary financial assistance, and lodging was arranged for him in the home of a Durban member of the academic staff of the University of Natal. But the attitude of his college was such that he thought it prudent not to attend.

Most South African departments of philosophy publish papers by their members of staff in journals sponsored by their universities, such as the *Bulletin* of the department of philosophy of the University of Cape Town, *Occasional Papers* of the department at Rhodes University, and *Bulletin vir die Suid-Afrikaanse Vereniging vir die Bevordering van Christelike*

Wetenskap of the University of Potchefstroom. Since 1964, however, *The South African Journal of Philosophy* (*Die Suid-Afrikaanse Tydskrif vir Wysbegeerte*) has appeared with an editorial committee consisting of Professor A. H. Murray, Professor J. J. Degenaar, and Dr. S. I. M. du Plessis. The editorial board consists of the heads of departments of philosophy of all South African universities (as distinguished from university colleges, which are still controlled by the University of South Africa). To this journal South African philosophers from various universities are able to contribute, and it is distributed also overseas. Tentative explorations are being made with respect to the possibility and feasibility of an inter-African journal of philosophy.

Visits from eminent overseas philosophers are encouraged, and South African universities have special funds to make such visits possible. Among such distinguished visitors have been Karl Löwith (Heidelberg), R. C. Kwant (Utrecht), C. A. van Peursen (Leiden), and H. van Riessen, S. U. Zuidema, and H. Dooyeweerd (Free University, Amsterdam). Many of these lecturing tours have been made possible by the *Genootskap Nederland-Suid Afrika*. Visits of South African philosophers to other South African universities are also encouraged.

Bibliography

Bfookes, E. H. *Apartheid: A Documentary Study of Modern South Africa*, 1968.
Cawood, L. *The Churches and Race Relations in South Africa*, 1960.
Conradie, A. L. *The Neo-Calvinist Concept of Philosophy*, 1960.
Davies, H. *Great South African Christians*, 1951.
Smuts, J. C. *Holism and Evolution*, 1926.

Public Address

A. L. McLeod

*P*ublic address, formerly called oratory or public speaking, has always been a determining factor in the development of any country's culture, though it was often late in being recorded accurately and completely and then becoming one of the principal components of national literature, often providing the basis for the development of a characteristic style or method of argument.

Great speeches are indeed few, yet those of important representatives of church, state, the courts—and even dissident organizations—in any society can often help us to understand the course of events and thus of history itself. "And what," asked Demosthenes in his famous oration "On the Crown," "is the duty of a statesman? To watch the inception of events, to descry their tendency, and to forewarn his countrymen." This obligation is not restricted, of course, merely to statesmen, but is to be expected of all who would participate in any controversy—but particularly in leaders of public opinion, such as preachers, legislators, and representatives of the vast majority of normally undemonstrative citizens, most of whom are uninstructed in the principles of rhetoric and dialectic yet eager to have their thoughts enunciated by their surrogates.

Throughout Africa there is a growing awareness of the role of speeches in the literary no less than in the political life of a nation. Julius Nyerere has issued at least five volumes of his principal speeches; Jomo Kenyatta published two collections; Nnamdi Azikiwi, Kwame Nkrumah, and Milton Obote have all had speeches issued in book form. And if the issues that they speak to are frequently the same as those that engaged the attention of the great British orators such as Pitt, Burke, Fox, Sheridan, and Mansfield, this merely suggests how slowly political and social changed has proceeded in the world. But their illustrations and examples, their supports and proofs, their lines of attack and defense—taken from their own experience or from those of their audiences and expressed in the idiom of their place and time often provide models of eloquence and persuasion not to be found for modern-day listeners in speeches of bygone ages.

South African poetry and prose have become familiar to readers both within and outside the country through the commercial publication of individual works and of anthologies; literary criticism reaches audiences throughout the world via the major scholarly journals; but because so many individuals are subjected to restraints, their speeches can not be freely circulated, they can not any longer address public gatherings, and their ideas are withheld from those who are free to hear them. While official government spokesmen have their speeches fully reported within the Republic and distributed abroad, opposition speakers can at best hope to find their speeches preserved beyond the moment of delivery in leaflets printed by job printers, in small-circulation journals of special-interest organizations, or in the massive and hence formidable volumes of *Hansard*. The effect is that the full range of South African thought as expressed in public speeches is rarely encountered by even a serious, interested reader.

However, in any consideration of South African public speaking one is constantly aware of two subjects—religion and race—that have been introduced into almost all speeches, regardless of their ostensible subject or theme, their place of delivery or audience. In few other countries can this phenomenon be so clearly discerned, but where considerations of race and of religion are so pervasive in the very life of a nation, it is only to be expected that these matters should find their way into the thoughts, the serious deliberations, and public discourse of the people, whether deliberative, forensic, homiletic, or epideictic.

In all the former colonies that now constitute the Commonwealth, creative writing is preceded by general prose (usually descriptive and statistical), and that, in turn, by speeches (normally sermons of thanksgiving and administrative discourses) in the evolution of their national literatures. The same phenomenon is to be noted in South Africa, and there as elsewhere the sermon rapidly developed into a literary artifact that combined the best qualities of the essay and of the rhetorical exercise, that was influenced by the examples of the dynamic Episcopal and Presbyterian preachers of Europe, and was guided by such works as Perkins's *The Art of Prophesying*, Aristotle's *Rhetoric*, and Blair's *Lectures on Rhetoric and Belles Letters* as well as the Dutch heuristics. As Brastow points out in *The Modern Pulpit*, "the freshness, the freedom, and the individuality that had characterized the preaching of the Reformation period vanished," to be replaced by more elaborately and formally argumentative sermons that appealed to the understanding through elaborate theological analysis. But in the sermons of the two Murrays we can see the "freshness, freedom, and individuality" of the post-eighteenth-century divines and then the more formal analytical method of the nineteenth century. Preaching, as they did, before vast audiences throughout their ministries, their influence can not be under-estimated: in their own way, they helped to make permanent the influence of organized religion on the very core of South African society. Yet their influence was restricted largely to white congregations, and they apparently did not see fit to broach the matter of race relations directly or often. Of course, in 1815 the London Missionary Society had advised Caribbean missionaries against sympathizing with slaves who were discontented with their roles and counseled them to "enforce upon them the necessity of being subject," and this attitude must have been widespread among the colonial clergy.

Sir George Rose, a British parliamentarian, published in 1823 *A Letter on the Means and Importance of Converting the Slaves in the West Indies to Christianity*, which bears on the problems encountered by preachers in all the outposts of Empire, including South Africa:

> Our clergy, educated at our universities on a scale necessary for the due performance of their regular functions to European audiences are raised too far above the level of the comprehension and reasoning of the heathen negro for it to be practicable for them to lower themselves to the standard of such mental operations as, however, are indispensable for the instruction of a being so enlightened and so little capable of thought and reflection as the uninstructed slave is found to be. (12)

But he thought that the clergy of the evangelical and nonconformist sects would be able to preach to Blacks:

> He is used to deal with ignorant men of coarse habits; he knows how to set about making himself understood by them; how to unrave their half-intelligible jargon and to descry and aid the first glimmerings of their reason and conviction. None of these things can be expected from the graduated member of an English university. (15)

There were, however, some Oxford-trained missionaries in Africa who managed to establish genuine identification with the native peoples (Arthur Shearly Cripps was one of the most successful), though such evidence as that presented in *They Led the Way: Christian Pioneers of Central Africa* attests to the greater success of Methodists at Umtali, Dominican sisters at Macloutie, the Salvation Army in Rhodesia, and the self-educated Scot, Robert Moffat, among the Matabele and Namaquas. As their outreach grew, their preaching increased in frequency, sophistication, and efficacy, and their concern for the native peoples was undiminished by the reluctance of government to consider the Blacks as deserving of those considerations that were thought minimal for Whites. So it is not astonishing to read, in Rhodes's "The Bases of South African

Government," that he thought that the missionaries were overstepping their mark by advocating even limited franchise for advanced and qualified natives.

Clearly, where the rudiments of English alone were familiar to converts, preaching of a high order was impossible; nonetheless, preaching of some merit has been no less rare in South Africa than elsewhere, especially in the larger English and Afrikaans congregations. Perhaps the most agreeable sermons to non-Afrikaans readers are those by the Anglican bishops Joost de Blank and Ambrose Reeves, who have been in the very vanguard of the liberal movement for political and social reform. In their sermons and diocesan addresses they addressed the fundamental issue of Christian recognition of the rights of all peoples, regardless of race or color, rejecting the Victorian concept of trusteeship by Whites, which is implicit in even the most enlightened versions of apartheid, or "separate development," propounded by the Nationalist party and theologians of the Dutch Reformed Church in South Africa. Nonetheless, as Arthur Pollard notes in his *English Sermons*, "The secular trends of our day have all but destroyed the sermon as literature": it has become a polemical tract or essay in some pulpits and an exegetical exercise in others; this transformation was heralded in William Plomer's *Turbott Wolfe* (1926), in which the Rev. Mr. Friston, a missionary, confides to Wolfe:

> I believe that the white man's day is over. Anybody can see plainly that the world is quickly and inevitably becoming a colored world. I do not assert that miscegenation should be actually encouraged but I believe that it is the missionary's work now, and the work of any white man in Africa worth his salt, to prepare the way for the ultimate end. Let us take the native, and instead of yapping to him about Jesus Christ and Noah's ark, let us tell him about himself, not in relation to Hebrew folk-lore, but in relation to himself and the white man. That is where my work lies. (123)

While Cecil Rhodes's statement, "We must adopt a system of despotism, such as works so well in India, in our relations with the barbarian of South Africa," is perhaps the most candid statement of a belief all too widespread in his era, it can be argued that the attitude that it represents has not altered fundamentally in the intervening years—at least in the dominant group. Some years later Rhodes said that he was prepared to offer the natives the franchise when they could operate the telephone system, but today such employments have been withdrawn from those to which Blacks can aspire. And Kruger, in his long "Fourth Inaugural Address" made it clear that full enjoyment of the richness of South African life he envisioned only for Europeans. Fundamentally, the equal opportunity that people seek is dependent upon that liberty that Smuts wished for all people towards the end of his days and which itself was impossible without what his intellectual colleague Jan Hoymeyr identified as the "fifth freedom"—freedom from prejudice based on race and color.

While most Nationalist oratory is couched in terms of Christian trusteeship motivated by a genuine concern for the unfettered development of tribal or racial culture, this pseudo-benevolence is presented by Dr. Verwoerd in a more realistic focus in his 1948 exposition of the policy of apartheid; here, camouflaged by irrelevant considerations and false analogies, he states the fundamental issues: "South Africa is a white man's country, and he must remain the master here," and "Once [the natives] are given the vote...the opportunity is given to them to get the balance of power into their hands." Hence, the policy of apartheid, or separate development, is not so much a reaction to race or to color as to fear of loss of authority and status, or power.

Only now is the Dutch Reformed Church re-examining its own past genteel acquiescence in this political policy, which it had equated with the law of God, and questioning whether what had been presented as Christian principle was not merely Nationalist expediency. That it has allowed itself to be used so long and not spoken up sooner is to be regretted; that it is now speaking up at all is commendable.

Fortunately, there are signs of change. The Rev. C. F. Byers Naude, formerly a member of the Nationalist party, has reexamined his political and religion position and now leads the Christian Institute of Southern Africa, having been deprived of pastoral privileges by the Dutch Reformed Church on account of his activities in behalf of a more "Christian" approach to race relations; the dean of Johannesburg cathedral, the Very Rev. Gonville French-Baytagh was sentenced to five years in prison for questioning the nation's racial legislation: Rev. Brian Brown and Rev. Theo Kotze of Cape Town have been "banned" (severely restricted in movement and expression) for preaching at Methodist church gatherings in favor of liberal reform and gradualism in ending the policy of apartheid. And some theologians of the Cape Province synod of the Nederduitse Gereformeerde Kerk described racial discrimination as "an evil which is in conflict with the Biblical message of the equality of all people," and the synod itself passed a resolution opposing "all racial discrimination which is in conflict with the ethical norm of love for one's neighbor" or that conflicts with "justice."

In the development of South Africa the Dutch Reformed Church has always played a significant—and sometimes a crucial—role, and within both the church and the country the influence of the Reverend Dr. Andrew Murray (1794-1866) is always to be discerned. Originally his strong individual witness to evangelistic Christianity directly influenced the lives and thinking of his immediate congregations; subsequently, his religious and philosophical views—elaborated and propagated by his son—influenced those whose knowledge of the preacher was attenuated by time and distance alike, but who nonetheless sought a Scriptural basis for their lives and behavior. In a country in which contemporary social policy is frequently justified by allusion to Christian belief and text it could be argued that the influence of Andrew Murray has been more pervasive than that of any clergyman except his son. And the basis of his widespread, continuing effect was his great skill as a preacher.

Murray, whose family had long been sheep farmers in Clatt, Aberdeenshire, was brought up as an adherent of "Old Light," or evangelical Presbyterianism. His eldest brother, John, entered the Presbyterian ministry, and Andrew decided to pursue the same vocation. Accordingly, he entered King's College in Aberdeen and prepared for missionary work. For ten months he studied in Utrecht, so that he might become proficient in Dutch; and when, in 1821, Dr. George Thom was in Scotland in search of clergy to minister in the Cape Colony, Murray was selected as one of four Presbyterians for that purpose. He left London on February 27, 1822 for the four-month voyage to Cape Town. On arrival, he was re-ordained at the church in Graaff-Reinert, which he served without interruption for the next forty-five years.

In 1824 Murray participated in the first synod of the Dutch Reformed Church held in South Africa, after which the ties with the Netherlands were severed. At this meeting he was selected as a member of the commission which established church polity; in 1834 he became secretary of synod; in 1837 he became moderator. Largely because of his ability to speak with clarity and force in Dutch, Murray was one of those sent in the first delegation to visit the Voortrekkers north of the Orange River in 1848. On this journey some 800 children were baptized and large groups attended divine services at which Murray preached.

Murray was an indefatigable preacher; though most of his sermons were delivered in Dutch, a number of them, written out in full in his notably even and legible script, are retained in the NGK archives in Cape Town. Many of his sermon manuscripts are still in private hands, however. Because he married into an influential Cape Dutch family (that of Johann Stegmann), wholly identified with his parishioners, and never revisited Scotland, Murray adopted Dutch as his own primary language, and this at a time when English was being given preferential treatment that led ultimately to its ascendancy in 1865. As T. R. H. Davenport notes in *The Oxford History of South Africa*, "When Sir George Grey opened parliament in April 1857, his speech was gazetted in both languages; but when Sir Philip

Wodehouse opened the session of 1870, his speech was given only in English."

Davenport comments, also, that "A policy of thoroughgoing Anglicanization would have required the capture of the Afrikaner's cultural citadel, his church," but this was not attempted, and "gradually the English language came to be used with growing frequency in service of the N. G. Kerk, especially in the Groote Kerk, Cape Town."

Murray was an individual of profound piety and obvious sincerity: his Sabbath observance was in strict conformity to the dictates of Scottish puritanism, and he was tireless in his exhortation of his congregation to regular worship, frequent reading of Scripture, genuine repentance, and repudiation of the attractions of the world. Accordingly, his sermons have a pervasive fundamentalism that is often tinged with an apocalyptic vision and (from a modern standpoint) assume a far greater depravity in his audience than seems plausible.

His sermons contain many of those purple passages that were once considered the hallmark of inspired and inspirational preaching; are marked by frequent repetition and inordinate restatement; are supported by Biblical allusion, quotation, and paraphrase; and only rarely resort to structured argumentation of inductive or deductive form. More common is argumentation from exigency, as in a sermon on I Peter 4:7 ("The end of all things is at hand"), in which repentance is recommended as an urgent necessity for the soul's salvation. Nonetheless, the addition of examples and elucidations to his manuscripts suggests that Murray gave considerable thought to the total effect of his sermons and approached their composition fully aware of their potential as instruments of Divine power. Murray's biographer in *The South African Dictionary of National Biography* observes that

> Characteristic features of Murray's preaching were simplicity, warmth, and complete sincerity. The themes he preferred were spiritual rebirth, conversion, and sanctification; this is borne out of eight of his numerous sermons which have been preserved, as well as by his

synodal sermon, based on Zech. 6:12, and delivered at the historic session of 1862, the text of which was used once again for the opening address at the synod in Cape Town in 1962.

Without doubt, that text applied with particular aptness to Murray himself—especially the words, "he shall grow up out of his place, and he shall build the temple of the Lord."

Unquestionably, the most influential churchman in South Africa has been the Reverend Andrew Murray Jr. (1828-1917). As both preacher and pamphleteer he was indefatigable: a bibliography of his published works lists no fewer than 240 separate titles—mostly individual sermons, small collections of addresses, and tracts on contemporary issues, mainly in Dutch, though many in English. He was thus the quintessential pastor of the Tractarian Movement.

At age ten, Andrew and his brother, John, were sent to Scotland for their education and lived with their uncle, a minister in the evangelical wing of the Presbyterian Church, in Aberdeen. They attended Marischal College and took the M. A. degree in 1845, with special preparation in Evidences of Christianity, Moral and Natural Philosophy, and Logic, and proceeded to Utrecht to study both Dutch and theology—being cautioned by their father against the liberalism even then permeating Dutch Christianity.

In a letter of November 14, 1845, the younger Andrew wrote to his father and advised him, "I have been led to surrender myself wholly to Christ." But because he could not be ordained as a parish minister before age twenty-two, Murray was stationed at Bloemfontein upon his return to South Africa and was inducted by his father. However, before he proceeded beyond the Orange River, to become the first regular pastor of the whole territory between the Orange and the Vaal, he assisted his father in preaching at Graaff-Reinerts. In *Andrew Murray and His Message: One of God's Saints* (1926), W. M. Douglas observes:

> While his two sons were with him in Graaff-Reinert, the father would often ask one or the other of them to preach

for him, and the sexton always wanted to be told which of them was to preach, for, said he, 'If it is Mr. Andrew, I must remove the lamps, for in his fiery zeal they will be in his way.' This characteristic marked his preaching till the end. About the year 1904, he was invited to preach the annual sermon in connection with the Christian Endeavour Convention, which was meeting that year in Cape Town. Two elderly men were present; one of them had known the preacher for only 10 or 12 years, and he remarked to the other, after the service, on the vigour and power with which the aged preacher delivered his message. 'Yes,' said the other, 'but if you had heard him fifty years ago, you would have said he was indeed vigorous in those days.' (51)

And although Murray observed in another letter to his father that "my voice is stronger than that of John," yet Douglas felt competent to note that "He was never violent or unrestrained, but just glowing with intensity."

At Wynburg, Murray assumed his pastorate with a sermon from I Corinthians 1:23: "We preach Christ crucified," and this text was, in effect, his primary inspiration for the remainder of his active ministry. Abstemious in the midst of a viticultural community, Murray attacked intemperance with as great zeal as he attacked any shortcoming in belief or other excess in behavior. Missions, education, repentance all attracted his attention, and by 34 he was appointed moderator of his synod, the leading exponent of orthodoxy in a religious environment under attack from both liberalism and modernist rationalism.

Two years later, in 1864, Murray defended the church's traditional theology against a modernist challenge with a celebrated four-hour courtroom address in Cape Town that was praised by the judge, Sir Sydney Bell; subsequently, he acted as advocate in the appeal before the Privy Council, in London, and preached at Surrey Chapel, where he gained fame as a "Holiness" speaker.

Back in Cape Town, Murray undertook to answer the challenge of liberal theology, which had been encouraged by the writing and speaking of the Reverend David Faure, founder of the Free Protestant, or Unitarian, Church and author of *Modern Theology*. In response to a series of lectures by Faure, which applied a rationalist dialectic to theology, Murray inaugurated his own lecture series, which strictly followed the same subjects and order, among which were Human Reason, Divine Revelation, Miracles, The Miracle of the Resurrection, The Eternity of Punishment, and Prophesy. As Johannes du Plessis, author of *The Life of Andrew Murray of South Africa* (1917), notes, "thus the conflict between liberalism and orthodoxy was transferred from the forum to the pulpit and the lecture hall and took the shape of controversy rather than of litigation" (232). Murray's lectures, delivered in Dutch in the Adderley Street church on Monday evenings, attracted widespread interest, and for those who were not fluent in that language, he gave a lengthy conflation in English at the Commercial Exchange. Du Plessis writes:

> Of the great ability displayed in these discourses, there cannot be two opinions. Mr. Faure himself, whose writings were chiefly assailed, confesses that both as regards matter and manner, Mr. Murray's lectures were far superior to those previously (given against his own) and they represent the only serious attempt made to meet argument with argument. (246)

Murray's lectures were published as *Modern Unbelief* (1868), in the preface to which he sought for himself and his readers "life and strength...in these days of temptation and apostasy." It was from this time that he decided to preach in a more restrained, less frenetic manner, though still with pentecostal power. Throughout seven years' ministry in Cape Town, during which he founded the local YMCA branch, Murray was concerned for the physical and social well-being of his parishioners, yet he strenuously opposed the identification of religion and politics, being concerned for the effects of establishment, subvention, and control.

In September 1871 Murray was inducted at Wellington, his fourth parish, where he remained for the rest of his life, though contributing to the religious and educational development of the whole of the nation. Here, his induction sermon was given on the text "And it came to pass, as they so spake, a great multitude believed" (Acts 14:1). Few texts could have been as appropriate to the occasion.

Murray was instrumental in founding the Dutch Reformed Church seminary; the Huguenot Seminary at Wellington; several churches, colleges, and organizations for church members. During five overseas tours, he spread his fame as a preacher: he stirred Pentecostal audiences in Scotland, England, Canada, and the United States and was described by John R. Mott, founder of the YMCA, as "the world-renowned spiritual leader...a flame of spiritual light for many years." On his fellow ministers his influence was overpowering, and on his audiences his effect was long-lasting. Appropriately, he is said to have cherished even more than the honorary degrees awarded him by the universities of Aberdeen and Cape of Good Hope the simple religious award, V. D. M.—Minister of the Divine Word, for he was pre-eminently a preacher, a master of exegetical and heuristic address.

His contemporary A. Moorrees, himself a distinguished pulpit orator, wrote of Andrew Murray that his preaching was less characterized by elegant phrases and histrionic delivery than by lucid and logical development, genuine vivacity, and sincere fervor. "The sedate and venerable minister disappears," wrote a Presbyterian minister who heard Murray preach at Keswick in 1895, "and an ancient Hebrew prophet rises up before us... The audience bows before the torrent of his words."

Murray's favorite theme was the necessity and efficacy of personal prayer as a means to eternal salvation. In his earlier years he wrote his sermons in a somewhat crabbed longhand; later, he resorted to broad outlines; finally, he dictated to one of his daughters, "speaking in a powerful voice and even gesticulating as if he had an audience in front of him," we are told by one biographer. The resultant harmony between content and delivery was his reward.

I   La Provence (c. 1750). Fransch Hoek Valley, Cape Province.
    Courtesy, South African Railways.

II Old Cape furniture. Marie Koopmans de wet House (c.1750). Cape Town.
    Courtesy, South African Railways

III South African Institute for Medical Research (1912).
Sir Herbert Baker, architect.
Johannesburg.

IV "Minon Theme in Yellow and Black" (1964). Cecily Sash.
Courtest the artist.

V Schlesinger Center (1960). Monty Slack, architect, Johannesburg
   Courtesy, J.G. Boss

VI "Hollow Torso" (1955). Lippy Lipshi
Courtesy, the sculptor.

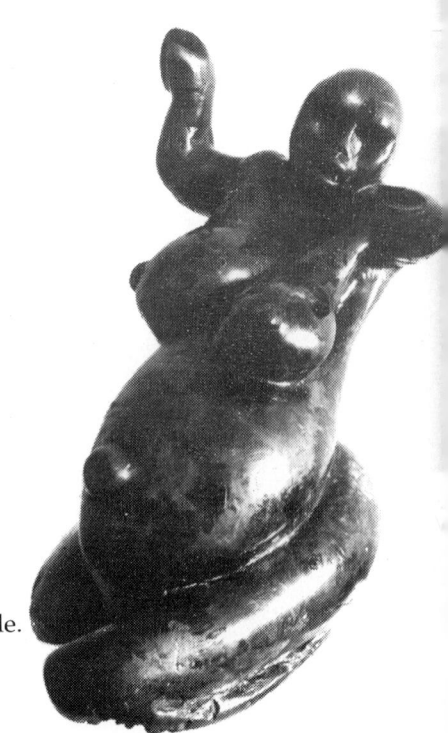

VII "Pregnant Woman" (1960). Lucas Sithole.
Courtesy, the sculptor.

VIII "Cat and Nasturtiums" (1932). Maggie Laubser. *Courtesy,* the artist.

IX   "Mother of the Tribe" (1969). Walter Battiss.
Courtesy, Artlook.

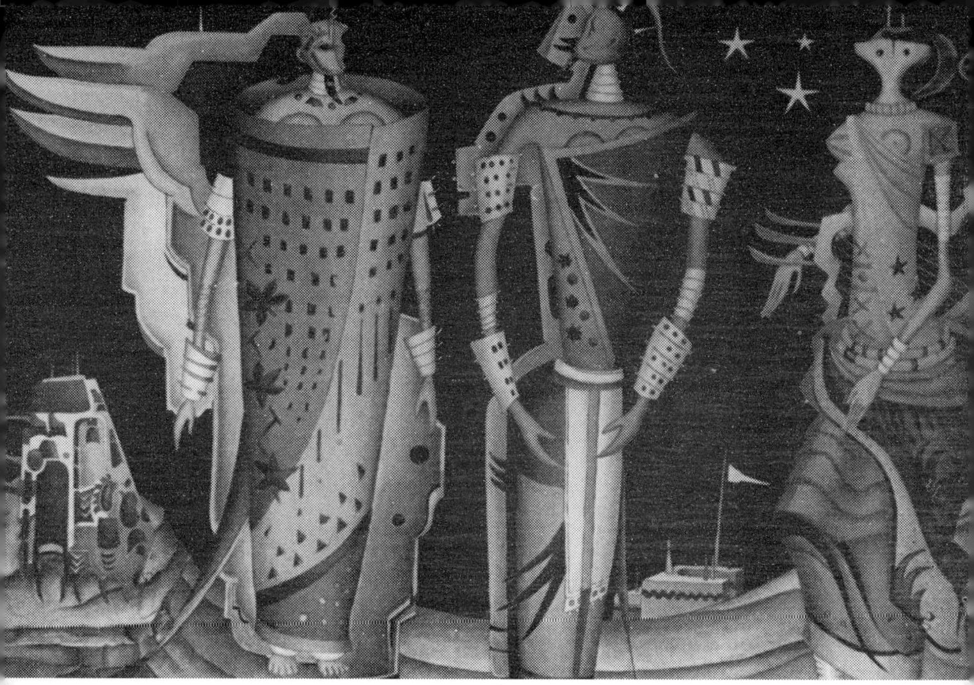

"Hieratic Women" (1966). Alexis Preller.
Courtesy, J.G. Boss.

House Le Roux (1950). Revel Fox, architect. Llandudno, Cape Peninsula
Courtesy, the architect.

XII "Fire Bird" (1968). Helmut Starcke. *Courtesy*, Martin Gibbs.

According to the *South African Dictionary of National Biography*,

> All his preaching, writing, and prayers emanated from a striving to mobilize the spiritual life and work of the church, lacking which the church would remain powerless to fulfill its task in the world. Through all the years, those who knew him can still hear his powerful voice issuing from his delicate frame...and can recall a prophet whose strength lay in his speech when action was no longer possible. His contemporaries recall the stream of molten eloquence which overflowed the glowing crucible of his soul.

Notwithstanding this testimony of his contemporaries, Murray confessed, in a latter-day self-assessment, that "Though all around me looked upon me as one of the most earnest preachers, my life was one real discontent. I struggled and prayed as best I could." This, it will be noted, is the frank testament of a truly pious evangelist: others have been more generous in their judgment of the man, his message, and his ministry. One of his theological adversaries, quoted by Douglas, gave this picture of Murray:

> Eloquent, quick, and talented, he has an acute mind and clear judgement. He instantly divines the weak points in his opponent's arguments and knows how to assail them; he is too clever for most of them; he carries the meeting with him. He understands the art of making his ideas so attractive to the elders and small minds among his ministers (who all look up with reverence towards him) that they very seldom venture to contradict Demosthenes—or, another called him, Apollos. There is no member of the assembly who possesses more influence than Andrew Murray. (105)

"Modern Unbelief and Human Reason" was the first lecture in the series delivered in Groote Kerk, Cape Town, in April 1868 and published that year as *Het Moderne Ongeloof: Dertien Leerreden*. The influential *Advertiser and Mail*, which provided generous reporting, including excerpts and paraphrases, described the series as "keen in thought, scientific in treatment, and as profoundly philosophical in its essence as it was eloquent in its expression." Plans to publish an English-language edition of the lectures apparently did not materialize; however, the Cape Town YMCA issued the text of the Commercial Exchange address of April 28 as a tract, *A Lecture on the Modern Theology*, which its preface described as "a high-toned advocacy and vindication of that vital Christianity, old but ever new, which is as philosophical as it is orthodox, and which is as indispensable to meet man's deepest needs in these modern times as it was in the earliest and most primitive ages."

One of the few South Africans familiar to ordinary citizens and school children as well as to historians of imperialism and African nationalism, Cecil Rhodes (1853-1902) was motivated not so much by a desire to amass great personal wealth as by a desire to amass great public property: specifically, he sought to see fulfilled his abiding vision of British territory "from Cape to Cairo," as he so memorably phrased his goal. Before he had accumulated any fortune, he drew a first will in 1877 in which he made provision for a secret society to extend the British Empire throughout the world, to recover the United States, to inaugurate colonial representation in Westminister, and to establish a political entity of such power that wars would henceforth become impractical. Truly, he wanted for Britain, which he saw as the one "Land of hope and glory," the goals made popular in song: "Wider still, and wider, shall thy bounds be set/God who made thee mighty, make thee mightier yet."

The son of a Church of England vicar, Rhodes was educated at the local grammar school in Bishop's Stortford; and though his father apparently proposed a ministerial career for him, his own goal was a university education not related to the church; but his somewhat precarious health dictated a visit to a farmer brother in South Africa that resulted in permanent settlement there, interrupted only by return to Oxford, from which university he graduated in 1881.

While at Oxford Rhodes developed a very personal concept of religion which melded the elements of Darwinism and those of Christianity: he saw a divine plan in evolution, which had produced the Anglo-Saxon "race" as a means of assuring the world of peace, prosperity, and moral leadership. British imperialism was the political means for the achievement of this end.

In a short speech on the occasion of the laying of the cornerstone of the Presbyterian Church at Woodstock, in the Cape, on July 29, 1899, Rhodes said he accepted the invitation because he admired the "most practical idea of your church; that is, work," and confided that in a conversation with the bishop of Derry on one occasion he declined an invitation to hear the bishop preach, preferring his own "chapel," Table Mountain, for

> I find that up that mountain one gets thoughts—What you might term religious thoughts, because they are thoughts for the betterment of humanity, and I believe that is the best description of religion, to work for the betterment of the human beings who surround us......
>
> There are those who throughout the world have set themselves the task of elevating their fellow-beings and have abandoned personal ambition, the accumulation of wealth, perhaps the pursuit of art and many of those things that are deemed most valuable. What is left for them? They have chosen to do what? To devote their whole mind to make other human beings better, braver, kindlier, more thoughtful, and more unselfish, for which they deserve the praise of all men.

So that he himself might help improve mankind's lot, Rhodes entered politics. In 1881 he entered the Cape parliament for Barkly West, a predominantly Afrikaner electorate that he represented for the remainder of his career. He argued that the stronger imperial government should exercise control over Basutoland and Bechuanaland, and it took years of negotiation, guerrilla warfare, and manipulation before his position was adopted, but betterment was questionable.

Rhodes became prime minister of the Cape Colony in 1890 and was supported actively by the Afrikaner Bond and its leader, J. H. Hofmeyer. His primary, frequently expounded goal was the United British and Dutch ("the two races") states in South Africa (something that was consummated eight years after his death); a secondary one was the paternalistic administration of the "Natives" (or Kaffirs, or Bantu, as they were later termed), and to this end he himself accepted the Native Affairs portfolio in addition to the premiership, thus providing him with opportunities to control the destinies of the "children" of Africa, as he frequently alluded to the indigenes, and to deliver major speeches.

Maybelle Katzen comments in the *Encyclopaedia Britannica* that "Rhodes was not a great orator, but he was able to express his large ideas in popular phrases," and she cites "painting the map red," "British from Cape to Cairo," and "philanthropy plus 5%" as examples. But this viewpoint is challenged by Rhodes's biographer, the noted author Sarah Gertrude Millin, who wrote in 1936:

> He was effective because his matter was good, and he could now and then flash a phrase. But he began and ended awkwardly. He was rambling and repetitive. He had a voice that broke startlingly into a high falsetto.
>
> We are, on the other hand, assured that his speeches...were not edited. But, unless his manner was quite inescapably bad, there can be no explanation of why those speeches seemed so indifferent when they were delivered and read so well now, except that fashions in oratory have changed in the last fifty years.
>
> For Rhodes's speeches are not only bold, wise, direct, and epigrammatic in the reading, they give an impression of almost contemptuous sincerity...When Rhodes made his first speech on northern expansion, he was thirty. But he was already in what Conrad, thinking of a man's forties, used to call 'the force of his life.' In experience, achievement, habit, thought—and body too—he was a middle-aged man. (51)

Public Address

This assessment has considerable insight, as a reading of Rhodes's speech "The Basis of South African Government," will reveal. Clearly, the speaker is rambling and repetitive in both the introduction and the peroration; there are succinct turns of phrase and memorable, quotable passages that approximate aphorisms and maxims; but there is a forthrightness that occasionally suggests self-righteousness, a firmness that is hard to distinguish from inflexibility and doctrinaire stubbornness. But as he was well aware, a man of firm opinions should not be reluctant to express them: "I defy any one to make a speech as prime minister of this colony without hurting the feelings of some one," he observed in an address at Paarl, April 23, 1891, which shows that he was not a pusillanimous politician but rather the confident speaker whose efforts had been recognized by a gold medal for elocution at grammar school.

Because Rhodes was so adept at shaping the catchy phrase, his ideas were often misrepresented by his political opponents and detractors: perhaps no South African speaker can be "more easily or more grossly misrepresented by a detached quotation," says the compiler of a collection of his public statements, before assigning reasons:

> In part this is due to the imperfect state of reporting in South Africa, in part to the fact that the speaker does not help the reporters with typewritten or printed copies of his speeches, for the simple reason that he never prepares what he has to say, but throws his ideas and facts before the public in such words as come on the spur of the moment. 'No one ever accused me of preparing a speech, though, no doubt it is the proper thing to do,' is his own admission in one of his speeches. (Vindex iii)

Ability to speak at length and with specific evidence soon became a widely acknowledged ability of Rhodes: for instance, he delivered one ten-thousand-word speech on diamond production, replete with technical detail and statistical supports, without any outline or notes.

Just twelve days after entering the Cape parliament, Rhodes delivered his maiden speech. Lewis Mitchell, in *The Life and Times of the Right Honourable Cecil John Rhodes* (1910), reveals that one parliamentary reporter judged it "bluff and untutored in style, with no graces of oratory," but added that "he became the most effective speaker in the House without ever being eloquent." Mitchell himself observes:

> Rhodes never became a conventional orator. But, having the root of the matter in him, and never speaking unless he had something to say worth saying, he gradually acquired the ear of both sides. As a speaker I should compare him with Cromwell, without Cromwell's puritan fervour for he was rapid, occasionally obscure, with here and there a glimpse of the fire that consumed him. It is noticeable that his very first speech should have been in defence of what he considered native rights. (97)

Actually, Rhodes's "defence" of native rights was not entirely altruistic: the government proposal to restrict sales of armaments to the native peoples was seen by Rhodes as a probable cause of their reluctance to work in the mines. Later, when he introduced his own "Bill for Africa" (1894), Rhodes raised the economic qualifications for the franchise among Bantu, attempted to remove access to alcohol, and introduced a tax intended to encourage unlanded natives to seek employment outside their own traditional tribal territories. But because of widespread opposition, this tax ("Not slavery, but a gentle stimulus," Rhodes termed it), it was not imposed. Incessantly, Rhodes encouraged the migration of natives to provide cheap and seasonal labor for mining and other labor-intensive industries.

Notwithstanding Rhodes's frequent speaking in public, he was apparently never really at ease before audiences, never the self-confident performer. One of his contemporaries has left us this view, recorded by Mitchell:

> He was an exceedingly nervous speaker; there is a twitching about his hands, and he has a somewhat

ungainly way of turning his body about. That he is a man of extraordinary energy is clear to every one who takes observation of him; he is in a continual state of restlessness. (100-101)

On one occasion, after encountering a decidedly hostile audience, Rhodes "reasoned out his position and justified his conduct with so much force and spirit that he carried the audience with him and sat down amid repeated cheers." The *Cape Argus*, reporting the event, referred to the speaker's "exhibition of oratorical skill and dialectic power."

In "The Basis of South African Government" Rhodes speaks against the extension of the franchise to Africans—a proposal that had attracted the support of a great number of missionaries—arguing that the vote should be restricted to "all civilized persons," those defined as those owning a dwelling worth at least 25 pounds, which he, the wealthy businessman, deems "literally nothing."

Quite explicitly, he expounds his belief that "we have to govern the natives as a subject race" and suggests that if there were not Dutch-British animosities, "we would have given the native his vote because we are afraid of him." Further:

> We are to be lords over them. These are my politics on native affairs, and these are the politics of South Africa. Treat the natives as a subject people as long as they continue in a state of barbarism and communal tenure; be the lords over them and let them be a subject race, and keep the liquor from them.... The native is to be treated as a child and denied the franchise.

It is unfortunate that Rhodes was not more advanced in his understanding of social anthropology and in his perception of causal relationships, for if he had been, his pronouncements may have less frequently exhibited that "unctuous rectitude" that he discovered in the missionaries who opposed him. Yet, though times have greatly changed, South African public (and hence political) sentiments have not progressed far from Rhodes's oft-repeated position, which he asseverated was based on "precedent, justice, and policy" and supported by the natives themselves, for whom he believed he could state of the franchise, "They do not want it." Today South Africa's black citizens *do* want it, and they cite "precedent, justice, and policy" in their behalf.

The universal recognition of the justice of total adult franchise and the adoption of this as policy can not be ignored.

Stephanus Johannes Paules Kruger (1825-1904), like Lucius Junius Brutus, might properly be termed the father of his country. Magisterial in appearance and avuncular in demeanor, he is generally recognized as the most influential figure that Afrikanerdom has produced, and to him more than to any other public figure do we owe the unique admixture of religion and race in public rhetoric that is to be found in South African discourse. Patriarchal in pronouncements, he was no less so in his personal life: to Kruger, Moses's leading of his people to the promised land was the paradigm for the Boers' Great Trek of 1835-36 from under British suzerainty to full national ('racial' in Rhodes's lexicon) independence and integrity. His vision was constant, his labors indefatigable, and his encouragement incessant. Though he and his people were temporarily discouraged and disappointed by the South African War's outcome, nonetheless they had that indomitable purpose, buoyed by religious inspiration and succor, that sustained them for another two generations until Kruger's vision was fulfilled. Though Dante might complain, in the *Paradiso* (XXXIII, 121), "How inadequate is speech, and how feeble towards my conception," it was through the power of his public speaking that Kruger was able to direct and sustain the political development of first the Transvaal and then the entire nation.

Kruger and his parents participated in the Greak Trek, which gave them undeniable credentials among their own people. At age 15, Paul was recognized as a burgher, and at 17 he married, took up farming, and raised a family of sixteen. He became a member of the Dopper sect, in whose churches he remained a lay preacher for the duration of his life. His build, exuberance, and religious conviction combined to provide him with all the requisites of leadership and persuasion in a society that was little short of theocratic.

As D. W. Kruger notes, "He grew to manhood in the shadow of a struggle against wild barbarians, against untamed natives, during which a new land was converted from pioneering conditions to a liveable heritage. He was reared in the traditional Calvinism of the religious Afrikaner, with its strong Old Testament leanings." One consequence of this background was a proclivity to view matters in antitheses: there were seldom any opportunities for compromises—particularly where he perceived the application of some basic principle. Accordingly, he cautioned the Boers in 1878 against allying with the Zulus against the British (which at the time would have been a tactical advantage), saying that "one must never join with savages in war against a civilized nation." And when the Dutch Reformed Church initiated evangelical hymns in the Cape, Kruger and the Doppers saw this as a threat to their sober and conservative orthodoxy and sought their own dominies from Holland. Again, when T. F. Burgers, a clergyman, stood for the presidency, Kruger opposed him on the basis that his views were too liberal in theology and too worldly in education.

In politics, Kruger worked unsuccessfully for the unification of the Orange Free State and the Transvaal, for fair treatment of foreigners who declined to accept citizenship (the uitlanders), against the expansionist policies of Rhodes, and for the acquisition of a rail link with Delagoa Bay on the Indian Ocean. The uitlander question was probably the most vexing and misunderstood: these temporary immigrants, intent upon quick fortunes in mining and similar pursuits, could well have outvoted the permanent settlers and changed the very nature of the Transvaal if they were accorded the franchise after just a year or so, as the British government proposed. Kruger's halving of the residency requirements to seven years respected the principle of commitment to the country, was in concord with other nations' qualifications, yet was rejected by Britain. Thus the South African War was inevitable and broke out on October 12, 1899.

In May 1900 Kruger addressed the volksraad for the last time and took the railway from Pretoria to Delagoa Bay en route to Europe to advocate the Boer cause. He was politely received in Germany, was popularly acclaimed in France, and was accorded every civility in the Netherlands. But his mission was no more successful than that of Lajos Kossuth, the Hungarian patriot, who sought American assistance in his nation's fight for independence in 1848.

The war was costly for both antagonists and for the black populations of southern Africa that were caught in the conflict. It dragged on for two-and-a-half years, involving 448,000 British and colonial troops against 87,000 Boer commandos in trenches, on horses, and living off the land. There were over 22,000 British fatalities and between 25,000 and 35,000 Afrikaner deaths.

But the British role was not commendable: essentially, the war was waged in order to protect the dream of British High Commissioner Alfred Milner and Cecil Rhodes of an imperial dominion from Cape to Cairo and to provide the means for Alfred Beit, Julius Wernher, and Cecil Rhodes to gain and maintain a goldmining monopoly in the Rand.

Kruger's mission to Europe was unproductive, and the course of the war, together with the death of his wife, showed their effects on the ageing statesman. He died in Switzerland in July 1904. His biographer, D. W. Kruger notes:

> His death was the end of an era in the history of South Africa. His career encompassed the entire history of the Boer republic of the Transvaal. As the political heir to the Great Trek, he more than anyone else saw to it that the ideals and principles of the Trek were preserved and handed on to posterity. He embodied the republican tradition in South Africa and maintained republican independence for a quarter of a century in the face of mounting British imperialism. In this he laid the foundations of an Afrikaner nationalism which revived strongly in the first decades after his death.... As a Boer he was typical of the period and among his own people he is still regarded as one of the greatest Afrikaners of all time.

The "ideals and principles" that Kruger transmitted to his country are most clearly stated in his famous speech on the occasion of his installation as president of the South African Republic for the fourth time on May 12, 1898. This speech, which "took almost three hours to deliver...set forth my religious and political views on the actual situation and on the problems confronting the State," says Kruger in his *Memoirs*. Actually, the speech is a political, social, and religious testament and it is in the form of a series of speeches addressed to discrete audiences—burghers, teachers, jurists, clergy, children—so that we can see the application of his personal and public philosophies to all branches of society. That Kruger himself thought of this speech as the major statement of his long and distinguished career can be observed from his taking the precaution at the outset to request a secretary "to take down my words, that my speech may not later, for one reason or another, be misunderstood." Furthermore, he selected it from his countless speeches for inclusion in his *Memoirs*, where it is given first place of a number of other speeches, proclamations, and similar state documents.

In introducing Olive Schreiner's *Story of an African Farm*, Bergen Evans wrote:

> No other book in our language, with the possible exception of Emily Bronte's *Wuthering Heights*, leaves us with quite the same impression of pain, beauty, protest, and passion.... It has great value as a historical and social document, being one of the few contemporary pictures we have of the life of the Boer settlers in South Africa a hundred years ago. But it is in its literary qualities—its passion, insight, and wild beauty—that make it a classic. It is not as widely known as most of our classics, but since its first appearance it has been prized by the knowing who, indeed, regard a knowledge of the book as a sort of touchstone of taste.

And, *mutatis mutandis*, the same observation could be made for her short, great speech on the Boer War; for it, too, is marked by passion, insight, and literary beauty and gives vent to not-inconsiderable pain and protest. Though it is not widely known, it is one of the truly moving statements on the liberties of colonial peoples, the rights of women, and the relationship between capitalism and economic and political exploitation.

Born in Basutoland, Olive Schreiner (1855-1920) was the sixth of twelve children of a German missionary father and an English mother. The Boer War had on her an effect similar to that of the Second World War on Virginia Woolf: it caused her the greatest anguish; and she, too, became suicidal.

In one of her letters to Havelock Ellis, she asks, "Are not the words *stepmother* and *mother-in-law* the two bitterest words in the world?" And elsewhere she said, "My mother has never been a mother to me; I have had no mother." Accordingly, it is not amazing that in her writing the aggressor-figure is almost always portrayed as a mother and the victim as a child. This comes out in her pamphlet, written just before the Boer War, *An English South African's View of the Situation*. The same imagery is used with great poignancy in her speeches on the war, in which she portrays the Boer republics as the stepchildren of Great Britain and repeats (with slight modification) the refrain that "The England of our love is dead."

Schreiner's sympathies were uniformly against the aggressors and for the victims, whether women, Boers, or Blacks. "Rhodes," writes Friedman, "was for her the incarnation of aggressive strength, and in the decade preceding the Boer War, she attacked him unceasingly, laying at his door corruption, betrayal, plunder, and even murder: it was verbal aggression, but aggression nonetheless" (50). Her own defense was that writing and speaking were forms of passive resistance, and that "If the use of force is ever justified, it is justified in fighting against social oppression" (*Letters*, 316).

In her speeches on the Boer War (one given in Cape Town, the other at Somerset East), Schreiner develops the same themes as in her earlier *View of the Situation*; namely, that political and economic imperialism are the basic motivational factors, that British military tactics have been unsurpassed in their treachery, that public criticism has been silenced by being declared unpatriotic, that justice and peace are being subverted, that independence has been crushed by the so-called defenders of liberty, and that the ultimate price of the Boer War will be that "this land will be the home of a strong and independent nation" because "the future is with the republicans."

In "Our Love is Dead" one can only admire the speaker's forthrightness at a time when candor was perilous and her prescience when jingoism precluded almost any attempt at honest evaluation and prognosis.

Perhaps the most striking quality of this speech on the Boer War is its very personal sense of direct communication: the feeling that the speaker is conveying forcefully, yet honestly, her most deeply felt opinions and emotions. Thus emotional, personal, and logical proofs have almost equal significance. Though there are ample instances of specific examples in support of her theses, yet she resorts with considerable effect to the use of most vivid illustration. This development of the factual by the figurative she has commented on in *Women and Labour* (1911): "In addition to the prose argument, I [use] one or more allegories; because while it is easy clearly to express abstract thoughts in argumentative prose, whatever emotion those thoughts awaken I have not felt myself adequately to express except in the other form" (9). And there are few more emotional illustrations than that of parricide, few more homiletic than that of the lioness and the meerkat. Her "allegories" are commendably apposite. It is clearly defensible to conclude that this speech, like her *Story of an African Farm*, "is in its literary qualities" no less than in its rhetorical, a classic.

Yet the remarkable fact is that Olive Schreiner was not a practiced orator. As her husband notes in his edition of her *Letters*,

> As Cape Town's delegate against the war she attended a people's Congress at Graff Reinert at the end of May 1900. The meeting was a wonderful one. She disliked public speaking, though she had the gifts of the orator, and did not mean to speak; but the people wanted to see and hear her; and she was called up. Once on her feet, all her nervousness disappeared; she saw only the outraged, quiet

people before her. I can recall only two occasions when she spoke publicly (315).

This first speech was very brief: it was in English, and to no more than about one hundred words, if the version in the Cape Town newspaper *Ons Land* is accurate. Her peroration, "If we remain steadfast in our attitude, and if we continue to persist, then I say the day will come that the republics will have their independence," was greeted with applause, and as the paper reports, "the storm of cheering broke loose again."

A second speech was delivered at the protest meeting in Cape Town on July 9, 1900 in the Metropolitan Hall. One member of the audience, H. W. Nevinson, has provided in *Changes and Chances* (1923) some account of the occasion and the speaker:

> Indeed, though she stood perfectly still, she was transfigured into flame. Indignation can make the dumb speak and stones be eloquent. But this woman was not dumb and was no stone. I have heard much indignant eloquence, but never such a molten torrent of white-hot rage. It was overwhelming. When it suddenly ceased, the large audience...about 1,500 men and women...could hardly gasp. If Olive Schreiner had called on them to storm Government House, they would have thrown themselves upon the bayonets.

Three months later, she sent the manuscript of her Cape Town speech to be read at the Somerset East women's meeting on October 12. The audience response was again extraordinary, and we can only regret that the times and her inclinations militated against her greater involvement in public affairs and her more frequent appearance as a public speaker. If she was not the most logical speaker of her time, she excelled in the heuristic mode, marshalling the most persuasive arguments and supporting them with undeniable personal and emotional proofs and eschewing casuistry.

Pixley Ka Isaka Seme, a Zulu born in Inanda, Natal, was one of a group of talented young South Africans who shared a vision of leading the native peoples of the continent towards political enfranchisement, tribal cooperation, and full and equal participation in a multi-racial society in which the benign influence of religion would reduce factional animosities and ensure the progressive attainment of material well-being.

In 1902 Seme was admitted to Columbia University, having been sponsored by the Reverend Joseph Pixley, a member of the Board of Missions of the African Methodist Episcopal Church. After his graduation, he was admitted to Jesus College, Oxford, and subsequently read law in London and was admitted to the Middle Temple. He returned to Durban, where he established his practice. But his return to South Africa provided something of a culture shock: he was appalled at the treatment afforded to Blacks and at the bickering among their purported leaders. "We are one people," he declared; "These divisions, these jealousies are the cause of our woes." This analysis, of course, was somewhat simplistic, but it motivated him to call a meeting in Bloemfontein on January 8, 1912 (at which he delivered the principal address) that resulted in the founding of the South African Native National Congress, later simply the African National Congress.

Seme became vice-president of the A.N.C., editor of its journal, *Abantu-Batho*, and one of its principal spokesmen, advocating for almost forty years a centrist, responsible policy of racial cooperation that was almost indistinguishable from that of Dr. Booker T. Washington, president of Tuskeegee Institute, who rose to national fame following his 1895 speech to the Cotton States Exposition in Atlanta, Georgia. That speech was largely replicated in Seme's 1932 speech to the A.N.C. But just as Washington's philosophy of gradualism and vocationalism had its opponents, led in the main by Dr. W. E. B. DuBois, so did Seme's; and as the economic and social ills of the 1930's increased, Seme's policies became increasingly irrelevant in the eyes of his leftist adversaries. After three years of his presidency, the A.N.C. was moribund: the disaffected had left, and his supporters were reduced to about thirty.

Though he was indefatigable as a speaker during his long public life, perhaps no speech surpassed in rhetorical excellence the Curtis Medals Oration that Seme delivered at Columbia University on April 5, 1906. It states with brevity, clarity, and force the quintessence of his lifelong philosophy, so that it can justifiably be considered his most representative public statement. (In the tradition of the time, it was published by the university as a booklet; but the university library no longer owns a copy.) Fortunately, the speech was printed in *The Colored American Magazine* and in J. M. Webb's *The Black Man: The Father of Civilization, Proven by Biblical History.*

Seme's oration, entitled "The Regeneration of Africa," has many of the stylistic characteristics (parallelisms, analogies, recapitulation) common to most eighteenth- and nineteenth-century speeches in the "high" style: this is not especially remarkable. But he does make greater use of comparison and contrast, of exemplification, and of literary tropes than his predecessors. As a result, his style at times has a decidedly poetic quality and enjoys the hue and heft of inspired, inspirational eloquence. The several passages that utilize parallelisms and antithesis would be easily committed to memory, and so it is understandable that the oration seems to have become known to other Africans studying in America in later years; and more than half a century later, it could be quoted in its entirety by Dr. Kwame Nkrumah of Ghana.

"The Regeneration of Africa" presents material that is today commonplace: that an adequate and honest history of Africa will demonstrate the achievements of the black race; that unity is a prerequisite to strength; and that science and technology must be harnessed for the common advancement. Seme himself sought to establish a united black African church, but failed; it, too, was an ingredient in his recipe for regeneration.

Yet Seme's evident pride in Africa is apparent, and his erudition is clear. He reveals an advanced understanding of cultural anthropology, noting the integrity of all cultures and denying the validity of any hierarchy based solely on Eurocentric criteria; he stresses the accomplishments of African art and architecture, going beyond the then normal limitations to utensils and personal adornments to include the Ethiopian pyramids and their elaborate decoration; he emphasizes the need for racial pride and self-consciousness, anticipating Alain Locke's clarion call for these in *The New Negro* exactly twenty years later; and he recognizes the inevitability of martyrdom before the achievement of individual liberty and racial respect. To him, industry and education, science and religion, churches and colleges, commerce and business, peace and war, were all necessary for the achievement of pan-African solidarity and racial self-fulfillment. In observance of the principles of Ciceronian rhetoric, he provides a succinct recapitulation of the substance of his oration in his peroration:

> Agencies of a social, economic, and religious advance tell of a new spirit which, acting as a leavening ferment, shall raise the anxious and aspiring mass to the level of their former glory. The ancestral greatness, the unimpaired genius, and the recuperative power of the race, its irrepressibility, which assures its permanence, constitute the African's greatest source of inspiration. He has refused to camp forever on the borders of the industrial world....
>
> The regeneration of Africa means that a new and unique civilization is soon to be added to the world.

Admittedly, Seme's remarkably clear vision was somewhat premature; but that, of course, is in the nature of inspirational leadership and without which progress is slow and uncertain. More commendable, surely, is the fact that this vision was that of a twenty-year-old undergraduate, that it has proved so accurate in particulars, and that it was so impressively stated.

It is to be regretted that Seme's leadership potential was never fully realized. The cause was probably his firm belief—held with religious conviction, it would appear—in the legitimacy of only his own vision of African development and his disparagement of other, less-reactionary views. When he died in 1951 he was duly honored for his efforts, but hardly lamented. Nonetheless, his 1906 oration, "The Regeneration of Africa," fully deserves to be retained in any collection of major or representative speeches by Africans.

Perhaps the most famous South African outside his country for fifty years, Jan Christiaan Smuts (1870-1950), early established a reputation as a soldier, politician, and philosopher and long seemed the only individual who might be able to bring a measure of harmony among the races and cooperation between the Afrikaner and British segments of South African society. He was descended from a long line of Dutch immigrants (the founder of the South African branch arrived from Holland some time prior to 1692) and received what might be regarded as a model English education: he majored in literature and science at the University of the Cape of Good Hope, gaining double first-class honors and winning the Ebden Scholarship to Cambridge University. He read widely in poetry, wrote a little undistinguished verse, collected botanical specimens, taught Sunday school classes, and was much taken by the issues involved in both religion and politics.

At Christ's College, Cambridge, Smuts read law and distinguished himself in the examinations, but his interests were far-ranging. He prepared essays on the future of South African literature (before Sir Herbert Warren, president of Magdalen College, Oxford, wrote in his chapter of the *Cambridge History of English Literature* that South African literature amounted only to poetry and "shows today the promise and the potency of achievement"), on the historical Christ, on the nature of life, and (in 1894-5) a pioneering work, *Walt Whitman: A Study in the Evolution of Personality*.

Back in Cape Town in 1895, Smuts began the practice of law. His first appearance on a political platform occurred when he went to Kimberley in October to defend Cecil Rhodes, who had been publicly attacked by Olive Schreiner.

Smuts was much influenced by Rhodes's concept of a united South Africa and was critical of Kruger's intransigence; but when he was unsuccessful in an application for a law lectureship at the South African College (now the University of Cape Town) and when Rhodes's part in the infamous Jameson Raid became public knowledge, he became disillusioned and moved to Johannesburg where—having surrendered his British citizenship—he became one of Kruger's nationalized burghers, was appointed state attorney at age 28, and accompanied Kruger in the discussions that preceded the outbreak of the Boer War—a war that Smuts vainly tried to prevent. He wrote an anti-British tract, *A Century of Wrongs*.

In his *Memoirs*, Paul Kruger writes of Smuts as a representative of the younger generation of Afrikaners:

> Smuts is one of the cleverest lawyers in South Africa and a man of versatile attainments besides. He is personally a very simple man, and to meet him, one would not suspect that he possesses so firm a will and so determined a character as he does. Although scarcely thirty years of age and without the slightest previous experience of military affairs, he developed, in the later phases of the war, into a most brilliant general, so that he added to his position as State Attorney that of an assistant commandant-general of the South African Republic. Smuts will yet play a great part in the history of South Africa (264-65).

When it became apparent that the Transvaal was moving towards withdrawal from the customs union, Smuts saw political separatism as an inevitable end and so hastened discussions on political union and submitted a draft constitution. His own view was that native franchise would become a difficult issue: his often-stated position was that "I don't believe in politics for them," while the Transvaal politicians categorically denied any representation to the Blacks and the Cape Colony constitution made no distinction on the basis of race or color. His solution to the apparent impasse was to place the problem "on to the shoulders of the future." At the time, this was probably the only pragmatic solution. His dream of a Union of South Africa was realized in 1910.

In a fashion, the Union was an expression of Smuts's growing philosophy of "the whole"—nowadays called holism, after the title of his treatise *Holism and Evolution* (1926). Smuts declared that the idea of the whole had become unfashionable: the classical philosophers' concept of a unitary universe had been discarded in favor of the separation of subject and object. Ironically, however, his vision of a united South Africa did not include the native peoples, who constituted even then an overwhelming numerical majority.

On December 16, 1918 Smuts's plan for the League of Nations was published: it was one of his fondest inventions and brought him into close relationship with Woodrow Wilson. Like Wilson, he traveled, wrote, and spoke in its support to the point of personal exhaustion. The League scheme paralleled Smuts's advocacy of a British association to supplant the anachronistic Empire: his "A British Commonwealth of Nations" was delivered as an after-dinner speech at a banquet given in Smuts's honor by both houses of parliament in London on May 15, 1917. That same evening Lord Harcourt wrote him a note: "My dear General Smuts: I would sooner have made your speech of tonight than anything I have ever done or attained in my life." This praise clearly pleased the speaker, and he quoted the note in a letter to his wife, written just two days later. The speech has the elements of the best after-dinner speeches: a friendly, casual style; an anecdotal introduction that establishes rapport and common ground with the audience; a substantial content presented in a light manner; and a balance between the twin goals of entertainment and instruction. In some details, Smuts proved not entirely prescient, but in others he was remarkably accurate as a prognosticator: "Public opinion will be more powerful," he suggested; the Crown will become a visible head of the Commonwealth; there should be freedom within the Commonwealth for a grand variety of forms of national government. Union, Commonwealth, and League were all part of a system.

In the aftermath of the war, Smuts fought a lonely battle for what he believed to be a more just peace than that favored by the principal British and Allied statesmen: he wanted a peace treaty that would not jeopardize "the civilisation that we are out to save." His passionate and repeated speeches against the victors' proposals were ineffective.

The death of Botha in 1919 made Smuts prime minister for the next five years, during which the Nationalist party moved towards republicanism and secession from the Empire. He advocated what later became known as the Statute of

Westminster, though in 1921 the other dominion governments were not with him. And in 1924 he and his government were defeated in an election, whereupon he resumed his interest in science and philosophy and gave numerous addresses and papers at scholarship meetings, conducted a lecture tour of the United States, and received a number of academic and scholarly honors.

In the wake of the stock market crash and the deepening economic depression, Smuts and Hertzog formed a coalition that won the 1933 election. Later, Smuts proceeded to Britain to attend the world economic conference, and while there he went north to Scotland to deliver his rectorial address at the University of Saint Andrews on October 17, 1934.

In this major speech, the characteristics of all of Smuts's discourses are present: the conversational mode, the anecdotal introduction, analogical development, the statement of contemporary problems as universal principles, the summary of major points in aphorisms, and the prediction of events in the event of either acceptance or non-acceptance of his line of argumentation. Occasionally, of course, he was wrong: he indicates to his Scottish audience, "I do not agree with the common view that we are on the verge of another great war"; yet he did foretell a cataclysm resulting from the development of the "cult of power" that was becoming ever more insistent in Europe and from the even greater danger, "lassitude and disillusion."

Back in South Africa, Smuts (as minister for justice under Hertzog) was faced with severe problems, problems which he had to accept as a personal challenge when he became prime minister in 1939. The fundamental problem was, of course, the future role of the native population (though this impinged on the relationship between Afrikaner and British South African).

In the 1920s Smuts was a convinced segregationist, and his own early native legislation was predicated on the belief that Blacks and Whites should be kept apart "socially, territorially, and politically." During the 1930's, as B. J. Liebenberg has pointed out, "Race relations in South Africa had deteriorated rapidly during Smuts's government"; but in a speech in January

1942 Smuts proposed to provide for Bantu as permanent townspeople and to increase the expenditure of general revenue for their education. The Bantu, however, wanted political equality and called for the abolition of all discriminatory legislation. By 1946 the National party manifesto called for *apartheid*, and so Smuts set up a commission to study racial policy. It concluded that true apartheid was impractical and that true integration was not feasible, hence a compromise had to be found. This, he suggested, would allow permanent existence of black and white communities in contiguity and the minimum social and legislative discrimination that would be required to take into account the different educational, social, and economic levels of the several peoples. But in May 1948 Smuts's government was swept out of office and the policy of apartheid—propounded so forcefully at a time when the rest of the world was finally abandoning it—became the basis of modern South African political life.

Jan Hofmeyr (1894-1948), deputy prime minister of the Union of South Africa, was long regarded by Smuts as his right-hand man and intellectual successor, so that his death in 1948 left no apparent heir to Smuts's position of leadership in developing a new philosophy of government and social relations for South Africa in the changed post-war international climate.

But Hofmeyr was not a mere carbon copy of Smuts; he often differed with his mentor on fundamental matters: when bills against mixed marriages and the employment of white girls by Asiatics were introduced, Smuts did not oppose them, though Hofmeyr did.

From 1924 to 1929, Hofmeyr was administrator of the Transvaal, and from 1933 to 1936 he served as minister of the interior and minister of health and education. "At this juncture of his career he regarded total separation of races as morally defensible, but doubted its practicability," one commentator notes, but he thought that the amity of Briton and Boer was the fundamental need to assure the continued development of Western civilization in southern Africa.

On 6 April 1936 Hofmeyr made one of the most important speeches of his career, arguing that the bill (which removed qualified Bantu men from the Cape electoral roll and allowed them to elect three white representatives) was wrong in principle, rooted in fear, and dangerous in that it implied a divergency rather than a community of interests in South Africa. Rejecting both white supremacy and racial egalitarianism, he advocated the distinctive development of the Bantu in their own areas and the economic advance of those in the towns. This, he argued, would be safer than repression, though no policy could guarantee white survival. Neither liberal nor conservative whites were satisfied with his attitude. (Paton 145)

Six months later, Hofmeyr's portfolio of interior affairs was changed to mines and labor.

In 1938 Hofmeyr became chancellor of the University of the Witwatersrand, and his inauguration address, which has been judged one of his most important speeches, was a defense of freedom of opinion, the democratic process, and of the individual's right to self-expression.

During the war, as minister of finance, he introduced severe taxation policies but made greater provision for social services and especially for Bantu education—which for the first time came from consolidated revenue. Eighty per cent of Hofmeyr's own parliamentary salary he paid into the Deo Gratia Fund, which he himself established, for the purpose of advancement of Bantu education: to him, the most meaningful social action possible for post-war South Africa.

In 1946 the Asian Land Tenure and Representation Bill at last gave Indian South Africans some legal rights, and so he supported the legislation; but in the course of the parliamentary debates he made one of those crucial statements that frequently change the course of political fortunes: "I take my stand for the ultimate removal of the color bar from our constitution," he declared, and the United Party felt incommoded, while the Nationalists saw in this an election-winning opportunity. Apartheid, he argued, would only result in a series of small white enclaves surrounded by large black communities; the solution that he advocated was white Christian trusteeship in the interests of the Bantu. But on November 27, 1948 he had a heart attack and died within the week, leaving a legacy of intellectual achievement, administrative efficiency, liberal thought, and indefatigable speaking in behalf of what were often advanced and hence unpopular causes.

There is little question but that Hofmeyr was one of South Africa's most distinguished speakers: sound substance; careful organization; full development by illustration and example, comparison and contrast: appropriate adaptation of language and idea to the immediate audience; elevation of the immediate issue to the level of universal or even cosmic principle all of these attributes made his speeches take on a lasting rather than merely a passing importance. The *Address Delivered by the Chancellor, The Right Honourable J. H. Hofmeyr, M A., Hon. D.Sc., Hon. D.C.L., M. P., On the Occasion of the Summer Graduation Ceremony of the University of Witwatersrand, Johannesburg, 16 March 1946*, later entitled "The Fifth Freedom," eloquently states the main tenets of his life's thought and work—that the greatest conflicts are between freedom and order, liberty and imperialism; that race prejudice is a basic cause of the failure to achieve freedom for all in society; that "the plain truth, whether we like it or not, is that the dominant mentality in South Africa is a Herrenvolk mentality"; that "the greatest evil of all is the tyranny of prejudice"—has all the characteristics of a philosophical and political testament. It is also a manifesto for a new liberalism and another example of the *vox clamantis in deserto*, a plea for freedom from prejudice. *Hofmeyr* (1965), by Alan Paton, is a detailed, sympathetic biography of the man.

Though he was born in the Netherlands, Hendrik Verwoerd (1901-1966) lived in South Africa from the time he was one year old. His father was a Dutch Reformed Church missionary in Bulawayo, Zimbabwe, but the son attended the University of Stellenbosch in Cape Province, where he studied psychology and philosophy and became president of the Union Debating and Philosophical Society as well as president of the Students' Representative Council. He obtained both the B.A. and M.A. degrees in philosophy and psychology: his master's thesis was on the theory of values. In 1923 he was appointed a lecturer in logic and psychology at the University of Stellenbosch. He obtained his Ph.D. and became a professor of sociology.

In 1935 Dr. Verwoerd organized the National Conference on the Poor White Problem and became chairman of its executive committee; thereafter, he served on Cape Town committees for housing and charities, problems of Coloreds, and against the admission to South Africa of Jewish refugees from Central Europe.

Die Transvaler, an Afrikaans daily newspaper, was established in 1937, and Verwoerd became its editor. The paper was the official organ of the National party, and it wielded considerable influence in Johannesburg and Pretoria, supporting the German cause almost without exception throughout the war—which the Afrikanerbond had tried to keep South Africa from entering. In 1942 he published a proposal for a republican constitution of the Union and became a vocal advocate of both Afrikaner causes and national independence. Although he was unsuccessful in an attempt to win election to parliament in the great 1948 landslide, his incessant and effective advocacy of Afrikaner policies assured the election of many others, so that Dr. Malan (who became prime minister in 1948) was greatly in his debt. In 1950, nonetheless, Verwoerd was elected to the senate, and he became a member of the cabinet as minister for native affairs. In this role (which he held for the next eight years) he became the chief spokesman of the policy of apartheid.

In the 1958 election, Verwoerd stood for the Heidelberg (Transvaal) seat in the Assembly and won. Prime Minister Strijdom (who had succeeded Dr. Malan in 1954) died suddenly in 1958 and Verwoerd was elected to his position. He declared that the main policies of the government would be enforcement of the policy of apartheid and the attainment of republican status. It was at the premiers' conference in London in 1961 that he announced South Africa's withdrawal from the Commonwealth and its reconstitution as a republic. On September 6, 1966 he was assassinated in parliament house, Cape Town, by a temporary government worker.

Perhaps no policy of the governments of South Africa has caused so much concern throughout the world as the apartheid policy formally inaugurated by the Malan government in 1948. And because the policy was conceived in its modern form by Verwoerd and implemented by his department and subsequently by him as prime minister, it has properly been identified almost exclusively with him. Therefore, the definitive statement on the policy of apartheid remains the minister's very long speech to parliament on September 3, 1948, which followed two days' discussion of the policy.

At the conclusion of the extended debate, Dr. Verwoerd provided his long speech on the meaning of the policy of apartheid, which has become the classic statement of modern South African social policy. "The Meaning of the Policy of Apartheid" appears in *Verwoerd Speaks: Speeches 1948-1966*, ed. A. N. Pelzer, and in Hansard (Senate Proceedings), September 3, 1948, cols. 223-55.

In *Out of Africa* (1964), a book of sermons, lectures, and addresses delivered while archbishop of Cape Town, the Very Reverend Joost de Blank notes:

> For more than two hundred years after the Cape was settled in 1652 the idea of *apartheid* in worship was rejected. It was proposed at a synod of the church in 1829, and the proposal was turned down. Not until the synod of 1857, when a Scotsman, Dr. Andrew Murray, was moderator, was it resolved that, as a temporary measure for the hardness of men's hearts, separate facilities of worship should be provided for different racial groups. Alas, the temporary nature of the measure has lasted over a hundred years, and shows no signs to coming to an end. (106-7)

Although the N. G. Kerk synod in 1970 reaffirmed its support for the government's policy of "separate development," or apartheid, the Cape Anglican synod rejected racial discrimination which is "in conflict with the ethical norm of 'Love thy Neighbour' or conflicts with the principle that all people enjoy equal status before God." The Anglican communion has consistently opposed apartheid.

It was into such an environment that Richard Ambrose Reeves arrived upon his appointment as bishop of Johannesburg in 1949 and which he left in sadness shortly after the infamous Sharpeville "massacre" of March 21, 1960.

Reeves attended Sidney Sussex College, Cambridge, and took second-class honors in history and moral sciences before enrolling in the General Theological Seminary, New York, in 1926. He later worked in Gibraltar and London and was appointed canon of Liverpool Cathedral (1944-49) before proceeding to South Africa.

From shortly after his arrival in Johannesburg, Reeves took a firm stand against the application of apartheid to religious worship and activities, and perhaps the clearest statement of his position—based both on moral and pragmatic grounds—is his statement to the diocesan synod of the Province at Johannesburg on Sunday, October 23, 1955. So succinct a statement was this that another notable South African churchman, the Very Reverend Joost de Blank, quoted it in full in *Out of Africa*. And de Blank was himself a militant campaigner against apartheid in all its forms. In 1957, soon after his enthronement, he placed a large sign outside St. George's Cathedral in Cape Town that read, "This Cathedral is open to welcome men and women of all races to all services at all times." Dr. Verwoerd interpreted the sign as open confrontation, especially as the parliament building is just a few yards away from the cathedral, and in 1960 the archbishop refused to offer prayers for Dr. Verwoerd, who had been injured in an assassination attempt. Together, Reeves and de Blank led the Anglican communion in the first important assaults on the policy of apartheid.

After the inglorious Sharpeville episode of 1960, Reeves wrote a book entitled *The Agony of Apartheid*, which was promptly banned in South Africa, and which became the basis for his expulsion from the country. As de Blank saw things, "Reeves was outlawed for obedience to the Christian gospel as he sees it...Dr. Reeves's vision, insight, concern for social justice and love for the underprivileged will never be forgotten and South Africa will be immeasurably the poorer for his going." His being exiled was, in the eyes of the archbishop, "an act of religious persecution—an act abhorrent to all faithful churchmen."

Bishop Reeves was a preacher of simple yet profound eloquence whose personal Christian qualities became apparent immediately to all who met, saw, or heard him. Though his pastoral sermons did not have large immediate audiences, his messages themselves certainly affected the relationship between church and state in South Africa.

Reeves's most representative sermon must be "Segregation and Separation Are Impossible," which was delivered in November 1955 and published in *The Watchmen* that month.

Albert John Luthuli (1898-1967) was born in Rhodesia and grew up on the Groutville Mission station in the Umvoti mission reserve near Durban, Natal. His father was an interpreter for the Congregationalist missionaries; his mother, Mtonya, was a member of one of the most honored Zulu tribes. As a youngster, Luthuli attended the local mission school, then the Methodist mission school at Edendale, near Pietermaritzburg; he became a devout Christian, a master of the English language, and ultimately an instructor at Adam's Mission Station College for fifteen years.

In 1936 Luthuli was elected as chief of his tribe of 5,000 members; in 1938 he visited India as a member of the International Missionary Council; and for several years he served on administrative organizations of the Congregationalist Churches of Africa. In 1947 he joined the African National Congress and soon was elected president of its Natal branch. Five years later he helped organize the "defiance campaign" through which Africans protested the segregation of races in post offices, railways, libraries, and similar public facilities in South Africa by non-violent means. As a result, the government deposed him as chief of his people and subsequently banned him from free movement and imprisoned him ultimately on a charge of treason—in peacetime.

After he had been deposed, the African National Congress issued a tract by Luthuli under the title *Our Chief Speaks*. Parts of this document have been quoted and reprinted frequently, for it is a most eloquent statement. The chief recalls that he has never been anti-White and that he has always sought change by peaceful means, even though government actions, such as the Hertzog Bills 1936 (the Native Representation Bill and the Native Trust and Land Bill) took away the hope of Africans that they would achieve the universal franchise that they had been promised since 1853. Then he says, most persuasively:

> Insofar as gaining citizenship rights and opportunities for the unfettered development of the African people, who will deny that thirty years of my life have been spent knocking in vain, patiently, moderately, and modestly at closed and barred doors? Has there been any reciprocal tolerance or moderation from the government, be it Nationalist or United Party? No! On the contrary, the past thirty years have seen the greatest number of laws restricting our rights and progress until today we have reached a stage where we have almost no rights at all, no adequate land for our occupation, our only assets cattle—dwindling, no security of homes, no decent and remunerative employment, more restrictions to freedom of movement through passes, curfew regulations, influx control measures; in short, we have witnessed in these years an intensification of our subjection to ensure and protect white supremacy.

It is with this background and with a full sense of responsibility that I have joined my people...in the spirit that revolts openly and boldly against injustice and expresses itself in a determined and non-violent manner.

A month after being deposed, Luthuli was elected president-general of the A.N.C. As one writer put it, he went into the defiance campaign a tribal chief and emerged from it as a national leader. But he was soon barred from all important towns and cities and thus prohibited from addressing public assemblies. The ban on him expired in July 1956, but he was immediately re-arrested and incarcerated in Johannesburg Fort. Later, he was charged with treason, though the charge was withdrawn when it became apparent that if the moderates were all removed, the extremists in the African freedom movement would probably gain leadership roles.

Early in 1959 he was beaten up by hooligans when he was addressing a white audience, and in May of that year he was banned from all public speaking and confined to his home village. He appealed for a day of national mourning for the Sharpeville shootings in March 1960, and this and similar peaceful actions brought him into ever-more-ominous confrontation with the government, which painted an image of Luthuli that was far removed from reality. As Nadine Gordimer wrote in *The Atlantic* in April 1959:

> Among his less obvious characteristics is a sense of repose; sometimes a monumental quiet. If more white South Africans could meet him, or even hear him speak on a public platform, they would be astonished (and perhaps even a little ashamed—he makes that sort of impression) to measure the real man against the bloodthirsty demagogue that is the African leader as they imagine him. (62)

In announcing its award for 1960, the Nobel Peace Prize Committee declared that Luthuli was being honored "because in his fight against racial discrimination he had always worked for non-violent methods." The government reluctantly granted a ten-day passport for the nominee, but not before the minister of the interior, Senator Jan H. de Klerk declared that "The government fully realizes that the award was not made on merit and must necessarily rob the Nobel Prize of all its high esteem in the judgement of objectively minded people." Luthuli was dressed in the traditional attire of his tribal chiefs when he delivered his acceptance speech in the Great Hall of the University of Oslo on Monday, December 11, 1961—the first African to be so honored. It is, without a doubt, one of the great speeches in advocacy of liberty, democracy, and peace.

(The Reuters text of the speech, published in *The New York Times* on December 12, 1961 is somewhat different from that of the London *Times* of the same date; a conflated text appeared in Edward Callan's *Albert John Luthuli and the South African Race*

Conflict, 1968, and the official text was published by the Nobel Foundation.)

Nelson Mandela (b. 1918) is the eldest son of a Tembu chief, one of the royal family of the Transkei. At an early age he ran away from his home in Mvezo, Eastern Cape, to Johannesburg to avoid an arranged marriage and started his formal education by taking the B.A. degree by correspondence from the University of South Africa after being sent down from Fort Hare University College; he later was awarded the LL.B. degree by the University of the Witwatersrand and established a law practice in Johannesburg.

In 1944, Mandela joined the African National Congress and soon rose to positions of management. For his role in the 1952 campaign of defiance of apartheid laws, he was banned from attending public gatherings and from speaking and subjected to constant surveillance by the security police. In 1956 he was again arrested and was one of the defendants in the infamous "Treason Trial" that lasted four-and-a-half years and ended in acquittal of all 28 defendants. Thereupon, Mandela was elected secretary of the African National Action Council, an organization formed to activate black resistance to apartheid, and became leader of the Spear of the Nation, a paramilitary offshoot of the A.N.C.

In 1960, Mandela was charged with having left South Africa without a valid travel document and with having incited South Africans to strike. The trial, which turned into an attack on the government policy of apartheid, was held in the Old Synagogue in Pretoria, which had been converted into a courtroom, and opened on October 22, 1962. Mandela conducted his own defense through the four-day trial. Judgment was reserved until November 7, and on that occasion, before sentence was pronounced, Mandela delivered his famous speech to the court, a speech that is equaled in logic, passion, and power only by his subsequent "No Easy Walk to Freedom" speech, which was delivered before he was sentenced to life imprisonment.

The result of the Pretoria trial was a sentence of three years in jail for traveling without a passport and two years' imprisonment for incitement to strike. The prisoner was forced to spend twenty-three hours daily in solitary confinement in the Pretoria Central Prison, and while in confinement was further charged with conspiracy to overthrow the government of South Africa after a police raid on June 11, 1963 of an African underground headquarters in Rivonia, a suburb of Johannesburg. Again, Mandela opened the defense of all eight brought to trial. The case lasted eleven months after the raid, and six Africans, one Indian, and one White were sentenced to life imprisonment on Robben Island, the South African "Devil's Island" some six miles out in the sea off Cape Town.

At Pretoria, the judge described Mandela with great insight as "the leader and figurehead of his people"—not just the Xhosas, but all South African Blacks. The *New York Times* commented that Mandela and his colleagues were "the George Washingtons and Benjamin Franklins of South Africa." And just as the speeches of Washington, Franklin, Jefferson, and Adams contain succinct and memorable statements of the principles that have guided the American nation over the years, Mandela's speeches provide his followers and supporters with moving words of witness. As he said in his final statement at Rivonia:

> There is no easy walk to freedom anywhere, and many of us will have to pass through the valley of the shadow of death again and again before we reach the mountain-tops of our desires.... During my lifetime I have dedicated myself to the struggle of the African people. I have fought against white domination, and I have fought against black domination. I have cherished the ideal of a democratic and free society in which all persons live together in harmony and with equal opportunities. It is an ideal which I hope to live for and achieve. But if need be, it is an idea for which I am prepared to die.

It is some measure of the effectiveness of Mandela as a public speaker that the South African government's initial restriction of his democratic rights was to prohibit him from addressing meetings and that, to minimize his influence on the more literate and affluent, his printed speeches were not allowed to be circulated. By these and similar infringements on individual liberty, the South African government has created a martyr, a hero, and a legend that will surely outlast the memory of the midget men who have inadvertently created their opponents' strength and their own nemesis.

Both of Nelson Mandela's speeches to the courts on sentencing are outstanding examples of that genre, which includes such well-known orations as those of John Brown, the abolitionist whose exploits at Harper's Ferry in 1859 have become world famous; Eugene V. Debs, the renowned American socialist and pacifist; William Calley, the Vietnam veteran; and "Ned" Kelly, the celebrated Australian bushranger. As one critic has said, "Their speeches shine."

Perhaps no contemporary South African writer is better-known throughout the world than Alan Paton (b. 1903), author of *Cry, the Beloved Country* (1948), *Too Late the Phalarope* (1953), *Tales from a Troubled Land* (1961), and *Sponomo* (1965). But though his reputation rests largely on these books, he has made great and lasting contributions to the development of a realistic and enlightened political environment in South Africa as speaker, pamphleteer, educator, and social activist. The range of his speaking engagements in impressive, and the titles of some of his speeches will illustrate this: "The Treatment of non-European Crime," "The Prevention of Crime," "Juvenile Delinquency and its Treatment," "Christian Unity: A South African View," "The Abuse of Power," "Liberals Reject Violence," and "The Third Force" (the presidential address to the Liberal Party). In addition, Paton delivered the Stafford Cripps Memorial Sermon in St. Paul's Cathedral and the eulogy at the funeral of his close friend Albert Luthuli.

> Paton was born in Pietermaritzburg and attended the Natal University College, graduating B.Sc. with distinction in physics, and obtaining the Dip.Ed. While an undergraduate he belonged to the Student Christian Association; contributed poetry, prose, and drama to the university literary journals; and was sent to the first Imperial Conference of Students in England. From 1925 to

1935, he taught mathematics and physics at Ixopo High School and Maritzburg College, and in 1935 he was appointed principal of Diepkloof Reformatory, a Johannesburg institution for African boys. This last appointment stimulated his interest in race relations, in social policy, and in the relationship between religion and politics: he addressed the World Council of Churches in Evanston, Illinois, in 1954, and contributed to such journals as *Christian Century*, advocating a democratic, multi-racial society in South Africa.

In 1956 Paton became chairman of the Liberal Party, a trustee of the Defense and Aid Fund, and a founder of *Contact*, a liberal fortnightly journal; in 1960 he lectured in Britain and New York, and had his passport withdrawn on his return to South Africa; since then he has been under virtual house arrest, so great have been the restrictions on his activities.

As Mrs. Paton has written, "My husband feels...that the best speech that he has delivered in recent years is the one he delivered at the University of the Witwatersrand on June 6th, 1968, on the sixth annual Day of Affirmation of Academic and Human Freedom." Though relatively short, it is a forceful statement not only of Paton's personal belief but of the universal philosophy of liberalism; as he says, "The important question is not whether the dream is to be fulfilled. The important question is whether we should go on dreaming."

Remarkably, this speech was printed in full in the *Rand Daily Mail* (Johannesburg) on June 7, 1968 and was widely acclaimed.

Richard L. Strout, veteran correspondent of the *Christian Science Monitor*, recently commented on political oratory:

> Where are the great phrases of today, the rolling periods, the dramatic pause, the sequence of rhetorical questions that enlist the audience, the majestic peroration?...It is all very well to say that government proceeds more smoothly without emotion, conducted by quiet technocrats appealing only to logic; but that isn't the way governments are run, masses moved, or conventions ruled. There is good

reason that statesmen should be logical and clear-thinking—we all feel safer if they have plenty of ballast in the hold—but wind of eloquence in the sails helps enormously, too.

The speeches of Helen Suzman (b. 1917), a trained economist and new parliamentarian from the Transvaal, may not be remarkable for their frequent rolling periods, their impressive dramatic pauses, or their memorable and moving perorations, but they combine in a most effective way the principal elements of successful deliberative rhetoric: they reveal an incisive mind exploring others' speeches and policies for fundamental ideas and intrinsic weaknesses; they reveal the ethos of the speaker herself by demonstrating her abiding concern for individuals of all races and economic groups: they show her ability to thrust and parts with political opponents; they introduce a fine balance between seriousness and humor or satire; they make use of clear organizational patterns and cogent argumentation (emotional, logical, and personal proofs being utilized to advantage); and they invariably relate even the most apparently mundane issue to the broader and more general ones of liberty, freedom, and equality before the law. When we hear her speak or read her printed speeches we feel compelled to respond in the words of Macbeth: "Stay, you imperfect speaker, tell me more."

While politicians and theologians offer theoretical and practical justifications for apartheid, there are others who invoke Scripture and political or sociological reasons for its abandonment; for its demise the United Nations and other organizations have spoken in not uncertain terms, and new leaders of African and Colored groups have been as vocal as the older ones, such as Paton, Suzman, and Reeves. Among them is Desmond Tutu (b. 1931), born in Klerksdorp, Transvaal, and a resident from age 12 of Johannesburg.

Tutu studied at the Pretoria Bantu Normal College, 1951-53, and became a teacher at the Johannesburg Bantu High School and subsequently in Pietermaritzburg. He resigned in protest after the passage of the Bantu Education Act, which he believed augured ill for Africans, and took up the study of theology at St. Peter's Theology College: he was ordained as an Anglican minister in 1960. He obtained his bachelor's and master's degrees in theology from the University of London and served as curate at St. Alban's Cathedral. On his return to South Africa he delivered sermons that highlighted the disparity between the positions of the Dutch and Anglican churches and the increasing oppression of the non-white groups, counseling Prime Minister John Vorster that the situation was a "powder barrel that can explode at any time." He has become one of the most vocal of the new generation of preachers—and one of the most respected and effective, demonstrating that the sermon is no less influential than the deliberative or forensic speech—and notably devoid of demagoguery.

As can be seen from the preceding, South Africans of all racial groups have contributed to a remarkable oeuvre of oratory; public address is arguably as highly developed in South Africa as in any other nation, and the nation's public speakers have demonstrably mastered the classical canons of rhetoric in the several forms of oratory.

Bibliography

Callan, Edward. *Albert John Luthuli and the South African Race Conflict*, 1968.
Davenport, T. R. H. *The Oxford History of South Africa*, 1960.
Douglas, W. M. *Andrew Murray and His Message*, 1926.
Du Plessis, J. *The Life of Andrew Murray of South Africa*, 1917.
Friedman, Marion V. *Olive Schreiner: A Study in Latent Meaning*, 1956.
Kruger, S. J. P. *Memoirs*, 1902.
Millin, Sarah G. *Rhodes*, 1936.
Mitchell, Lewis. *The Life and Times of the Right Honourable Cecil Rhodes*, 1910.
Paton, Alan. *Hofmeyr*, 1965.
Pelzer, A. N., ed. *Verwoerd Speaks: Speeches 1948-1966*, 1966.
Smuts, Jan Christiaan. *Holism and Evolution*, 1926.
Verschoyle, F. (pseudo. Vindex). *Cecil Rhodes: His Political Life and Speeches*, 1900.

10

Bantu Culture

F. J. Language

The Bantu-speaking peoples inhabit practically the whole of the area from the Equator to the Cape of Good Hope, or about one third of Africa as a whole; and while South Africa constitutes a little more than one-tenth of Bantu Southern Africa, it is inhabited by about one-sixth of the total Bantu population.

Racially, the Bantu are classified as negroid, together with such peoples as the West African Negroes, although the physical characteristics of these groups vary considerably as they do also among the Bantu themselves; thus skin color varies from light to dark brown, but in most cases is chocolate brown, in contrast to the West African Negroes, whose skin color is generally black.

A peculiarity of a number of Bantu is that, in addition to their typically negroid features, they also reveal physical characteristics that resemble those of the Hamites of North Africa. This gave rise to an old theory that the origin of the Bantu must be ascribed to miscegenation between some West African negro tribes and peoples of Hamitic stock, probably in the vicinity of the interlacustrine areas of East Africa about two thousand years ago. This theory was substantiated by certain cultural phenomena that are peculiar to the Bantu: among others, that their traditional economic system was a mixed one, consisting of agriculture and animal husbandry.

Many other theories have hitherto been put forward as to the origin of the Bantu as a separate race and people, but none of them have been conclusive. One fact, however, stands out clearly, and that is that the Bantu must be accepted as a race and people indigenous to Africa clearly distinctive and easily distinguishable from all other races and peoples of both Africa and the rest of the world.

The South African Bantu are, however, not indigenous to South Africa. Their ancestors migrated from East Africa, and they traveled along a three-forked overland route southward in numerous small groups or tribes, wave after wave, over a long period of time. The vanguard of this large-scale population shift probably reached South Africa some four or five centuries ago. In those days practically the whole of the country was occupied by wandering bands of Bushman hunters and gatherers as well as by some scattered tribes of nomadic cattle-keeping Hottentots. Both the Bushmen and the Hottentots have, since the middle of the nineteenth century, completely disappeared from the South African scene simply because they could not resist the impact of Western and Bantu civilizations: the Bushmen have taken refuge in the almost impenetrable semi-desert of the Kalahari and some part of Southwest Africa, leaving behind them only their rock paintings and engravings; the Hottentots became practically extinct as a result of epidemics of smallpox and Dutch settler appropriation of their pastoral lands; they retreated into the interior, where their numbers declined and they engaged in herding.

Towards the beginning of the nineteenth century a considerable number of separate and independent Bantu tribes, large and small, were already settled in various parts of the country. Soon disputes over tribal territory and grazing areas arose among them, cattle raids ensued, and within a short time many tribes lived in enmity with each other and warfare was invariably resorted to. Hostilities reached a climax when an ambitious and despotic chief in Natal, Chaka (and after him Dingaan) succeeded in mercilessly conquering almost 300 tribes and subjecting them to the rule and paramountcy of himself, thereby depriving them all of their independence. This was the birth of the fearless and fearful Zulu empire, which at one time had at its disposal an army of about one hundred thousand well-trained and dauntless warriors.

During those years a couple of Chaka's most competent generals fled the Zulu country with a following of warriors, establishing large empires of their own. The tribes of the interior were thrown into confusion; many became famished and fugitive, and this led to the building of yet another powerful and influential Bantu nation in South Africa, namely the Ba-Sotho. Moshesh, chief of the Kwena tribe in Lesotho and a man of outstanding statesmanship and diplomatic ability, offered refuge and protection to fugitive tribes, which he permitted to settle in his country, provided they agreed to acknowledge him as their paramount chief—which they did.

Brief mention should also be made of a few other Bantu nations that came into existence in South Africa during the past century. Sekhukhune, chief of the Pedi tribe in the northeastern Transvaal, brought a number of tribes under his paramountcy to form the Pedi nation; and the Swazi nation was created out of a number of separate tribes, all under the rule of one paramount chief.

Apart from the tribes which were amalgamated to constitute these large states, there were still a considerable number of separate tribes that continued to live in their own areas. In 1838 Dingaan, the Zulu chief, slaughtered about five hundred Boers; he and his followers were then killed by Andreas Pretorius. Dingaan's successor, Mpanda, became a vassal of the Republic of Natal, but his son, Cetewayo, resumed warfare and was defeated by British forces in 1878.

Contact between the Europeans and the Bantu over a long period has given rise to many changes in the traditional life and culture of the latter. Bantu culture at present can be correctly understood and appreciated only if it is studied against the background of the old or traditional culture of these people as it existed before it was influenced by Europeans.

Whenever a classification into ethnic or cultural groups of the South African Bantu is made, it is essential that the one and one-half million Bantu of the three neighboring countries—Lesotho, Botswana, and Swaziland—be included with the thirteen million Bantu of South Africa on the ground of their close cultural affinity.

On the basis of phenomena that can be described as partly linguistic, partly cultural, and partly historical, the Bantu of South Africa and these adjacent territories can be classified into four distinctive main groups, generally referred as the Nguni, the Sotho, the Tsonga, and the Venda. On the basis of cultural similarity, each main group can be subdivided into a number of subgroups, and each subgroup can in turn be divided into a number of separate tribes, the total of which in a subgroup may vary from about a dozen to well over several hundred.

The Nguni main group is generally divided into the following subgroups: (a) the Xhosa-speaking tribes of the Transkeian and Ciskeian territories in Cape Province; (b) the Zulu-speaking tribes of Natal and Zulu-land; (c) two sections of Ndebele tribes occupying some parts of the Transvaal; and (d) the Swazi tribes of the independent kingdom of Swaziland just across the Southeastern border of the Transvaal.

The Sotho main group is divided into three subgroups, namely: (a) the Northern Sotho, which is made up of a number of Ba-Pedi tribes speaking dialects of the Se-Pedi language and inhabiting parts of the Northern and Eastern Transvaal; (b) the Western Sotho, in which is included all the Tswana-speaking tribes of the Western Transvaal, the northern Cape, and the Orange Free State as well as all the Tswana tribes of the Republic of Botswana on the western borders of the Transvaal; and (c) the Southern Sotho, consisting of a great many Ba-Sotho tribes, speaking various dialects of the Se-Sotho language and inhabiting Lesotho, a mountainous country situated in the center of the Republic of South Africa.

The Tsonga main group of the eastern Transvaal can be divided into three subgroups, and the Venda of the northern Transvaal can be also.

According to Dr. A. Winifred Hoernlé, one can expect to find the greatest degree of cultural similarity between the tribes belonging to the same subgroup, minor cultural differences between the subgroups within the same main group, and major cultural differences between the main groups: "At the same time, even the basic (main) groups have certain types of institution in common, though these appear in each group in distinctive forms." Cultural similarity does, in fact, exist between these major groups of Bantu, but then only in respect of a few basic institutions, and with regard to these, only in very broad outline. In reality, there is nowadays, as in the distant past, more diversity than similarity in culture between these major ethnic groups of Bantu people in South Africa. Any attempt, therefore, to generalize about Bantu culture on the supposition that there is uniformity of culture among all of them will be misleading.

The problem is further complicated by the fact that not all Bantu in South Africa can culturally any longer be classified in any of the above-mentioned major groups, subgroups, or even tribes, inasmuch as quite a considerable number of them have become completely detribalized and divorced from every semblance of Bantu culture and way of life. These detribalized Bantu—the majority of them have taken up permanent residence in the European urban areas—have come to regard it as being beneath their dignity to be associated with Bantu life in any way. They must therefore be classified as entirely separate from the tribal Bantu in the reserves, who still adhere to a changed form of their traditional culture.

The main economic pursuits of the Bantu were limited to animal husbandry and agriculture, supplemented by the hunting of wild game and the gathering of edibles from the veld. Trading by barter on a very limited scale was resorted to only in very exceptional circumstances; commercial trading and industrial undertakings were entirely unknown. Some crafts, such as the smelting of iron and the working of metals, were confined to a few specialists in some of the tribes, while the manufacture of clothing, domestic utensils, and personal effects was done manually by the members of every household as and when the need arose, or as a means of passing the time.

The economic system of the tribe was closely bound up with the system of land use. Every tribe occupied its own territory, which was owned by all the members of the tribe collectively and administered by the chief as trustee. The system of individual ownership in land was unknown and never practiced. The area selected for tribal settlement had to conform to a few basic requirements: among others, it had to be vacant and unoccupied land; it had to be sufficiently extensive and fertile to provide for the agricultural activities and the pastoral pursuits of the tribe; and it had to afford natural protection against possible raids and attacks by hostile tribes. The final decision as to the suitability of a particular area rested with the chief. Similarly, whenever the tribal territory became exhausted through over-stocking, denudation, impoverishment of the agricultural fields, scarcity of wild game, or lack of natural resources (so that the existence of the tribe was threatened) it was the chief, on the advice of his council, who would issue an order for the tribe to move to another territory in order to ensure their safety and survival. Actually, there was nothing or nobody that could prevent the tribe from exercising its prerogative to move to new and suitable territories from time to time as the need arose.

It was customary for every tribe to demarcate various sections of its territory in such a way that each of the main branches of the economic system would best be provided for. Among the Sotho, the chief, as head of the tribe and trustee of the tribal territory, would set aside part of the territory as the grazing areas where tribesmen could pasture their cattle; parts of the territory most suitable for cultivation would be reserved for agricultural purposes; the most outlying areas were regarded as the hunting grounds, and usually a site would be specially set aside as the headquarters of the tribe, and here the chief would put up his residence. It was customary for the tribe as a whole to live together in one large town with the chief's residence more or less in the center, while among some of the Nguni tribes the residences of the households were scattered among the corn fields and grazing areas.

The means of existence; the methods employed in agriculture, animal husbandry, hunting, and domestic industries; the division of labor, the standard of living; the type of house, its erection and the materials used; the type of dress; domestic utensils, and so on, were with very few exceptions the same for every tribesman, woman, or child, as the case might be. A uniform pattern of economic thought, organization, activity, and life in general existed throughout the tribe as a whole. And yet the basic economic unit within the tribal establishment was not the tribe as such, but the individual *family*, which consisted of a man and his wife together with their children. Not even a *household* as such, which consisted of a man and as many wives as he had married, together with their children (in the case of polygenous marriages), could be considered as an economic unit; in every household each wife, together with her children, constituted a separate economic unit, the husband sharing to some extent in the economic pursuits of every family.

The division of labor was the most discernible in the family as a social and economic unit. The principles on which it was based were the same for every family throughout the tribe, so that in this respect also a uniform pattern was observed. Broadly speaking, it was based on a differentiation between the sexes, but also to some extent on age, rank, and status.

Every Bantu family engaged itself in the production of food with but one object in view: to provide for its subsistence from one season to the next, and no more. A self-sufficient subsistence economy par excellence! If the last crop was a poor one, food had to be rationed. Usually, families or households would share among themselves all food that might be available. On the other hand, if food was plentiful, it had, of necessity, to be consumed, as there were no other means of disposing of it.

The portions of the tribal territory that were earmarked for agricultural purposes were allocated by the chief in large blocks to his headmen, whose duty it was to sub-divide them into smaller plots and to distribute these among the family heads residing in their respective areas of jurisdiction. Every family head was entitled to as many plots as equaled the number of individual families under his care. Similarly, each family was entitled to demand a plot of land to cultivate for the sole benefit of its own members. But it could never be sold or alienated in any way; it had to remain the property of the tribe.

Cultivation of the plot and the production of food devolved mainly upon the wife in the family. According to Professor Schapera, it was her responsibility "to break up the soil, plant the seed, remove the weeds, keep off the granivorous birds and other pests, and finally reap and thresh the crops" and carry the same to the granaries. On occasion the wife would organize a party of relatives and friends to assist her in completing some major or urgent task on the plot; in return for their services she would treat them during intervals to food and beer.

The crops cultivated for consumption consisted mainly of kaffir corn and maize, supplemented by pumpkins, melons, calabashes, beans, peas, sweet cane, and millet. The methods employed were rather primitive: the only implement used for all agricultural purposes was a kind of hoe made out of iron or wood; of fertilizer or manure they knew nothing; the lands were never irrigated. Rotation of crops was never practiced; instead, in order to ensure good crops, the Bantu resorted to magic and all sorts of ritual practices, such as the doctoring of the lands and the seed. Certain taboos were observed, and in cases of drought the chief would summon some renowned rainmaker to perform the necessary ceremonies that would cause the rain to fall.

The most impressive ceremony of all, called the festival of the first fruits, was performed towards the end of the agricultural season. Until this ceremony was performed and concluded, it was prohibited for anybody to eat or even touch any food that was prepared from the staple crops of the new season—kafir corn or maize—the other food products being excepted. In some tribes, such as the Zulu and the Swazi, this ceremony was performed on a national basis inasmuch as the tribe as a whole participated in it at the headquarters of the chief, who was the central figure in all the festivities, which sometimes would last as long as a week.

Besides their agricultural holdings and pursuits, the Bantu also kept livestock (in the form of cattle and goats) for their subsistence as well as for other essential purposes. Cattle, especially, were esteemed as their most treasured personal possessions; cattle filled them with pride and gave them intrinsic satisfaction and gratification as nothing else could do. No small wonder that every Bantu man cherished the ambition of amassing as many cattle as was within his means and ability. Cattle were not only kept for the sustenance of the family; they were regarded as part of the household.

As a rule, cattle were very seldom slaughtered for the purpose of providing meat for the family; meat supplies were obtained by killing goats and wild game or using cattle that died of disease. Cow's and goat's milk was regarded as a very nourishing food, and it figured prominently in the daily diet of the family.

Animals had many uses for the Bantu. Skins were used as material to make clothes, blankets, sleeping mats, and carrying- or storage-bags; fat was usually rubbed on the hair and body as a cosmetic; ornaments and articles for personal or domestic use were made from horns, bones, and sinews.

Usually a very personal relationship existed between a man and his beasts; he would always call them by their names and often he would eulogize them. He would never harm or ill-treat them and, although he knew each one by sight, he would slit the official mark of his clan on the ears of every beast lest it be claimed by somebody else should it stray.

The Bantu attached a peculiar economic value to their cattle. The wealth or prosperity of a person was gauged in terms of the number of cattle he possessed, irrespective of whether they were as thin as laths or as fat as pigs: quality was of no great concern. Cattle were also used to settle big debts or to pay court fines; the Bantu of olden times employed no currency other than cattle, goats being of minor concern.

For the Bantu, cattle also had a social and ritual significance, which was much more important than their economic value. The number of cattle a man possessed determined his wealth, the respect he commanded, and the influence he exerted among his fellow men in social life and at tribal meetings. A man rich in cattle could easily afford to marry many women, for in Bantu society a man could get married only if he had enough cattle to transfer to his bride's family as *lobola*, or *bogadi*—a custom which not only legalized a marriage and its offspring, but also created a great many rights, duties, and obligations between the relatives of the husband and those of his wife. The more women a man had married, the greater was his prestige and the larger the number of people and adherents who treated him with respect and deference.

The only means by which a man, a family, or the tribe could make and keep contact with the ancestral spirits in order to ensure their continued interest in and their benevolence towards personal and national welfare and prosperity was by periodic sacrifices of cattle. Sacrifices of this nature were regularly made on the death of the chief, during ceremonies of a national character (such as the ceremonies of the first fruits and the rain ceremonies), and on occasions of family or tribal affliction.

The Venda tribes of the northern Transvaal believed that their ancestors were personified in particular beasts; and in order to keep them pacified or to gain their favor, sacrifices of beer would regularly be poured over the back of such an animal. The Bomvana, a Xhosa-speaking tribe from the eastern Cape province, used to keep a special herd of cattle at the chief's headquarters; this herd they regarded as sacred, and the animals were kept only to be offered as sacrifices to the ancestral spirits.

The cattle pen, or kraal, occupied a venerable place in the social, spiritual, and political life of the household or tribe. In the layout of any village, which was invariably built in the form of a circle or semi-circle, the cattle pen was as a rule erected in the center. A further enclosure, called the *kgotla* in the Tswana language, and also in circular form, was erected around a big tree at the main gate of the cattle pen. Both the cattle pen and the kgotla were taboo to women. The adult men of the village or tribe spent most of their day in the kgotla, gossiping, drinking beer, and discussing family affairs. In the chief's kgotla, in addition, the adult men would come together to assist the chief in the settlement of serious court cases.

The chief's kgotla also served as a place where the adult tribesmen would gather in a tribal meeting (*pitso*) under the chairmanship of the chief to deliberate upon matters of national concern. If the meeting was to be held in great secret, it would move from the kgotla into the cattle pen.

Finally, the cattle pen was regarded as the most appropriate place for the chief of the tribe to be buried after his death. His body would be wrapped in the skin of a bull ritually slaughtered for the purpose and put away in a hole dug in the center of the kraal or underneath its fence near the gate. After the ceremony the cattle would be brought into the kraal and kept there until they had obscured all outward signs of the grave. Thereafter specially selected cattle would at regular intervals be sacrificed to the departed spirits of the chief and his predecessors.

Cattle were regarded and treated as a special legacy from the ancestral spirits; they could not be disposed of lightly; at all times they had to be protected and defended against both wild animals and marauding bands; their care had in all respects to be undertaken with the greatest solicitude and reverence. Ritually contaminated persons—and especially grown women—were prohibited from mingling with the cattle lest the tribe be struck with disaster. Other taboos with regard to the cattle were imposed and strictly observed; magical rites were regularly performed in respect of the pastures, the cattle pens, and the cattle in order to promote their health, fertility, and general well-being.

The hunting of wild game and animals was quite extensively engaged in by the Bantu in olden times, mainly as a supplement to the meat, skins, horns, and other useful articles they obtained from their own domestic animals. Sometimes a hunt was undertaken with the object of getting the skin, limbs, or fat of a particular animal, to be used for special purposes. For instance, the skins of all leopards killed in a hunting expedition had to be handed over to the chief as his insignia of royalty; the astragali of some species were widely used for divination purposes; the fat of crocodiles and lions, mixed with other ingredients, was indispensable for the preparation of certain potent medicines used in magical rites and ceremonies.

The hunting of small game was a relatively easy task for any individual; even the boys were very fond of it. But the killing of big game, such as elephants, rhinoceroses, and buffaloes, as well as wild animals such as lions and leopards, was indeed a dangerous undertaking, considering that the weapons employed were of a very crude and primitive nature: the spear, the axe, and the wooden club.

In order to minimize the danger and enhance the success (and perhaps the excitement as well), the chief would on occasion organize large parties of men to undertake a hunting expedition on a collective basis. The game killed would be divided among the participants and the chief according to the customary rules of the tribe.

Many precautions of a magical nature had to be taken before an individual or a party embarked on a hunting trip: the bonethrower, or witchdoctor, had to be consulted for a divination; the weapons had to be doctored with medicine; certain taboos had to be observed before, during, and after the hunt; special attention had to be given to certain omens; various charms had to be carried, and so on, with a view to ensuring success in the chase and averting any possible accidents, injury, or calamity.

The smallest, but nevertheless the most conspicuous, social unit among the Bantu was the family or household, which was composed of a husband, his wife or wives, and their minor children, together with any other relatives or unrelated dependents. Within this household the individual family, consisting of a mother and her children, could be easily distinguished; and such a family or household could only come into existence by virtue of one or more legal marriages—marriages that a man had contracted in accordance with tribal law and custom.

Among the Nguni tribes no marriage was allowed with people related through any of the four grandparents; marriage with a blood relative less than at least four generations removed (be it on the father's or the mother's side) was regarded as incestuous and strictly prohibited. Among the Sotho tribes, on the other hand, the position was just the reverse. These tribes showed a strong preference for a man's marriage with his mother's brother's daughter or with the father's sister's daughter or with the father's brother's daughter, and they even encouraged marriages between the children of two sisters. Such cross-cousin marriages, as a result in which either the maternal or paternal uncle might also be the father-in-law, were never tolerated by the Nguni tribes.

Needless to say, as a consequence of the system of preferential marriages among the Sotho tribes, the custom of infant betrothal was widely practiced to such an extent that, in some cases, infants would be betrothed to one another by their parents even before they were born. Their marriage, as was the case with all marriages among all the Bantu, could not be contracted until they had complied with certain prerequisites. One inexorable requirement of tribal custom was that young people could be permitted to get married only after they had been ceremonially initiated into adulthood. Without exception boys and girls, on attaining the age of puberty, were initiated separately.

All the boys of the tribe were taken together as a group and kept isolated from the tribe in a specially constructed camp away from the nearest residences or villages for a period of approximately three months, usually during winter. The camp was in the charge of a senior and experienced elder of the tribe, assisted by a magician and a number of initiated men who acted as guardians and instructors of the boys. No women or uninitiated men were allowed in or near the camp. An outstanding feature of the initiation ceremonies and other activities performed at the camp was the profound secrecy in which everything was kept. Even the deaths that occurred in the camp during its duration had to be kept secret. Any person found guilty of divulging anything about the camp and the initiation ceremonies could be punished by death.

The boys were escorted to the initiation camp by the adult tribesmen and, on their arrival, amid deafening uproariousness, they would be circumcised by a magician in the order of their seniority. This was the first test of their power of endurance; many other tests would be applied during their course of training. (Circumcision was practiced by all the South African Bantu in olden times, but the custom has been abolished by the Zulu, the Swazi, and some Xhosa and Tswana tribes during the past century and a half, though the majority of tribes still observe the custom.)

While in the camp, the boys were instructed in the laws and customs of their tribe and emphasis was laid on the relation between the sexes—especially on the customary behavior of men and women in and out of wedlock. At the conclusion of the initiation ceremonies the boys who had been initiated together were formed into a regiment of the tribe with a close relative of the chief as its leader. Such a regiment could at any time be called up by the chief to perform any duty of a public nature. The Xhosa tribes were an exception to this almost universal custom.

The initiation of girls was begun shortly after the completion of the ceremonies for the boys. The ceremonies that they had to go through varied considerably from tribe to tribe, but the underlying principles and objects were the same among all tribes; the girls could pass from youth to adulthood only through a series of rites and ceremonies. In their course of training they received detailed instruction from the old women on sexual matters and on the duties and responsibilities of women in adult and married life. Among the Sotho tribes, the girls were usually initiated as a group, but among the other tribes this was done on an individual basis.

Another indispensable feature of a traditional Bantu marriage was the institutionalized custom known as *bogadi* among the Sotho and *lobola* among the Nguni tribes. In essence, bogadi consisted of some tangible property—almost without exception a number of cattle—that the family of the bridegroom was obliged to pass over to the family of the bride. The significance of this custom has often been mistakenly interpreted as a dowry, or as a purchase price of the wife. In a sense it could be regarded as a form of compensation to the girl's family for the loss of a useful member. Its primary function, however, seems to have been to legitimize the marriage and its resultant offspring. In addition, bogadi served the useful purpose of strengthening the marriage ties between husband and wife; it guaranteed the stability and continued existence of the marriage union; it ensured the good treatment and support of the wife by the husband and vice versa. If the woman gave her husband any good and sufficient reason to divorce her, she would have to return to her family, in which event they would, to their dismay, regret, and utter shame, be compelled to return the bogadi-cattle to their original owners. If, on the other hand, the husband, through ill-treatment or neglect of duty, compelled his wife to flee back to her people, he would have no claim to the return of the bogadi-cattle, which would be retained by the wife's people for her sustenance and benefit—a material loss to the husband and a slur on his name.

Cattle in the form of bogadi thus had far-reaching consequences, not only for a married couple but also for both their families and wider kin. If a man did not possess enough cattle to make up the full bogadi, he could either turn to the members of his family to make up the deficiency or he could wait until one of his sisters got married and, with his father's consent, appropriate her bogadi. Also, the bogadi that was given in respect of a bride did not all belong to her father alone, as some of her relatives could lay claim to a portion of it—especially if they had on a previous occasion made contributions to the bogadi of her brother. Bogadi, like marriage, was therefore an institution in which not only the husband and his wife were concerned; the families and relatives of both of them were socially and legally implicated in it in more than one way. For instance, when a man died, or when he was found impotent, or when he was unable to beget children with his wife, his younger brother (or another close male relative) could stand in the breach. And the children so borne by the woman were regarded and treated as the offspring not of their physiological father, but of the man who had given the bogadi at the time of the marriage. Again, when a wife died childless, or when she was proved to be barren, her husband was entitled to request her parents or family to replace her or to provide a substitute in the person of her younger sister or another close female relative. No bogadi was given in respect of such a substitute wife, and the children borne by her were regarded as the children of the wife who had died childless or could have no children of her own.

According to Bantu opinion, a marriage without offspring, a family without children, or a family head with neither issue nor a successor was unthinkable. The individual family, as a biological unit, produced and reared children; as a social unit it fitted into the structure of the village and the tribe; as an economic unit, it was self-sufficient in the production and consumption of food; in religion it performed the customary ceremonies connected with the life of the individual from birth to death and thereafter. In all matters pertaining to the family or household the father was the head and legal representative, greatly respected as such by his wife or wives, his children, his kin, and his adherents.

Polygamy was universally recognized by the Bantu as a feature of their social system. Every man was at liberty to marry as many wives as he could pay bogadi for. It follows that only the more or less well-to-do men in the tribe were polygamists. The number of wives a man had married was always an index of his wealth, social status, influence, and importance, not only among his kinsmen and adherents, but in wider circles as well.

Seniority was a matter of great importance in any polygamous household. Every individual family was regarded as a separate unit: it occupied its own hut or huts, grouped together but fenced off from the others; it had its own lands and produced its own food; it possessed its own cattle, household effects, and so on. But there never was equality of status among the various wives in such a household, otherwise chaos would have ensued. Among the Sotho tribes the seniority of the various wives was determined according to the order in which they were married, the wife first married being regarded as the senior or great wife. Whenever a man married the daughter of his maternal uncle, however, she would take precedence over all the others. In the case of a chief, his great wife was the one chosen for him by the tribe and whose bogadi was also paid by the tribe.

Among the Xhosa also, the wife first married was regarded as the principal wife except in the case of a chief, whose principal wife was chosen after he had firmly established himself; the cattle to be paid for her were also collected from the tribe. In addition, the Xhosa had a "right-hand" wife selected from among the others. The remaining wives were affiliated to these two principal wives as their subordinates.

Among the Zulu tribes, the household was divided into three separate sections: those of the great wife, the "left-hand" wife, and the "right-hand" wife, each with a number of subordinate wives or "houses."

The rules of succession laid down that the eldest son of the principal wife was the legitimate successor of his father as head of the household. He not only inherited all the property of the household but also assumed all the duties and responsibilities connected with the administration and smooth running of the affairs of the household. Likewise, in each individual family the eldest son was the heir and successor to the property of that "house," and he also was the guardian of the interests of every member of it.

Besides the closely integrated family or household, the Bantu also recognized in their social system a large body of kindred, the members of which were related to each other either by birth or by marriage. Kinship formed the basis and laid down the pattern of many social units and institutions; it intimately affected marriage regulations and customs and it regulated to a fine degree the personal relationships between and the customary behavior of tribal members in social and political life, in economic pursuits, in magic, and in religion.

Descent among the Bantu was reckoned through the father: a person belonged to the kinship group of his father, while the kinship group of his mother embraced all his relatives-in-law. Marriage was not an affair in which only a man and a woman became involved; it entailed the bringing together, into close relationship, of two different kinship groups between whom a long list of duties, rights, and responsibilities as well as a fixed pattern of behavior was mutually created. Although the children in a household all belonged to the kinship group of their father, that of their mother was nonetheless of great significance to them.

Among the Sotho tribes, the marriage that was most preferred was that between a man and one of his cousins, more particularly the daughter of his maternal uncle. This woman, upon her marriage, immediately became the great or principal wife in the household of her polygamous husband, taking precedence over all the wives he might formerly have married. Even if such a cross-cousin marriage did not or could not ensue, a special behavior pattern would nevertheless continue to exist between the mother's son and her brother (*malome*, or "male mother," in the Sotho language). Thus the mother's brother would make a substantial contribution to the bogadi that his nephew might require; he would take a leading part in the wedding ceremonies and festivals of his nephew as well as any ritual ceremonies that might have to be performed from time to time; at his home he would, at all times, receive and accommodate his nephew to the best of his ability; the nephew, in turn, would always treat his uncle with great familiarity, give him presents, and render him all kinds of services; and the nephew might even some day inherit one of the wives of his uncle.

The system of kinship terminology was demonstrated at its best within the family or household. But it was extended far

Bantu Culture

beyond the family circle to include a great many people who did not belong to the household. A distinctive feature of the Bantu kinship system and terminology was that many people outside the household were addressed as father, mother, brother, and sister. For instance, a man would address all his father's brothers as "father," and he would behave towards all of them in exactly the same way as he would towards his own father. And, if all these fathers' brothers were "fathers" to a man, naturally he would regard and treat their children as if they were his own brothers and sisters. Similarly, a man's mother's sisters would be "mother" to him, and all their children would be brothers and sisters to him. But the principle was also extended to include the sisters of a man's father and the brothers of a man's mother as well as all their children. Thus my father's sister would be my "female father," and my mother's brother would be my "male mother": all their children I would regard as my brothers and sisters.

It is obvious, therefore, that a Bantu man had many fathers, including female fathers, among the kin of his own father, and also many mothers, including male mothers, among the kin of his own mother. Likewise, he had many brothers and sisters among both kin groups.

Needless to say, a man's behavior was expected to be of the same general type towards all his relatives whom he addressed by the same term, and that it was expected of them all to reciprocate towards him in the same manner.

A behavior pattern that was strictly observed was that of a man towards his mother-in-law and of a woman towards her father-in-law. In Bantu society generally, and in any kinship group, both a father and mother-in-law commanded respect, and they had to be treated with the greatest discretion and circumspection. While the relationships between a man and his father-in-law and between a daughter and her mother-in-law were of a more or less easy and friendly nature, it was entirely otherwise between a man and his mother-in-law, especially between a woman and her father-in-law and men of his status. For instance, a man was expected to avoid his mother-in-law at all times; he was not supposed to look at her or to speak to her, or even to gossip in her presence. Among the Nguni tribes the relationship between a woman and her male relatives-in-law was of an extremely reserved nature, to the extent of almost causing tension. For instance, she was expected not to intrude upon the men's side of the hut, to enter the cattle pen, to mention the name of her husband, or to use words containing the main syllables of his name or that of her father-in-law. These restrictions in behavior could be lifted only after a long period of residence or by performing certain ceremonies.

The kinship system imposed many duties and responsibilities on close relatives. They were expected always to treat each other with respect and consideration, to make occasional gifts to each other, to offer assistance in times of need or illness, to share their food, to give advice in family affairs, to defend each other in court cases and—if need be—to assist in paying debts or court fines and to cooperate in major tasks, such as the clearing of new fields or building and thatching new huts.

In addition, kinship ties to a very large extent regulated and controlled customary behavior in the household and in the tribe at large. Relationship either by blood or by marriage imposed certain rules of conduct and mutual help; guaranteed every person support or protection in case of need; provided assistance in economic pursuits and undertakings; influenced the pattern of social, economic, legal, political, and religious practices and institutions; established and promoted greater social cohesion within the community and the tribe and, in the end, brought about the unity and solidarity of the tribe as a political unit.

Social groupings larger than the family or household and also based on kinship were a further feature of the tribe among the Bantu. For instance, among the Nguni tribes, the clan or sib was such a kinship group. It consisted of a group of people all claiming descent in the male line from the same ancient ancestor. Each clan was known by a laudatory name, and marriage between members of the same clan was strictly forbidden. Very often, however, a section assuming descent from a more recent ancestor would hive off to form a new clan, and intermarriage between the members of the senior and junior branches of the original clan would thereafter be permitted. All clans in the tribe were ranked in a regular order of seniority or precedence in accordance with their grade of relationship to the common ancestor, the clan of the tribal chief being the most senior. The clans were not organized into local or territorial or residential units inasmuch as most of the members of the same clan were intermingled with the members of other clans all over the tribe, and some of them would even be found to be residing with other tribes. Nevertheless, the bond of kinship and unity between them would and could never be broken; this unity was manifested in a common name, the same behavior patterns in social life, uniform marriage regulations, and joint participation in certain ceremonies of a ritual nature.

Within the comprehensive framework of every clan there existed a number of lineages the members of which generally had a common grandfather in the male line. As was the case with the clan, each lineage had its own praise-name, and marriage between its members was forbidden. The lineage and clan are extremely important groups, the lineage being, next to the household, the most intimate social group and principal ritual group within the tribe. The lineage undoubtedly is the most important purely kinship group among most of the Xhosa and Zulu tribes, the group which exercises most social control over the people and within which there is the most intimate social contact and the most stable system of reciprocal rights and duties.

It should be noted that the system of clan organization, as described above for the Nguni tribes, did not exist among the Sotho tribes. They would seem to have had a system of extended lineages which, to a large extent, fitted in with the political organization of the tribe.

Furthermore, the Sotho and Venda tribes had a system of totemic grouping that did not exist among the Nguni. The members of these groups had a notion that they were mysteriously connected with a certain species of animal or natural object, the name of which they used as a laudatory form of address. Such animal or object was greatly revered by the members of its group, though they never offered any prayers or sacrifices to it. Many taboos were observed in connection with such an object, and the members of its group had to pretend to know nothing about it. For instance, members of the group had to avoid "this thing" at all times, never to speak about it, never to touch it, and so on. Actually, such a "totemic" group was a group in name only; in social, economic, political, and religious life it was of no significance. No marriage restrictions were imposed on its members; in fact, there were no rules or regulations prescribing any line of conduct, duties, or responsibilities between members of the group. Yet the number of members of any such group could be considerable; it could extend beyond the limits of any tribe, and even several tribes as such could belong to the same group; but that did not affect the equilibrium or independence of such tribes nor commit them to any mutual obligations.

The tribe was the basic and at the same time the largest political unit among the Bantu. It could be described as a consolidated group of people who lived together under the rule and authority of a chief who exercised sole and independent jurisdiction over a particular territory that was regarded as the property of the tribe as a whole.

The nucleus of a tribe consisted of all the people who believed in their descent from the same ancestor as the chief. But, in addition, each tribe was composed of people or groups of people of foreign descent; there was hardly a single tribe that did not embrace some foreign elements and, especially in the larger tribes, these aliens often outnumbered the nuclear group. Membership of the tribe was therefore not confined to those who might be born into it; the tribe was not a closed unit, such as the lineage or clan, for instance. In fact, any stranger could become a member and a citizen of the tribe on condition that he confessed his loyalty and allegiance to the chief and obtained the latter's consent to settle in an approved place within the recognized boundaries of the tribal territory. And, as has already been explained, people or even whole tribes could by conquest be compelled to become subjects of a tribe to which they had not formerly belonged. Citizenship of a tribe could therefore be acquired by birth, voluntary association, or conquest.

An outstanding characteristic of the tribe was its unity and solidarity, of which every member was constantly aware. This unity found expression in concerted action in times of war as well as peace; in an economic system that was the same for all members; in a well-organized social structure and order that followed a traditional pattern; in religious beliefs that were common to all; in certain ceremonial practices that were regularly undertaken on a national basis; and it culminated in a common loyalty and allegiance to the chief, who was in charge of the government and administration of the tribe as a whole.

Apart from the central government, a system of local government was introduced in every tribe, more or less according to the following universal pattern: usually a number of households who were residing in a neighborhood that could be easily demarcated were constituted into the smallest unit in the political hierarchy of the tribe, namely the ward or subdistrict, with a judicial and administrative system of its own under the control of a headman or petty chief.

The duties, function, and privileges of such a ward headman were adequately described by Isaac Schapera in *The Bantu-Speaking Tribes of South Africa*:

> The headman is sometimes a member of the chief's family, sometimes a commoner. He is either formally appointed by the chief, or at least confirmed, the latter being the more usual since the office tends to be hereditary. The headman is responsible to the chief for the peace, order, and good government of his area, in which he is the chief's representative. He must help his people in their troubles, and sponsor them before the chief; he regulates their occupation and use of land, and controls the right of strangers to settle there; he prays and sacrifices on their behalf to his ancestors, and performs other ceremonies for their well-being and protection. He deals with cases which the kraal heads (household heads) have not been able to

settle, or have referred to him in the first instance; and he has the power to impose fines and other forms of punishment. But he must himself refer all cases of serious difficulty to his superior authority, and there is also an appeal from his verdict. He must further see that his people pay the customary forms of tribute and carry out the commands of the chief, conveyed to him by special messengers or at council meetings. He must himself visit the chief from time to time, not only to assist at the council, but also to report upon the affairs of his area.

His own privileges are relatively few. His home is built in the most favoured part of his area, and he has the pick of the land for cultivation and grazing. He can claim free labour from his people for such public services as building and repairing his official courtyard, taking messages or executing the verdicts of his court; but he does not as a rule receive any private tribute, either in labour or in kind, except with the special permission of the chief. By virtue of his office, however, he is as a rule greatly respected, not only by his own people but in the tribe as a whole; and if he had a large following he may play an important part in tribal politics generally.

The headman is assisted by a small council embracing his own senior male relatives and the more important kraalheads, together with any other elderly men of repute in his area. They sit with him in judgment over the cases that come to his court; he discusses with them all the matters relating to the public life of the group, and consults them on tribal questions generally in connection with meetings of the chief's council. They also keep check upon his own behavior. They can, if need be, reprimand him severely; but more generally, if he is negligent, incompetent, or unduly severe, they report him to the chief, who may then fine him or even depose him in favour of a more suitable man.

Local government within the tribe was further extended by combining a number of adjacent wards or sub-districts into a district and placing the administration thereof in the hands of a sub-chief. In some of the larger tribes a system existed whereby the various sub-chiefs were graded into what may be termed important and minor sub-chiefs, depending upon various factors such as their degree of relationship to the chief, their competency, their popularity, the size of the area, and the number of people under their jurisdiction. A sub-chief would, in the case of a small tribe, normally exercise jurisdiction over only the headmen in his district. An important sub-chief, in the case of a large tribe, would have several minor sub-chiefs as well as some headmen under him, while a minor sub-chief would have only a limited number of headmen under him.

Nevertheless, these sub-chiefs were all of them important people in status and rank: in the system of local government as a whole they occupied the highest positions; they had the power to overrule any decision of their subordinate headmen; they acted as courts of appeal over the courts of the headmen; most of them were members of the chief's council, and they had a right to be consulted by the chief on all matters affecting the tribe as a whole. They were themselves directly responsible to the chief in any matter affecting the interests of their followers and any decisions taken or verdicts given by them were subject to appeal to the chief, who had the final say in any matter. For the rest the duties, functions, and responsibilities of the sub-chiefs were in principle similar to those of the headmen. In the execution of their duties and functions the sub-chiefs were assisted by their headmen either in their individual capacities or in the form of an advisory council. By the responsibility for the smooth running of the affairs of the inmates of a district rested on the shoulders of the sub-chief alone. If he proved to be incompetent, he could be discharged by the chief and replaced by somebody else.

The system of local government among the Bantu was thus one of ever-widening jurisdiction starting from the smallest unit in the tribal hierarchy (the household), extending to the ward, from the ward to the district, and from the district to the tribal chief. Local government could also be described as a system of delegated authority from the chief downwards along the hierarchy to the sub-chief and from him to the headman, ending up with the head of a household.

The central government of the tribe was vested in the chief, whose office was hereditary in the male line. A chief ruled as such until his death when, as a rule, he would be succeeded by his eldest son borne by the principal or tribal wife—except among the Tsonga, where a chief was usually succeeded by his brothers in turn. If the heir was too young to be installed as chief, a regent, in the person of the late chief's younger brother, would be appointed by the tribe to act as chief until such time as the lawful successor became of age—after he had been initiated into adulthood.

The installation of the new chief was a very elaborate process that sometimes lasted for months before it reached its climax. The chief-elect, together with his family, had to undergo a series of purification rites and thereafter he would be ceremonially doctored from time to time in preparation for the high office he was about to assume. He was expected to present himself regularly at the *kgotla* (the gathering place of the tribesmen), where the late chief's counselors and the old men of the tribe would constantly remind him of the meritorious qualities and achievements of his late father, if any; and they would for the umpteenth time informally counsel him on the do's and don'ts appertaining to the office of chieftainship.

The day of the installation was an occasion for joy and great festivity at the headquarters of the tribe. Usually the tribe as a whole would gather to participate in the dancing and feasting, abundant supplies of beer and meat having been prepared for the occasion. At an appropriate time the new chief would be escorted into the cattle pen, or kgotla, where, in full view of the tribe, he would be draped with the insignia of office (among other things a newly softened leopard skin) and be entrusted with the sacred tribal medicines and regalia.

In the execution of his duties and functions the chief did not act alone. In the first place he had at his disposal the services and advice of a few close relatives, including a few trustworthy and influential sub-chiefs whom he would at all times informally and confidentially consult on the formulation of policy and the correct line of action to adopt in administering the affairs of the tribe. These private counselors also functioned as the eyes and ears of the chief; they had to keep him informed of public opinion among tribesmen and, in particular, to keep him posted on all happenings of importance both within the tribe and outside. In addition, they would keep a close watch on the behavior of the chief and, if necessary, they would warn him if he did anything that might antagonize the people.

Second, there was a formal council, which consisted of all the sub-chiefs and headmen in the tribe together with the chief's private advisers and the chief himself as presiding officer at all the meetings. On important occasions a meeting of the council was convened to deal with matters of public policy. Any matter of a public nature previously discussed by the chief and his advisers was laid before this council for further consideration and a decision.

The powers of this council were not the same everywhere. Among all the tribes, excepting the Sotho, this council was in effect the governing body of the tribe; any resolution adopted or decision taken by it became binding on the tribe as a whole, and all sub-chiefs and headmen had thereupon to ensure that it was made known and properly carried out by everybody in their respective districts and wards. Among the Sotho tribes, the position was somewhat different, inasmuch as the decisions taken by the chief's council on matters of public concern had to be ratified by the assembly (*pitso*) of all adult tribesmen, presided over by the chief, before they could be carried out.

Great freedom of speech was permitted at any meeting of the council or the tribe, and a proper decision could only be arrived at after the matter under discussion had been thoroughly thrashed out. People who might feel aggrieved at any proposals put forward by the chief would not hesitate to say so in no uncertain terms; they might even go so far as to take him severely to task for having the temerity to bring such an unpopular matter before the people. No ballot was ever taken in order to determine whether a proposal was carried or not. At the end of the deliberations the chief, in his capacity as chairman, would merely announce what obviously appeared to be the consensus and that would be accepted as a formal and final decision of the meeting. If the majority was against the chief, he would have no option but to accept the situation.

A person very intimately and indispensably connected with the chief and the administration of the tribe was what may be termed the chief's "orderly." Among some tribes he was a close relative of the chief; among others he was an ordinary citizen. But he had to be a man of unquestionable loyalty, integrity, ability, and trustworthiness. Apart from the chief, he was the most highly respected man. No member of the tribe could approach the chief except through this *induna*; all reports intended for the chief had to be made to this man first; court cases had to be filed with him, and he would then arrange for their hearing; in the absence of the chief, he would be the chief's deputy, presiding at tribal meetings and delivering judgments at the court. The induna was the chief's right-hand man and his principal consultant on all tribal affairs; he was the intermediary between the chief, the council, and the tribe. On account of his many and varied duties, he was required to reside close to the chief's headquarters so as to be immediately available whenever his services were required by either the chief or the public.

The chief occupied the most respected, privileged, and exalted position in the social, political, economic, and religious orders and life of the tribe. On the social ladder he was the head of the senior household of the senior lineage of the senior clan of the senior kinship group; in the political hierarchy he was the headman of the senior ward or sub-district, sub-chief of the senior district, and chief of the tribe in the final instance; in the economic field he was the wealthiest person and theoretically the owner of the tribal territory; in religion he was the only link and the sole mediator between the people and their gods. Among the Zulu, the Northern Sotho, and the Venda the chief was elevated to an almost godlike eminence: his person was regarded as sacred, his subjects bowed before him in humble adoration and obeisance, and his smallest gesture was greeted with a chorus of fulsome adulation. Among the Venda, indeed, not only is the chief regarded as semi-divine during the greater part of his life; towards the end of it, or sometimes before, he actually confers godhead upon himself.

But the chief's position was not merely one of outstanding eminence and privilege. As administrative and executive head of the tribe he had many duties to perform and many obligations to carry out. He had to watch over the interests of his subjects, treat everybody sympathetically and impartially, keep himself informed of tribal affairs generally, visit the kgotla regularly to listen to grievances and to receive petitions, and supervise the administration of wards and districts.

The Bantu had no prison or police system, but the chief was responsible for the maintenance of law and order and for the proper administration of justice; he was the chief justice of the tribe, and beyond his court there was no appeal; his judgments were final. All serious cases, such as assault, rape, murder, or sorcery could be heard by only his court. In military affairs, the chief was the head and leader of the tribal army; it was his duty to arrange for the ritual preparations of his regiments before a military expedition and for their purification thereafter; he had the final say in the disposal of any spoils of war. In all ritual affairs concerning the tribe, the chief had to take the initiative and at the same time play the leading role; he was the only living link between the tribe and their ancestors and, after his death, he would become a tribal god himself. It was his special duty, therefore, to ensure a continued and equitable equilibrium between the tribe and the spirits of their ancestors by regularly holding the customary tribal ceremonies and making the necessary offerings to the gods on behalf of the tribe, failing which any calamity might come down on the tribe at any time.

The Bantu had a firm belief in the existence of certain supernatural beings who were endowed with the power to influence the lives of the people on earth benevolently or malevolently. The most important of these were the spirits of the dead ancestors in respect of whom an elaborate system of belief and worship had been developed. In addition, the Bantu believed in a supreme being, as well as in some other deities. The latter, however, did not influence the lives and destinies of the living people as intimately and profoundly as did the ancestor spirits.

Magic played a significant role in the daily life of every individual as well as that of the community as a whole. While magic as such could be clearly differentiated from ancestor-worship, many beliefs and practices of a magical nature were intertwined with the latter, so that many of the religious ceremonies observed by the Bantu were of a dual character.

The supreme being, although generally regarded as impersonal, was referred to by a special name among all tribes (Sotho, *Modimo*; Venda, *Raluvhimba*; Zulu, *Unkulunkulu*; Xhosa, *uDali*). The Zulu also spoke of him as *inkosi pezulu*, "the chief or lord above"; they believed that he was the creator of all things, such as the sun and the moon, animals and birds, water and mountains; that he was the original ancestor of all people; and that he instituted the present order of society. It was also generally believed that this high god controlled the elements as well as the weather; that he manifested himself in lightning and that he could cause the rain to stop or to fall.

Yet this supreme being was never worshipped; no prayers or offerings were ever directed to him; he was not an object of any direct or regular cult. Some connection, however, does seem to have existed between the "sky god" and the ancestor spirits, as evidenced by the rainmaking ceremonies. It is doubtful whether the ancestor spirits themselves were able to control the heavens and the rain; this power was attributed to the high god, and he, according to traditional Bantu concepts, could only successfully be approached by the intervention of the ancestor spirits at the request of their descendants on earth.

The Bantu, without exception, believed in the survival of man after death in the form of a spirit. Death did not change the rank, status, occupation, character, or the range of influence of a person; what a man used to be during life, he would be thereafter, wherever that might be: a commoner would remain a commoner, a chief would be a chief. A man's spirit was a facsimile of the deceased. It was on the ground of this basic tenet of faith that ancestor-religion and ancestor-worship were interpreted by the Bantu as nothing else but a continuation or extension of earthly life and culture into the hereafter.

Ancestor-worship was based on the unshakable belief that the spirits of the dead continued to influence, if not control and regulate, the lives of their people on earth, for good or for evil. If the people on earth lived strictly in accordance with the traditions and moral codes left behind by the ancestors, the spirits would bless them with abundance of food and beer, with plenty of cattle and children, with good luck and prosperity. But if the people neglected their duties, if they failed to fulfill their obligations towards their kinsmen (including the spirits of their deceased relatives), or if they committed any breaches or infringements of tribal law and custom, the spirits were bound to feel offended and their natural reaction would be to punish the culprits through some visitation or other in the family, the lineage, the clan, or the tribe, as the case might be.

The extent of the power of a spirit to bless or punish corresponded to the position it occupied as a living being on earth. Thus worship and veneration were mainly directed to the spirits of those who had during their lifetimes held positions of authority in the household, the lineage, the clan, the ward, or the tribe.

Occasions on which the ancestors of a household had to be specially approached included such events as birth, initiation, marriage, illness, death, an accident, or a heavy fine in court. The ancestors of the tribal chief were regularly approached on such occasions as the planting of the fields, the eating of the first fruits, the harvesting of the crops, the initiation of young boys and girls, the occurrence of drought, or the outbreak of an epidemic.

The traditional method of communicating with the ancestor spirits consisted of a short prayer usually accompanied by the offering of some food or beer spilled on the floor, the ground, or on an animal.

These ceremonies were conducted with the object either of maintaining the friendship and ensuring the continued benevolence of the ancestors, or of restoring the normal relations between the spirits and the people where these had been broken off by the negligence or misbehavior of the latter. Furthermore, these ceremonies served to maintain the solidarity of every group from the household upwards, to and including the tribe itself or to re-establish and consolidate the order of seniority of the members of each group as well as that of every group itself within the social structure and the political hierarchy of the tribe as a whole. They also re-established and consolidated beyond doubt the lawful position of the authoritative head of every social and political group, and in the final instance they reaffirmed the traditional and unquestionable unity between an ordered society on earth and the supernatural beings in the hereafter. Ancestor worship guaranteed, furthermore, the perpetuation of the tribe as a unique system of social and political order.

It should be clear, then, why all ceremonies on a tribal basis had to be performed strictly in accordance with the traditional pattern. The first requirement was that all participants had to be ritually clean. The tribal chief himself, as the only living representative of both the tribal ancestors (his predecessors) and his people, especially had to be ritually cleansed and doctored with the sacred and potent tribal medicines containing, among other things, the bodily ingredients of the former chiefs, before he could venture to approach his ancestor spirits in the interests of and in behalf of his tribe. The cattle, specially selected as offerings, had likewise to be doctored beforehand; they had to be killed with bare hands and, after they had been slaughtered, the meat had once again to be doctored before all participants ate it in strict order of seniority, starting with the chief and working downwards. In his prayer, the chief would briefly dedicate the offerings to his ancestors, thanking them for a good crop or imploring them to cause the rains to fall, as the case might be.

According to the Bantu, magic was the firm belief that supernatural forces could by means of certain rites or spells be invoked to the advantage or the detriment of man. Magicians who practiced their art for the benefit of others were highly respected; their services were always in great demand and they were usually well remunerated. But those magicians who applied their knowledge to inflict harm on other people were the most dreaded persons of all, and anyone found guilty of sorcery or witchcraft by the chief's court would instantly be punished by death.

Magic, or the services of a magician, was at all times and in all circumstances employed by everybody in order to ensure success in life or a particular undertaking, or to avert danger, accident, misfortune, or disappointment. If anything went wrong, the person affected would call in a magician to establish the cause and to prescribe a suitable remedy. If the ancestor spirits were to blame, they had to be pacified with an offering; if a malicious person had been at work, he had to be smelled out and punished for his anti-social activities.

Traditional Bantu culture has inevitably undergone many changes during the past century and a half, mainly as a result of the contact between the Bantu and the Europeans who are the carriers of the typically South African form of Western civilization. The contact between the Bantu and the other population groups with different cultures, such as the Coloreds, the Asians, and the Malays, although intimate and of long duration, has not produced any changes in the traditional culture of the Bantu. The changes that have been produced, and which are still being produced, can almost exclusively be ascribed to the settlement of Europeans in South Africa: the establishment, extension, consolidation, and intensification of direct European government and control over the country as a whole; the introduction of an economic system that was entirely new and foreign to the Bantu; the spread of Christianity and, concomitant therewith, a system of Westernized education: in short, the imposition and impact of Western civilization in all its manifestations.

In the process of change many elements of Bantu culture have completely disappeared; others have undergone slight or radical modifications; and still many others, entirely new, have been borrowed from the Europeans. The nature and extent of the changes in culture that have been taking place differ from one major group of tribes to another, depending on the nature, duration, and intensity of the contact with the Europeans. But although the tempo of change may have differed from one area to another, the general trend in all cases has been the same.

One of the most conspicuous developments in modern times is the fact that the Bantu have become differentiated into at least three main classes or groups of more or less equal size: the de-culturated, the semi-culturated, and the acculturated groups.

The de-culturated group consists of all those Bantu who have become dissociated from their original tribes. They have severed all connections with tribal life, customs, and traditions. The majority of this group have become urban dwellers in European territory, although not all urban dwellers can be described as belonging to this group. In fact, many urban Bantu still regard themselves as stanch members of their tribes, despite the fact that they have been residing away from them for many years. Although the large group of permanently urbanized Bantu have discarded their traditional way of life, they have not as yet evolved a culture system of their own. They tend to live like Europeans, but they refuse to be designated otherwise than as Bantu. Whether they, or their offspring in the distant future, will ever assimilate Western civilization in full remains an open question. It was reliably estimated that out of a total of thirteen million Bantu in the Republic of South Africa at the end of 1968, 31 percent (or just over four million) were residing in the European urban centers, and that any number between 45 percent and 70 percent of the urban Bantu population about 14 percent to 22 percent of the total Bantu population could be regarded as having become permanently urbanized.

The semi-culturated group includes all those Bantu who still adhere to many of their old tribal customs while at the same time are in the process of taking over elements of European culture to an ever increasing extent. It would appear as if they are slowly moving away from tribal life towards the group of completely detribalized or de-culturated Bantu. Many Bantu falling into this class have been residing for some time in the European urban areas where they are in the permanent employment of Europeans in commerce, trade, or industry. A limited number are still living with their tribes and are employed by the government and the few Europeans who may be carrying on some economic activity or other. But the majority, approximately 4.5 million, are found on the European-owned farms, mostly in the rural parts of the country, where they are employed as laborers.

The acculturated group is made up of the many hundreds of different tribes living as such in reserves that have been specially set aside for them by the government. A statute adopted by parliament in 1913 lays down that no European may acquire any interest in land situated within these reserves and that no Bantu may acquire any land situated outside these reserves, without the approval of the State President. There are about 250 such Bantu reserves, and together they aggregate approximately 42 million acres. About 4,500,000 Bantu inhabit these reserves at any one time, the rest of the group residing temporarily in the European urban and rural areas.

These reserves are in the main the territories that were occupied by the various Bantu tribes at the time of the arrival of the Europeans during the first half of the nineteenth century. In colloquial language they are referred to as the Bantu homelands.

Bantu culture flourished at its best in these homelands before the arrival of the Europeans, but as a consequence of the impact of Western civilization many changes have been produced. As a result of European rule, the Bantu have lost their tribal autonomy and political independence. In tribal rule and the administration of justice the duties, powers, and responsibilities of the chief have either been abolished or diminished to such an extent that the institution of chieftainship has become a caricature of what it used to be. At the present time the State President, formerly the governor-general, is the Supreme Chief of all the Bantu. He is invested with extremely wide powers, the most significant of which is the power to proclaim legislation for the Bantu. In effect, the administration of Bantu affairs is in the hands of the minister of the Department of Bantu Administration and Development, which has been created specially for this purpose. The minister, in collaboration with the cabinet, lays down the policy, enacts the necessary legislation through parliament or the State President, and sees that it is carried out. There is hardly a single aspect of Bantu life in South Africa in respect of which a policy has not been laid down and carried into effect. A European state official of fairly senior status and invested with civil and criminal jurisdiction is stationed in every Bantu reserve. This Bantu Affairs Commissioner and his staff, consisting of both European and Bantu civil servants, are responsible for the direct administration of the tribe or tribes in the reserve, the implementation of government policy, the maintenance of law and order, and the carrying out of instructions that may be issued from headquarters in Pretoria.

In the South African system of Bantu administration the tribal institution of chieftainship is retained and employed as an instrument not of the tribe, but of the European government, and as such only to a limited extent. A chief no longer accedes to his office in his own right: he is officially appointed thereto by the minister of state who has discretion in the matter. Every chief so appointed gets a fixed salary from the government, and he usually remains in office until his death or until he has become physically and mentally infirm. In a sense, the chief has become a civil servant of the state and his administrative functions are limited to carrying out government instructions and to acting as a link between the government and his tribe. If he is neglectful in the carrying out of these duties, he will be reprimanded by the commissioner and, if he proves to be continuously untrustworthy or inefficient, the minister has the power to depose him and appoint somebody else in his place.

Apart from the chieftainship, the state also recognizes and employs the traditional system of tribal local government, but to a limited extent, as only a few sub-chiefs or headmen in each tribe may be officially appointed as such at minimal emoluments.

Until recently a system of local and general councils with elaborate administrative functions and responsibilities was in operation in the Ciskei and Transkei reserves of Cape province.

But this has been abolished in favor of a country-wide system of tribal, regional, and territorial Bantu authorities with extensive administrative, financial, and judicial functions. The tribal chiefs play a prominent part in this new system of administration. For instance, the regional authority of the Transkei consists of 109 members, 64 of whom are ex officio members by virtue of their being tribal or paramount chiefs; the remaining 45 members are elected by all men and women voters of the Transkei by means of a secret ballot. A few years ago this Transkeian regional authority (as well as a few others) was granted political independence from the white government in all respects excepting a few areas such as external affairs and defense, which still remain the responsibility of the European government.

The executive committee of this authority consists of a prime or chief minister (himself a tribal paramount chief) and five other ministers who are in charge of such portfolios as justice, finance, transport, agriculture, education, or internal affairs.

The system of self-government in the Transkei and elsewhere in South Africa is based not on any traditional Bantu institution, but on the principles and procedures of Western democracy. In the administration of justice the powers of the chief are severely limited. Bantu law is officially recognized only in so far as it is "not opposed to the principles of public policy or natural justice." Bantu chiefs and some headmen are permitted to determine cases of a civil or criminal nature between members of their own tribes, but an appeal lies from the chief's court to that of the local European courts from which further appeals lie to higher courts especially established for the settlement of disputes between Bantu only. Criminal cases of a serious nature in which only Bantu are involved and civil cases in which both Bantu and Europeans are involved are excluded from jurisdiction of a chief's court and are taken directly to the European courts.

In the economic life of the Bantu many traditional elements and institutions of culture have entirely or nearly disappeared; others have undergone material changes and many new elements have been introduced. The process of disappearance, change, and innovation in the economic field is assuming an ever-increasing tempo and it is more conspicuous and profound than in other aspects of culture.

Cattle raiding and inter-tribal warfare have completely died out among the Bantu; the hunting of wild game cannot be practiced any longer, owing to the dire scarcity of game and the severe controls imposed by the European government; the homecraft industry has become something of the past, since the Bantu can obtain what they need from manufacturers; traditional forms of dress have been discarded in favor of European fashions; European-type houses are fast displacing the traditional bee-hive or conical-roofed Bantu hut.

What used to be tribal territory has been demarcated by statute into reserves, and thus ownership and control have passed from the tribes and their chiefs to the European government. In some reserves the system of individual tenure and ownership of land has been introduced in the place of the traditional system of communal tenure—a profound change.

In agriculture a great variety of new products—such as sugar, sisal, cotton, lucerne, wheat, and table vegetables—have been introduced in addition to the traditional maize and millet. The old methods of soil cultivation and food production have become obsolete in all respects: all kinds of modern farming implements, from the plough to the threshing machine, are being used either on an individual or co-operative basis; more use is being made of good seed and fertilizer provided by the European government at nominal prices; wherever possible, irrigation of lands and crops is regularly practiced by the Bantu, assisted and encouraged by the government, which has initiated a large number of irrigation schemes, augmented by a widespread system of boreholes fitted with windmills and pumping plants.

The government also assists the Bantu in the harvesting, grading, and marketing of their surplus crops, which are considerable in some instances. Farming among the Bantu, then, has become a scientific undertaking, almost completely rid of the former crude methods, magical practices, and taboos.

Animal husbandry has likewise undergone some fundamental changes. The social and ritual values of cattle are being replaced by values of a purely monetary nature. The government has introduced new breeds of cattle in the reserves with the dual purpose of stimulating the production of dairy products and a good grade of meat. Many Bantu have consequently become quite successful cattle farmers in the European sense. But cattle will continue to have a special value for the Bantu: they are still used as sacrifices to the ancestor spirits, as *bogadi*, and as a means of giving satisfaction and pride to their owners.

The Bantu of olden times did not have any system of transport. To some extent they made use of cattle as pack-animals, but mostly they and their women carried their wares from one place to another themselves. Nowadays they are making use of all the forms of transport introduced by the Europeans, such as riding horses, horse-carts, oxwagons, bicycles, motor cars, trucks, tractors, trailers, taxis, and railways.

The introduction of European currency has revolutionized the traditional economic system of the Bantu. For more than a century it has become an indispensable commodity in Bantu life, and since it was not possible for the Bantu to raise capital in the reserves to meet all their obligations, a great many of them were compelled to look for money outside. The insatiable demand for labor on the part of the Europeans has always provided a necessary outlet with the result that almost two-thirds of the total Bantu population have become dependent for their subsistence on what they are able to earn among Europeans as unskilled, semi-skilled, and skilled laborers. In addition, a considerable number of Bantu men and women have set up their own businesses or have become absorbed into the teaching, nursing, and legal professions. However, in most occupations Bantu receive smaller remuneration than Whites and are discriminated against in promotions, but they are being prepared for inevitable changes.

In short, the traditional self-sufficient economic system of the Bantu is being rapidly transformed to a diversified system of capitalism more or less like that of the Europeans of South

Africa. The spirit and principles of communal responsibility and of mutual reciprocity that were so characteristic of traditional Bantu life are gradually giving way to a system based on the principles of individualism and of entrepreneurship.

Needless to say, the social and religious systems of the old Bantu have also been transformed from what may be termed tribalism and heathenism to a form of Western civilization and "Christianity"—more rapidly in recent times than ever before. With about two-thirds of the members of any tribe absent in the European areas at any one time, Bantu social life in the reserves has become far removed from what it used to be when the tribe lived together as a complete unit—either in one large town, as among the Tswana, or scattered over the tribal territory in households or small hamlets, as among the Nguni. And restrictions on travel by Bantu have created considerable social and psychological problems. With so many absentees from the tribe, the inference is not that the tribe as a unit has necessarily been broken up, but that its resident population has been depleted. But it should be clear that no social group, be it the family or the tribe, can be expected to function normally whenever most of its members are absent. Continued absence will lead to disruption and to the decay of moral behavior and religious practice.

The most profound influence on the social and religious lives of the old Bantu was exerted by the missionaries. Missionary work was started in 1774, and it is no exaggeration to say that there is hardly a single Bantu tribe in South Africa among whom the Gospel has not regularly been preached during the past hundred years and longer.

Missionary work was undertaken with the dual object of uprooting heathen beliefs and customs among the Bantu and of replacing these by Christian beliefs and ideals. But missionaries soon learned that success could only be achieved by providing auxiliary services such as welfare work, hospitalization, and education, in respect of which they were subsidized by the state government. Missionary effort was therefore designed not only to introduce a new religion among the Bantu, but also a new social order.

The missionaries taught the Bantu, among other things, that it was sinful to go about half-undressed, to purchase a wife, to practice polygamy, to inherit widows, and even to circumcise young men and put them through an initiation school. In other words, those Bantu who were prepared to renounce the fundamentals of their traditional social system were accepted as Christians, and those who became Christians were lost to their tribes, so that one observer could write: "Wherever one travels through native territory one finds heathen villages and Christian villages, often side by side but never a composite unit. The Christian gospel was, during the nineteenth century, the most powerful agency in the disintegration of the South African tribes."

Acceptance of the Christian faith by the Bantu does not necessarily imply that all of them have abandoned all customs and practices of the past. On the contrary, many Bantu Christians still adhere to the custom of bogadi after their marriages have been solemnized in the church; some still sacrifice to their ancestor spirits, and others still believe in magic and in the power of the magicians to control the supernatural forces.

There was a period in the history of Christian missions in South Africa when many Bantu joined the Christian church merely for the sake of gaining the benefit of the social welfare, medical, and educational services provided by the church. But since some services of this nature have been put at the disposal of the Bantu by the state, municipalities, and other welfare organizations—especially during the past three decades—the Bantu have become reluctant to accept Christianity. Meanwhile, ecclesiastical separatism and sectarianism have occurred among the Bantu on an unprecedented scale, so that at present close to two thousand separate Bantu churches are in existence apart from the one hundred recognized, or official, churches.

Bibliography

Ashton, H. *The Basuto*, 1955.
Bryant, A. T. *Olden Times in Zululand and Natal*, 1929.
Burchell, W. J. *Travels in the Interior of South Africa*, 1929.
Callaway, H. *Nursery Tales, Traditions and Histories of the Zulus*, 1868.
Engelbrecht, J. A. *Swazi Customs Relating to Marriage*, 1930.
Fritsch, G. *Die Eingeborenen Sud-Afrika's ethnographisch und anatomisch beschrieben*, 1872.
Hunter, Monica. *Reaction to Conquest: Effects of Contact with Europeans on the Pondo of South Africa*, 1936.
Junod, H. A. *The Life of a South African Tribe*, 1927.
Krige, Eileen J. *The Social System of the Zulus*, 1936.
Molema, S. M. *The Bantu, Past and Present*, 1920.
Schapera, I. *Western Civilization and the Natives of South Africa: Studies in Culture Contact*, 1934.
—. *The Bantu-Speaking Tribes of South Africa: An Ethnographical Survey*, 1937.
Stayt, H. A. *The Bavenda*, 1931.
van Warmelo, N. J. *A Preliminary Survey of the Bantu Tribes of South Africa*, 1935.

Notes on the Contributors

D. R. BEETON, who was born at Zeerust, South Africa, holds the B.A., M.A., and D.Litt. degrees. He is a Fellow of the South African Library Association and head of the department of English in the University of South Africa. Over the years he has contributed numerous articles on South African language, nineteenth-century literature, and aesthetics to the professional journals. He is a contributor to the *Dictionary of South African Biography* and is supervising preparation of the *Index of English Usage in Southern Africa*.

G. G. CILLIÉ took his B.Sc. and M.Sc. degrees in pure and applied mathematics at the University of Stellenbosch and was subsequently awarded a Rhodes Scholarship to Oxford, where he read for the D.Phil. in astrophysics under Professor E. A. Milne, and then studied astronomy as a Commonwealth Fund Fellow at Harvard University. His first academic appointments, in mathematics, were at the Universities of the Witwatersrand and Pretoria. Since 1939 he has held the chair of mathematics in the University of Stellenbosch and has served as dean of the faculty of science. Professor Cillié is a member of the Suid-Afrikaanse Akademie vir Wetenskap en Kuns, and was awarded the gold medal of the Suid-Afrikaanse Akademie for his work in music.

ANNA L. CONRADIE is a graduate of the University of Cape Town, from which institution she holds the B.A., M.A., and Ph.D. degrees. After graduate study in the University of Utrecht, she taught philosophy at Cape Town for some time before being appointed to the chair of philosophy in the University of Natal. Her special interest is the philosophy of religion, though she has published two novels, *Dans Makaber* and *Dambord*—both written in Afrikaans. Her philosophical works include *The Neo-Calvinist Concept of Philosophy* (1960), *African Philosophy* (1970), and *A Phenomenological Approach to Creativity* (1971).

J. B. DU TOIT, who is professor of sociology and dean of the faculty of arts in the University of the Western Cape, holds the D.Phil. degree in sociology of the University of Stellenbosch, in which university he lectured for several years. During 1957-58 he did research at the University of Chicago on an International House Fellowship, and in 1966-67 he studied mass communications in Germany under a grant from the German Academic Exchange Program. Professor du Toit's research has been primarily devoted to mass media, South African social problems, and family life.

ELLISON KAHN has been professor of law in the University of the Witwatersrand in Johannesburg since 1954 and dean of the faculty of law since 1967. He holds the degrees of B.Com. and LL.B. (Witwatersrand) and LL.M. (Natal), is an advocate of the Supreme Court of South Africa and a barrister of the Middle Temple, London. Professor Kahn is editor of the *South African Law Journal* and a member of the editorial board of the *Annual Survey of South African Law*. He is co-author of *The South African Legal System and Its Background* (1968) and of *Contract and Mercantile Law Through the Cases* (1970).

Notes on the Contributors

F. J. LANGUAGE studied for the B.A., M.A., and D.Phil. degrees from the University of Stellenbosch, where he taught anthropology, Bantu languages, and Bantu administration. Later he became Director of Bantu Affairs in Brakpan, in the Witwatersrand. In 1960 he was invited to become professor of anthropology in the University of the Orange Free State, which position he still occupies. Professor Language has published many papers in both English and Afrikaans about the Bantu, among whom he has carried out anthropological research for over thirty years.

HEATHER MARTIENSSEN received her B.Arch., B.A., and M.A. (Fine Arts) degrees in the University of the Witwatersrand, though she was born in Cape Town. She did additional graduate work at the Courtauld Institute of Art, University of London, and was awarded the Ph.D. degree. She was appointed to the faculty of the University of the Witwatersrand in 1941 and to that institution's chair of fine arts in 1957. During 1953 she studied in the United States under a Carnegie Grant. In recent years she has devoted considerable time to lecturing and broadcasting as well as to adjudicating art exhibitions throughout South Africa.

A. L. McLEOD, a graduate of Sydney, Melbourne, and Pennsylvania State Universities, has taught in Australia and the United States; he is now professor of English and speech in Rider College, and dean of its school of liberal arts and science. Dr. McLeod is author of *Rex Warner: Writer* (1960) and editor of J. C. Smuts's *Walt Whitman: A Study in the Evolution of Personality* (1972) and *The Achievement of Rex Warner* (1965). He is at present preparing *Representative South African Speeches: The Rhetoric of Race and Religion* for the Centre for Commonwealth Literature and Research of the University of Mysore.

JOHN C. POVEY is associate professor of English and assistant director of the African Studies Center in the University of California at Los Angeles; he holds his B.A. and M.A. degrees in English from the University of South Africa. He took his Ph.D. degree at Michigan State University, and his diploma in the teaching of English as a second language from Davis College, London. Professor Povey has given papers on contemporary African literature at conferences in Dakar, Berlin, Vancouver, Cape Town, Ife, and Brisbane and has been a prolific contributor to journals. He is editor of *African Languages and Literature* (1967) and *Black African Writing: An Anthology* (1969) and managing editor of the new journal *African Arts/ Arts d'Afrique*.

Index

Abrahams, Peter, 24, 25, 26, 27
Afrikaans, 184-194, 197-206
Afrikaners, 9-10
African National Congress (A.N.C), 289, 302, 303, 305
Anglo-Boer War, 285-287,
Appellate Division, 143-146, 151, 159-160, 165-166, 169, 176
Armstrong, F.W., 132
Atherstone, W.G., 51
Australia, 5-6, 41, 179

Bain, Andrew Geddes, 51
Baines, Thomas, 124
Baker, Herbert, 117-120
Bantu:
    art, 133-134
    acculturation, 344-345
    cattle, 319-322, 348-349
    chieftains, 322-323, 326, 327-328
    culture, 311-351
    family life, 210-212
    food, 315-317
    households, 322-324
    initiations, 323-324
    kinship, 322-323, 326, 327-328
    religion, 339-343, 350-351
Bantu Administration Act (1927), 160
Bantu Authorities Act (1951), 154
Bantu Education Act (1953), 100-101
Barnard, Lady Anne, 14, 189
Barnard, Christiaan, 70-71
Battiss, Walter, 129

Bible, Afrikaans trans., 37
Bills of Exchange Act (1964), 141
Blank, Joost de, 300
Bosman, Herman Charles, 18-19, 184-185
Bowker, T.H., 55
Bowler, Thomas, 124, 136
Breuil, Abbé, 56
Broadcasting, 232-235
Broom, Robert, 53-54, 55
Brutus, Dennis, 35-36, 39
Bryant, Daniel, 93

Campbell, Roy, 6-7, 16, 20-22, 38
Canada, 42
Cape Town, 14, 45, 66, 80, 82, 113, 135, 209, 231
Carnegie Commission, 217-219
Chaka, Chief, 312-313
Christianity, 76-92, 96-97, 106-109, 265-271, 276- 277, 350- 351
Christian Institute, 104-106
Cilliers, S.P., 211, 214
Cloete, J.D., 172
Clothing, 223-225
Code Napoleon, 138
Colenso, Bishop, 82-83
Companies Act (1926), 141
Conradie, A.L., 260
Costhuizen, D.J., 252
Council for Scientific and Industrial Research (CSIR), 70
Cricket, 243
Culture, defined, 1-2

Daniell, Samuel, 123
Dart, R.A., 54-55
Darvall, Denise, 70
Darwin, Charles, 50-51
Dingaan, Chief, 313
Degenaar, J.J., 253, 261
Delius, Anthony, 21
Diaz, Bartholomew de Novais, 2
Divorce, 220-221
Divorce Laws Amendment Act (1935), 147
Donkin, Rufane, 14-15
DuBois, W.E.B., 289
Du Plessis, J., 81, 273
Durant, Will, 247
Dutch East India Company, 43, 77, 115, 180, 199
Dutch Reformed Church, 76-81, 96-98, 102-104, 268-269

Education, 8-9
Eliot, T.S., 1, 135
Everard, Bertha, 126
Extension of University Education Act (1959), 155

Fallows, Fearon, 45
Family Life, 208-209
Fugard, Athol, 36
Film, 236-237
Folk music and dance, 237-240
Food, 225-226
Football, 241-242
Frye, Northrop, 1

Gereformeerde Kerk, 77, 80, 96, 97, 109, 219, 268
Gill, David, 46, 48
Golf, 243
Goode, William J., 214
Goodman, Gwelo, 125
Goodwin, A.J.H., 55
Gordimer, Nadine, 23, 28-30, 304

Gordon, Jacob, 67
Gray, Robert, 82-83

Harcourt, Lord, 294
Harvey, W.H., 57
Heever, F.P. van den, 142
Hellberg, Carl-Johan, 10-11
Henderson, Thomas, 45
Herschel, John, 45-46, 49
Hertzog, J.B. 108
Hershchel, William, 45-46
Hervormde Kerk, 77, 78, 79, 96, 98, 103-104, 106-107
Higgs, Cecil, 127
Hinduism, 94- 96
Hoernlé, A. Winifred, 175, 314-315
Hoernlé, R.F.A., 249-251
Hofmeyr, Jan Hendrik, 249, 296-298

Immorality Act (1927), 153
Indian Reformed Church, 79
Innes, Chief Justice, 143
Innes, R.T.A., 47
Islam, 94- 95

Jacobson, Dan, 28

Kipling, Rudyard, 16
Kolbe, Frederick, 85-86
Kooy, G.A. 218
Krige, Uys, 38
Kruger, Paul, 4, 65, 267, 282-285, 293
Kumalo, Sydney, 132

Lacaille, Abbé de, 44, 45, 48, 49
La Guna, Alex, 33-34, 35, 39
Lake, John G., 90-91
Langenhoven, C.J., 37
Lanham, L.W., 195
Lansdown, C.W.H., 173
Law:
    apartheid, 149-153
    Bantu, 156-161

Index

capital punishment, 172-176
contracts, 142
criminal, 171-172
desuetude, 144
English, 139, 140-142, 144, 145
judges, 166-169
magistrates, 169-170
matrimonial, 146-149
parliamentary, 161-163
provincial, 163-166
Roman-Dutch, 138-139, 141-144, 146, 174, 176
Leistner, G.M.E., 213
Libraries, 231-232
Lighten, Conrad, 1
Lipshitz, Lippy, 132
Literature:
    Afrikaan, 37-39
    censorship, 40
    diaries, 14
    drama, 36
    magazines, 40-41
    poetry, 14-17, 37
    prose, 24-35
Locke, Bobby, 243
Louw, N.P. van Wyk, 37, 205, 253
Lowe, C. van Riet, 55
Lutherans, 89-90
Luthuli, Albert John, 302-305
Lutyens, Edwin, 117, 119

Maclear, Thomas, 45, 48
Makeba, Miriam, 245
Malan, D.F., 258, 299
Malherbe, D.F., 37
Mandela, Nelson, 305-307
Martienssen, Rex, 119-120, 137
Matrimonial Affairs Act (1953), 147
Mayer, Eric, 125
McKerren, R.G., 145
Media, 226-31
Methodists, 86-88
Meyer, F.J., 235

Millin, Sarah Gertrude, 18, 184, 278
Mokene, Mangena M., 92
Molengraaf, G.A.F., 52
Moshesh, Chief, 313
Motor Carrier Transportation Act (1930), 152
Mpanda, Chief, 313
Mphahlele, Ezekiel, 31-33
Muller, H.P.N., 239
Murray, Andrew Jr., 80, 81, 85-86, 216, 271-275
Murray, Andrew Sr., 216, 249, 251, 261, 268-75, 300
Modisane, Bloke, 31
Molteno, John, 231
Muslims, 94, 95, 213

Native Laws Amendment Act (1957), 100
Naude, Hugo, 125-126
Nguni tribes:
    initiation, 323-324
    kinship, 330-331
    marriage, 323
    territory, 316
Nkosi, Lewis, 19, 39

Opperman, D.J., 38

Pappé, Ludwig, 57
Paton, Alan, 24-25, 27, 298, 307-309
Pellissier, S.H., 238
Peringuey, L., 55
Philip, John, 98-99
Pierneef, Hendrik, 128
Plomer, William, 21, 22, 266
Population Registration Act (1950), 102
Preller, Alexis, 129-130
Presbyterians, 88-89
Prohibition of Mixed Marriages Act (1949), 102, 153
Prohibition of Political Interference Act (1968), 154

Pronunciation, English, 195-197
Pringle, Thomas, 15, 16, 181, 183, 185, 226
Pugh, Herbert, 14-15

Reeves, Richard Ambrose, 266, 301-302, 309
Religion:
   African, 91-95
   Apostolic, 90-91
   Bantu, 339-343, 350-351
   Baptist, 90
   Congregational, 91
   Hindu, 94-96
   Islam, 94-95
   Judaism, 91
   Methodist, 86-88, 93
   Presbyterian, 88-89
   Roman Catholicism, 83-84, 86
   Zionism, 93
Rhodes, Cecil, 117, 267, 276-282, 284, 292
Riebeeck, Jan van, 3, 36, 43, 56, 62, 72, 75, 115, 180, 199, 223, 231
Rive, Richard, 34
Reservation of Separate Amenities Act (1953), 152
Rose, George, 265
Rothman, M.E., 218
Rensburg, M.C.G.T. van, 233
Rural Colored Areas Act (1963), 155

Schapera, Isaac, 333-334
Schonland, Basil, 49-50
Sculpture, 132-133
Schreiner, Olive, 17, 18, 183-184, 285-288, 292
Science:
   agriculture, 60-63
   archeology, 55-56
   astronomy, 43-48
   botany, 56-60

   biology, 66-67
   education, 72-75
   forestry, 63-64
   geology, 50-53
   medicine, 68-72
   meteorology, 48-50
   oenology, 62
   paleontology, 55
   zoology, 54
Seme, Pixley Ka Isaka, 288-291
Skotnes, Cecil, 131
Slater, Frances C., 16-17, 185, 188
Small, Adam, 255-256, 260
Smith, Andrew, 65
Smith, J.L.B., 66-67
Smith, Pauline, 184
Smuts, Jan Christiaan, 4, 6, 10, 19, 86, 258-259, 267, 292-296
Somerset, Lord Charles, 36, 65, 78, 86, 88, 97, 231
Sotho tribes, 314, 323, 324, 328, 337
South African Broadcasting Corporation (SABC), 233-235
Stel, Simon van der, 44, 50, 114
Stern, Irma, 127
Steyn, J.H., 171
Steyn, L.C. 141
Sundkler, B.G.M., 94
Sutton, J.G., 49
Stoker, H.G., 256-258
Suzman, Helen, 309
Swazi tribes, 313, 314, 318, 324

Tachard, Gui, 44
Theiler, Arnold, 67-68
Thom, George, 78, 88, 269
Thumberg, Karl, 57
Transkei, 154
Transkei Constitution Act (1963), 168
Tswana tribes, 314-324
Tutu, Desmond, 309-310

Index

United Nations, 309
Unterhalter, Beryl, 219-220

Venda tribes, 320, 331
Versfeld, Martin, 253-256
Verwoerd, Hendrick, F., 8, 218, 267, 298-300
Vigne, Randolph, 38
Vleeschauwer, H.J. de, 248
Vorster, B.J., 227
Vorster, John, 107, 244
Voortrekkers, 77

Washington, Booker T., 289
Washkansky, Louis, 71
Wilson, Woodrow, 10
Wodehouse, Philip, 51, 270

Workers' Compensation Act (1941), 160

Xhosa tribes:
    Eastern Cape, 320
    initiation, 314
    kinship, 331
    language, 185-186
    marriage, 327
    religion, 93

Young Men's Christian Association (YMCA), 81, 273, 274, 276
Yusuf, Sheik, 94

Zulus, 313